Nov 15 02

68 - 12126

crayshon

The White Conscience

THE
WHITE
CONSCIENCE

FRANK H. TUCKER

FREDERICK UNGAR PUBLISHING CO.

NEW YORK

Acknowledgments

I WISH to express my appreciation for the Colorado College Faculty Research Grants which enabled me to complete the writing of this book. I am also grateful to numerous colleagues of that faculty for their helpful ideas and advice.

The interpretive thrust of this study was guided particularly by the late Dr. Carl Jung's analysis of the white man's mind and conduct.

Acknowledgments are due to the University of Nebraska Press for permission to use material from pages 29–47 of my article "Sino-Soviet Relations as Conditioned by Competition of Factions and Pressure Groups in the U.S.S.R.," *Studies on Asia*, 1964; and to the Editor of the *Rocky Mountain Social Science Journal* for authorization to use material from pages 115–24 of my article "The Sino-Soviet Rivalry in Africa, 1960–65," published in Volume IV, Number 1, of the *Journal*.

Special thanks are due to my wife, Kathryn Libby Tucker, for the very important contributions she made to the preparation of this book.

· · · ··
· · · ··

Contents

---

vii

The White Conscience

:: I ::

White Offenses
in the Aggregate

INDICTMENTS

SOME VERY strong words were uttered in a speech to the United States Senate in 1890 by J. J. Ingalls: "The race to which we belong is the most arrogant and rapacious, the most exclusive and indomitable in history. It is the conquering and the unconquerable race, through which alone man has taken possession of the physical and moral world. All other races have been its enemies or its victims." Seventy-four years later, watching the lengthening record of Western civilization's works, Gerald W. Johnson could write that, of all the creatures to appear on this earth, the white man is the fiercest by far.

These are painful words for a white man to hear; it is always difficult to take a long, hard look at the misdeeds or failings of oneself or of one's group. Some Americans and Europeans profess to be heartily sick of hearing about interracial problems—about which they have, to be sure, heard much in the last few years. They want no more talk of segregation, discrimination, or imperialism. The wrongs of nineteenth century imperialism, they say, have been amply admitted and have receded into the welcome mists of the past. Similarly, many Germans do not want to be reminded of Nazi crimes. Those belong to the past, they say, and have nothing to do with the current problems of Germany and the world. Although former Russian Premier Nikita Khrushchev had denounced Stalin's crimes before the Central Committee of Russia's Communist Party in 1956, he was quite enraged to hear the matter mentioned again in 1959, when he visited the Press Club in Washington, D.C.

I believe, however, that these misdeeds call for a fuller, better integrated review than they have yet received. From the dawning of the modern age, our world has suffered a remarkable amount of criminal activity on a national, and often on a continent-wide or worldwide, scale. Criminal activity refers to offenses of the sort charged in the Nuremburg Trials of 1946. I would categorize these offenses as follows: (1) planning and waging of aggressive war, often unusually extensive or cruel war; (2) such crimes against humanity as genocide, slavery, and other servitude, not omitting many national enterprises of profiteering, plundering, or regimentation; (3) racism—sometimes more accurately labelled nationalism—not always criminal, but seldom trivial, even in its subtle forms of discrimination or presumption of superiority.

In Michel de Montaigne's *Essays,* written in the 1600's, when expansion of European power around the world was in an early stage, the philosopher characterized Europe's successes as "base and mechanical victories." He regretted the unprecedentedly horrible warfare and calamities even then being inflicted, he said, upon the newly discovered, often helpless, continents beyond the seas.

As the twentieth century dawned, British poet Wilfrid Blunt surveyed the progress of European civilization and concluded that the whole white race was "revelling openly in violence."[1] At about the same time, even such a careful analyst of imperialism as British economist John A. Hobson delivered his summary indictment that, wherever Europeans had found less highly organized peoples with promising mineral or agricultural lands, they had, if possible, taken over these lands, compelling the inhabitants to work for the Europeans' benefit. If the natives could not be reduced to useful forms of servitude, they were expelled or exterminated.[2] These were the alternatives throughout most of Africa, the Americas, and Australia.

Did the twentieth century bring an end to these dreadful patterns of behavior? By midcentury, Europe's colonial enterprises were abandoned, albeit reluctantly. However, the white man's racism has continued in new forms which at times have been worse than before, thanks to the awesome resources of modern technology. (Genocidal destruction of over five million European Jews would have been thought impossible in 1900; yet, in the 1940's, it was actually carried out.)

Also, the white man's warlike ferocity has in recent decades come to be served by new, impressive means of destruction—vastly improved guns, atomic bombs, and ICBM's. In addition, we now see in Europe and America the emergence of many amazing means of influencing or controlling human behavior through new devices of communication, conditioning of the mind, and surveillance.

Thus, today, we must entertain sobering thoughts, not only of past guilt, but of future consequences. The Western World is, in effect, appearing before the tribunal of history, with very little time to make amends for its misdeeds and ill-portending creations. Albert Schweitzer, in his preface to Rolf Hochhuth's play *The Deputy*, recently reminded us that our thought continues to be "founded on inhumanity," and therefore great inhumanities may be perpetrated by our civilization in the future.

One of the great Asian statesmen of the twentieth century, Jawaharlal Nehru, expressed his misgivings in an address to the Asian-African Conference at Bandung, Indonesia, in 1955: "In Asia all of us have many faults as countries, as individuals. Our past history shows that. Nevertheless I say that Europe has been in the past a continent full of conflict, full of trouble, full of hatred; and their conflicts continue. . . . Now are we going to continue to . . . tie ourselves to Europe's troubles, Europe's hatred, and Europe's conflicts? I hope not." Yet Nehru was readier than many Western observers to discern and share the burden of difficulties which still arise as a heritage of the colonial era. At Bandung, he put the centuries-long tragedy of the African slave trade in proper perspective, saying: "When I think of it everything else pales into insignificance, that infinite tragedy of Africa. . . . We have to bear that burden, all of us. We did not do it ourselves, but the world has to bear it . . . it is up to Asia to help Africa to the best of her ability because we are sister continents."

As for the United States and its burden of racist offenses, one sensitive observer, William Stringfellow, has recently spoken of the "terrible premonition I suffer about what lies ahead for all Americans in the harsh days which come upon the nation in the crisis of racism."[3]

DEFINING THE PROBLEM

HARD AS it may be for a European or American to accept the foregoing statements, we can expect that most thoughtful Afro-Asians think much the same things. You might ask how such harsh verdicts could be pronounced on nations which have given so much to the enrichment of mankind. Did not Europe and the United States foster the Christian faith, the democratic way of life, marvelous works of art and music, the Industrial Revolution, and the wonders of this century's scientific revolution?

Did not Europe and America give to many Afro-Asian lands an orderly, efficient governmental system? Have not the United States and a number of European countries given generously of their money and talents to help countries which needed assistance? The proper answer to all these questions is "yes." Why, then, do we deserve the adverse evaluations described above?

We should concede that the deeds of inhumanity, tyranny, or greed charged against Europeans or Americans have been equalled—in wickedness, though not extensiveness—by acts committed through the centuries in all parts of the world by the world's peoples. It may even be conjectured that if an Asian power had acquired modern weaponry before Europe did, its imperialism and tyranny might have exceeded everything the white man has done.

That may be so, but the real historical drama has, for five centuries, cast the white man in the role of domineering master. His burden of guilt is made more impressive by the interlinkages of

European *imperialism, racism,* and *totalitarianism.* These three terms can be reduced to one by coinage of the term "keeperism" to include all these modes of *being one's brother's keeper.* There are, for example, noteworthy connections between nineteenth century colonialism and the totalitarianism of Central and Eastern Europe. Not only have these distressing events been related as a matter of cause and effect, but their underlying motives seem interwoven. Most important, we should expect that, in the minds of most thoughtful Afro-Asians, the more impressive misdeeds—both those committed in Europe and those committed by Europeans around the world—appear as one cumulative burden of guilt, all matters to be blamed on, or associated closely with, "the white man."

Since the terms "white man" and "Western man" will come up repeatedly in this discussion, it is best to acknowledge that, while they are brief and handy as labels, what they mean here is "people of Europe and people anywhere of European descent." It is these people whose record we are examining, not the record of North African or South Asian groups whose skin happens to be light. Likewise, use of "Afro-Asian" is often sensible, but requires clarification. I would use it to cover groups not included in the preceding paragraph—Asians, Africans, and even Pacific islanders—but not the American aborigines. "Non-Western" can also be used in this way, but is a negative word and can carry an idea of a purely cultural affiliation.

It is important to distinguish Western culture from Western power. This book is concerned chiefly with exertion of malevolent power by the Western nations, whether this took the form of worldwide imperialism, totalitarian rule at home, or the socio-political pressures of racism. Naturally, where such assertions of power occurred, one also finds Western civilization. What is more, abrupt imposition of Europe's cultural modalities has often disrupted and aggrieved the non-Western world. (These disruptive effects have seldom been recognized by the "cultural invaders." The missionary, teacher, and other visitors bent upon good works saw themselves in a benevolent light and could scarcely conceive of their ministrations as an unwonted disruption of the old culture.) However, the culture of the West *has* finally become the common possession of most countries of the world. The quarrel of non-Western peoples can scarcely be with this culture as a whole, although they reject specific facets of it from time to time.

A few other matters of definition should be considered in this introductory chapter. Let us first concede that the terms "colonialism" and "imperialism" are often interchangeable, even though their usage sometimes differs. As for "empires," we should note that imperial expansion has occurred both overland and overseas. Russia and the United States expanded overland at the expense of many native peoples, an expansion which was no less wrong than, for example, British seizure of Kenya in Africa.

This point was overlooked by General Dwight D. Eisenhower in his *Crusade in Europe*, written shortly after World War II, when he attempted to visualize the future of Russo-American relations. He felt optimistic because, "historically," as he saw it, both nations "were free of the stigma of empire building by force." It is important to distinguish between "moving in" en masse, with its frequent consequences of enslavement, assimilation, or extirpation, and mere assumption of control in a colony by a minority of administrators and exploiters.

The broadest definition of "empire" holds that an empire must possess a ruling class which applies *unequal* laws to the diverse groups under its control. This can include forms of domination which are mainly economic, ideological, or racist in character. Profit returned to the dominant group is not an essential criterion; there have been colonies which consistently lost money for the colonizers. Nor does domination of one people by another necessarily mean that the controlling power is altogether injurious to the conquered people. However, in scanning the record of history, we often find that the empires which were almost wholly maleficent, destructive, or greedy—such as the Mongol Empire of Genghis and Kublai Khan—withered rapidly. Those which offered new fruitful modes of life or organization did not decay quickly. Even after their "fall," these "creative" empires were often reincarnated in modified forms. The Roman Empire, for all its failings, can be included in this category.

With this criterion in mind, how may the European empires be rated? It is true that the colonial enterprises of Europe endured, indeed, in an over-all sense expanded, over nearly half a millenium. But the modes of empire altered greatly through those centuries. The nineteenth century form of imperialism, which is most closely associated with the very word, achieved virtually complete global dominion for the white man by the end of that century. Yet, within two decades, reversal of the trend had begun. In evaluating another form of domination, Hitler's Germany, by its durability, we get a seemingly clearer answer—it endured only a few years.

Repression and its Consequences

THE REASON for attempting a recapitulation of white offenses here, and for stressing the collective, unitary nature of white guilt, is that we have forgotten or repressed so much of it. For the future, we badly need to examine the white record, and we must consider the Afro-Asian assessment of that record, even though it may lump together more events, and more responsibility, than we would like.

By repression or misunderstanding, or just lack of information, the people of the West may fail to see their record as others see it. As in psychoanalysis, the record should be brought out, reviewed, and seen from new points of view. Reappraisal can clarify the conscience of Western man, lightening the burden of his anxieties. Proper appraisal of the past record may serve as a corrective to future international or interracial actions which might otherwise be misdirected or misunderstood.

Recognition of repressed material is also valuable because it deprives that negative material of its persistent strength. According to Sigmund Freud, the wishes and impressions harbored in the *id* survive unchanged for decades. Only through the analytic procedure can they be "recognized as belonging to the past, devalued and robbed of their charge of energy by becoming conscious."[4]

In one of his last works, *Civilization and Its Discontents*, Freud called the sense of guilt "the most important problem in the evolution of culture." However, when another psychoanalyst, Theodor

Reik, wrote his *Myth and Guilt* 27 years after Freud's statement, he could find no significant research on the matter during that interval. Even the psychoanalysts evade the problem, Reik charges, ". . . as though they hope it will go away when they do not mention it."[5]

As for "collective guilt," whereby an entire people partakes of the responsibility for violent acts of its members, this idea occurred commonly among the ancient Greeks, the Hebrews of the Old Testament, and other Mediterranean peoples. Why is this concept avoided or rejected so much among modern nations?

Reik considers that men in the aggregate, like individual personalities, have a *superego* (a collective conscience, one might call it) which imposes high standards of virtuous conduct. Therefore, a group which, through innate aggressiveness and destructiveness, has failed to live up to these standards must, according to Reik, feel strong discontent and guilt. A further grim corollary to this theory is that extremism in the pursuit of virtue will itself often produce horrors. Reik quotes Anatole France's words, "Did you not realize that the greatest cruelties, the most horrible massacres are inspired by the idea that man is good and virtuous?"[6] The annals of modern imperialism and totalitarianism provide many illustrations of his thesis.

Why is virtue pushed to extremes so dangerous? One answer is that it becomes unrealistic, feeding the *superego* but neglecting the largely unconscious *id* and the *ego*, thus accumulating aggressiveness which must burst out unexpectedly. Humankind should, therefore, be careful not to expect too much of itself in a moral sense. To ignore human frailty only obliges human aggression to burst out again—*because* a further tragedy of repression is that guilt is often relieved by repeating, or at least acting out, the aggressive deeds or ideas which contributed to the guilt in the first place. Clearly, part of the hazard in this cycle of guilt and aggression can be removed through conscious awareness of the background of guilt. But Western man seems to avoid acknowledgment of the background of guilt most persistently.

Oliver Wendell Holmes once remarked, "The mind of a bigot may be compared to the pupil of the eye; the more light you pour on it the more it contracts."[7] In just this way, the evils of racism seem to thrive best when the guilty nation does not *recognize* the evil. Referring to American racism, James Baldwin speaks bitterly of "what white men do not want to know." In his *Nobody Knows My Name*, Baldwin describes eloquently how evasion of his fellow Negroes' humanity has damaged the nation as a whole, because America "has spent a large part of its time and energy looking away from one of the principal facts of its life." If the problems of race relations are to be solved, says Baldwin, "we must first crack the American image and find out and deal with what it hides."

Almost the same interpretation is made by psychoanalyst Jung, speaking of the self-deception of Western man who blinds himself to the truth with "illusions about our beauty of soul." As Jung puts it, "The Occidental burns incense to himself, and his own countenance is veiled from him in the smoke. But how do we strike men of another colour?"[8]

This willful veiling of reality was apparent even in the well-publicized civil rights campaigns in America during the 1960's. As these events began to percolate slowly into the consciousness of most Americans, one realized that, despite brief episodes of lurid publicity, the attention of the North had not been focussed on the abuse and degradation of the Southern Negro. Only when thousands of organized Northern demonstrators began to enter the South in the 1960's, to contact the abused minority there and experience Southern jails and Southern police actions, did the North begin to understand and acknowledge the condition of the Southern Negro.

Even then, a most dramatic event, the murder of three civil rights workers (two white and one Negro) near Philadelphia, Mississippi, in 1964, was met with widespread public refusal to face up to the plausible facts of the case. Many Southerners, *and* Northerners, would not believe that the three victims, who disappeared under sinister circumstances, could have been killed. It was some sort of trick, people said; the three men were merely hiding somewhere.

When, after long investigation, the three bodies were found, the fact of murder could scarcely be ignored. But even then it was commonly believed—at least in the deep South—that none of the good people of Philadelphia had committed the crime. When nearly a score of suspects were arrested after much careful detective work, the innocence of these people was stoutly maintained by a great many citizens.

Besides the "oblivious" and "forgetful" types of repression, there has been much use of "compartmentation of guilt." A subtle way of lightening a burden of guilt is to split up its components, so that even those which are not repressed are given only individual consideration. In the same manner, a felon might prefer to think of only one escapade at a time, while regretting a full recapitulation of his record in a court of law.

When the white man is confronted with the record of his aggressions against foreign peoples, he often eases the burden by this means, and by synthesizing a justification for any given act of imperialism in comfortable isolation from its many causes, related events, and consequences. John A. Hobson, in his scholarly analysis of imperialism, concludes that "This genius of inconsistency, of holding conflicting ideas or feelings in the mind simultaneously in watertight compartments, is perhaps peculiarly British; . . . it is a condition of the success of this [inconsistent] conduct that it should be unconscious."[9]

Closely related to the self-deception of the racist or imperialist is the artful compartmentation contrived by apostles of European totalitarianism. In 1956, a Hungarian Communist writer, Paloczi-Horvath, wrote a short piece, "A Meeting of Two Young Men," in which he charged the ruthless Communist leadership with precisely this deception. He stated the charge through the complaints of a character called Ivan Karamazov—borrowed, appropriately, from Dostoevsky, a nineteenth century foe of authoritarian rule. Ivan's complaint against his "leader" runs as follows: "Yours was an organized and directed schizophrenia. You did the splitting up yourself into a conscious and unconscious personality, into an honest private person and a ruthless, immoral happiness builder."[10]

It is notorious that people can ignore facts that conflict with their cherished ideas and interests. Even in merely seeing or hearing, we do not register or observe a thing that does not "fit in," and quickly forget matters uncongenial to us. The most widely discussed case of repressed European guilt in modern times involves the Nazi crimes. The opinion is often heard that, since World War II, the Germans have gone in for a massive national attack of amnesia, forgetting the horrors of Hitler's Third Reich. Just as important as repression of past events, however, is the universal habit of filtering from one's current experiences bits of data which are useless or repugnant. It seems that the Germans under Hitler often did not notice death camps or gas chambers, or did not *believe* what they saw.

In fairness to those who preferred to ignore such crimes, we should note that even the victims of Hitler's horrors were incredulous. Bruno Bettelheim, himself a former concentration camp inmate, writes in his "Dachau to Buchenwald": "The prisoners had to convince themselves that this was real, was really happening and not just a nightmare. They were never wholly successful." Among the perpetrators themselves, excuses were easily found in organizational circumstances. Almost everyone engaging in organized violence or tyranny can point to a superior official compelling him to act. The claim can be made that, if one didn't carry out orders, others would do the job, and that others *are* in fact concurrently doing similar deeds.

Carl Jung gives the psychoanalyst's view of the Nazi and post-Nazi phenomena in *Essays on Contemporary Events.* He notes that a large proportion of Germans, including the responsible or educated Germans, refuses to listen to the evidence of German barbarities all around Europe during World War II. He says that they acknowledge only: "All kinds of regrettable things did happen, it is true, but that was during the war." He complains that even those who did admit to real German crimes will still project the evil on others, in that they proceed to dwell upon outrages committed by the British, for example.

Especially relevant to the present study is Jung's concept of participation by non-Germans in the guilt of Hitler's Reich. Jung was a Swiss citizen, but felt a *participation mystique* with the Hitlerian events and experienced a full range of the "psychological

13 :

concept of collective guilt." Jung compares the record of the Third
Reich to "the case-sheet of a hysterical subject's illness." He sees
this hysteria as related to a strong German feeling of inferiority
from which sprang a *hysterical dissociation* of the personality.
This dissociation led to an obsession with guilt, even though the
guilt was projected upon others. All that was dark or charged with
guilt was sought and found in others, notably Jews, Bolsheviks,
and American financiers. Jung declares that this diagnosis of the
mental condition "applies to the whole nation [i.e., the Germans]
and beyond that to the whole of Europe, whose general mental
condition for some time past has hardly been normal."

Dr. Jung's methodical discussion explaining his particular
usage of the word "guilt" does a lot to clarify the matter of guilt
for us all. He says that the psychological concept of guilt means
an irrational presence of a subjective feeling of guilt. He is careful
to say that this psychological usage should not be confused with
"guilt" in the legal or moral sense alone. He gives the example
of a man who belongs to a family, one member of which has committed a crime. Though this man is not legally or morally responsible, an atmosphere of guilt does reach him, in that his family
name has been sullied. Even less rationally or precisely, the crime
committed may involve a village, a house, or a locale; the involvement is real in that it extends to the people of that location in addition to those directly concerned.

In regard to political and social matters, Jung broadens his
application of collective guilt; in the case of the Nazi horrors he
sees all Europe and the Christian church as a whole to be involved.
He points out that an Asian would see most Europeans as sharing
responsibility for the crimes of Dachau Concentration Camp, just
as we might have blamed India, or all Indians, for the Black Hole
of Calcutta episode, instead of limiting this unpleasant association
to Suraja Dowla, the Nawab of Bengal. Jung's comparison is gener-
all borne out by the fact that the Indian subcontinent and Europe
have been comparable in numbers of inhabitants and ethnic
diversity.

Dr. Jung is aware that the psychological concept of collective
guilt will be regarded poorly by many persons, who may call it

an unfair, sweeping judgment. He acknowledges that this criticism is correct in a sense, but is able to point out that prejudice and sweeping judgments are indeed part of the substance of collective guilt.

Another non-logical, but equally real, aspect of collective guilt is the involvement of ordinary citizens in sensational crimes. Of course the ordinary citizen has had nothing to do with the criminal event, but psychologically he is much involved. He is often passionately interested in the chase after the criminal, the detective work, and the trial. The lurid crime has an exciting effect on the average citizen. Furthermore, involvement of the beholder in matters of crime or brutality will contain what we might call a feedback factor. Jung feels that the evil in the beholder determines the degree of hateful response to the wickedness observed. Environmental evil may operate as an infection, stirring up the evil acts or thoughts of the observer.

The wickedness of one's neighbor or one's neighbor country can be harmful in still another way. As Jung sees it, if one's rival or antagonist, or the rival of one's fatherland, is accepted as the repository of all evil, then the guilt or anxiety which one is harboring anyway will probably be projected upon the antagonist.[11] In this all too common situation, whatever wicked steps have to be taken by one's own side can be justified as a supposedly unavoidable consequence of the foul deeds or menaces of the other party.

Brand new ways in which repression of guilt may interfere with human progress are considered by atomic scientist Edward Teller in *The Legacy of Hiroshima*. He fears that Western man has been forced by the nuclear bomb and other radically new, destructive weapons into the equivalent of a sudden transition from childlike security to insecure adulthood. Teller recognizes the danger that men may flee from the menacing array of new realities, taking refuge in unreality, with repression of uncongenial memories and denial that the more horrendous problems exist at all. All the suppressed anxieties and guilt left untreated by such tactics then interfere, says Teller, with man's urgently needed constructive endeavors.

We have found two ways in which the white man's guilt

is important: as a body of grievances which the non-white world may hold against the white man, and as a burden of anxieties in the minds of Europeans and Americans. In the latter respect, the anxiety is probably reinforced by a sense of unearned or unmerited riches and comfort. Europeans and Americans are, after all, the world's best-fixed people—far better off than the rest of the world and, in fact, far more comfortable than their own forebears of 50 or 100 years ago.

The question therefore arises: To what extent do these unprecedentedly affluent people feel unworthy of their comforts and, consequently, uneasy? Also, to what extent might this sense of unworthiness bring about—especially in the leadership groups of Western nations—an unclearness of purpose, a vacillation or weakness in pursuit of national goals? Other related questions are these. Has the self-confidence of the West been faltering in the mid-twentieth century because the intense feelings or faith of its adversaries have made a deeper impression than anyone thought possible? Is it in consequence of this impression, or guilt-feeling, if you will, that a Western nation, even a most powerful one, may falter even when its physical forces are intact, so that it neither fights nor negotiates effectively?

THE COLLECTIVITY OF THE PERPETRATORS

BEFORE GOING ON, in ensuing chapters, to review offenses committed by Europeans and Americans in recent centuries, I must ask the reader to consider two questions: Are these "white" nations to be held collectively responsible for their respective aggressions and tyrannies, in one great, unitary Western body? Are the non-Western nations inclined to view these aggressors as a single, closely involved, or homogeneous group?

To answer briefly, let us focus for a moment on Nazism in Germany. Was it just an accident, a regression to primitive violence? Reinhold Niebuhr, for one, does not think so, but believes that the modern Western peoples share a taste for violence.[12]

It appears entirely plausible that Nazism constitutes a continuation of the revolt against the Judæo-Christian tradition which picked up momentum in the eighteenth century, when philosophers of the Enlightenment tried to substitute *reason* for *faith*.

A general concession that other powers shared the Nazis' responsibility was heard at Nuremberg, when Chief Prosecutor Jackson said, at the outset of the war crimes trials: "The real complaining party at your bar is Civilization. In all our countries it is still a struggling and imperfect thing. It does not plead that the United States, or any other country, has been blameless of the conditions which made the German people easy victims to the blandishments and intimidations of the Nazi conspirators."

Even more eloquent testimony to this joint involvement was provided when the Four Power Agreement for prosecution of Nazi war criminals was signed in London, August 8, 1945, because the world had just heard about the dropping of the first atomic bomb on a city of Japan. The following day, August 9, would witness the dropping of a plutonium bomb on a second Japanese metropolis.

Now the Hitler Era had receded somewhat into the past. Are there heirs to Hitler's ideals in the Western camp? The following observations, made by Prime Minister Verwoerd of the Union of South Africa in an address to his country's House of Assembly, March 10, 1960, are noteworthy less for their extremism than for the likelihood that a large portion of Europeans and Americans concur in them:

> The West, which once abetted the "whites-must-go" theory for independence, has since come to realize how important is the need for its continued aid and ministrations in Africa if the new states are not to fall prey to avid Communist aspirations or become exploited by traders and colonists from the East.
>
> Non-white people have outnumbered white people on this earth for more than 400 years; nevertheless, it was the white people who through that time played the dominant role, as indeed they still do, on the ground of their superior strength in other respects—strength of character, initiative, creative genius and intellect.

Other Verwoerd statements, of a more radical sort, would doubtless fail to get broad Western support; but the ideas quoted above show that there is still much common ground between the Verwoerd mind and a large segment of the Western community.

To the Afro-Asian observer, the white world seems to have been of one mind in modern times. You could hardly persuade him, for example, that fondness for military glory is peculiarly French, that dictatorial rule is most of all a German habit, or that Russians are more cruel than British in warfare. Despite various differences in national customs and languages, one can argue effectively that modern Europe is homogeneous in an ideological sense and in a general cultural sense. Such a point is generally conceded with regard to Medieval Europe.

More recently, modern European nationalism has dramatized antagonisms among European nations, and there have been two World Wars to show that the antagonisms were genuine. However, the depth of European solidarity is apparent from the fact that, from the end of the Napoleonic Wars until World War I, the powers of Europe limited their quarrels and fought only short or inexpensive wars. During that entire span of 100 years, the only war *within* the Western community that could be called cataclysmic, in losses of men and property, and lasted more than a couple of years, was the Civil War in the United States.

The European powers all had similar concepts of propriety *and* expediency in the relationship among their homelands. Vis-à-vis their colonial victims, however, they dropped their intra-European politesse and diplomatic restraint. The egalitarian relationship of intra-European international law was not supposed to apply to the "lesser breeds without the law" in Africa and Asia.

A detailed demonstration of the diplomatic rapport of Europe is found in the voluminous diplomatic histories of modern Europe, especially as concerns nineteenth century European acquisition of colonies. Repeatedly, in the 1880's and 1890's, statesmen of Europe gathered at great conferences to determine the fate of the non-European world. Africa, in particular, was parcelled out in a series of these conferences.

To cite just a few examples of how this cooperation worked and how essential it was in the progress of imperialism, German support was probably indispensable in the French seizures of colonies in West Africa, Madagascar, and Indo-China during the nineteenth century. Without Bismarck's endorsement of these projects, British resistance would have been strongly felt. Bismarck, without even concealing his motives, put himself in this role of accessory to French colonialism because he hoped to divert France's attention from her losses in the Franco-Prussian War and maintain German predominance on the European Continent.

India's Jawaharlal Nehru recognized this European collectivity practiced by the colonialist. Describing India's plight under British rule in his book *The Discovery of India*, Nehru commented, "Racialism in India is not so much English versus Indian. It is European as opposed to Asiatic. In India every European ... is automatically a member of the ruling race." Nehru observed during World War II that thousands of European prisoners of war, mostly Italians, were kept in India. He compared their treatment, under the guarantees of the Geneva Convention, with the frequently inhumane treatment of the thousands of Indian political prisoners then in British jails. This latter group were often victims of inadequate diet, corporal punishment, and other cruelties. For them, said Nehru, "There was no convention or law or rule to govern the conditions under which [they] had to exist."[13]

It is interesting to find Nehru sizing up the principal Western nations in terms of their national animals—the British lion and bulldog, the eagle of Germany and the United States, the Russian bear, and the fighting cock of France. Nehru suspected that these creatures were national symbols because they reflected the national character, and noted that all of those just named were "aggressive, fighting animals, beasts of prey." Nehru believed that people who lived with these as symbols were, in fact, people who "strike up aggressive attitudes, roar, and prey on others."[14]

With the advent of Fascism and Nazism, did Nehru and the multitudes of Asian intellectuals who shared his thoughts consider these dreadful movements to be entirely separate and different from the main body of Western thoughts and acts? Sad to relate, they did not.

Expressing the revulsion of his people to Fascism and Nazism,

Jawaharlal Nehru said that the Indians' own experiences "were enough to teach us to what these Nazi principles and theories of life and the state ultimately led. For our people had been the victims for long of those very principles and methods of government." Indeed, Nehru believed that the appeasement of Hitler in the 1930's was due not only to fear, but also to the Western powers' "sneaking admiration for him."[15] What of the United States? Writing in 1933 concerning Franklin D. Roosevelt's program for saving America from the Depression, Nehru seems to admire the President personally, but identifies his program as "state socialism" and opines that "He seems to represent forces which, as the crisis develops, may turn more and more to fascism."[16] Of course, this fear of 1933 did not materialize in any clear and immediate way during the ensuing decades. Meanwhile, however, a succession of noisy and influential American expansionists or jingoists had said enough to show their ideological identity with the imperialists of Europe.

At the beginning of the twentieth century, it was evident that the American expansionist Senator Albert J. Beveridge had a special regard for his fellow expansionists of Russia and Germany. Only these two powers, said he, "had a clearly defined Asiatic policy." He also credited the Germans with "the keenest commercial minds ... the steadiest energy ... the most assertive national spirit, and the most vivid racial *esprit de corps* in Europe."[17] Such men as Beveridge met with widespread disagreement among their fellow citizens; however, their words, when read by Asians or Africans, sound authentically American, because they were, for three decades after 1898, underscored by quite a few concretely aggressive acts by the United States.

Besides taking a careful look at white expansionism in the chapters which follow, it is going to be necessary to find out to what extent the same motives underlay those other pernicious features of the West in modern times, racism and totalitarianism.

Imperialism, says Robin Winks, is a matter of "Gold, God, or Glory." A. P. Thornton relates imperialism to "Profit, Power, and Civilization," which comes close to being the same three factors, differently arranged. This three-way explanation is, I believe, more reasonable and more complete than various attempts to account for imperialism as mainly economic or little more than a series of military and ideological thrusts.

I would also like to stress that this threefold explanation can be made to account as well for other abuses discussed in this book—racism, nationalism, and totalitarianism. However, it is possible that the basic motivation behind all this is more subtle, perhaps best expressed in what Carl Jung heard from an American Indian friend of his, who was governor of a pueblo: "We don't understand the whites; they are always wanting something—always restless—always looking for something. . . . We think they are all crazy."[18]

The Indian had identified one of the central reasons for the white man's obstreperousness—his restless, questing, crusading drive. Sometimes this is called a Faustian or Promethean urge—the will to extend one's power, discover, and master. Did this Faustian ambition produce both the great cultural and industrial developments of Europe *and* the white drive for dominion over men? Perhaps; or you may prefer to identify as "Messianism" most of the problems under study here, thus stressing the white man's habitual view of himself as heaven-sent deliverer.

Sigmund Freud, like many another student of human nature, is aware of the adaptability of human aggressiveness whch can pretend, as he says, to be in the service of "some other purpose, whose goal might also have been reached by milder measures."[19] This we may take as Freud's way of accounting for several rationales of imperialism or racism—the need to spread the Gospel, share the benefits of civilization, or glorify one's homeland. Carl Jung explains Messianism as being derived from man's proneness to identify with God himself "that still small voice" within his own mind. In man's uncritical heeding of the inner voice, says Jung, "he even runs the grave risk of believing he has a Messianic mission, and forces tyrannic doctrines upon his fellow-beings."[20]

A similarly Messianic explanation has been formulated by French statesman and historian Georges Sorel in his *Reflections on Violence.* He found that promoters of great revolutionary movements always foresee an apocalyptic conflict from which they will emerge triumphant. This myth of the cosmic conflict appears effective in enlisting popular support for "the cause," as totalitarians through the ages have discovered. As Sorel explains it, striving for a certain kind of future becomes hardest to resist when the designs for the future take the form of "myths, which enclose with them all the strongest inclinations of a people, of a party or of a class, inclinations which recur to the mind with the insistence of instincts. . . ."[21]

Turning again to the psychoanalysts, one reaches an explanation that may be most basic of all. Carl Jung often refers to *archetypes*, that is, patterns of instinctual human behavior, to explain social trends. According to Jung, there is a *collective* (or public) *unconscious*, made up essentially of archetypes, while the *personal unconscious* consists mostly of complexes. Having defined these forces, Jung proceeds to illustrate their fateful application to the problems of our time:

> There is no lunacy people under the domination of an archetype will not fall a prey to. If 30 years ago [that is, 30 years before Hitler's genocides] anyone had dared to predict that our psychological development was tending towards a revival of the medieval persecutions of the Jews, that Europe would again tremble before the Roman fasces and the tramp of legions, that people would once more give the Roman salute, as two thousand years ago, and that instead of the Christian cross an archaic swastika would lure onward millions of warriers ready for death—why, that man would have been hooted at as a mystical fool.

The general theory outlined above does cast light on our problems, and appears to fit the facts very well indeed. Of less certain applicability, but worth mentioning as an attempt to explain the problems of Western man in more specific terms, is the derivation of modern European Messianism from the Protestant Reformation, or, alternatively, from the long-simmering conflicts in Christian Europe among the ill-absorbed, pre-Christian paganism, the Græco-Hebrew religious tradition, and militant Protestantism.

Jung believed that Protestantism had deprived its adherents of too many essential symbols; to him the health of the mind depended on the dynamic contribution of symbols and rites which, like those of traditional Christianity, fitted the needs of the human personality. Says the psychoanalyst, "The desymbolized world of the Protestant produced first an unhealthy sentimentality and then a sharpening of the moral conflict, which because it was so unbearable, led logically to Nietzsche's 'beyond good and evil' [that is, unbridled use of power in any expedient way]."[22]

:: II ::

Europe's Discovery of
the World around it

WHY EUROPE EXPANDED

ALMOST ALL of the major misdeeds under discussion in this book have been connected in some way with the expansion of European power that began with the discovery of America and da Gama's voyage of 1498 to India. Rapid seizure of most of South and Central America by the Spanish and Portuguese followed these expeditions, with consequent enslavement and highly profitable exploitation of the conquered peoples. Though in some areas full conquest and occupation was still almost three centuries away, eventually almost all Indian inhabitants of the Western Hemisphere were dispossessed of their lands, a process in which most of Western and Central Europe took some part.

It might have been difficult in the first years of the fifteenth century to prophesy that a great age of expansion lay ahead of Europe. Europeans were hard-pressed by non-Christian powers on many of their frontiers, and were certainly not equal in civilization or power to the mighty empire of China. In the early 1400's, Islam appeared to be a great expansionist force. The Moslems were in the process of taking over India, and Islamic influence was also expanding through the Indonesian Islands. Islam and Buddhism were the dominant religions of Central Asia, while Christianity seemed to have lost its chance for expansion in Asia when the Dynasty of the Mongols came to an end in China, being supplanted by a native Chinese dynasty. The Mongols had allowed considerable latitude to Christian missionaries; after their fall the scope for Christian missions was very much narrowed.

In Western Asia, of course, the Moslem Turks had in 1453 demolished the remainder of the Byzantine Empire by their capture of Constantinople, nor was that the end of their expansion in that region. They went on to conquer the Balkans and, at times, even threaten the Hapsburg capital of Vienna. Syria fell to the Ottoman armies, and their conquest of Egypt in 1517 cut off that last useful, open route for trade between the Eastern Mediterranean and Asia. The disruption that had begun with the fall of Byzantine Constantinople to the Turks in 1453 was now complete, and European trade had to follow entirely new paths to Asia.

Even at this time, however, the most profitable and wide-ranging oceangoing trade in the world was the Arab commerce, reaching from Southeast Asia along the entire northern and western shores of the Indian Ocean. Many essentials of the future, oceanborne expansion of the Europeans, such as the compass, gunpowder, and lateen sails, were in Asian or Moslem hands, unknown to Europeans until the thirteenth or fourteenth century.

One might wonder what could have launched the Europeans on their course of expansion. An early inspiration was the crusade concept, an idea which helped to inspire European expansionism throughout its entire development. The original crusades, though they had ended in the thirteenth century, had left Europeans imbued with the idea of organized warfare against non-Christians, warfare sanctified by religious objectives, a mandate from God Himself. This is an idea to keep in mind when observing the subsequent development of European colonialism and imperialism.

Besides the crusades in the Eastern Mediterranean, there came a whole series of crusade-like campaigns against the infidels of Spain, the Moslem Moors who had for centuries prevailed against the Christians in much of Spain. Beginning in 1415, the Portuguese organized a campaign which claimed to be a crusade, and which did attain its objective of capturing Ceuta in Morocco.

The crusading idea had much to do with early Portuguese interest in Africa, because, in addition to the obvious presence of infidels in the Iberian peninsula and Morocco, there were supposedly fabulous Christian kingdoms deep within Africa, and good Christians felt obliged to make contact with them. Further related to these considerations was the desire of Europeans to have a better route for trade with Asia, now that the Turks controlled the Eastern Mediterranean. The movement of European exploration down the African coast is generally credited more to Prince Henry the Navigator of Portugal than any other single man. This Prince had served in the Ceuta campaign, and it was he who encouraged pushing exploration farther and farther down the West African coast.

Aside from the ambitions and desires of the Europeans, there were some practical and technical developments which had to take place before European expansion would be possible: improvements in the three closely related fields of geography, navigation, and astronomy were the first great requirements; shipbuilding and ship handling were the second; and improvements in firearms, including naval ordnance, were the third of these key developments. The details of these developments are very well described in J. H. Parry's *The Establishment of the European Hegemony, 1415–1715*.

The Greeks, in the time of Eratosthenes, had made a good beginning in the first of these fields by reckoning the circumference of the earth quite accurately. Ptolemy, in the Egypt of A.D. 130, produced important works on astronomy and geography, and Islamic scholars whose culture was the light of the Mediterranean world in early medieval times put Ptolemy's book on astronomy to good use. As with so many important cultural matters, the Arabs preserved the source material and thus enabled the Europeans to use it later. The Ptolemaic book of geography became availablt again in Europe in 1410, when it was translated into Latin.

The related technology of mapmaking began its slow improvement in Renaissance times. In the thirteenth century, if not earlier, Italian and Spanish cartographers began to produce charts called portolani. These were not mathematically precise, but were very careful drawings which recorded all observations of coastal and island landmarks. Later, in the sixteenth century, Mercator's new technique of projection made it possible to put systematic indications of latitude and longitude on the charts, with both latitude and longitude drawn as straight lines.

Without all these developments, further voyages beyond the coasts of Europe and Africa would have been just about impossible. The thought of proceeding far out to sea in the vast waters of the Atlantic, without a means of knowing one's location, was understandably appalling to the navigator of the fourteenth century. Of course the Viking voyagers had succeeded, hundreds of years earlier, in reaching North America, but they had done so by long, indirect routes. In part, their voyages followed the coasts (of Greenland and Labrador) and utilized stopovers at the Faroes, Iceland, and other islands, so that their uninterrupted ocean voyage in the North Atlantic was much shorter than one might suppose.

By the end of the fifteenth century, the better navigators could determine latitude fairly accurately, and had serviceable charts on which they could record positions and plot courses. Although longitude could not be estimated with accuracy until the eighteenth century, navigators could now combine observation of latitude with the well-explored process of dead reckoning, and thus fear of unknown ocean waters was much reduced. As for the compass, it had been known to Europeans since the 1200's, but it was in the fifteenth century that the compass and other navigational instruments reached a state of development making possible fairly precise navigation.

The fifteenth century was also notable for progress in ship construction. The Europeans had begun that century with ships that compared poorly with those of some Asian nations, but the end of the century found them in possession of ships equal to any in the world. The Arabs had developed a lateen-type sail—a fore-and-aft rigged sail—and they continued for centuries to use that rig alone. Europeans of the late fifteenth century, however, were flexible enough to use combinations of their old square-rigged sails and the lateen rig. They were thus able to build much larger ships, rising in tonnage from a few hundred tons to a thousand before the sixteenth century had ended. With such vessels, the Europeans had maneuverable ships which could take them anywhere in the world, and could outperform African or Asian craft.

As for naval gunnery, this too really began to develop in the fourteenth and fifteenth centuries, and by the sixteenth century the number and size of guns had increased so much that stability of the ship was best served by placing them below the open deck, to fire through gun-ports.

Not only did the Portuguese lead European traders to Asia, but, according to Professor Parry, they probably were the first to realize that guns, not men, were the primary resource in naval warfare. He notes that the Indian Ocean was the scene of the first naval battles ever fought with a primary view to sinking ships by naval gunfire. Therefore, in the very process of arriving in Asia, Westerners became equipped with superior ships which had a formidable armament.

THE PORTUGUESE EMPIRE

THE PORTUGUESE COLONIAL EMPIRE grew rapidly after the first voyages of discovery. Pedro Alvares Cabral crossed the Atlantic in 1500 and discovered the coast of Brazil. This was territory which belonged to Portugal by virtue of her treaty of 1494 with Spain, and was to be a large and long-term Portuguese possession.

In the New World, besides discovery of Brazil by Cabral, the Portuguese should be credited with a voyage in 1500 to Greenland and Labrador, followed by other explorations of Labrador and Newfoundland during the next two years. Also in that two-year period came the voyages of Amerigo Vespucci, an Italian explorer in Portuguese service, which achieved further exploration of the Brazilian coast, not to mention eventual bestowal of the name "America" on the continents of the New World in his honor.

Within a few years, the Portuguese empire in South and Southeast Asia also developed greatly. Its cornerstones were laid by Afonso de Albuquerque, who began to direct the building of Portugal's Asian empire in 1509. The following six years found

Albuquerque's forces spreading out in all directions. It was he who took Goa on India's west coast. In Indonesia he acquired Malacca, while in the West Indian Ocean area he provided important links for Portugal by seizure of Muscat on the eastern end of the Arabian Peninsula, as well as Ormuz on the Persian Gulf. He tried to take Aden, strategically located at the entrance to the Red Sea, but was unable to do so. A little later, in 1511, Albuquerque dispatched a force to the Banda Islands and the Moluccas, important spice sources. The same fleet soon afterward entered the Pacific Ocean proper.

In 1518, the Portuguese received reluctant permission from the ruler of Kotte, one of the principal kingdoms of Ceylon, to build a fort. After that, the Portuguese position in Ceylon and South India became strong. Portuguese merchants and missionaries alike were successful, and politically the Portuguese portion of the island was under the rule of their Viceroy in the Indian city of Goa—the Portuguese capital for South Asia.

Siam, Java, and Formosa also came within the area of Portuguese visitations and trade. In 1514 the Portuguese representative arrived in Canton, and somewhat later, in 1557, Macau, near Canton on the China coast, was made a permanent Portuguese colony.

Had the Portuguese held on to all territories in which they had this initial interest, their empire would have been a mighty colonial network. Even Japan and Abyssinia would then presumably have been taken by Portugal. However, the Portuguese were more gifted as voyagers and reporters than as traders and colonizers. Perhaps it was simply not possible for a country located and composed as Portugal was in Europe to become a great colonial power. Her capital of Lisbon was just not well located to be Europe's prime trading center with the continents beyond the seas. First Antwerp, and later Amsterdam, in the Low Countries did become such a primary center, and Portugal inevitably became a second-rate colonial empire.

SPAIN AND THE NEW WORLD

THE VOYAGES of Columbus, which discovered several islands of the Western Hemisphere and made the existence of New World lands known to Europe, naturally also meant the foundation of Spain's empire in the new lands. Besides numerous islands of the West Indies—those found by Columbus and others—we should note Ponce de Leon's discovery of Florida in 1512, followed the next year by Balboa's crossing of the Panamanian Isthmus to discover the Pacific Ocean (not quite the first European sighting of that body if we count the Portuguese sighting of it during Indonesian voyages in 1512). In 1519, Alvárez Pineda completed his voyages of exploration in the Gulf of Mexico all the way from Florida to Vera Cruz, and in that same year Magellan began the first round-the-world voyage in history.

The first Spanish capital in the West Indies was established on San Domingo. Other notable conquests were Puerto Rico, fully occupied by 1511, and Jamaica, colonized about the same time. Beginning in 1509, the Spanish placed a settlement in Panama and, within the decade, had set up a trans-isthmian route. (This route was naturally important as a link with the west coast of South America, where other major Spanish colonization was shortly to come. Both this isthmus and the Tehuantepec Isthmus of Mexico were also to be important as routes of transit for valuable cargoes en route from Asia and the Philippines to the Spanish homeland.)

In 1518 Hernando Cortes took a force of 600 men from Cuba to the coast of Mexico. After setting up his authority at what is now Vera Cruz, he made contact with the ruler of the highly de-veloped Aztec empire. Before approaching the capital, Cortes gained the support of certain subject peoples of the Aztecs, after which, in 1519, he was in a position to move on to the capital, Tenochtitlan. Although his initial entry was peaceable, Cortes soon betrayed the trust of his hosts. He made the ruler, Montezuma, a prisoner, and overzealous destruction of "heathen" temples by the Spaniards caused the Aztecs to rise against him. After some narrow escapes from complete defeat, Cortes' forces were able to fight their way out of the capital city. They still had the support of the non-Aztec people of Eastern Mexico, and received further reinforcements from Cuba. Returning to the capital, they besieged it and gradually overwhelmed the Aztec forces, until by 1521 the city was entirely theirs. Their destruction of the great city's buildings was so ferociously complete that almost nothing remained for future archaeologists or historians to study. On the same site, Cortes established a city which we now know as Mexico City, the capital of Mexico.

This new Spanish possession, Mexico, became highly prosperous. Cortes was a clever administrator able to rule the Indians, once they were conquered, with a fairly moderate level of violence and cruelty. By the middle 1500's, the already considerable production of precious metals in Mexico was augmented by the opening of productive silver mines at Zacatecas and Guanajuato. In Mexico, as in the other New World colonies of Spain, trade was a monopoly, but not a direct monopoly, of the King. The monarch permitted this monopoly to be held by the merchant guild of Seville. Not only Spain, but other colonizers of the New World maintained thoroughly monopolistic trade arrangements of some sort from the sixteenth into at least the eighteenth centuries.

In the 1520's, Cortes sent conquering forces through Central America which took over the chief centers of population and other worthwhile places there. They often proceeded with less diplomacy and even more brutality than Cortes had used in the conquest of Mexico itself. The Mayan peoples in the Yucatan were beaten into submission in the long period from 1527 to 1535, and were ruled so oppressively that they revolted in 1546, but without success.

Spanish explorers and settlers also moved northward from Mexico into what are now the southwestern states of the United States, the vast region extending from Texas to California. This development gained impetus, not only from the usual interest in precious metals and other possible riches of the region, but also from seizure of the Philippine Islands by the Spaniards. Trans-Pacific trade made the western coast of both Central and Northern America a region of strategic interest to the Spaniards.

A notable instance of Central European participation in early operations of colonization came in 1527, when Charles V, Hapsburg King of Spain and Holy Roman Emperor, leased Venezuela to the German banking house of Welser. The Welsers were given this truly king-sized leasehold as security for a debt, and for nearly 20 years had Venezuela for their very own. Such Welser employees as Speyer, von Hutten, Federmann, and Alfinger pioneered settlements there and explored Venezuela's interior. Before Charles finally canceled the lease, these German overlords had built a reputation for cruel exploitation of the Venezuelan Indians. Their ruthlessness must indeed have been great to distinguish them in an age of cruel Spanish conquests.

As Spanish power moved into South America, the Chibcha Indians, living in the highlands of Colombia, were especially likely to attract the plunder-hungry Europeans. They had observed an annual rite for installation of their ruler wherein they coated his entire body with gold dust. Although the rite fell into disuse long before the coming of the Spaniards, the aura of wealth created by rumors of this practice was sure to bring conquistadores to Chibcha lands. Arriving in 1538, a Spanish force failed to find the anticipated wealth but did begin seizure of the region for the Spanish Crown.

Moving farther south, other Spaniards had entered the Peruvian area sufficiently to be aware of the importance of the empire of the Incas. Pizarro had done preliminary exploration of this area from 1524 to 1528, after which he obtained from the Spanish Crown very specific rights to the conquest of Peru. In 1531 Pizarro led his expedition against the Inca empire. He met its ruler, Atahualpa, and although the Inca was accompanied by a great army, Pizarro was successful in seizing the person of the Inca. That great king had such centralized, autocratic power that there was no satisfactory means for continuity of government when he was captured; Incan power lay moribund in the face of the Spanish intruders.

In 1533, having been promised release, the Inca raised a ransom in precious metals, but was killed by the Spaniards anyway. Peru was added to Spain's empire; there followed years of plundering this rich conquest of its vast stores of gold and silver. In 1545, great silver mines were put into production at Potosí, now a city of Bolivia. Such intervening lands as Ecuador were explored and conquered, and in addition to all the conquest and plundering, the Spaniards found time for civil wars among themselves. There was a long struggle between Pizarro and his former collaborator Almagro which ended in the execution of Almagro in 1538. Other rivals also fought against Pizarro, and in time they too were executed. Seldom did the coming of Europe's civilization mean that peace or harmony were to reign.

Although the Spaniards were resisted strongly by Indian inhabitants almost everywhere in the Americas, by 1550 Spain controlled all the principal cities and strategic points in tropical America, except the Portuguese holdings. Spanish expansion southward from Peru was stopped only in southern Chile, where the Araucanian Indians held out successfully to preserve their freedom. Spanish progress north of Mexico was slow but steady. There was a setback in New Mexico, where the natives revolted in 1680 and drove out the Spaniards, but the latter reconquered the region by 1696. Settlement of Texas from Mexico was not really undertaken until the first quarter of the eighteenth century, and the more important settlements of the modern American state of California were made by colonizers from Mexico in the late 1700's.

Though there were various competitive forces at work in the Spanish colonial empire—clergy, soldiers, traders, desperadoes, and administrators—there was something of a totalitarian approach to administration of the empire, insofar as Madrid could manage it. The Spanish Crown, like the French, had been at some pains to cut the Spanish nobility down to size and establish a strong, centralized rule. Consequently, the Spanish Government was most anxious to avoid real decentralization of authority in the New World, and certainly the Spanish King had full rights to his New World holdings, in European and Christian terms. Like all rulers who were beneficiaries of New World treasure, the monarch had ample means for hiring armies, financing military operations, and, in short, policing his domains. The King had the right of prior exploration and settlement in almost every case, and the Pope had, by his Bull of 1493, formally given the King of Spain the sacred duty of Christianizing and governing the New World.

The geographic immensity of global European empires from the sixteenth century onward obliged the rulers to organize bureaucratic machines of greater complexity and impersonality. The rulers, and even their most trusted assistants, could not visit their worldwide domains, or even communicate rapidly with them, before the twentieth century.

Even within the European homelands, consolidation of large national governments was sure to bring elaboration of administrative apparatus, but the additional need to coordinate overseas empires brought forth especially refined systems of directives, supervisory devices, and reporting systems. The ruler had to exact not only personal loyalty to himself, but also impersonal loyalty to the dictates of his bureaucracy. Thus, very early in the saga of Europe's global expansion, we see colonial conditions promoting the growth of centralized, authoritarian bureaucracies.

Spanish overlords in the New World naturally found ample justification for keeping the Indians under a brutally tight rule. Although the Spanish missionaries recognized the Indians as fellow men and candidates for salvation, many Spaniards firmly believed the Indians to be animals, not rational humans. As evidence of this, they pointed to the Indians' way of life on the lowest level of subsistence, with no apparent desire to become rich or live in a better or different way. The Spanish authorities often felt that stern rule and systematic economic development, imposed from above, was best for all concerned. To show the effect of this Spanish rule, take as an example Mexico. Its state is best summarized by the total population figures for central Mexico, which show a decline from about 11,000,000 in 1519 to 3,700,000 in 1793.[1]

Contrasted to the plundering and profiteering Spanish entrepreneurs were such idealists as Father Bartolomé de Las Casas, who insisted that the Indians were proper objects of Christian mission work, but were as much entitled to the protection of their sovereign, the King of Spain, as any other Spanish subjects. Las Casas even insisted that the conversion of Indians to Christianity be voluntary. He made a deep impression with his reports of horrible Spanish mistreatment of the Indians. The Spanish Court was interested, and the Pope supported Las Casas' allegation that the Indians were human beings who possessed immortal souls. The English took up the good Father's charges of cruelty and incorporated them into the traditional British view of the "cruel Spaniards."

In opposition to Las Casas, aggressive colonialism obtained support from an eminent Spanish humanist and philosopher, Juan Ginés de Sepúlveda, who in 1542 undertook to explain the colonial obligations of Spain on the basis of natural law. He was not unusual among traditional European philosophers in founding concepts of law and moral obligations on natural law. It is interesting that he believed only the ablest men of the higher races could properly determine what was or was not natural law. Thus, he was really calling for a natural aristocracy in which the lower races would be governed by the higher. The end result of this philosophy seems to be a mandate for the higher races to conquer lower forms of humanity, if need be, so that those lesser folk can enjoy the superior way of life of the more civilized race. Sepúlveda believed that a superior civilized government was justified in conquering barbarous nations by force by the innate servility of barbarians, crimes of barbarians against natural law, the obligation to rescue various victims of the barbarian rulers (who might be oppressing or enslaving them), and the duty to make available to the barbarians the preaching of the Christian gospel.

In 1550, a great debate was staged between Sepúlveda and Las Casas on the question of the morality of conquest as a means of spreading the faith. The debate was inconclusive at the time, but by 1570 Las Casas' work bore some fruit: Indian slavery was much reduced, as was imposition of forced labor in the American mines in lieu of tribute.

In the temperate lands of the New World, the Spanish entrepreneurs often left farming in the hands of Indians and turned to animal husbandry as a chief interest. This became a great industry, producing vast quantities of horses, sheep, and cattle. In the West Indies and some parts of the tropical coastlands of the American continents, cultivation of sugar and tobacco under a plantation system became the rule of the day. Since sugar production required complex cane-crushing and extraction equipment, very large plantations were the logical arrangement. Sugar and tobacco also seemed to lead logically to use of black African slaves as the primary labor source. Father Las Casas had managed to obstruct the cruel exploitation of the Indians as slave labor. Indians may not have been ideal plantation laborers and, indeed, were virtually exterminated through overwork, abuse, and even straightforward massacres. Their thinning ranks were filled by imported African slaves whose fate, for some reason, disturbed the Spanish conscience even less than the sufferings of Indians.

The Spanish settlers in the New World wished to be left alone as much as possible by officials who acted for the King. The settlers wanted the Crown to give them protection and grants of land, and make those grants hereditary estates on which they would have the freedom to enslave and oppress the Indians as they wished. However, oppression of the Indians seldom had a truly racist flavor. The Spanish, and their French neighbors in North America, often married Indian women, and there arose a large class of inhabitants of mixed race. Although this class was identified permanently by the Spanish name Mestizo, segregation of the Mestizo class from pure Spaniards and from pure Indians was essentially a question of social stratification rather than a matter of race prejudice.

THE FRENCH COLONIES

THE EARLY colonial efforts of France were concentrated upon North America. As early as 1524 a French group sponsored the voyage of Verrazano to look over the North American coastline from Nova Scotia in the north to the Carolinas in the south. After this preliminary exploration, Jacques Cartier accomplished some exploration of Canada proper. In the 1530's, he not only surveyed the coast of Labrador and Newfoundland, but also went up the St. Lawrence River as far as the present site of Montreal. Later, on a return voyage, Cartier made a settlement where Quebec now stands, but this was not a lasting colonization.

There followed a long hiatus before French Canada actually became a colony. The real foundation of Quebec was done in 1608 by Champlain who, with his associates, did a great deal of the initial exploration of the vast North American interior.

That great French statesman, Cardinal Richelieu, did much to further French imperial expansion in the first half of the seventeenth century. In his administration, France gained what we now call French Guiana, as well as the West Indies Islands of Martinique and Guadeloupe. Later, Haiti was to become a part of France's West Indian holdings. Another capable minister of France, Colbert, promoted development of French Canada in the latter part of the seventeenth century. He tried to increase the flow of French colonists to that region and was successful in some degree, though Frenchmen were never really much inclined to leave their homeland to build a new France overseas. Through Colbert's efforts, Canada was taken from the trading corporations which had previously run it and made an official French colony.

During the same period, another explorer, La Salle, helped to explore the Mississippi River basin, and developed ambitious plans for a great French colonial belt that would extend from Louisiana through the Great Lakes region into Eastern Canada. Although reaction to his plan was slow in coming, the French did found New Orleans in 1718, and established a few settlements along the Mississippi and its tributaries. By the early 1700's, the French had spread loosely through the Midwest and had made a junction of sorts with the edge of Spanish settlement in New Mexico. In the mid-eighteenth century, the French completed their exploration of Central Canada, going as far as the Rocky Mountain range.

In Africa, Cardinal Richelieu had authorized a trading company which began operations in the Senegal region of West Africa. Although the French continued to do business in that region, this was primarily a sphere of trade for slaves and gold, not the building of a large colony.

A similarly prolonged but tentative operation occurred in the French approach to Madagascar. Although the French occasionally traded with that island as early as the 1500's, they established merely a vaguely proprietary interest in it. The local inhabitants were well-organized and numerous enough to keep the island from successful penetration so long as the efforts were casual. Elsewhere in the Indian Ocean, the French acquired several islands, including Réunion and Mauritius. Until the nineteenth century, that was the extent of the French effort.

COLONIZERS FROM NORTHERN EUROPE

IN SHOWING that movements of colonization were almost a Europe-wide endeavor, it should be pointed out that even such small countries as Denmark and Sweden colonized to the best of their ability. Even Prussia, seldom heard of as a colonial power until the late nineteenth century, managed to join in the process of establishing settlements and trading in slaves in the seventeenth century.

The operations of Denmark were quite widespread; her Asiatic company lasted from 1732 to 1844. In India, Denmark had established her Tranquebar station in the early 1600's, and did not dispose of it until she sold it to England in 1845. Another Danish post was located near Calcutta, and the Danes persistently tried to annex the Nicobar Islands in the Bay of Bengal. Finally, in 1869, they surrendered this claim to England. On the West African coast, Christiansborg was founded by the Danes in 1657 and held until they gave it to England in 1850.

In the Caribbean, the Danes began their Virgin Island holdings with the colonization of St. Thomas in 1666. At first it was a failure, although the Danish Company sent out as settlers various groups of convicts, refugees, and Negroes. For a time in the 1670's the British took it, but the Danes soon regained it. Like the other nations, Denmark let her West Indies Company exercise almost sovereign powers in colonial territories. After a few years, the Brandenburg Company of Prussia obtained from the Danes a concession to use St. Thomas Island as a slave-trading station. We gather the arrangement did not work out very well, because the Danes later found it necessary to seize the Brandenburg Company's goods in payment for debts which were past due. St. Croix Island in the Virgin group had a history of various European owners, being under Spain, the Netherlands, and England during the quarter century which began in 1625. The French had it for a while, and in 1653 even granted it to the Sovereign Order of the Knights of Malta! In 1733 Denmark added it to the Danish Virgin Islands.

The English colonizers represented a fast-rising power—a nation which, by 1500, was better unified than most of its neighbors, and was welded closer together as the sixteenth century went on. English seafarers were able to relieve many Spanish treasure galleons of their cargoes of precious metals en route from the New World. It was, in fact, as hijackers of two enormously profitable Spanish operations, the eastward movement of treasure from America and the westward movement of slaves from Africa to America, that the British made their debut upon the imperial stage. By fighting off Spain's "Invincible Armada" in 1588, they established England's position as a world power. The seventeenth century brought the beginnings of England's onslaught on the French colonial position, a siege which produced vast gains by the mid-eighteenth century.

Concomitantly, England's textile and lumber industries developed, and her copper, lead, tin, and zinc processing techniques enabled her to become a prime supplier of ships and guns for the rest of Europe. This industry, together with the flourishing of English commerce and finance, helps to explain how London increased its population from 180,000 in 1550 to 700,000 in 1700, the latter figure amounting to about one-tenth of England's population.[2]

Although there was an abortive attempt by Sir Walter Raleigh's colonists to colonize Virginia in 1584, the first successful and lasting English colonial establishment on the North American coast came with the founding of the Jamestown colony, sponsored by the London Company, in 1607. When cultivation of tobacco began in 1612, its new popularity among European consumers assured the economic future of the colony. In 1619, the first Negro slaves were brought to the Virginia colony to assist with the raising of tobacco and other crops.

The next English colony was established at Plymouth in 1621 by the Pilgrim Fathers. Other immigrations into New England, the Middle Atlantic, and Southern regions of the Atlantic coast made the British hold in North America quite secure. It is interesting that the Pilgrims got their original foothold because an epidemic of disease had driven much of the population from the Massachusetts coast where the English landed. Their first experiences reflected considerable dependence on Indian neighbors, who not only welcomed the Pilgrims but also provided useful knowledge about cultivation of corn, and other wilderness technology. The cordial Thanksgiving gathering of the Pilgrims with the Indians under Chief Massasoit is a familiar historical picture. Decidedly less cordial was the relationship of the New England colonists with Massasoit's son, known as Philip. In 1675 and 1676, Philip, like his father chief of the Wampanoag tribe, realized that the white settlements were increasing and advancing into the wilderness so fast that Indian territory was being disastrously reduced. Philip, apparently convinced that either whites or Indians must perish, made an alliance with most of the principal tribes along the New England coast from Maine to Connecticut.

The Indians raided many white settlements, and the settlers attacked the fortress-village of the Narragansetts, one of Philip's allies, in the Rhode Island area. They managed to wipe out nearly all inhabitants of this town, and the anti-Indian campaign was so successfully pursued that, by summer of 1676, the Indians were completely defeated. Philip was killed in August, and his head displayed for a long time on a pike in Plymouthtown—a grim sequel to the friendship of his father with the Pilgrim Fathers at that first Thanksgiving.

The Indian defeat in King Philip's War left the losers at the mercy of the English. Hundreds were killed, and many sold into slavery, even the nine-year-old son of Philip. To justify this last act against an innocent child required careful argument by the colonists' religious leaders. The leaders, like most of Europe's colonists through the years, were not lacking in rationalizations which would bestow divine sanction on whatever crimes might be expedient. In the case of King Philip's child, the clergy of Massachusetts mixed some thoughts about collective guilt with a wholesome reference to God. The ministers John Cotton and Samuel Arnold submitted that "The children of . . . principal leaders and actors in such horrid villainies, and that against a whole nation, yea, the Israel of God, may be involved in the guilt of their parents. . . ."[3]

The last link in the chain of British colonies in what is now the Eastern United States was the founding of the Georgia colony in 1733. There was now a compact area of British settlement from Maine on the north to Georgia in the south.

The many wars which occurred in Europe in the late seventeenth and eighteenth centuries involved not only English and French settlers in North America, but inevitably their Indian allies as well. For example, King William's War, lasting from 1689 to 1697, was brought on in North America by the European conflicts known as the War of the League of Augsburg. In the colonial conflict, Canadian Indians and the Abenakis of Maine fought in behalf of the French, while the Iroquois Confederation sided with the British. When the War of the Spanish Succession began in Europe, it was reflected in the New World as Queen Anne's War, and lasted from 1702 to 1713. The Treaty of Utrecht, which ended that conflict, resulted in English acquisition of Newfoundland, Acadia, and French recognition of British claims to the Hudson Bay region. Other colonial conflicts came in 1739, when the Spanish and English fought the so-called War of Jenkins' Ear, and from 1743 to 1748, when the European War of the Austrian Succession brought on King George's War in the colonies. Each time, it might be noted, many Indian lives were lost, as well as those of white settlers and soldiers on both sides.

Finally, in 1763, there was a definitive settlement in North America between the British and French. In that year the European Seven Years' War, or French and Indian War, as the colonists called it, was concluded by treaty arrangements which gave the British all of France's Canadian possessions except the two small islands of Saint Pierre and Miquelon in the St. Lawrence River estuary. England also gained all of the French Louisiana Territory east of the Mississippi River, except the "Island of Orleans" area.

No sooner was the war over than the Indian tribes of the old Northwest Territory—the territory east of the Mississippi and north of the Ohio River—arose en masse in revolt against the British, apparently provoked by dishonest operations of British traders in the area as well as the evident intention of white settlers to expand into their lands. The revolt was quelled in 1765, but long before the end of this Indian war the British Government had decided to forbid entry of white settlers into the territory west of the Allegheny mountain chain. This was intended to minimize conflicts with the Indians, though it must be noted that several settlements existed west of those mountains before the American Revolution. After the Revolution, the trans-Appalachian territory as far as the Mississippi River became part of the United States, again with the exception of Louisiana, and American settlers continued their advance through that region.

Like the other Europeans, the Dutch carried on some of their most significant colonial developments through trading companies rather than as governmental enterprises. Their United East India Company was established in 1602, receiving full and exclusive rights to develop Dutch trade in the Indian and Pacific Oceans. The chief leader of early Dutch colonial efforts in the Indian Ocean and Southeast Asia was Jan Coen, who founded Batavia on Java— long to be the center of Dutch colonial enterprises in Indonesia. Besides conquering Java and Banda, Coen established Dutch control in the Moluccas and other Indonesian Islands.

Exploration of the Australian coast was furthered by a later Dutch governor in Indonesia, Van Diemen. It was he who caused Captain Tasman to explore the vicinity of Australia. Earlier voyagers had seen parts of the continent, but no one knew its shape or extent. Tasman circumnavigated the Australian continent and also discovered New Zealand.

In North America, the Dutch West India Company, established in 1621, spearheaded its country's efforts. The Dutch colonized much of what is now New York State, founding New Amsterdam on the present site of the city of New York. Their territory also extended into the present states of New Jersey, Pennsylvania, and Delaware, where in 1655 they had seized a Swedish colony founded in the Delaware Valley in 1637 and known as New Sweden.

Although the Swedish colonial experience was brief, its records yield typical European views on the status and rights of the indigenous peoples. New Sweden's Governor, Johan Printz, made no secret of his views regarding Indians. Though he did find it expedient to reach a modus vivendi with them, he said that, if he could have his way, he "would not let a soul of them live." In 1664, England seized the Dutch holdings, including both the original New Amsterdam and the former Swedish colony.

In South America, the Dutch strategy was to seize Brazil, if possible, and, by operating plantations there, complement the African posts through which the supply of African slaves for plantations was obtained. For a brief time they were successful, taking much of Brazil from the Portuguese and also seizing the Portuguese colony of Angola in southwest Africa. These Brazilian and African acquisitions were soon regained by the Portuguese, however, leaving the Dutch effort in the New World limited thereafter to Dutch Guiana, Curaçao, and other small West Indies islands. At the southern tip of Africa, the Dutch were more successful. The other European powers had established no permanent colony by the Cape of Good Hope, and the Dutch proceeded to do so in 1652 with the foundation of Capetown.

In Ceylon, beginning in 1638, the Portuguese were driven out by the Dutch, in cooperation with the King of Kandy (a part of Ceylon). The Kandyan monarch found that the new European invaders, determined to control the island's cinnamon output, simply took over much of the Portuguese domain. By 1765, after several wars, the Dutch controlled all the coastal lands, leaving Kandy a much-reduced, landlocked kingdom.

The Dutch introduced an efficient administration and were notable for their keen, aggressive planning concerning Ceylon's cinnamon production. Securing this spice at negligible expense, they marketed it in Europe at enormous profit. They also monopolized the trade between South India and Ceylon and controlled all distribution of cloth on the island.

The English, like the Dutch, did not place salvation of heathen, non-European souls high on the list of colonial aspirations. Both of these countries were, however, interested in making permanent settlements, built up with the emigration of numerous Englishmen and Dutchmen from the homelands. The religious aspect of their colonization was usually the conviction that a divine mandate or divine sanction stood behind their efforts to settle a new land in the wilderness. Identifying themselves with the chosen people of the Old Testament, they believed that, as God's Elect, they were destined, even obligated, to dislodge the heathen and found their own commonwealths. It was not much of a step from labelling the indigenous people as heathen to identifying them as virtually non-human, outside the pale of divine protection and human rights.

Puritan preacher John Winslow declared the Indians to be "sons of Satan" who had no souls and were therefore to be destroyed by good Christians.[4] Another Puritan clergyman, John Cotton, in his sermon "God's Promise to His Plantations," justified the taking of land from its pre-European inhabitants as follows: "God makes room for a people ... when He casts out the enemies of the people before them by lawful war, but this driving them out without provocation depends upon special commission from God." Cotton also said that God made a country available when it was "though not altogether void of inhabitants, yet void in that place where they reside. ... Abraham and Isaac, when they sojourned amongst the Philistines, they did not buy that land to feed their cattle." How were people to know that they should have the land? Cotton said, "God's people take the land by promise: and therefore the land of Canaan is called a land of promise. Which they discerned, first, by discerning themselves to be in Christ, in whom all the promises are, yea, and amen."[5]

The North American Indians did not have the European concept of land tenure, whereby lands were owned for exclusive and permanent use of the owner. Property, for the Indian, was largely personal goods; if land was tilled by him, then he "owned" the crops he produced on it. But when the white man "purchased" land, often for merely a few trinkets, he appropriated it for exclusive use. This was shocking to the Indian, who usually supposed that "sale" just allowed the European to share the land and till such parts of it as he needed for a time.

Whether lands were bought, acquired through trickery, or peremptorily seized, the Puritans of New England justified their preemption of Indian lands by viewing themselves as "chosen people," a view exceptionally well expressed by the town meeting of Milford, Connecticut, in the following resolutions of 1640: "Voted, that the earth is the Lord's and the fulness thereof; voted, that the earth is given to the Saints; voted, that we are the Saints."[6]

The idea of venturing into the wilderness, like the Israelites of the Old Testament, to find a promised land and build a holy city of God, doubtless originated partly in this inclination of many European Christians to identify themselves with the Chosen People of the Scripture. (This habit was long indulged in by Russians and many other Europeans besides the English Puritans.) An advantage of the "divine errand" argument to Governor Winthrop, in those early days when he was pulling his contingent together for migration to New England, was that he needed an answer for those who claimed that these Puritans were turning their backs on the difficulties of their co-religionists in England.

Governor Winthrop made it clear to his people that they had a covenant with God and were to be "a city set on a hill," a new Jerusalem or Holy City for the world. Consequently, he explained, ". . . the eies of all people are uppon us; soe that if wee shall deal falsely with our god in this worke wee have undertaken and soe cause him to withdrawe his present help from us, we shall be made a story and a by-word through the world."[7]

Less extreme, but tending toward similar views, were the words of that stern churchman of Puritan New England, Cotton Mather, who said that the churches of New England might not be ideal but were "very like unto those that were in the first ages of Christianity." Thus, the Lord "might there, to them first, and then by them, give a specimen of many good things which he would have his churches elsewhere aspire and arise unto."[8]

Although the Puritan Theocracy of New England contributed more than its share of interesting formulations about a God-given right to expand, it would be wrong to consider the New Englanders as an exceptional group among the men building the global hegemony of Europe. Among the North American colonies, Massachusetts was not immensely different from Virginia, for example, in its religious commitment. Like the New Englanders, the Virginian settlers came with a sense of a divinely ordained mission. The Virginia Colony, like Massachusetts, had meticulously formulated rules for church attendance and other religious or moral standards.

The famous marriage of colonist John Rolfe to Indian Princess Pocahontas was an event for which divine sanction was sought in Virginia, even as it would have been sought in New England. When Rolfe wrote Sir Thomas Dale, applying for permission to marry Pocahontas, he went to great pains to explain that he was motivated not "with the unbridled desire of carnall affection, but for the good of this plantation, for the honour of our countrie, for the glory of God, for my owne salvation, and for converting to the true knowledge of God and Jesus Christ, an unbeleeving creature." John Rolfe had the "chosen people" concept all right, as we see from his description of the Virginia settlers as "a peculiar people, marked and chosen by the finger of God, to possess [Virginia], for undoubtedly He is with us."[9]

Most colonies, and indeed most of Europe, remained theocratic in this colonial period. Church and state were not yet separated; God's requirements were generally supposed to be paramount, and salvation through service to God was still considered as the great end of human endeavor. We have previously discussed evidence of the Messianic view among apologists of the Spanish Empire. When the Dutch occupants of South Africa are considered later in this book, their Messianism will be seen as chronic. Even in Eastern Europe, the Russians—whether under Czars or Communists—have been consistently Messianic. They, too, had a "city on a hill" in their concept of Moscow as the Third Rome, and spoke of their leadership as "a beacon which will illuminate the entire world." (This last phrase was uttered by a Patriarch of the Church in Moscow, not only in the seventeenth century, but in 1950, when the Patriarch "wholeheartedly thanked" Joseph Stalin for his "wonderful service to all Christians.")

EUROPEAN EXPANSION AND
THE GROWTH OF EUROPEAN STRENGTH

THERE IS a very tangled skein of cause and effect which we should try to untangle so that the interaction between round-the-world expansion and European home development can be understood. Analysis of this interaction will show that the processes of colonization, slave trading, technological development, and imperialism are intricately related to one another.

One could also mention as relevant almost any of the developments which helped to produce modern Europe—the Crusades, the Renaissance and Reformation, the evolution of capitalism, or the invention of printing. However, we will stress those events and processes which were immediate links in the evolution of Europe from its pre-modern status as a backward, poor, isolated corner of the world to its twentieth century peak of power as arbiter of the world.

Relevant in this connection are those technological changes, discussed at the beginning of this chapter, which made worldwide explorations possible—the fifteenth century improvements in navigation, mapmaking, ship construction, and guns. Arnold Toynbee reminds us that, through the ages, until the Europeans began their voyages of discovery in the fifteenth century, the vast steppes of Central Asia were the "dry sea" over which the civilizations of the Eastern Hemisphere communicated. From this central area, the Turkic nations moved out to conquer their neighbors, from North Africa to China—the Otttoman Turks, the Safawi Dynasty of Iran, the Mogul Emperors of India, and the Manchus, whose Dynasty controlled China from 1644 to 1912.

After 1498, when da Gama reached India, there followed such improvements in European mastery of the oceans that waterborne communication, dominated by Europe, came to bind the world together much more tightly than the steppes had done. Nevertheless, when European interlopers invaded that long belt of territories from North Africa to China they were, so to speak, invading the invader. At any rate, they were resisted less heartily or less effectively in parts of that belt because they were only substituting one yoke for another.

We should next consider the profits Europe received from opening all the world's continents to exploitation or trade. The late Professor Walter Webb's "Great Frontier" thesis can serve as a means of accounting for the ensuing European prosperity. He points out that the age of discovery made available to European exploitation several almost uninhabited or sparsely inhabited continents: North and South America, Australia, and the southern end of Africa. Leaving aside the question of the rights of Indians, Bushmen, and others who had prior occupancy in these Great Frontier regions, the main problem of settlers from Europe in these regions was subduing the new environments, not conquering the native inhabitants.

In terms of land alone, the Great Frontier regions expanded five- or six-fold the amount of arable land available to Europeans. In precious metals, the New World mines and other sources around the world so expanded the supply of gold and silver that, if we estimate European supply in 1500 at 200 million dollars and call that 100 per cent, by 1930 the supply had swelled to 18,308 per cent. As we read in The Great Frontier, "This sudden, continuing and ever-increasing flood of wealth precipitated [on Europe] a business boom such as the world had never known before and probably can never know again."[10]

Besides land, gold, and silver, the slave trade was a further source of boom conditions. Seen from the point of view of individual merchants in Europe, this trade meant profits of hundreds of per cent to individuals and firms involved over a period of many years. During the three centuries beginning in 1619, when Virginia plantations began utilization of slaves for tobacco cultivation, approximately 50 million black Africans were exported from Africa to labor in the plantations of North America, South America, and the West Indies. These were a great source of wealth for Europeans, and a cause of impoverishment for a number of African regions. Those regions were losing one of their most valuable assets in an economic as well as a personal sense, their younger and most vigorous population, often as it had just reached the adulthood in which the new generation becomes productive. In return, Africa often received goods useless in economic development, such as guns or alcoholic beverages. The notorious three-cornered trade worked well for Europeans and North Americans, who took slaves to the New World, where they might be in effect exchanged for sugar, then processing the sugar into rum and returning to Africa to exchange the rum for more slaves. In addition to this profitable triangle were such vital commodities as tobacco, which really gave British North America its vital economic start.

Other key factors in this early pattern were the seventeenth and eighteenth century production of textiles and firearms in Europe. This production provided further commodities for the African slave trade, and the improvement in weapons also led toward the day of great European military predominance.

Profits of the slave trade, like the production of New World gold and silver mines, provided essential capital for the advancement of European technology and industrialization. (It was not uncommon for a slavery operation to return a 300 per cent profit in a year.) Moreover, diffusion of technology was a slow process in those early centuries, and so the Europeans overseas usually had the advantage of being equipped with guns and other devices somewhat before the local peoples were able to receive the improvements. Although various Afro-Asian peoples and the Indians of America were often equipped with firearms when they resisted European invasion, their equipment tended to be much inferior.

The largest single boost to the influx of capital into Europe seems to have come in the 1760's, after the British seizure of India's Bengal region. After conquering Bengal, the British proceeded to profiteer rapidly and extensively. They did so through taxes, which they drove higher and higher, as well as seizures of valuable property and a variety of wrongful practices, including trade monopolies. Their financial success may be measured by the export-import figures for 1766–1768, when exports from India aggregated over 6,300,000 pounds, while imports were about 625,000 pounds. It is entirely possible that this gain of capital was a major cause of the Industrial Revolution in England. Certainly this immense transfusion of capital helped entrepreneurs get loans, open factories, and install better equipment. It is significant that the first 20 years after the conquest of Bengal saw the appearance, in rapid succession, of these key developments—the flying shuttle, the spinning jenny, Watt's new steam engine, and Crompton's mule.

Baines' *History of the Cotton Manufacture* has told how, before 1760, the machinery for spinning cotton in Lancashire was almost as simple as in India. Baines also noted that in 1750 the English iron industry was in full decline.[11]

Strange to relate, some of Europe's great new store of precious metals had been, as of about 1700, drained off to Asia—chiefly China and India—simply because, for centuries, Europe had bought more from Asia than it could sell there. The looting of India in the 1760's was an ironic repetition of plunder; much of the same silver that had previously been plundered from the New World was now replundered from India![12]

Going a step farther in the technology of white aggression, we can see that improvements in England's textile machinery, together with Whitney's invention of the cotton gin in the United States at the outset of the nineteenth century, actually resulted in prolonging slavery by making intensive production of cotton profitable in North America. Raw material sources, technical processes, and markets were all closely interlinked. Under British control, India could now become a vast market for British textiles.

The new technological improvements had far-reaching effect whether they were essentially simple devices or highly sophisticated. In the American West of the nineteenth century, for example, four very important devices were the newly invented barbed wire, with which the fencing of cattle ranges became feasible; the improved axes, which assisted the frontiersmen; and the six-shooter pistol and repeater rifle, which gave the white settlers greater fire power than their Indian antagonists.

It is also relevant that enrichment of Europe was helping to produce an ever more rapid population explosion. This would provide a greater manpower resource for the countries involved, and was also going to encourage industrialization of such lands as the

United States of America. After the devices mentioned in preceding paragraphs had made settlement and development of the American West technologically feasible, the population explosion provided the one missing piece: Europe now needed to import grain, and the American Midwest could provide that grain if an efficient means of getting it to the European market were available.

The demand for grain thus ushered in a great period of railroad building in America, as the transcontinental railroads provided the means of moving the grain toward the European market. The railroad building also caused rapid development of many related industries, such as iron and steel, which would produce the rails and other metal parts needed by a railroad system. A similar process occurred in the development of the Russian railroad system a little later in the nineteenth century. In both the Russian and the American cases, exportable grain and railroad construction were critical factors in producing further industrial development.

One could mention many things in the realm of sophisticated technology, but two good examples are ocean transportation and explosives, because both had a close bearing on the exertion of European power around the world in the nineteenth and twentieth centuries. This development can best be shown through contrast. In 1492, Columbus crossed the Atlantic in 71 days on a 200 ton ship, 80 feet in length. In 1938, the Queen Mary crossed the Atlantic in less than four days, and this was a ship of 80,000 tons, 1,018 feet in length.

With respect to artillery, in the Elizabethan era a gun might fire a 24 pound projectile a distance of 250 yards, while by the mid-twentieth century a 16-inch gun could fire a 2,461 pound projectile as far as 35,000 yards. Furthermore, discovery of nitroglycerin and nitrocellulose in 1846, development of dynamite in 1866, and development of the first modern, steam-powered armored turret ship, the Monitor, in 1861, are several of the impressive developments in ordnance which enabled Europe to dominate the entire world in a military sense.[13]

While we are tracing causes and effects, it is timely to note that, by a cruel irony, sub-Saharan Africa, which had been so impoverished by the slave trade, was scarcely recovered even in the late nineteenth century. In this wretched state, probably brought on in large part by the Europeans' own operations, she appeared to be in need of help and guidance, or so the Europeans saw it. This became their justification for completing the colonization of Africa in the late nineteenth and early twentieth centuries.

All in all, it is clear that, for all of Western Europe, there were many interconnections between worldwide expansion and the long process by which the West became technologically predominant. Europe's round-the-world operations before 1800 involved extensive settlements only in the "Great Frontier" regions—the sparsely settled lands. Because most of the great scientific and industrial development of Europe came after 1800, invasion of densely populated regions beyond the seas was, with the notable exception of India, more than Europe could manage in those earlier centuries.

After 1800, Europe was superior to the non-Western world in armament. transportation, and much other technology. Almost any act of invasion became technically possible for the Europeans after 1800, and at the same time those Europeans already installed in North America could proceed to industrialize mightily on their own.

:: I I I ::

Indians and Negroes:
Five Centuries of Dishonor

THE UNITED STATES AND ITS ABORIGINES

"FIVE CENTURIES of dishonor!"—an echo, somewhat amplified, of Helen Hunt Jackson's famous title for the book in which she censured the United States Government for its cruel handling of Indian tribes during the first hundred years of American independence. My use of "five centuries" stems from the historical record—from the coming of Europeans to the American continents until the present year, nearly half a millenium, there has been an unbroken record of duplicity and disregard of Indian rights. The recent record does show important mitigations; the straightforward plundering and awful cruelties of earlier centuries have been stopped. We no longer hear arrogant claims that God made the white settler a crusader for His Kingdom, a privileged instrument of His will, but a look at even recent events will reveal that the filching of rights and property through legalistic trickery never stopped.

Why take up injuries to Negroes here, together with Indian matters? To be sure, the Negro population of the United States is much larger than the Indian minority, and the problems of the two groups are very different, but the white record of nearly five centuries again reveals constant oppression. As with the Indians,

...vil has become more subtle. A century ago, the Negro ceased to be legally recognized as an item of property, an object of legal enslavement. In the 1950's, the United States Government gradually began to liberate him from a comprehensive set of inequities and indignities which had been maintained by the laws or usages of regional and national authorities. In the late 1960's, the British Government found it appropriate to take similar steps against such discriminatory usages.

Besides this common pattern of continued, but mitigated, abuse, the epics of Indian and Negro share the distinction of being the longest continuing of several kinds of white offenses against the non-white world. Imperialistic moves into the territories of Asia and Africa have been much more recent, and seemingly of much shorter duration.

The reader will recall that enslavement of Indians was sequentially connected with Negro slavery—when conquerors of the New World found their supply of Indian workers inadequate, they imported African slaves to fill the gap. The racism of white Americans was often directed against all non-whites, making the Indian and Negro "targets in common." In fact, some of the military campaigns of American Forces against the Cherokee and Seminole Indians were brought on by the presence of escaped slaves among these Indians.

A "general racism" appeared early in American history. For example, the good Benjamin Franklin regretted that the number of "purely white" people in the world was proportionately very small. "I could wish their numbers were increased," said Franklin. "In America, we have so fair an opportunity, by excluding all blacks and tawnys, of increasing the lovely white and red. [I don't think he means Indian by 'red' here.] But perhaps I am partial to the complexion of my country, for such kind of partiality is natural to mankind."[1]

Of course, America had received help from Europe in developing its ideas about non-white races. The two most common myths, generated in Europe and exported to the New World, were the bipolar ideas of the noble savage and the dangerous, churlish savage. These two concepts occupied innumerable places in the literature of Europe. There was Shakespeare's *The Tempest*, where twin extremes were embodied in the characters of Ariel and Caliban. The very name "Caliban" appears to be a rearrangement of the letters CANIBAL, and the word "cannibal" was in fact derived from the *Carib* or *Caribal* Indians, who lived in the West Indies. This was an apt label, in a psychological sense, for the savage. Aside from his generally debased character, remember that Caliban had allegedly made menacing advances toward Prospero's daughter.

The aggressive savage recurs in Defoe's *Robinson Crusoe*, where the horrid cannibals appear in sharp contrast to Crusoe's cooperative native friend, Friday. In French literature, the idyllic aspect of the savage was stressed by Rousseau, Chateaubriand, and others. Here, more was involved—it was not just a picture of non-white persons, but the idea of how wonderful it could be for *any* men to live in an unspoiled, simple state of nature.

Thomas Jefferson's observations about characteristics of the Negro, in his "Notes on Virginia," sound remarkably similar to the ideas of later American racists: "The Negroes are equal to the whites in point of memory," said Jefferson, "but much inferior in general reasoning ability. They are ardent in love, but it is merely a sensual sort of love; they are lacking in imagination, and their griefs are transient."

Professor Leslie Fiedler's analysis of Indian and Negro characters in American literature indicates that several of the white American's cherished, oft-repeated myths, which for some time utilized Indian characters, later transferred their characterization to Negro figures. The much-loved myth of the benevolent savage occurred in such favorite tales as the Pocahontas-John Smith love story, or in the idyllic friendship of Wawatam and Trapper Henry described by Thoreau. Subsequently, Americans treated themselves to a variety of comparable personalities in blackface, such as Huckleberry Finn's good friend, Nigger Jim.

Then there is the contrasting myth of the hateful, violent, or sex-mad savage onto whom white persons like to project their own aggressions, fears or frustrations. Early in American history, the white raiders at the Boston Tea Party used Indian disguises. It is also symptomatic, says Professor Fiedler, that American children regularly play "Cowboys and Indians," and that the American father is accustomed to calling his noisy children "wild Indians."[2] The white concept of the sex-crazed Negro is so familiar that examples are scarcely needed, but certainly this theme received one of its classic treatments in the immensely popular motion picture epic of 1915, *The Birth of a Nation*. This film's more dramatic episodes featured a whole series of arrogant acts, attacks, and attempted rapes by Negroes and mulattoes.

If the Indian and Negro are so intertwined in the white conscience, how could such a champion of the Indian as Helen Hunt Jackson do nothing to defend the downtrodden Negro? A scholarly commentary of 1965 on Mrs. Jackson's monumental work of commiseration for the Indians observed, "Curiously never interested in the Negro equality with whites, she was almost immediately attracted to the cause of these Indians."[3]

Actually, Mrs. Jackson became acquainted early in life with Ralph Waldo Emerson and Emily Dickinson and was, in fact, deeply concerned about the slavery question. However, her first husband, Lt. Edward Hunt, whom she married in 1852, abhorred all abolisionists. He forbade Helen from engaging in any defense of Harriet Beecher Stowe's anti-slavery polemics. Hunt was determined, as an officer in the Regular Army, that his wife should not get involved in any controversial matters which might interfere with the advancement of his military career.[4]

Major Hunt was accidentally killed in 1863, and soon thereafter defeat of the Southern Armies had made abolition of slavery an accomplished fact. In the 1870's, Mrs. Hunt traveled in the American West and also heard from a lecturer about the scandalous treatment of the Ponca Indians. She proceeded to attack the series of wrongs inflicted upon the American Indians, especially injuries done to the Lenni Lenape, Cheyenne, Nez Percé, Sioux, and Winnebago tribes. Her account was not merely sentimental or a group of horror stories, but was carefully researched as to the legal issues involved. (Meanwhile, she married again, to a William Jackson.) Mrs. Jackson's special ire was directed at the United States Government. She engaged in a fairly acrimonious correspondence with officials of the War and Interior Departments long after *A Century of Dishonor* was written, trying without much success to get officials to deal fairly with the Indians.

Significantly, it was at the hands of the Federal and State Governments that the Indians suffered their gravest wrongs. One might more easily forget crimes committed by individuals or non-governmental groups. What have "governmental crimes" included? Most importantly, imposition of one enforced treaty after another. Some Indian treaties were made voluntarily by both parties, but more often the Indian signatories affixed their names under threat or were not valid representatives of their full tribe. Furthermore, successive treaties (or decisions) frequently deprived the Indians of territories which had been solemnly guaranteed them in previous pacts with the Government of the United States.

Consequent to this great crime of stealing of territory, there had to be deportations of the "former owners." In systematically deporting Indians to the West, the United States Government wished to appear benevolent, not aggressive. Andrew Jackson offered a formula for this, declaring in his "Farewell Address" that the removal program would save the Indians "from the degradation and destruction to which they were rapidly hastening while they remained in the States." Deportation to the West would place the Indians "beyond the reach of injury or oppression."[5]

Removal to lands far to the west and north of their old territories was a terrible ordeal for such tribes as the Cherokees and Seminoles. In enforcing deportation, the Army often found it necessary to shoot some recalcitrant redskins, while others died of starvation, either en route to their new homes or after arriving there.

This brings up the notorious corruption of U.S. Government agencies dealing with the Indians—President Grant's crooked Indian agents were just one group of cases. The corruption was most serious when it diverted essential rations from the Indians to thieves in official positions. Not only did the Indians starve because of graft, but at times their rations were stopped because of official decrees. This was done "to enforce" regulations which forbade the Indian religious rite known as the Sun Dance. Freedom of religion?

Equal rights? At that time—the 1870's and 1880's—most Americans were not interested in extending to Indians the rights and immunities guaranteed by the Constitution of the United States.

Recurrent American programs for extermination of the Indians were best reflected by continual public offers of bounties for Indian scalps. Entire Indian communities were exterminated in order to earn this money. In Pennsylvania, Verrill tells us, a man's scalp brought $134 in 1764; women's scalps were rated at $50, and that of an infant only $20. In Indiana the bounty was $50. In Denver, by 1867, the rate had declined to $10, presumably because so many hundreds were presented for payment. Yet, in Central City, Colorado, a fee of $25 was paid on over 200 scalps.[6] (Of course, the Indians habitually took white scalps over the long centuries of warfare, primarily as trophies—although during the American Revolution British agents paid bounties to many Indians for the scalps of colonists.)

Lastly, the Army and Militia carried out various killings, judicial murders, and massacres. Some were unprovoked or a peacetime incident; others were carried out because certain Indians had rebelled, or were violating official regulations. Let us note here just two of many massacres. General Custer reported that he had fought the "Battle of the Washita" after he attacked a village of Cheyennes and Sioux, all of whom were unarmed, and 100 of whom his men killed.

Any slaughter of Indians by white forces, even when the dead included women and children, was customarily referred to as a "glorious victory," while an Indian victory was reported as a "massacre." In the fall of 1864, hundreds of Cheyenne and Arapahoe tribesmen reported to United States authorities at Fort Lyon in Colorado. There were rebellious Indians in Colorado, but those who came to the Fort desired peace. The Chief in charge, Black Kettle, took his people to the camping area nearby, on Sand Creek, as instructed by the authorities. His people turned in all weapons except a few hunting pieces which officials permitted them to keep. A white flag and an American flag flew over the Indian camp.

Without warning, at dawn on November 29, 1864, about 1,000

soldiers under Colonel Chivington fell upon these helpless Indians and killed or wounded most of them.[7] Over 100 scalps were displayed in Denver. The U.S. Government regretted the incident and tried to make amends by granting land to the survivors. The Colonel went free, though much later, in Denver, he was unaccountably murdered.

What justifications can be found for these various acts against the Indians? Theodore Roosevelt's justification of expansion over the North American continent at Indian expense is of special interest. Not only was he President of the United States and an expansionist who desired to extend aggressive American influence into many parts of the world, but he had a special interest in the American West, where he lived long enough and learned enough firsthand to call himself an "expert."

Roosevelt was willing to admit that the Indians had suffered terrible injustices from white settlers and travelers. He mentioned, as true crimes, the way Georgians dealt with the Cherokees in the early 1800's, and the mistreatment of Chief Joseph's Nez Percés. In general, though, he felt that historians apologized too much for what our race did in North America. He claimed that it would have been really impossible to avoid conflict and battles with Indians unless we were content to let the North American continent be taken over by other strong powers, who would inevitably have been even more aggressive. He felt that the Indians would have fought us whether we wanted to fight them or not.

In Roosevelt's opinion, the Indians did not really *own* the vast prairies and forests. He speaks of "the dozen squalid savages who hunted at long intervals over a territory of a thousand square miles." Such wretches could not properly be considered as owning their hunting grounds, he says, pointing out that various Indian tribes would not and could not define their own tribal borders.

Actually, Roosevelt thought that United States policy on Indians was mostly to be blamed for its weakness and occasional readiness to follow sentimental humanitarian policies, rather than for what he calls "wilful wrong-doing," of which he thought there had been very little. Federal authorities allegedly controlled white settlers on the edge of the Indian country far better than the

Indian chiefs controlled their warlike braves. Roosevelt really doubted that the Indian had any personal honor or reliability. He writes, "The most vicious cowboy has more moral principle than the average Indian."[8]

What have the Indians themselves had to say in recent years? At the American Indian Chicago Conference, June 13–20, 1961, there gathered 460 Indians belonging to 90 tribes. The assembly produced a "Declaration of Indian Purpose" in which the United States Government was reminded of the U.S. Supreme Court decision in U.S. v. Kagana (1885) 118 U.S. 375,383. The decision stated in part: "Because of the local ill feeling of the people, states where they [the Indians] are found are often their deadliest enemies. From their very weakness and helplessness, so largely due to the course of dealing of the Federal Government with them . . . there arises a duty of protection." The Indians' Declaration admonished the Government, "The repeated breaking of solemn treaties by the United States has also been a concern which is disheartening to the tribes, and it is felt that there is no apparent concern by the Government about breaking treaties."[9]

The complaint about breaking of treaties was still timely in 1961. At about that time, a remnant of the Iroquois Nation, living on the Niagara River, was being deprived of lands guaranteed to them in perpetuity by a treaty with the United States. The lands were needed for a hydroelectric project, but the Indians insisted on their rights. The U.S. Supreme Court decided against the Indians—not on grounds of law, but on the basis of public needs. The Kinzua Dam on the Allegheny River in northwestern Pennsylvania was completed in 1966, despite protests of Seneca Indians whose lands would be flooded by the dam. The Supreme Court ruled that Indian lands were subject to the laws of eminent domain, despite the treaty concluded by President Washington with Chief Cornplanter in 1794, guaranteeing this land to the Senecas forever.

In 1964 and 1965, Indians in the State of Washington were defending their rights, solemnly guaranteed by treaties, to fish freely along certain rivers. The State Government had forbidden use of nets by the Indians, and was supported in this treaty violation by the State Supreme Court and the U.S. Department of the Interior.

In September, 1964, the Hopi Tribe of Arizona held a conclave of its traditional leaders to protest steps taken by a rigged tribal council to lease Hopi lands to oil companies without the consent of Hopi village leaders or clan leaders. Traditionally, the Hopi have balked at treaty-making and have been so cohesive that their oil-rich land could not be taken away through subversion of individual tribesmen. By December, 1964, however, it appeared that the Hopi were losing their fight and that the Federal authorities were not responding—or could not respond, in any substantive way—to appeals from the Indians. Indian Affairs Bureau collaborators who complied too easily with wishes of the whites were criticized as being "Uncle Tomahawks"!

As a last example of Indian affairs, recall the Seminoles of Florida, who fought a stubborn war with the United States from 1835 to 1842, and never did surrender or conclude a proper treaty. Their principal leaders were eventually captured, most notably Chief Osceola, who was taken by the convenient device of violating a flag of truce. Osceola died while still a U.S. Army prisoner, and the Army doctor who treated him detached the head of the noble savage as a souvenir. (He kept it at home, as a device for frightening his children if they were disobedient.)

Those Seminoles who managed to remain in Florida, in spite of deportation programs, are still technically at war with the United States. In July, 1959, 12 members of the tribe journeyed to Cuba, where Fidel Castro was freshly come to power. They gave him a buckskin document recognizing his government, and he in turn recognized the independence of the Seminoles. This unexpected complication in an already nasty Cuban situation may be the reason why the U.S. Indian Claims Commission began to function with even greater speed than usual. By 1964, the Commission had tentatively offered a settlement payment of 25 to 45 cents per acre on the 32,000,000 acres of Florida land the Seminoles claim to own. (The total area of Florida is 37,478,000 acres.) The Government appealed the Commission's decision, but in June, 1967, the United States Court of Claims upheld the Commission. While ruling that the Seminoles had indeed held title to most of Florida in 1823, the Court left it to the Commission to make a precise determination of the acreage and land values involved.

Further sympathy for the poor Indian came from red Vietnamese prisoners of war in South Vietnam. When their white captors showed them "Western" movies, the prisoners cheered for the Indians in the film battle. One guerrilla, who had claimed to become anti-Communist in captivity, gave himself away by crying when the Indians lost at the end of the show.

From some Indians, 1967 brought a gesture of sympathy for the Viet Cong. Indians joined massive demonstrations against President Johnson's war policy in the Spring of that year, carrying such signs as "Paleface President speak with forked tongue." These Indians may have been unrepresentative of their people— may have been hired to demonstrate, in fact—but their role in the demonstrations is in itself interesting.

There are now more than 600,000 Indians in the United States. Since 1924, they have held full U.S. citizenship. In addition, they enjoy such benefits as lifetime medical care by the U.S. Public Health Service. However, Indians have higher disease rates and a shorter life span than any other major segment of the nation's population. (Their average age at death is 43, compared to a national average of 63.) Modern devices have scarcely reached some Indian lands—on one reservation of 2,700,000 acres there were, in 1966, only 12 telephones.

As for education, the 1966 Conference of the Association on American Indian Affairs revealed that the average Indian attends school for only five years. The Conference criticized the readiness of the Bureau of Indian Affairs to remove children, even those under nine years of age, to one of its 81 boarding schools. The Bureau's workers often remove children to these schools, as much as 600 miles from home, without consulting their parents, according to the Conference.

The average Indian family's annual income was $1,500 in 1964, just half of the average for Negro families and a quarter of the income of the average white family. Worse still, there continued to be exceptional hardships among some tribes, such as the Oglala Sioux of South Dakota, with their annual toll of deaths from cold and starvation. So Indian grievances have endured as long as the white presence in the New World. They are of lesser extent now, but are still far from negligible.

NEGRO SLAVERY

NEGRO SLAVERY began in the Americas in the 1500's and lasted four centuries. During this time, the slave trade, conducted by some seven European nations, probably removed from Africa at least 50 million victims. Of these, only about 35 million actually reached their American places of servitude, because mortality during voyages to the Americas was high. The life of a slave was fraught with hard labor, maltreatment, and all sorts of indignities. Sickness and death must have been frequent visitors to the plantations. In Dutch Guiana in about 1800, for instance, a British report found that the population of 50,000 slaves had to be completely replaced every two decades.[10]

Which European nations participated in the American slave trade? The following had slave-collection stations in Africa or slave-handling depots in the New World: France, England, Spain, Portugal, Netherlands, Denmark, Sweden, and even a Brandenburg-Prussian Company.

Aside from its inhumanity, the slave trade was decisive in wrecking the economy of three regions: The East African Coast, the Congo, and parts of the "Guinea Coast." In economic terms, impoverishment was caused by the vast exports of recently matured persons, which represented a great capital loss. Wares obtained in exchange for slaves were of little good to the local economies, being chiefly equipment for warfare and articles of conspicuous consumption.

Not only was economic growth suffocated; African potentates who provided slaves at the source also made profits and were further strengthened by acquisition of better weapons from Europe. Thus, the grip of feudalism was made tighter as normal development and political changes were inhibited. In such regions as the Congo, somewhat different, but equally baneful, effects occurred; general disorganization set in. It was really a compounding of injuries when Europeans proceeded, in the late 1800's, to make colonies or "protectorates" of previously free parts of Africa, often justifying these moves by reference to the disorganized and wretched state of their prey. The slave trade itself had done much to spoil or retard development of many areas.

In the 1400's and 1500's, Europeans who dealt with the rulers of African nations or tribes commonly thought of the African authorities as equal in general standing to Europe's own feudal rulers. The buying and using of slaves did not then imply, either to sellers of this human merchandise or to the purchasers, any clear idea of racial superiority. Slavery was a universal institution, as old as civilization itself. However, slavery as practiced in Western Africa, Latin America, and within Europe in the 1500's was not the *total* form of servitude it came to be in America.

The slave within Africa was usually like the serf of medieval Europe, i.e., he retained customary rights and might accumulate property. Sometimes this slavery was effective for limited periods, but not for life. In France, in the sixteenth and seventeenth centuries, law provided that a slave who reached the French homeland and was baptised as a Christian became free automatically. Under such conditions, slave-masters were not inclined to believe in racial superiority, nor were slaves likely to believe that their inferiority was on a racial basis, or that their subordination had been ordained by divine providence. Tragically for modern Europe and America, these pernicious doctrines gained acceptance as the peculiar institution of slavery took shape in North America. The institution was motivated by powerful economic forces; profits which Europe amassed from it helped to create Europe's Industrial Revolution.

In England, merchants, shipbuilders, and slavers profited richly from the trade; in France, profits from slaving voyages, on which the original investment was often tripled, made capital available for establishment of new industrial facilities. In America, the millions of enslaved workers did much to convert an undeveloped wilderness into a rich, modern country. American products for which there was a heavy demand in Europe—sugar, cotton, and tobacco—required abundant field labor. Slavery filled these needs.

But what were the terms of servitude in America? Why were they so rigorous? First, the slave was to serve all his life. This was affirmed in the laws of the American colonies during the late 1600's. The slavocracy even frowned on masters who liberated individual slaves. In Georgia, an owner who did this or who dared to make a will that would free his slaves when he died was subject to heavy fines. Other laws provided that *a Negro was a slave* unless he could prove that he was free, and that a free Negro was to be re-enslaved if he committed a crime.

Second, the Negro slave's marriage and family arrangements were entirely at the discretion of his owner. A family of slaves had no *right* to remain together. The offspring of slaves were born into slavery, as the law saw it. Third, slaveowners enjoyed full disciplinary powers. The courts would seldom take action, even against a man who murdered his slave, the legal assumption being that a proprietor would not destroy his own property. Last, the slave had no property rights, or essentially any privileges beyond what the owner's personal inclination or self-interest allowed.

These were the legalities. Behind them were uncodified, but generally accepted beliefs—call them myths, if you wish—which justified the institution in the white mind. These beliefs implied that the Negro was an inferior type of human being, or that he was *not* really human, in some sense. There was a widespread idea that black men were descendants of Adam's sinful offspring Cain, and thus bore God's curse as placed upon Cain's progeny, according to the holy writ. Other scriptural references were quoted to show divine sanction for slavery.

The inferiority theme was mixed with assertions that slavery was "the best thing" for Negroes. Their minds and dispositions made them naturally suited to be slaves of the white race, while their bodies were supposedly designed by nature for the hard labor of the plantations. Then there were benevolent apologists of slavery, who explained that plantations were ideal institutions for training and uplifting the African savage. There was also the claim that the ferocious qualities of Africans required ironclad subjugation and rigid controls.

The foregoing myths were supplemented by public unwillingness to think about the plight of Negroes—that apathy and repression which has accompanied all the great crimes of our people. Apathy reigned almost as strongly in the North as in the South, and had to be somewhat willful; it did not arise merely from lack of knowledge. The North had known slavery at first hand, and both North and South saw enough episodes of Negro unrest to prove that the Negroes were not satisfied with their lot.

Although slavery had not really flourished in New York and adjacent colonies, there were 1,300 Negroes (as against 7,767 whites) in five counties about New York City in 1703. In New York itself there had been no slave rebellion under Dutch rule, but the English rulers did become worried about possible insurrections. Indeed, in 1712 there were plots by Negro slaves, and violence in which nine whites were killed, whereupon 20 of the rebels were captured and hanged, burned, or broken on the wheel. Again in 1741, when the 2,000 slaves of New York City represented about one-fifth of its population, fear engendered by a largely imaginary "Great Plot" motivated whites to jail 154 slaves, burn 14, and hang 18.[11]

There were constant indications in Southern newspapers and court proceedings of Negro efforts to retaliate against their oppressors by setting fire to houses, barns, and other property. Many rebellions of Negro slaves occurred in the eighteenth and nineteenth centuries; some had as many as 500 rebel participants. The highly vocal, earnest agitation of American abolitionists also served, in the nineteenth century, to indicate the evils of slavery with perfect clarity for those who would listen. Then there were the examples of the European powers; Denmark prohibited the slave *trade* in 1792, England in 1807, France in 1818, and Portugal—the last to do so—in 1836. (The United States forbade importation of slaves as of 1808.) Abolition of slavery was decreed by England in 1833, and by France in 1848.

However, there were regressions in the movement against involuntary servitude. A sudden rise in the demand for tropical products in the mid-nineteenth century made the plantation labor supply inadequate. English, French, and Spanish merchants, colonists, and officials had to devise many tricks to increase servitude in their colonies. They brought in "apprenticed Africans" and coolies from Asia, and relied upon various systems of compulsion. Many of these schemes for illegal importation of Africans into the European colonies were devised by the merchants of New York and Boston.

The commercial motivation behind slavery in America at this time remained strong enough for serious efforts to be made to reopen the slave trade in the face of abolitionists' efforts to extirpate slavery altogether. The most telling blow at the unyielding façade of public apathy toward slavery in America was struck by a book that was polemical and at the same time psychologically subtle and effective, *Uncle Tom's Cabin*. When Harriet Beecher Stowe's forthcoming book was announced in the *National Era*, the subtitle was "The Man That Was a Thing." Mrs. Stowe took pains to reveal her enslaved characters as unique and distinctly human personalities, and as Severn Duvall says, she trapped the white man into admitting this humanity, so that the "thing" turned out in her pages to be definitely a man.[12]

Mrs. Stowe also contended with a somewhat different postulate of the pro-slavery debaters, the idea that the slave was a childlike being who must be cared for and supervised by a patriarchal slaveholding society. This point of view seems essentially like Rudyard Kipling's characterization of the lesser folk of the British Empire as "half devil and half child." The author of *Uncle Tom's Cabin* demolished the patriarchal thesis with her vivid illustrations of highly unpaternal slaveholders who abused and even killed their "children" in unfatherly fashion, and unhesitatingly broke up their "families," selling a mother here, a father there, and children elsewhere. Thus, slavery in America was brought to public notice, and revealed in all its heartlessness. Actual eradication of slavery was not to come, however, until the blood bath of the Civil War brought emancipation in its wake.

THE AFTERMATH OF SLAVERY
IN THE UNITED STATES, 1865–1967

FROM EMANCIPATION until very recent years, my American compatriots have managed to disregard the Negro and his plight. In North and South alike, the Negro continued to be relegated to the fringe of American life. The white mythology continued to treat him as subhuman, and this meant that economically he would enjoy only crumbs from the bountiful American table. How can we then be surprised at the verdict Robert Hutchins pronounced in 1963 at the Center for the Study of Democratic Institutions? "The Negro in America is not a part of the American society. This is the greatest single crime that the American people have ever committed, and one of the greatest crimes that any people has ever committed."

The position of American Negroes has improved since the Civil War, but very slowly and with incredible setbacks. *Full equality* was the standard set by Northern leadership in the immediate aftermath of the War, but in the 1870's the South found ways to segregate and regiment its Negroes once again. Even the liberal-appearing Woodrow Wilson agreed, in his *History of the American People*, that Southern whites were justified in doing this as a matter of "self-preservation." The Negro was not ready for full citizenship, said Wilson.

During the last quarter of the nineteenth century the position of the American Negro got worse in important respects. This deterioration was not merely a reversal of abrupt pro-Negro steps taken at the end of the Civil War; it was the shaping of a consensus in which the view of Woodrow Wilson was the common view of most state and national leaders in both political parties. The consensus was also shared by the great labor organizations and most of the social and philanthropic organizations of the American people.

Contributing to this consensus were such developments as increases in the number of Negroes in Southern cities from 1890 to 1900. This bred white anxieties, just as Northerners' fears were stirred in later decades by Negro influxes into their cities. Another contributory factor was global expansion of European and American power, which at this time was reaching its culmination. The displays of white supremacy and non-white impotence which imperialism entailed will be reviewed in later chapters of this book. Suffice it to say at this point that Europeans and Americans were more certain than ever of their racial superiority.

The racist consensus led not only to greater segregation, but also to provision of *inferior* facilities for the Negro minority. For instance, Wilcox County, Alabama, had 2,482 white children of school age in 1890–1891, and salaries for their teachers came to a total of $4,397. By 1907–1908, the County had 2,285 such children, for whom a teacher payroll of $28,108 was provided. In contrast to this considerable progress, the colored school-age children of the County increased from 9,931 in 1890–1891 to 10,745 in 1907–1908, but the payroll of their teachers actually went down from $6,545 to $3,940.[13]

During the last decade of the nineteenth century, the States of Mississippi, North Carolina, South Carolina, and Louisiana revised their laws to require that a would-be voter be able not only to read and write, but also demonstrate an understanding of such documents as the Constitution of the United States. This requirement, not only more stringent but also lending itself to denial of the vote to any Negro citizen, may have been designed to "compensate" for the rise in Negro literacy from 18.6 per cent in 1870 to 55.5 per cent in 1890.[14]

As the nineteenth century ended, there were many indications of the new low of the status of the American Negro. In 1901, Congress saw the departure of its last Negro member, and would not see another for many years. Before leaving the halls of the United States Congress, he introduced the first resolution for a federal statute to forbid lynching. No one else had done so, although nearly 100 colored persons were being lynched each year.

It is not surprising that Southern white opinion would approve of segregation, and that a large fraction of that opinion would condone positive discrimination and mistreatment. The remarkable thing about the 1877–1901 period is that Northern opinion was very little better, as Logan confirmed by his study of 12 representative Northern newspapers. These papers, published in Boston, New York, New Haven, Philadelphia, Cinncinnati, Pittsburgh, Indianapolis, Detroit, St. Louis, San Francisco, Washington, D.C., and Chicago, were almost unanimous in opposing the Civil Rights Act of 1875 when it was under litigation in 1883. Their reasons varied somewhat, including the allegation that the Act had produced no real benefits for colored people, the claim that there was no serious problem of Negro rights, and the flat statement that the Negro and white races had been made so different by nature that it was pointless for the law to intervene in their relationship. In 1883, the Supreme Court declared the Civil Rights Act unconstitutional, a decision supported by all but one of the papers cited above. Some editors declared that this would stop "fanatical" Congressional efforts to legislate equal rights for colored persons in public places. Others were afraid that the "supremacy of the Negro" would still be enforced in areas under Federal jurisdiction—the territories and the District of Columbia—while still others concluded that the public was simply tired of hearing about the race question.[15]

But the public was not so tired in the ensuing period, 1900–1930, that it refrained from racist acts. The situation deteriorated even more, in some respects. The Charleston *News and Courier*, which had scorned the growth of Jim Crow practices in the late nineteenth century, was by 1906 persuaded that segregation was *not enough*. The proper remedy, said this influential paper, was deportation of Negroes en masse; they should be separated geographically from the white population.[16]

Other Southerners had recommended that Cuba be taken by the United States as a place of deportation for the Negro population. (The Cubans, presumably, were to be mere bystanders in this massive operation.) Later, in the Wilson Administration, a resolution was introduced in Congress authorizing the President to acquire territory in Mexico for resettlement of Negroes. No action was taken on the resolution. This geographic solution, deportation en masse, has been a common stategy of racists and totalitarians in many lands, and we shall see more of it in later pages of this volume.

Segregation continued to be the rule in all Southern schools and colleges, and in many in the North. When the State of Kentucky prohibited mixing of white and Negro persons in classes at Berea College, no less a prestigious, enlightened figure than President Charles W. Eliot of Harvard supported the South, saying, "Perhaps if there were as many Negroes here as there, we might think it better for them to be in separate schools."[17]

Meanwhile, none of the nation's presidents did anything to really disturb the "separate and inferior" status to which colored persons were relegated. President Taft declared that the Fourteenth Amendment had been "generally enforced." The Fifteenth had not been, he conceded, but noted happily that the right to vote of "intelligent and well-to-do" Negroes would be "acquiesced in."[18] Woodrow Wilson had at least made presidential campaign promises that, if elected, he would protect Negroes from being placed under "any greater political disadvantage" than they had suffered previously. In office, Wilson accepted a recommendation that Federal workers of Negro ancestry be methodically segregated by assigning them to work in all-Negro sections and providing separate eating places and washrooms. This was done in all agencies which had sizeable numbers of Negro employees.

When the United States entered World War I in 1917 over 360,000 American Negroes were taken into military service, while the manpower needs of war industries brought multitudes of Negroes from South to North. There resulted much more contact between the races on an interim basis of racial equality, or at least of fluid relationships. All this new experience contributed to the pride and confidence of America's Negroes, as did inferences they sometimes drew from wartime slogans about democracy, freedom, and justice.

The U.S. Army mental tests of World War I, and the study of all data gathered by these tests, provided more ammunition for apostles of racism. Americans of North European ancestry scored higher on the tests than all other groups, and the eminent expert on education and testing, E. L. Thorndike, was emboldened to declare that "race directly and indirectly produces differences so great that government, . . . and almost every other feature of . . . civilized life have to take account of a man's race." Intelligence, declared Thorndike, was due 80 per cent to heredity.[19]

After World War I there was greater hostility toward Negroes, just as the war had sharpened hostility to foreigners, minority groups, and political radicals in general. Possibly the latter group of animosities encouraged growth of anti-Negro sentiment. A race riot in Chicago in 1919 caused the death of 23 whites and 15 Negroes, and injury of 537 persons. In fact, from June to December, 1919, there were 25 race riots in the cities of the United States.[20]

In the 1920's the Ku Klux Klan rapidly began to increase its membership. This white supremacy, terrorist organization had a membership by 1923 of between four and six million, and was strong for years, not only in the South, but in such states as Colorado and Oregon as well. The Governor of Indiana was a Klansman. Senator Underwood of Alabama dared, at the Democratic National Convention of 1924, to condemn this organization, and so forfeited all chances of being nominated for the presidency. In this heyday of the Klan, plenty of violent racist acts carried out what the racist theorists and hatemongers had talked about. In the decade that ended in 1927, Americans lynched 455 persons, of whom 416 were Negroes. Elven of the victims were Negro women, and 42 of the victims were burned alive. Gossett cites a particular pathetic newspaper advertisement of the NAACP in 1922, containing the appeal, "Do you know that the United States is the *Only Land on Earth* where human beings are Burned at the Stake? In four years, 1918–1921, twenty-eight people were publicly BURNED BY AMERICAN MOBS."[21]

One of the more interesting white supremacy theorists in twentieth century America was Dr. Theodore Lothrop Stoddard (1883–1950), who was a member of an old New England family and had received both a law degree and a Ph.D. from Harvard. He was probably led toward race questions by his doctoral thesis, which examined the Negro revolt against French colonists in San Domingo in the eighteenth and nineteenth centuries. Stoddard believed that the white races, especially the Nordics, were in danger of inundation by the inferior races with their high birth rates.

In his book, *The Rising Tide of Color*, Stoddard said that white men could see that the Japanese defeat of Russia in 1904 was "... an omen of evil import for their race-future." Although Stoddard believed fervently in the superiority of the so-called Nordic race, he does not seem to have been dismissed by reviewers so summarily as one might wish. His books were, on the whole, favorably reviewed. *The New York Times'* reviewer said that Stoddard's *Social Classes in Post-War Europe* was "rich with collected facts and observations and illuminating with its philosophical discussion of their significance."[22]

Until World War II was over, so little had been done for the colored minority that the American public was not acquainted with the words "integration" and "desegregation." The acquaintance really began when the Truman and Eisenhower administrations carried out extensive integration measures in the armed forces. In 1954 came the Supreme Court ruling requiring integration of public educational facilities. Discarded was the formula of the 1896 Supreme Court, that separate schools for white and Negro pupils were legal if they were of equal quality. Nor did the Court rest on that single decision, but zealously issued further rulings to define and implement it.

Desegregation of trains, buses, and waiting rooms serving interstate passengers came about by a straightforward ruling of the Interstate Commerce Commission in 1955. Good progress was made in economic terms, too. In the period 1942–1962, the median income of Negro families increased six-fold, while the figure for white families multiplied only four times. On the other hand, vast areas of inertia remained. Eight years after the Supreme Court forbade segregation in schools, only 256 of the 2,265 school districts in the states of the old Confederacy had even *begun* desegregation.

The most dramatic moves toward recognition of the Negro as a full-fledged citizen came in the 1960's. "Sit-in" tactics were used to secure integration of lunchrooms and restaurants, and in 1964 a new Civil Rights Act prohibited discrimination in these and other public accommodations. Year after year, Negro demonstrations were backed up by white students and other volunteers. The most famous leader of the protests was the Reverend Martin Luther

King, Jr., whose techniques of non-violent resistance are taken up in Chapter Ten's comparative analysis of the reactions of victims. His 1963 campaign in Birmingham, Alabama, attracted far more public attention to the civil rights issue than had any previous moves.

Of course, it was not just the demonstrations, but rather the shocking, brutal response of authorities and the deeds of violently segregationist individuals which really enlivened the white conscience. This fortunate effect was produced by indiscriminate use of police dogs, high-pressure fire hoses, tear gas, and clubs against the demonstrators, and even against non-participating bystanders, as well as widespread burnings and bombings of Negro churches. The Birmingham dogs set onto Negro demonstrators by the notorious "Bull" Connor, head of that fair city's police force, gave Americans a better understanding of the whole racial issue.

Why? It was not only that millions of Americans saw on television the dogs being set upon people. It was the combat of animal against man which brought out so vividly the *humanness* of the Negro minority that the purblind prejudices of TV viewers were at least modified a little. This, I suppose, is why the late President Kennedy could tell top American Negro leaders that "Bull" Connor should get the most credit for improvement in the attitudes of white Americans.

There were other conscience-searing events still to come—the murder of the three civil rights workers near Philadelphia, Mississippi, in 1964, and the many brutalities inflicted upon campaigners for Negro voting rights in Selma, Alabama, in 1965. The violence in Selma included the fatal beating of a white minister by hoodlums. As with the Birmingham events, these dreadful proceeding had their fortunate consequences. The murder in Selma led President Johnson to demand, and obtain, enactment of the first really effective Federal law to enforce Negro voting rights. By August, 1965, less than 10 per cent of school districts in the South and border states had failed to make plans for integration.

With all this we have a good beginning. The near hopelessness and helplessness which beset the Southern Negro as late as the 1950's have been relieved; Southern segregationists have been curbed; and Northern whites have found that in their great cities, where thorough antidiscrimination laws have existed for years, there are still terrible, unsolved problems.

Each year, occurrence of bloody, destructive riots in the cities compels us to remember that something is wrong. The continuing issues, all extremely hard to resolve, consist chiefly of inequities in housing and source of livelihood, plus difficulties in the psychology of race relations. (Much as we are concerned with continuing patterns of racial separation in education, these are really traceable to the foregoing underlying problems.)

Inequities in housing for American Negroes derive primarily from poverty or unavailability of mortgage loans for Negroes. To break this latter bottleneck would seemingly require massive regimentation of the financial community—a difficult and unlikely prospect.

The interracial gap in employment opportunities is getting narrower, particularly in such white collar jobs as government positions and teaching. However, as many as 60 per cent of the companies surveyed by the Equal Employment Opportunity Commission were not making an effort to hire Negroes. Worse still is the stubborn resistance to admission of Negroes to many skilled, blue collar fields. The plumber, bricklayer, and crane operator have usually been white, and numerous union organizations have meant to keep it that way. To attack this evil, Presidents Kennedy and Johnson forbade job discrimination in Federally assisted construction, and the Civil Rights Act of 1964 prohibited all job discrimination. These remedies were slow and hard to utilize. A more effective approach was suggested in 1967, when a Federal District Court Judge enjoined the State of Ohio from entering into construction contracts with four employers who *had agreements with unions that practiced discrimination*. This went to the real source of the inequity; with enough pressure from decisions along these lines, the unions might be more fair.

As for the lingering psychological problems, we consider these at many points in this volume, but let us take note of the special resentments which produced the "black power" movement among American Negroes in the late 1960's. "Black power" implied impatience with the unfair treatment and privations of Negro life, and also meant readiness to take more aggressive steps under strictly Negro leadership. Was there some dissatisfaction with white participants in the civil rights movement? Yes, indicated Dr. Alvin Poussaint, in papers delivered to the 1966 and 1967 meetings of the American Psychiatric Association. Poussaint, a professor of psychiatry at Tufts University, had several years' experience as a field director of the Medical Committee for Human Rights in Jackson, Mississippi. He found that many white volunteers went South with "racist distortions in their personality and behavior." The condescending attitudes, sense off superiority, and other indiscretions of some of these well-meaning people were labelled by Poussaint as the "White African Queen" and "Tarzan" complexes attributed to white female and male volunteers respectively. These terms seem to require no more clarification.

EUROPE WELCOMES THE NEGRO

IF AMERICA'S handling of its non-white minorities is part of a greater pattern applicable to the whole Western world, it is natural to expect that non-white persons settling in Europe would encounter some racism, even though we make due allowance for the ease with which small groups can be absorbed in large countries. Actually, European racism directed against colored persons does exist. It varies from nation to nation, just as there is variation among regions in the United States. One thing the European nations have in common, however, is that their worst mistreatment of non-white races has occurred largely in colonies remote from the homeland. This has permitted Europeans to ignore or repress various abuses in their colonial domains, and allowed formation of a special, better standard of treatment for persons of color in Europe. This special treatment tends to compare favorably with the handling of Negroes in the United States, and has enabled many Europeans to indulge in self-righteous remonstrances against American racists.

But through the self-righteousness, even through the generally cordial reception given the Negro by Continental Europeans, one can discern the outlines of those same myths cultivated by earlier generations: The delightful, noble savage and the menacing, sometimes *thrillingly* aggressive savage.

The "welcome" tendered the Negro by Europeans has its pitfalls. Says James Baldwin, in *Nobody Knows my Name*: "Someone, someday, should do a study in depth of the role of the American Negro in the mind and life of Europe, and the extraordinary perils, different from those of America but not less grave, which the American Negro encounters in the Old World."

Nineteenth century England had, among its apostles of racism, some who expressed anti-Negro sentiments. For example, Rudyard Kipling described the Negro as "a big, black, vain baby and a man rolled into one." The common tendency to pretend that little or nothing is wrong in race relations was especially well exemplified when ex-slave Josiah Henson, who had been a model for Harriet Beecher Stowe's *Uncle Tom's Cabin*, arrived in England and was presented to Queen Victoria as the "first Negro slave to enter England." This completely overlooked the thousands of slaves brought to Liverpool en route to servitude in the New World in colonial days. Neither did it acknowledge the residence in eighteenth century England of almost 20,000 Negro slaves.

Twentieth century England has its race prejudices, too; English custom and prejudice has closed to Negroes many types of service work which are practically reserved *for them* in parts of the United States. Consequently, Negro maids, cooks, porters, and taxi drivers are seldom seen in England. As for the better jobs, government positions and most white collar jobs are rarely occupied by Negroes.

To deal with English racial discrimination, an organization of colored persons of the British Commonwealth, the League of Colored Peoples, was founded in 1931. It held a conference in 1944 which was attended by colored subjects of Britain from many African lands, as well as those residing in the British Isles. The delegates adopted a "charter" which in its demands summarizes neatly the troubles of colored persons under British rule. The charter requested "the same economic, educational, legal and political rights" as those enjoyed by other races. It requested that authorities put a stop to discrimination in employment, and "in places of public entertainment and refreshment, or at other public places." The group neither expected nor got any definite action from British authorities.[23]

Until the 1950's, the non-white resident in Britain was such a minute fraction of the population that he was not a noticeable problem; he could be regarded merely as a charmingly exotic visitor from the far-flung British Empire. In the fifties, though, Africans, dark-skinned West Indians, and Asians began coming to England in droves from the colonies and former colonies.

There resulted all sorts of complaints about violence and ruination of neighborhoods by the newcomers, worries about "mongrelization" of the nation, and some genuine, though small, race riots. Public concern led to passage of the Commonwealth Immigration Act of 1962, with its unprecedented limitation of the right of the Queen's subjects to enter England. Even so, in 1964 some Conservative members of the House of Commons called for more severe limitations. At the current rate of increase, they feared, the colored population would reach 3,000,000 by 1980. These "unassimilable immigrants" were, they said, "a grave danger even in a country as free from racial prejudice as Britain." The Labour Party had originally opposed the Immigration Act in 1962, but by late 1964, with the colored population approaching 1,000,000, Labour politicians found it expedient to extend the Act.

At about the same time, Prime Minister Harold Wilson took an over-all look at the broader field of interracial relations. In a speech at the Lord Mayor's Banquet, he referred with satisfaction to Britain's "prodigious and unparalleled record of de-colonization" since 1948. However, he warned, interracial problems continue to offer a multi-faceted and subtle challenge.

> Our approach to this challenge, whether in world affairs or in our domestic life, cannot be conditioned by cowardice or compromise; this is, for every nation, the great moral imperative.... If we are going to speak with authority abroad, we have a duty at home to show our deep loathing and to condemn by our words, and outlaw by our deeds, racial intolerance, colour prejudice, anti-Semitism:

whether they be found in the activities of squalid relics of pre-war Fascism, in the behaviour of politicians of any party—or in the attitudes of a so-called Labour Club.

In October, 1964, a candidate for the British House of Commons, Patrick Gordon Walker, was defeated by an opponent whose campaign slogans included, "If you want a Negro for a neighbor, vote for Gordon Walker." In a district which had seen quite an influx of colored persons, the slogan apparently had its effect. Consequently Mr. Walker, who was Her Majesty's Foreign Secretary, had to leave the Cabinet, because a British Cabinet member must have a seat in Parliament.

The Labour Party arranged to have another seat vacated so that Mr. Gordon Walker could try again in a by-election in January, 1965. This seat was in a "safe" district, where the Labour Party usually enjoyed a large majority. He was "an odds-on favorite to win," said a prediction in *The New York Times*; yet he *lost again*, regrettable evidence of dynamic racism.

Other recent issues in Britain involved lack of colored members of police forces and fire departments. As of May, 1965, the sole representation consisted of three part-time constables. The Government explained that the public was not so ready for colored officers as the American people had been. An English opponent of discrimination explained that policemen in England "are more a father figure, a symbol of authority." Trying to improve matters, the Labour Government planned to add colored policemen. It also secured passage of a bill to prohibit discrimination "on the grounds of color, race, or ethnic or national origins" in restaurants, theaters, and public housing. Passage of the bill in the House of Commons in May, 1965, came by a narrow margin—261 to 249.

Two years after this event, the Government's Race Relations Board received the results of a methodical survey of racial discrimination in the United Kingdom. The survey, commissioned by the Board, included extensive interviews and field tests. The tests revealed a regular pattern of discrimination in employment, housing, and financial services. To see if colored persons participating in the tests were being turned away for reasons other than race, the survey planners sent out white applicants with the same qualifications. Also, thinking that a general "anti-foreign" feeling might be involved, they sent foreign European applicants, only to find that the latter suffered little or no discrimination in comparison. At two-thirds of the advertised properties visited by test groups, colored persons were turned away. At one-twelfth of the places, higher rents were asked.

The Chairman of the Race Relations Board commented on the report, "The abiding impression which this report leaves on me is of a whole series of people passing the buck. The employer blames his employees, the real-estate agent his clients, the retailer his customers. Everybody behaves unjustly because of someone else." The Board proceeded to call on Parliament for new legislation to fight this discrimination, and the Home Secretary indicated that action would be taken.[24]

As for racial problems on the Continent of Europe, we should note that in France the Revolution of 1789 had made a complete end of officially sanctioned anti-Negro discrimination. Subsequently, however, the nineteenth century imperialism of France, and its general mistreatment of French colonial peoples, produced some reflection in metropolitan France. There are, of course, thousands of non-American, African Negroes residing in France. Even more effective in developing a certain racial sense in France was the presence of many thousands of Algerians in the country. A disadvantaged group at best, these Algerians were galvanized into agitation and violence during the war waged in Algeria to expel the French, 1956–1962.

It is interesting to read the detailed, on-the-scene observations of a Negro traveler, Roi Ottley, concerning racism in Europe. Unexpectedly, we learn that no stigma was attached to the Negro in modern Germany, and Negroes were treated about the same as other Germans. Ottley realizes that Hitler's Nuremberg Racial Laws applied to all non-members of the so-called Indo-European races, and therefore could have been used against Negroes. However, he has the impression that such applications of the Laws were not widespread. Even so, the racism of Germans under Hitler naturally brought about some deterioration in the status of

Germany's small Negro minority, and there was private discrimination in employment and social matters.[25]

Of course, the German record on handling of and attitudes toward Africans has some great blemishes in the twentieth century. We have already spoken of the massacres by Imperial German troops of thousands of inhabitants of the German African colonies. It is also well-known that the French forces which occupied certain parts of Germany for a time after World War I included personnel from Senegal in West Africa. The presence of these Negro troops was apparently much resented; Nazi propagandists, from the 1920's on, never ceased to complain bitterly about this French abuse, which they characterized as a malevolent attempt to corrupt the pure German race by Negro importations.

As another aspect of the relationship between racism on the Continent of Europe and the plight of non-whites outside of Europe, we might note that Adolf Hitler sent observers to the United States to see how the Jim Crow system worked in the American South. He apparently felt that this well-developed, effective system could be copied in his efforts to reduce Jews and other European minorities to the status of a subrace. Roi Ottley reports that, in 1932, Hitler invited Dr. S. J. Wright, a Negro professor doing research at Heidelberg, to join him at dinner. Not surprisingly, Hitler included in the long after-dinner conversation a number of insulting statements as to the general inferiority of the black race, but he also asked a great many questions about the status of American Negroes.[26]

More recently, in the 1960's, the reactions of Europeans to stirring developments in American race relations are illustrated by newspaper responses to the Harlem riots of July, 1964. The Austrian *Arbeiter-Zeitung* offered a very grave interpretation: "The conflict between colored and white is becoming a more serious problem. It is possible that the problem will replace the East-West conflict" [as a focus of world attention]. This newspaper recommended a geographic solution for the problem, i.e., "the transplanting of part or all of the eighteen million American Negroes to South Africa in exchange for three million white South

Africans." For such a solution to be at all possible, utterly totalitarian means of compulsion would have to be used.

Elsewhere in Europe, phrases used in headlines at this time often revealed highly negative symbolism, to say the least. The headlines included: "A Cancer Called Harlem," in Madrid's *ABC*, and "In Harlem the Devil is Loose," in West Germany's *Frankfurter Nachtausgabe*. In Europe and America alike, people have been more inclined to view such events as these riots with alarm or annoyance, rather than with a feeling of joint responsibility. Not surprisingly, many well disposed white persons are miffed at hearing that they, too, share responsibility for problems of race relations. What could the non-white brethren expect of them now, they wonder?

In the stark judgment of James Baldwin, the problem is not *just* a matter of race relations. In *The Fire Next Time*, he says: "White people will have quite enough to do in learning how to accept and love themselves and each other, and when they have achieved this—which will not be tomorrow, and may very well be never—the Negro problem will no longer exist, for it will no longer be needed."

:: IV ::

The Imperialist Advance
in Africa

NORTH AFRICA

LET US consider what happened when modern European powers thrust their way into fairly populous regions of the world, where intricate patterns of civilization had existed for thousands of years. The last few decades of the nineteenth century brought vast additions to European empires. The principal powers enjoyed gains as follows: British colonial acquisitions from 1870 to 1900 amounted to 4,754,000 square miles, containing 88,000,000 people. During the period 1880–1900, France acquired 3,500,000 square miles, with 37,000,000 inhabitants; Belgium appropriated 900,000 square miles, containing 30,000,000 inhabitants; and the Germans took 1,026,220 square miles, populated by 16,687,100 persons.[1] Most of these territorial additions were in Africa.

Until the defeat of Turkey in World War I, most of North Africa and the Near East was under some form of Turkish influence. Either the territories were Turkish, or the Sultan had influence through his position as Caliph, religious leader of Moslems.

An important objective of British foreign policy during the nineteenth century was defense of the Ottoman Empire's position. France and other nations of Western Europe were also involved in this solicitude for the security of Turkey. The reason for this great interest was, of course, the security of Britain's lifeline to her holdings in India and other parts of Asia. A large share of British colonial territories and colonialist operations in Southwest Asia and North Africa centered around this concept of the defense of India. Territories to the north of India were considered necessary to the defense of that subcontinent. The territories around the Isthmus of Suez were vital because of their position athwart the route to India, and the Ottoman Empire as a whole was important because if Russia—Turkey's aggressive neighbor to the North—could reach Turkish defenses, she would jeopardize the India lifeline. Oil later became an important consideration, and was menaced occasionally by Russian power and defended by Britain and her allies of the time.

The North African and Near Eastern nationalism which developed in the twentieth century was compounded of two things. It was naturally a movement to counter foreign influence, whether French, British, or Russian, and was also a movement of unification of Arabs. The Turkish Empire was not an Arab organization, and Arabs all through the North African and Near Eastern lands found the idea of Arab unity very attractive.

There was a serviceable basis for Arab unity. The religion of Islam was a common possession of all Arabs, as was the Arabic language and literature. The latter was tied up, in some respects, with the Moslem religion, but it also encompassed an entire cultural heritage. Though the spoken language varied considerably from the northwestern corner of Africa to the Arabian peninsula, the literature and culture were substantially the same in all regions.

Let us see how, under the Turkish suzerains during the nineteenth century, the position of West Europeans became so strong in this great region. As early as 1833 there were proposals to build a Suez canal in Egypt, but they were resisted so long as the Khedive Mohammed Ali reigned. When his son became Khedive in 1854, Egypt had a ruler more inclined to welcome West European assistance and advice. In 1854, most notably, French diplomat and entrepreneur de Lesseps received a concession to build the Suez Canal, and four years later the Suez Canal Company was organized. Railroad construction in Egypt began with a line from Alexandria to Cairo in 1857.

The Canal was not finished until 1869, by which time there was a new Khedive named Ismail. His rule, too, was a period of westernization. Aside from the Canal, expansion of railroads and other public works took place, financed by such large loans from European bankers that it was unlikely that the Khedive could maintain payments on the interest and principal out of current income. Indeed, by 1875, he was obliged by financial difficulties to sell to the British his shares in the Suez Canal Company. In spite of profit from this sale, his troubles were so aggravated by the following year that British and French controllers had to be designated to manage Egyptian debts and revenues. Egypt's peasantry had to pay such high taxes in order to repay the European bondholders that, in 1879, a wave of popular unrest led to the deposition of Khedive Ismail. Though the European financial advisers were dropped for a while, they were reappointed before the end of 1879, with the fateful provision that only with English and French consent could they be removed again.

In 1881 came the first of several coups d'état led by Egyptian Army officers, of whom Arabi Pasha was the most influential. The Army officers, usually of middle-class origin, often had sympathy for the Egyptian people as victims of excessive taxation and other exploitation. They also resented foreign influence, whether Turkish or West European. In addition, a movement called Islamic modernism developed under the leadership of famous teacher Jamal ud-Din Afghani, and his disciple Mohammed Abdu. The work of these men supplemented political and military actions of the time by linking nationalism with an Islamic revival.

Although Arabi Pasha was able to force appointment of a new, nationalist ministry in which he himself was War Minister, by the end of May, 1882, the English and French brought about the fall of that government. When the Khedive was forced by popular feeling to recall the nationalists, the British undertook further action, culminating with a bombardment of Alexandria and British occupation of Cairo. From 1883 on, superior British strength prevented further growth of liberal Western political institutions, and aborted the development of a free Egyptian nation. The British resident, Lord Cromer, was the power behind the Khedive for almost a quarter of a century thereafter, and under him other British advisers guided lesser Egyptian officials in all policymaking matters.

Immediately south of Egypt lay the Sudan, where there was strong resentment of Egyptian rule. In this situation, the British seem to have tried not to be aggressive. They endeavored in 1884 to withdraw all Egyptian forces from the Sudan, and restore the authority of Sudanese chiefs under nominal Egyptian control. The British were even willing to let the customary slave trade proceed as usual, in and through the Sudan. However, a conquering prophet known as the Mahdi wanted complete control for himself. He continued his military campaigns, seizing Khartoum in 1885 and killing General Charles Gordon and his garrison. Meanwhile, the British went on with prolonged negotiations with other European powers to settle the status of the Suez Canal. In 1888 they arrived at the agreement known as the Suez Canal Convention, to which France, Germany, Austria-Hungary, Italy, Russia, the Netherlands, and Turkey were also signatory. This convention made the Canal a free route, open to all vessels of all nations, both in peacetime and wartime. To understand the diplomatic tangles of the 1950's, note that this agreement forbade blockading of the Canal at any time, and prohibited all other acts of hostility around it. However, the convention did leave the Sultan of Turkey and the Khedive of Egypt free to take such steps as were "necessary for securing by their own forces the defense of Egypt and the maintenance of public order."

At last, in 1896, Lord Kitchener proceeded with British reconquest of the Sudan, inaugurating a period during which Britain took great interest in Ethiopia and the Sudan as regions where the Nile River had its sources. The Empire of Ethiopia managed to remain independent during most of the period of European predominance. Only from the Italian invasion of 1935 until its liberation during World War II was this Empire as a whole subjected to colonial treatment. However, its boundaries, and those of the Sudan, were ill-defined. The Italians and French infringed upon territory which Ethiopians claimed along the shores of the Red Sea and Indian Ocean. French plans for colonization of Equatorial Africa brought them into conflict with the British in this troubled region. Consequently, many diplomatic démarches and agreements were required to iron out boundaries among these competing nations. Although Ethiopia lost territory in the process, it remained independent. In 1862, the French acquired Obock, a port which would later form part of French Somaliland. In 1882, Italian colonizers seized territory on the Red Sea coast which they would later enlarge and call Eritrea, and within a few years both British and Italians appropriated more coastal areas, known respectively as British and Italian Somaliland.

The Italians thought they were carving out a goodly sphere of influence within Ethiopia. Moreover, in 1889, the Abyssinian Emperor assented to the Treaty of Uccialli, which, as the Italians saw it, gave them a protectorate over the whole Empire. In 1891, the British completed two agreements with the Italians whereby the Italian protectorate over Ethiopia was recognized—but only up to a point 100 miles from the Nile River, and also subject to the Italians not interfering with the flow of other Nile tributaries lying within the assumed protectorate.

Soon, however, Emperor Menelek of Abyssinia confounded the Italians by declaring that the Treaty of Uccialli, written in his own language, did not substantiate the claim of a protectorate. After encouragement from the British, the Italians invaded Ethiopia in 1895, but their army was wiped out at Adowa in Northern Ethiopia. The invaders therefore had no choice but to sign a new treaty, acknowledging Ethiopia to be a sovereign empire.

Meanwhile, the British and French had to settle the division of spoils across the interior of Africa. The French had placed a force at Fashoda, on the edge of the Sudan, in 1898. In a gigantic game of tic-tac-toe, they were moving to extend their equatorial holdings from the Atlantic Coast to the Indian Ocean, if possible. The British, whose General Kitchener had retaken the Sudan, now approached French-held Fashoda. They wanted to extend their Sudanese holding until it merged with other colonies farther south, to form a solid belt from Egypt to South Africa.

After an acute crisis, the French Government found itself compelled to evacuate Fashoda. They gave up the territory along the Nile, claimed by the British as part of the Sudan, and received very little as a quid pro quo, only an augmentation of their colonial holdings in the Sahara region—nothing that the British wanted, in any event. The ill-will left between British and French by this episode did not end until the Anglo-French Entente of 1904, which settled problems between these two nations across the entire north of Africa. It provided for French acquiescence to control of Egypt by the British, while the French were to be allowed to take Morocco, which had remained free of complete domination by any one European country during the nineteenth century because of rivalry amongst the powers. Spain had occupied a small part of Morocco in the 1400's, and her presence there continued into the twentieth century. However, Spanish holdings were but a small fraction of Morocco, and many European nations competed for economic or political influence elsewhere in the country. Each European nation gladly undertook public works for the Moroccan government, and made loans to it. The inability of the Moroccan government to repay these great loans was followed by the usual European pressures and efforts to convert financial default into political domination.

During the first decade of the twentieth century, the rivalry between France and Germany for predominance in Morocco was so keen that it repeatedly raised the specter of a Europe-wide war. By 1911, there was such a preponderance of French financial and administrative advisers in Morocco that France seemed likely to win this contest. Furthermore, the Anglo-French Entente had given France a measure of British support. Finally, in 1911, the French and Germans concluded a treaty which allowed a French protectorate over Morocco, in return for which Germany received part of the French Congo. France accordingly collected her new Moroccan award by exacting a protectorate from the Sultan. Spain, of course, retained her portions—Spanish Morocco on the Mediterranean and Ifni on the Atlantic Ocean. The powers declared the Moroccan city of Tangier an international zone.

Because World War I occurred within two years after imposition of France's protectorate, Morocco was spared immediate consolidation of French authority and ownership. However, in the early 1930's it became clear that France was not merely operating a protectorate, but was absorbing the country in many ways. The French obtained much of Morocco's best farmland, to the degree that, in 1950, 2,500,000 acres out of 11,000,000 under cultivation were owned by 6,000–7,000 Frenchmen, while 850,000 Moroccans owned the rest. Although two-thirds of the French owners had acquired this land by some sort of purchase, other land owners had picked up holdings which were summarily requisitioned by French authorities during the years 1918–1935. As with European programs of land acquisition in Southern and Eastern Africa or America, the French method of acquisition consisted of little more than arbitrary staking of claims, without careful check on prior titles.

The joint interest of the European nations in Algeria became clear as early as 1815, when Europe's diplomats, assembled at the Congress of Vienna, took up the subject of the Barbary Pirates. In 1827, the French found it timely to begin their move into Algeria. They used as a pretext the rudeness of the ruler of Algiers, who struck the French envoy with a fly swatter. The French sent expedition after expedition into Algeria, but resistance was so stubborn that not until the 1840's did they bring really large regions under their control. Algerian recalcitrance was displayed by repeated revolts in 1864, 1871, and the twentieth century, but none could bring about dislodgement of French power.

The French maintained that all the Moslems of Algeria were French subjects, but in practice their citizenship was of a lower degree than that of Frenchmen. The many Frenchmen settling in Algeria constituted a powerful interest group which steadfastly resisted any effort to give equality or freedom to the Moslem majority within the country.

In Algeria, we encounter the characteristic land robbery which European settlers performed on all the continents. In 1841, French General Bugeaud recommended that, wherever there was a good supply of water and fertile land in Algeria, the government install French colonists, without any concern as to previous land ownership. Three years later, in 1844, the French seem to have moved extensively to take the general's advice. They issued a law incorporating as French public domain all lands on which there were no buildings, and to which Moslem owners could not prove a firm title dated earlier than 1830. The next year, a law authorized French military authorities to take the lands of any Moslems guilty of "hostile acts." Naturally, lands seized by these processes were readily turned over to European settlers, who by 1954 owned about one-third of the farmland, including nearly all the prime land. Although 97 per cent of the farm people were Moslems, half of the agricultural output came from lands of Europeans. The French deserve credit, however, for greatly improving the farmlands of Algeria and adding millions of acres to cultivation. From 1,400,000 acres under cultivation in 1830, the farmland increased to 7,000,000 acres in 1954.[2]

In Tunisia, European domination came primarily through financial infiltration. There was rivalry among Europeans in Tunisia, but this was chiefly a Franco-Italian contest, and the French were in a good position to win. They actually had the backing of that arbiter of European diplomacy in the 1870's and 1880's, Bismarck, who considered French expansion into Tunisia an acceptable safety valve to relieve the frustration arising from France's losses to Germany in 1871.

The Bey, or local ruler of Tunis, made European infiltration easier by his manifold financial troubles and weaknesses. Tunisians found themselves compelled to secure their unmanageable debts with customs revenues and taxes; then England, France, and Italy found it expedient to supervise collection of the Tunisian obligations. The European powers scarcely helped the Tunisians financially by lending additional money at interest rates as high as 15 per cent. When the powers of Europe gathered in 1878 at the Congress of Berlin, the British offered freedom of action in Tunisia to the French in return for French acquiescence in British seizure of Cyprus. The Italians, wanting Tunisia for themselves, resisted extension of French control, but in the years 1881–1883 the French were able to make a definitive move in this area. Full financial control by France came first, and then some alleged violations of the

Algerian border by Tunisian tribesmen were used as a pretext for general seizure of power by the French. The Bey of Tunis retained only titular sovereignty after 1883.

In Tunisia, as in Morocco and Algeria, a considerable European takeover of land occurred. By 1956, just before the country regained its independence, 26 per cent of the farmland was held by Europeans. As in Algeria, the French had invested a lot of capital in improvement of the land, especially in provisions for water, such as deep wells and building of dams.[3]

The last large European acquisition in North Africa was in Libya. Italy went to war with Turkey in 1911, supposedly because the Sultan had not offered proper protection for Italians in the Tripoli area of Libya. In reality, Italy meant to keep up with French acquisitions by taking part of North Africa for herself. In 1911 the Italians announced that they had annexed Libya, and the Turkish Government reluctantly recognized this change. However, for several years the Italians had the task of repressing revolts by Arab inhabitants.

Not only did Arab independence fighters all around North Africa reiterate their dissatisfaction with colonial rule by innumerable large and small armed actions during the first three decades of the twentieth century, but World War I also gave greater scope to Arab nationalism in North Africa and Southwest Asia.

SUB-SAHARAN AFRICA

WE HAVE SAID that the stage was set for European takeover of Africa below the desert belt by the depredations of the slave trade and new problems created by the cessation of slavery. The 400-year experience of the African slave trade had conditioned Africans—especially in the West Coast regions from which most of the slaves came—to depend upon this trade as a major prop to their economy. During the slaving era, other promising lines of economic endeavor were pushed aside by the consuming financial value of the trade to vested African interests. Manufactured goods imported in exchange for slaves also had some tendency to limit the growth of indigenous manufactures.

The end of the slaving period in the nineteenth century brought further damage and disorders to Africa. Not only was export of slaves ceasing to be a source of trade and profit, but recurrent efforts by Europeans to put a stop to slaving caused forceable intervention in African affairs. The British Navy, in particular, kept trying to catch ships which were wrongfully carrying slave cargoes out of Africa, but it was clear that the best way of wiping out slave exports was to exert power within Africa to stop the taking and exchanging of slaves.

The British, and to a lesser extent the Danish and Dutch, became involved in still another consequence of the end of the slave trade. They tried to develop other trade in its place, and were thus motivated to uphold such west coast tribes as the Fanti, with whom they had maintained an alliance and trade agreement for slaving purposes. The Fanti, in turn, were increasingly under attack from their inland neighbors, the powerful Ashanti, who were now more aggressive because their profitable role as middlemen in the slave trade was coming to an end. In the first decade of the nineteenth century, and again in the 1820's, these European nations felt obliged to intervene and take action against the Ashanti in order to uphold their coastal allies.

Chapter One contained a general discussion of the technological developments which made modern imperialism possible and profitable. In addition to these developments, stress should be laid on the availability of quinine in the nineteenth century. Without it, European domination of malaria-ridden tropical Africa would scarcely have been possible. Together with such devices as the river steamboat and much-improved weapons, this enabled the Europeans to move swiftly into Africa in the 1800's.

Paradoxically, projects for liberation of American-held and British-held slaves in the early nineteenth century actually produced a number of attempts to colonize or control Sub-Saharan Africa. It was common, in those days, to plan on retransplantation of Negro slaves back to Africa after their liberation. Of course, they could not simply be restored to localities from which their ancestors had been removed into slavery. About the only region in which the population was scanty enough to admit of such Negro returns was the part of West Africa between the Ivory Coast and Senegal.

The British planned on such a colony of Negroes in the 1780's and were able, in 1791, to begin a settlement in Sierra Leone. Curiously, the Sierra Leone Company, which was resettling ex-slaves from Nova Scotia and England in this region, could meet the costs of transportation and operations only by the decidedly nonhumanitarian procedure of seizing more slaves within Africa, and marketing those. The English Parliament, apparently recognizing the inconsistency of this, in 1800 granted the Sierra Leone Company a subsidy, sparing it from playing further the concurrent roles of liberator and enslaver. In 1821, the British Government designated Sierra Leone, together with the Gold Coast and Gambia, as the "British West African Settlements."

In the United States, the American Colonization Society received its charter in 1816. Its program was not precisely one of liberation, since it concentrated upon removal from America of Negroes already freed. The Society received some Southern, even slave-owner backing, which is not surprising, since the Society's objectives resemble (in effect) those of later racists who aimed to keep an alleged race pure by entirely removing any minorities of another race.

The American Colonization Society issued a report in 1819, which reflected the smug feeling of superiority or condescension which accompanied later programs of imperialism. The report noted that, in the Society's projected African colony, "new forms of government, modeled after those which constitute the pride and boast of America, will attest the extent of their obligations to their former masters."[4] The Society acquired territory south of Britain's Sierra Leone project, and a settlement was established for American Negroes. Other charitable American societies set up settlements in the same vicinity, and in the 1830's most of these were merged to form Liberia. Although the new country declared its full independence in 1847, the United States Government did not formally recognize Liberia until the American Civil War was over.

As early as 1860, German colonizers got into the act in West Africa when one of their trading companies opened a factory in the Cameroons, but it was not until a generation later that the German Government proclaimed protectorates over the Togoland coast and the Cameroons. In the 1860's, the British took the Lagos coast of Nigeria, and the French set up a protectorate on the Dahomey coast. The Dutch finally left Africa by selling their posts on the Gold Coast to Great Britain. As for the Spaniards, they renewed their colonial activity by establishing protectorates in Rio de Oro and Spanish Guinea.

Meanwhile, in the Congo region, the Belgians were most active in forming the "International Association for the Exploration and Civilization of Central Africa," founded in 1876 for such benevolent purposes as suppression of slave trade. Within a year after its founding, the Belgians began to set up posts on Lake Tanganyika in Central Africa. The International Association, although dominated by Belgian interests, became a diplomatically recognized territorial power during the 1880's, when most of the great European powers and the United States recognized it as a sovereign entity.

The Berlin Conference, which convened in 1884, included representatives from most governments of Western Europe and from the United States. Bismarck brought this conference together to settle many pending problems involving African territories. Great Britain secured confirmation of her claim to the delta of the Niger River, while France got a northern portion of the Congo. Belgium was to have domination in the vast central Congo, where the "International Association" now redesignated itself as the "Congo Free State." Spain was given recognition of her claim to Rio Muñi, just south of the Cameroons, and Spanish Sahara, south of Morocco. Here once again was a prime example of the European nations, in conference assembled, disposing of territory to which they had no right.

Beginning in 1885, the King of Belgium assumed personal possession and sovereignty in the Congo. A large part of this vast country was set aside as Crown land or a private domain of the the King. An elaborate system of extortion was adopted to promote economic development of the Congo. A system of forced labor was established, while agents of the King and his concessionaires determined, at their pleasure, the quota of rubber or other products that each village had to turn in at trading posts. Nominal payments might be made in return, but often the goods were merely considered tax payments. The agents had unrestrained power, if demands for products were not met, to punish the "delinquent" by flogging and other barbarous means. These gangster-like programs, directed by the King of a "highly civilized country," undoubtedly succeeded in procuring rubber and other products in continually increasing quantities. Exports of the Congo State grew, imports remained small, and the Belgian profiteers did very well indeed! Soon the scandalous administration of the Congo became so notorious that it could not be ignored. The Aborigines Protection Society in Great Britain protested, and in 1903 the House of Commons called upon the Government to take action.

The ensuing investigation by Sir Roger Casement, then a British consul, revealed that the natives were being treated inhumanly. When a native village did not produce its quota of rubber, native soldiers were sent to punish the offenders; they commonly brought back villagers' hands as proof that they carried out their orders. In other cases, wives of villagers were seized as hostages for delivery of the required rubber tribute by their husbands. Most damning of all information gathered by Casement was the news that the population had diminished by 60 per cent as a result of starvation, thousands of executions, skirmishes, and the flight of tens of thousands out of this Belgian Congo—all in a country which the powers of Europe had pledged, at the Berlin Conference of 1884–1885, to lead to "moral and material well-being."[5]

King Leopold attempted to deny all these charges. When he was unsuccessful in his wily efforts to whitewash the affair, he consented to transfer of the Congo from his *own* custody to control by the Government of Belgium, a change that could not be expected to relieve the abuses very much. If this step appeased the consciences of Europe's leaders, one has to suppose that their consciences were not very active.

It would be reassuring to believe that the Belgian Congo was the only colony where involuntary servitude persisted long after official abolition of slavery, but let us not indulge in any such reassuring illusion. Forced labor was still common in many colonies in the early 1900's and lasted in some places as late as the 1940's. For example, Belgium agreed with reluctance to the International Labor Organization's Draft Convention of 1930, pledging suppression of forced labor. The French had still not ratified this Convention in 1940, saying that it was "out of harmony with French colonial labor problems." French authorities then admitted that such servitude was continuing by stating, "forced labor may be said to be on the decrease."[6] Equally guilty at this time were the colonial administrations of Italy and Portugal. As for the British colonies, their administrators at least tried, at times, to investigate such practices.

In 1912, the British East African Government appointed a "Native Labour Commission" to look into labor problems. The Commission obtained testimony from planters, farmers, and natives, which showed clearly that forced labor was regularly made available to European planters. When the natives proved recalcitrant, officials and their soldiers enforced these labor drafts. Pay for the laborers seldom exceeded one penny a day for boys and threepence a day for adults. To make this enslavement worse, it was not uncommon for the workers to be confined in locked, overheated freight cars during many hours of transit to their places of "employment."[7]

Another form of involuntary service arose from conscription of Afro-Asian colonial subjects to serve in the armed forces. This service was inequitable in several respects. France exacted longer service from her colonial conscripts than she required of Frenchmen in France. The colonials were habitually used in wars which did not directly concern their native land. For example, African troops were sent to Europe for the Crimean War, the Franco-Prussian War, and the World Wars. In World War I, 680,000 such troops were used by France in Europe. An obnoxious feature of colonial conscription was the typical unwillingness of European governments to permit "native" soldiers to prepare for higher rank or responsibilities. The Belgian Congo, even on the eve of its independence in 1960, had not one Congolese commissioned officer in its large forces.

In this examination of modern European expansion, there is little more to say about Portuguese holdings in Africa—Portuguese Guinea, Kabinda, and Angola on the west coast, and Mozambique on the east coast. Portugal was established in Africa several centuries before this time; her role in modern imperialism has been simply to resist change and quell revolts.

So let us look beyond Angola to the colonies at the southern end of Africa. The Dutch had founded a colony at the Cape of Good Hope in 1652, but the colony remained little more than a supply station for Asia-bound ships. Its slow growth was not due to resistance by natives, because the Cape area was virtually vacant. To the east and west, along the coasts, were the very primitive Hottentots, and between them, a little way inland, Bushmen. Both of these native types were in such a low state of political organization, and so small in number, that they were scarcely any problem for the settlers. Indeed, the original natives formed so inadequate a labor supply that it was found expedient to bring in slaves from the Bantu tribal areas of Africa, farther north, as well as forced labor from Asia. The more typical black Africans of Bantu stock were, in the seventeenth and eighteenth centuries, located far north of the Cape Colony, and it was only in the 1830's that their movement southward coincided with white expansion northward.

The white settlers had a considerable background of religious earnestness or fanaticism even before arriving in Africa. One principal group of South African settlers had been a Protestant minority in predominantly Catholic areas of the Low Countries back in Europe. They had developed a tough, somewhat fanatical belief in their own values, a frequent consequence of continuous existence as a religious minority. Their ideology was consequently rigid. Several thousand Huguenots had escaped French persecution by emigrating to South Africa at the end of the seventeenth century, adding even more religious fanaticism among the Cape settlers.

The settlers developed a viable economy, but, because it relied so heavily on its black working force, doctrines of racial superiority were necessary to justify and perpetuate a ruling class which really differed from its exploited people only in color of skin. The Boers seem to have filled this doctrinal need by thinking of themselves as the chosen people of God, finding their model in the Israelites of the Scriptures. They firmly believed that God had ordained them as His elect, and set them over the lesser folk of the land.

The Napoleonic Wars enabled the victorious British to take the Cape Colony from the Dutch, and the new proprietors pushed their holdings as far north as the Orange River in 1826. The Dutch, or Boers, desiring both new lands and escape from British rule, made their Great Trek in the 1830's, pushing northward into Zululand and Natal. Sporadic wars between the Dutch and British in the 1840's tended to be won by the British, who were, however, willing for the time being to recognize Dutch settlers beyond the Vaal River as an independent nation. This was the Transvaal Republic, later called the "South African Republic." Another independent Dutch entity included the lands north of the Orange River, and was known as the Orange Free State.

British interest in South Africa was greatly stimulated by discovery of diamonds on the Orange River in 1867. Within a year, the British began to take advantage of friction between the Boers and native tribes, and under the pretext of protecting the natives or adjudicating quarrels they added to their colonial holdings. The tribe of the Basutos, for example, had been at war with the Boers, but the conflict was terminated by a supposedly benevolent British annexation of Basutoland. Tribesmen found British protection somewhat oppressive, and soon began a war to expel the British, a three-year struggle which naturally ended with full British control.

The primary object of British expansion was, of course, the region most rich in diamonds, which the British were able to take from the Orange Free State in 1871. Six years later they annexed the Boers' South African Republic, but after a few years a Boer revolt resulted in restoration of independence to that Republic.

As the British extended control farther north, they had to contend with that powerful Bantu tribe, the Zulus. Zulu tribesmen were highly effective warriors, and against them the British were obliged to wage a difficult struggle. In 1879 the British were able to depose the most capable Zulu leader, King Cetywayo, but in 1882 Cetywayo regained the kingship. He was soon murdered, allegedly with British inspiration or connivance. With this courageous leader gone, Zulu resistance stopped for a while. British interest in the Transvaal became much keener in the late 1880's when rich gold deposits were found there. Brilliant entrepreneur Cecil Rhodes was able to gain control of the gold mining industry, and before long promoted a merger of the diamond interests, forming a company through which he controlled the diamond extraction enterprises.

Not only did Rhodes trample on native African sovereignty and land rights, but he also advocated compulsory labor by the natives to provide a labor force for his mines. In 1890, Rhodes, as Prime Minister, became political leader of the Cape Colony. He sponsored various territorial additions to British South Africa, and conducted intrigue aimed at a political merger of the Boer nations with the British colonies. Thoroughgoing racist that he was, Rhodes hoped that a great Anglo-Saxon Empire might eventually control the entire world.

The multilateral conference, a regular feature of imperialist diplomacy, goes far to prove in the minds of Afro-Asians that the European nations worked together *against them*. Another aspect of Pan-European collaboration which has been similarly obvious to Afro-Asian observers is financial collaboration involving many European nations. Cecil Rhodes' operations provide excellent examples of this. In one situation, he planned to buy out the holdings of a French company in Kimberley, South Africa. To do so, he sold some of his de Beers Syndicate shares through German financiers. He completed raising the necessary funds by borrowing money from the London branch of the international banking firm of Rothschild.

British imperialism changed its tactics more than once during the nineteenth century, but throughout that century there was no cessation or abatement of imperialism. The mid-Victorian period did bring occasional reluctance to acquire new colonies, but British power was then often extended by informal domination based upon latent commercial, military, or naval strength.

When Joseph Chamberlain took charge of British colonial affairs in 1895, imperialism became more forthright; Her Majesty's Government took more direct responsibility for administration of colonies. British interests in Africa were less likely to be considered transitory and allowed to rest in the hands of trading companies. Within a few years South Africa was seized from the Boers, and the unclaimed remains of the African interior assigned to specified European nations. Chamberlain's aggressive imperialism brought his fellow-countrymen to the apex of their global hegemony.

Only on the western coast of South Africa was there an exception to extension of British dominance. German Southwest Africa had been established in the 1880's, first as a creation of the German Colonial Company and later as a governmental colony.

The Boer-British rivalry culminated in the Boer War of 1899–1902. Because of effective Boer resistance, a third of a million British troops had to be sent in to win the war. After victory, however, the British were generous in their treatment of the Boers; the Rhodes concept of a Boer-British partnership was gradually carried out. In the Union of South Africa itself, the Boers gradually came to predominate (within the framework of British imperial control) so far as foreign relations and economic planning were concerned.

Aside from the rivalries of Boers and British and Bantu tribes, other major problems affected the large Indian and Chinese minorities. Indentured laborers from India who immigrated to work on Natal sugar plantations were initially welcomed by the white operators of plantations. However, when more and more Indians worked off their indenture and became merchants, the dominant white minority was increasingly disposed to resent the Indians and discriminate against them. In 1893, to encourage these workers to return to their homeland after completion of their indenture, a three pound annual tax was imposed on Indians. The 40,000 white inhabitants of Natal were, at this time, outnumbered two to one by the Indians and ten to one by the Negro Africans. The white minority consequently found it expedient to restrict the right of other ethnic groups to vote. As of 1896, the Indians were, for practical purposes, deprived of their vote, although, by passing "civilization tests," the Indian could supposedly earn the franchise. Actually, only a handful were ever found acceptable.

Mohandas Gandhi, later the hero of the Indian struggle for independence, came to Natal in 1893 on what he intended as a short visit to conduct a legal proceeding. He soon found that the Indians of Natal, subjected to extreme forms of discrimination, needed his leadership in their struggle for equal rights. He remained for some time in South Africa, and developed his historic non-violent resistance techniques. During the Boer War and the Bambata Rebellion, Gandhi volunteered to support the British war effort in a non-violent but active capacity. He organized for both of these conflicts an Indian Ambulance Corps which rendered valuable service. Although cooperating with the British, Gandhi's ambulance personnel also took care of wounded Africans during the Bambata conflict; hundreds of Zulu fighting men had only the care of the Indians when they fell wounded in battle, or when, as happened to hundreds more, they were flogged by British authorities after being captured.

Gandhi's organization of the Indian population of Natal had its first widespread test when, in 1906–1907, the Transvaal Government enacted a discriminatory law requiring Indians of the province to carry passes at all times. In fairness to South Africa, we should acknowledge that in many colonies the inhabitants were regimented as to place of work, residence, and movement. ID cards and movement permits were required in most colonies, under a variety of conditions. Sometimes the cards or permits became a means whereby an employer could prevent an African worker from leaving his property. Union of South Africa requirements have included separate passes for seeking employment, for circulation outside prescribed residence areas, and for being on the street when curfew began.

At any rate, when the Government of Natal directed that all Indians register under this law, Gandhi's organization was so effective that only 500 of the 13,000 Indians registered. Cooperating with Gandhi at this time was the Chinese minority in Natal, which had been coupled with the Indians as victims of this law since both were categorized as Asiatics. The Government repeatedly arrested Gandhi and jailed his followers en masse. When the Indians organized a strike among their countrymen working in the mines, the Government simply arrested the strikers and compelled them to work in the mines as prisoners.

However, the non-violent movement was so effective that indignation was focussed on the South African authorities, not only from India itself but from Europe and America as well. The three pound poll tax was abolished, as was the Transvaal pass law.[8] The South African Government gave Gandhi written assurances that Asian minorities would be treated justly. Although much discrimination against Indians would continue, Gandhi's success had been considerable, and he could now move on to India to apply his non-resistance tactics in a much larger arena.

In the early nineteenth century, the future colonial areas of Kenya and Tanganyika were under the rule of the Arab Sultan of Muscat, who controlled them from his homeland in Southern Arabia. All along the east coast of Africa, and far into the interior, Arab slave traders operated in large numbers, providing the black cargoes taken from the East African coast by Europeans during the centuries of slave trade. When the British fought the slave trade in the 1800's, they exerted increasing pressure upon its East African practitioners. In 1861, they prevailed upon the Sultan to detach his African domain, which was thereafter ruled by a separate sultan with a capital at Zanzibar, off the Tanganyika coast. This new Sultan was easily influenced by the British; within a few years, they had prevailed upon him to stop export of slaves from his sphere of control.

Establishment of German influence on the East African coast began with explorations by Germans in the 1860's and establishment of trading posts in the 1870's. German explorer and developer Karl Peters established a legal basis for German colonization in the 1880's by signing agreements with native chiefs to secure German protectorates in East Africa and Witu.

It became expedient for the British and Germans to come to an understanding about their conflicting ambitions in East

Africa. The British East Africa Company had, in 1887, secured a lease from the Sultan on a portion of the coast opposite Zanzibar. In 1890, diplomatic agreements heavily influenced by the ambitions and fears of these great powers in Europe disposed of East Africa. Zanzibar itself was placed under a British protectorate with German acquiescence. Germany's claim to Uganda was also given up, as was her hold on Witu. Back in Europe, as a quid pro quo, Britain ceded to Germany the island of Heligoland, in the North Sea. While this island had strategic value, it was considered to be of little importance at this time, and without a detailed analysis of diplomacy within the continent of Europe, one must simply conclude that Germany felt that her diplomatic position made concessions in East Africa expedient. France also agreed to the British protectorate, but received a more valuable counter-concession—recognition of her protectorate over the large island of Madagascar, off the eastern coast of Africa.

The Germans did retain the territory they had acquired opposite the island of Zanzibar. It was designated as German East Africa, and was usually referred to later as Tanganyika. This territory was the only piece lacking to fulfill Cecil Rhodes' dream of an unbroken British Africa extending from Capetown to Cairo. (Eventually, Germany had to let Britain have it when she yielded up her colonial empire after World War I.)

The French had established bases on Madagascar in the early 1600's, but for many years their interest in the island was shared by several European countries and the United States. At the time of the American War of Independence, a Polish adventurer, Benowsky, escaped from Russian captivity in Siberia and came to France, where he was entrusted with responsibility for setting up a French colony on Madagascar. He went too far with the colonization, it appears, for when he returned to France to report that he controlled the entire northeastern coast of the island, the French Government refused to support him. The United States Government then gave him a subsidy with which he attempted to continue administering the territory as an independent ruler. Finally, the French sent an expedition which defeated and killed this freelance imperialist.

During the Napoleonic Wars, the British seized French holdings in Madagascar, and the London Missionary Society had great success in Christianizing the natives. In the mid-nineteenth century, we find both the British and French established on Madagascar, but meeting determined resistance from the native Government. The dominant tribe there, the Hovas, controlled nearly the entire island, and were thus able to resist in a coordinated and effective manner.

The greatest ruler of nineteenth century Madagascar, Queen Ranavalona II, reigned from 1868 to 1883. She and her successor, of the same name, were able to slow down French penetration. In the 1870's, the French could do little more than recognize the Hova Government. In 1882 they claimed northwestern Madagascar as a protectorate, but even after vanquishing the local forces in a two year war they merely demanded control of the nation's foreign relations. After 1890, when Britain and Germany withdrew all objections to French seizure of the island, that seizure was only a matter of time. The French began their final war of conquest in 1894, and in less than two years were able to smash all resistance, exile the Queen, and designate the entire island as a French colony.

Although some colonies in Africa were gained with limited warfare, the land-grabs of the 1890's seem to have occasioned widespread and prolonged resistance by Africans. In that decade, the French fought two wars with the inhabitants of Dahomey in order to control that region. Although their colonies of French Guinea and Ivory Coast were easily seized, the powerful tribe of Mandingos in the interior behind the Ivory Coast proved very difficult to defeat; their resistance was not broken until 1898. The British, on their part, fought no less than four wars with the Ashanti. These militarily effective tribesmen of the Gold Coast resisted intermittently from 1824 until 1900, after which the colony became quiet.

The French faced many instances of stubborn resistance by local peoples whom they overcame as they pushed southward from Morocco and Algeria, and inland from their west coast colonies of Senegal and French Guinea. Although they were eventually able to overcome all major resistance, stubborn pockets remained well into the twentieth century in such places as the mountain regions of Morocco. Nevertheless, a large interconnected block of French colonial territory was established, including all the afore-mentioned colonies and reaching from the Mediterranean to the shores of the South Atlantic Ocean. Inland, it extended eastward to the borders of the Sudan.

Other insurrections, during the first five years of the twentieth century, included those in Nigeria, Cameroons, Angola, the French Congo, and German Southwest Africa, where systematic robbery by emissaries of civilization was the cause of revolt by the Herero Tribe. The Herero people had owned about 90,000 head of cattle in 1897. By 1902, after ten years of German settle-ment, they had about 46,000, and the 1,051 German traders and farmers had over 44,000.

To deal with the shocking revolt of the savages, the Govern-ment sent in an officer named von Trotha, who had played a role in suppression of the Boxer Rebellion in China. He appears to have kept in mind instructions issued by the Kaiser to German forces leaving for China at that time: "Just as the Huns a thousand years ago, under the leadership of Attila, gained a reputation by virtue of which they still live in history, so may the German name be-come known in such a manner in China that no Chinese will ever again dare to look askance at a German."[9] Von Trotha opened his action against the Hereros by inviting their chiefs to confer with him about peace terms. When they came to the conference, he had them shot. There followed a war of planned extermination, the results of which are shown by German estimates of the tribal popu-lations in 1904 and 1911, reflecting the massacres of 1904–1905: Hereros were reduced from 80,000 to 15,130, Hottentots from 20,000 to 9,781, and Berg-Damaras from 30,000 to 12,831.[10]

On the east coast of Africa, resistance in the 1890's included the so-called Wahehe War in German East Africa, as well as up-risings in Portuguese Mozambique and British Uganda. German East Africa was also the scene of a major uprising in 1905, which the Germans dealt with by exterminating the Angoni tribesmen of that colony.

In summary, it is fair to say that Europe's empire builders had seized almost the entire African continent in the course of 100 years of invasion. Ruthless military campaigns were carried on to secure the colonies, and additional campaigns were required periodically to deal with native revolts. Colonial rule was usually attended by the crassest economic exploitation, imposition of involuntary servitude, and little or no effort to foster the progress of the inhabitants.

:: V ::

The Achievement of White Dominance
over Asia and the Pacific

SOUTH ASIA

HERE WE BEGIN a review of the steps by which Asia came under European domination. Until about 1760 in India or 1840 in China, the Western role was of mercantile visitor. Before those years, the visitors' profits were great, but their power in Asia was limited and their possessions on the mainland of Asia just a few forts and port areas.

How then could Asia, home of most of the world's people, fall prostrate before the white invaders in 100 years? The over-all reasons for the burgeoning of Europe's strength have been discussed earlier. For Asia there is another factor, not attributable to the special strengths or driving determination of the invaders. Asia had a proneness to invasion, traceable to the fact that so many of her peoples had come under the rule of non-indigenous overlords: India's Moguls, the Manchu Dynasty in China, and the Turkish Sultans in Southwest Asia.

Consequently, European interlopers were not resisted in Asia with the single-minded opposition that a united people can offer to safeguard its independence. These Asian lands were not independent anyway. In some cases, local leaders hoped to get help from the newcomers to overthrow incumbent despots. Political disunity, corruption, and public apathy also made Asia an easy target.

British acquisition of India may have been inadvertent, in that the British Government did not plan ahead and schedule expansion there. Although forces of the East India Company had triumphed over the French at Plassey in 1763 and dominated much of India, they did so mostly through native princes who were their puppets. Indeed, the desire of the East India Company was not precisely territorial dominion, but just cooperation of local potentates who would let the Company have a highly privileged trading position and give large sums to the Company's staff in the guise of presents.

It is true that on three occasions the Company deposed the Nawab of Bengal, and that gradually desire to exploit led to increasing acts of administration, such as the tax law of 1764. So far as the Parliament of England was concerned, the Company was not really intended as an instrument of territorial expansion. A Parliamentary act of 1784 prohibited the Company from engaging in any aggressive war. When Lord Wellesley was the Company's Governor, Lord Castlereagh criticized his annexations, saying, "It bears the features of a systematic purpose of extending our territories in defiance of the recorded sense of Parliament." Later, in 1815, the Company itself was still opposed to expansion of the areas of Company control. In 1823 Lord Amherst was told, "No further acquisitions of territory can be desirable."[1] Even so, expansion of the areas of definite British control continued under the very governors and officials who were so firmly instructed not to annex, expand, or aggress. Probably all this was a result of a political-military situation both complex and unstable—a matter of unclear boundaries, inadequate control over subjects by various Indian potentates, or the alleged Russian threat against India.

All sorts of pretexts for British expansion—unfriendliness of a native prince, murder of a British subject, insult to the flag— sufficed, once the Europeans were inclined to solve all problems by further aggression. With an entire subcontinent falling under the control of a private company, how long could the British Government restrain itself from taking charge? It had taken preliminary steps toward exertion of sovereignty by investigating the plundering of Bengal and enacting the Regulating Act of 1773 and the India Act of 1784. Did the plundering and corruption of the Company oblige the Government to move in?

The early operations of the Company were as inhumane as could be. Famine had struck Bengal in 1770. The East India Company, far from planning famine relief, bought up vast food stores and sold them only with a steep mark-up. Ten million persons died of starvation before this disastrous affair ended. Through it all, the Company uncompromisingly collected the customary revenues, even increasing the rates in some cases to compensate for reduction in the taxpaying population. In 1772, Warren Hastings could report that the collections of 1771 had been greater than the 1768 receipts, even though the population was less by one-third.

Although the Company's man in charge, Clive, had greedily amassed a fortune during his first period in Bengal, he tried to behave better when he returned. The East India Company directors had given him agreements to present to the Company staff in India whereby the employees were forbidden to accept presents and engage in trade within the Indian hinterland. Clive enforced these directives of the Company, and thus reduced corruption and lessened the stultifying effect the Company people had on the Bengalese economy through their monopoly on inland trade.

A successor of Clive, Verelst, reproached the East India Company for enjoying possession of a vast territory without exercising responsibility and protective functions. To profiteer in this fashion was, he thought, "highly injurious to our national character . . . and absolutely bordering on inhumanity."[2] Complete assertion of Government power came finally as a result of the "Indian Mutiny," as the British called it, which nearly swept the interlopers out of the subcontinent in a holocaust of revolution, 1857–1858.

Restoration of British control was most difficult, requiring all the resources and arts of a modern government. There were rebels to be massacred and leaders to be executed. The sons and grandson of the native emperor had to be executed to prevent recurrence of disorder. Of course, in assuming sovereignty, the Government had to display the customary tender solicitude for the welfare of its new subjects, a solicitude reflected in the very title of the "Act for the Better Government of India" under which the Government took charge.

The British Government in India produced some beneficial, modernizing results. One was the gradual imposition upon virtually the entire subcontinent of a fairly well coordinated administrative machine. True, the original idea of nationwide bureaucracy and civil service, staffed by experts recruited under a system of merit, emanated from European observations of China in the seventeenth and eighteenth centuries. Nevertheless, the British did apply this useful form of political organization to their Indian possession. Somewhat later, in the twentieth century, India was allowed limited forms of representative governmental institutions. Even had these not been allowed, her politico-cultural association with the British should have given India a most useful acquaintance with a progressive and enlightened Western form of parliamentary democracy. Other gifts also flowed from British overlordship, such as modern railways and telegraph systems. In Jawaharlal Nehru's opinion, the best gift of all was the imparting of Western scientific knowledge to the people of India.

Negatively, the coming of British power in the 1760's had resulted in destruction of the old Indian economic structure. It was archaic, perhaps, being based upon exchange between the peasantry and localized fabrications by artisans. Even so, its destruction by monopolistic and discriminatory British practices severely damaged the Indian economy at the time, and delayed further economic development within India to a degree impossible to measure, but which must have been considerable.

The Indians themselves got the impression that the British were determined to prevent development of a modern industrial system in their country. Beginning in the 1880's, such Indian entrepreneurs as the Tata family undertook the building of large-scale modern industry. The Tatas had found in eastern India an ample supply of coal and iron ore required by a modern iron and steel industry, and proceeded to develop their mills. The entire process had to be carried out with Indian capital, while the British

declined both financial support and other official backing. Naturally, new endeavors of this kind can move ahead much better if
officialdom tries to facilitate them. British authorities, however,
saw no reason for a colonial regime to promote such industrial
development. It was not until World War I had diverted British
industrial capacity from production of consumer goods that India
obtained sufficient tariff protection to make it profitable to build
up a large textile industry.

Jawaharlal Nehru observed bitterly that, whereas in progressive
countries the industrial era has increased the portion of population engaged in industry, the British rule of India brought about
the reverse. He acknowledged that the growth of India's population also played a part in the country's deepening poverty, but he
underestimated the importance of that factor. Instead, he placed
the major blame on damage done by the British to Indian industry
and trade.[3]

What of labor practices in India during Britain's first century
of mastery? The new masters were able to apply their considerable
experience gained from the working of slave labor in the North
American and West Indian colonies. The Indigo Commission be-
latedly looked into the consequent harsh practices in 1860,
prompted by unrest and violence on the part of the victims. The
Commission heard many witnesses testify that they had been used
as slaves and variously mistreated.

And what of India's "self-employed" masses of farmers? Instead
of relieving the peasantry from the heavy exactions of native func-
tionaries who had traditionally collected rents and taxes, the
British Government frequently combined the worst features of
Oriental tenant farming and absentee landlords. The Government
recognized as true landowners men who formerly controlled the
lands as government beneficiaries. In some regions, they designated
the previous tax collectors (zamindars) as owners of lands over
which they had had fiscal jurisdiction. By and large, the opportunity for encouraging ownership of land by the cultivators was
lost. Sometimes the authorities did give the farmers title to land
they occupied, but all too often the financially weak and unpro-
tected peasants lost or sold this land.

Under the predominantly large-scale land ownership fostered by the British, the actual cultivators were left with neither the means nor the incentive to maintain soil quality, and yields per acre decreased. Irrigation canals and flood-control works were neglected by the British during all but the last few years of their rule. In the delta of the Ganges, for example, the excellent pre-British canal system deteriorated, and many areas became either waterlogged or deprived of the loam-bearing Ganges water. Another resultant problem was widespread erosion. When the Government did see to the fixing of canals, dams, or ditches, it often charged fees so high that the farmers could not afford to make use of the benefits involved. Admittedly, the woes of the Indian people were not due just to the inertia or callousness of the Government. The population had increased from about 100,000,000 in the 1600's to about 300,000,000 in 1900. Resultant pressure on the means of subsistence was terrific. The people, in a chronic state of semi-starvation, suffered disastrous famines when the harvests were poor—in the 1890's, for instance.

Hobson, in his careful analysis of imperialism, concludes that British rule in India was both efficient and benevolent to a great degree, yet he considers it a failure in that it did not materially assist in warding off "the chronic enemy, starvation, from the mass of the people."[4] Certainly it is proper to complain *if* this great suffering of the people was accompanied by immense British profits, and *if* these profits were remitted to England.

A portion of the British gains were plowed back into the Indian economy as investments. By 1909, the London *Economist* could report investment of British capital as totaling 475,000,000 pounds, and this figure had doubled by 1939. Profits to the investors were often huge. In the years before World War II, at least $750,000,000 was transferred annually to Britain from India in one form or another. How appropriate that the word "loot" was borrowed from the Hindi language of India!

In view of the poor treatment India received, it was natural that a strong Indian nationalism should arise, yet modern Indian nationalism was not the renewal of spirit of a nation that had always been fully united. It was, paradoxically, to Europe that India owed the maturation of her nationalism in the nineteenth century. Much of Europe itself—Italy, Germany, Greece, and other lands— was achieving its own unification, and the idea of national unity constantly appeared in the European literature and newspapers which Indian intellectuals were reading. The British within India also helped unite the country by bringing modern apparatus of communication and transportation which made prompt contact among all Indians feasible. Lastly, Indian nationalism was en- riched by rediscovery of the glorious cultural past of ancient India. In this, too, the research and exploration of European scholars pro- vided notable contributions.

The principal organization through which Indian nationalism developed was the Indian National Congress. This body was ac- tually brought into existence at the suggestion of a British Governor General, A. O. Hume, who suggested to students of the University of Calcutta that such a body be formed. The first session was held in 1885, with full British approval. Although at times the Congress was heavy with members from Western India, it was generally a Pan-Indian body. From its foundation until World War I, the Congress was dominated by moderates; it enjoyed British good will, and emphasized reform, not revolution.

There were also clear indications that the British overlordship was far from being a benevolent period of tutelage aimed at early bestowal of independence. Especially demoralizing to Indians was the modus operandi of the Indian Civil Service. In 1877, the maxi- mum age at which candidates for office in this Civil Service might take its examination was lowered from 21 to 19. This applied to examinations for which one must appear in England itself, and the practical difficulties for Indian persons were such that the result —and indeed the intent of the law—was to curtail Indian par- ticipation in administration of the country. In 1870 there had been only seven Indian candidates for the Service, and in 1880 there were only two. By 1913, fewer than 10 per cent of the officers of the Service receiving more than $266 a month were Indians.[5]

In reaction to decreasing rapport with British rule, one de- veloping trend among the Indians was the characteristic rever- sion to "old-time customs and ideals" so often found among victims of colonialism. The Indian revivals included most particularly a fusion of nationalism and traditional Hindu religion. Swami Dayanand Saraswati is usually considered the founder of this nationalistic Hinduism. He wished to purify Hinduism, cleansing it of what he considered the wrongful practices of caste, idolatry, polytheism, and child marriage. B. G. Tilak, whom some British historians called the "Father of Indian unrest," also revered ancient Indian institutions as well as working determinedly for political independence. Typical of Tilak's cultural nationalism was his move to establish a "cow-protection society," unquestionably a 100 per cent Hindu measure.

Aside from these internal reactions, let us not overlook what was occurring elsewhere in Asia. Modernization of Japan, her rise to the status of world power, and particularly her triumph over Russia in 1904–1905 greatly encouraged nationalism in India, and indeed throughout Asia. A Turkish consul of long experience noted that all over northern India the "most ignorant peasants tingled with the news" of the Russian defeat.[6] The slogan "Asia for the Asiatics" was taken up by Asian nationalists everywhere.

To a great extent, India was the center of Britain's empire. Not only was it necessary to form and maintain policies for India's neighbors in Asia, thus involving Britain in Asian affairs all the way from Iran to Southeast Asia and even China; it was also necessary to control the Indian Ocean and plan for all manner of affairs around its shores, almost as if the Ocean were a British lake. Then there was the most important matter of the "life-line of empire" from England to India. The Suez Canal was an essential life-line, and in order to control the Canal, England had to dominate Egypt and be much concerned about Egypt's neighbors. This concern extended to the Sudan on Egypt's southern border and to the group of territories around the borders of Ethiopia. The Somali territories and Kenya were important both as a center of power to the south of Egypt and as parts of the western shore of the Indian Ocean. Ethiopia and the Sudan also contained parts of the Nile River system, another way in which they figured in planning for the life-line.

The life-line concept had still another corollary. As Joseph Chamberlain said, the route around the Cape of Good Hope was an alternate route from England to India, and Chamberlain felt that European war would probably make it impossible for England to use the Suez route. Therefore, she must be able to count on the route around the Cape as a backup. Another British statesman, Foreign Secretary Kimberley, told the German Ambassador in 1894 that the Cape Colony was vital to England because it contributed to reliable communications with India. On the negative side, such British officials as James Stephen or Lord Salisbury were convinced that the territories in the southern portion of Africa were of little or no value except in safeguarding the way to India. Stephen felt that even the whole of Africa would be worthless to England as a possession. Lord Salisbury ridiculed Cecil Rhodes' plan for British domination all the way through Africa from Egypt in the north to Capetown in the south, with the intention of building a railroad along the entire length of that great north-south axis. Salisbury thought the idea curious, and more specifically he considered that the Transvaal territory would not add to the wealth or power of England. While there was much gold to be mined there, Salisbury recognized that British financiers had been able to profiteer on this gold when the South African area was under Boer rule, prior to the Boer War.

We may further demonstrate that there were no strong British interests in Eastern Africa aside from the Indian concerns by noting that the British considered trade in that area of very little importance to them. It was control of the coast which concerned the British, or control of the Nile River system as a backup to their dominance of Egypt. Lord Kimberley underscored the fact that the coast was an essential area of control for Britain in East Africa, while another Englishman, Dilke, told Herbert Bismarck in 1885 that Germany might have a free hand in the hinterland, but Britain must control the coast.

The British waged three wars against Burma in the nineteenth century, allegedly made necessary by Burmese raids against British India. They claimed that it was necessary, in 1826, to take over Arakan and Tenasserim in western Burma. The second invasion, in 1852, was supposedly to protect Englishmen from cruel treatment within Lower Burma; Lower Burma was accordingly annexed.

In 1885, the British made their final conquest, absorbing the remainder of Burma in order, as nearly as one can tell, to protect it from possible French occupation.

South of India, it was altogether natural that English forces should take Ceylon rather than leave it in the hands of any unfriendly power. The Napoleonic Wars in Europe gave the British a pretext to take Ceylon, because of domination of the Dutch homeland by the French. Seizing it in 1796, they were confirmed in possession by the treaties which ended the wars with France. The local Kandyans found their monarch and laws supplanted by British authorities, who went farther than the previous European masters in trying to dominate the entire island. This was, to the British, a natural accompaniment to their concurrent expansion of power over all of neighboring India. To the Kandyans, rebellion was the only course to resist complete subjugation. The rebellion had widespread popular backing, but was finally crushed in 1818 with ruthless repressive measures. British rule brought some benefits, such as abolition of slavery, while inflicting new grievances. The new masters chose to label much of the uplands as "crown lands," selling such lands to plantation operators. Since most of these were already being used by peasants, the new allocations of title were resented, leading to extensive disorders on the island in 1848.

In addition to the strategic and diplomatic considerations which testify to India's central point in British imperial planning, we can easily find day-to-day colonial operations in which Indian personnel and money did much to keep the empire together, and in which Indian resources were freely interchanged with those of related components of the empire. For instance, Indian laborers built railways in East Africa, and Indian clerks staffed British offices in East Africa. In Southeast Asia and British-controlled centers on the China coast, Indian policemen were assigned. Indian troops were used in China in 1839, 1856, and 1859. They served in Persia in 1856, in Ethiopia in 1861 and 1867, in Egypt in 1882, in Nyasaland in 1893, and in the Sudan and Uganda in 1896, as well as in the Boer War.[7]

This coordination by the British of the affairs of South Asia and so much of Africa was bound to have a constructive effect aside from what the British directly intended. By coordinating so many lands in this great region, the British undoubtedly reduced the amount of armed strife to a much lower level than had prevailed before their seizure or domination of these territories. Wars between neighbors, conquests by local empire builders, and trade wars became very nearly passé under British rule. Of course, there were rebellions in many areas, of which we speak in a number of other places in this book, as well as initial wars of conquest and wars between European powers which vied for control. On the whole, however, this centrality of British planning and control did make for a reduction in the active employment of force and violence.

The Russians in Asia and on the Shores of the Pacific

The conquest of Russian Asia was just about as rapid as other global expansions of European power. Except for the very first and last stages of this movement, no great and well-organized power barred its way. Initially, it was necessary to overcome the Tatar (Mongol) khans, with their capital at Kazan, and this was a difficult task. From 1240 until 1480, in fact, the Tatars had been overlords of Russia itself, though in its last decade the overlordship had been only titular.

Paradoxically, while Mongol power was decaying, its baleful ideological influence was becoming stronger in Russia. Three Mongol principles—totalitarianism, service to the State, and messianic imperialism—were perhaps the most important of many points in which the Russians emulated their former conquerors. Two of these principles, totalitarianism and imperialism, were already known to the Russians from their Byzantine contacts. From the Byzantines, in addition, they absorbed the important ideology of Caesaropapism, that relationship of Church and State in which the latter is arbiter of the former. Russian adherence to this Byzantine ideology was encouraged by the example of the Mongol overlords, who subordinated everything to the State.

The Russian leaders, steadfast Orthodox Christians, disapproved vehemently when the Byzantine Church announced in 1439 that it was uniting with the Church in Rome. When Constantinople fell to the Turks in 1453, the Russians regarded this as a punishment of God for the "heretical act of union with Rome." They themselves were, by then, nearly free of the Tatar yoke.

One conclusion drawn from these events was that Russia should fill the gap where Byzantium had fallen. God was expected to select a nation, a "Third Rome," to restore the Byzantine Empire and deliver the Christians from the Moslems. The marriage of Ivan III with Sophia Paleologina took place in 1472, giving the Grand Dukes a claim of succession to the Byzantine Imperium, since Sophia was the niece of the last Emperor. After this marriage, many "imperial" features were added in Moscow. The Byzantine coat of arms, the two-headed eagle, was adopted by the Grand Duke. The most significant phenomenon was the wider use of the title "Czar" or "Tsar," derived from the Latin "Caesar," which had originally been applied only to Byzantine emperors and Mongol khans.

The first forthright statements of the "Third Rome" idea as such came from the Abbot Philotheus, who wrote to Ivan III: "The church of old Rome fell because of impiety;... that of the Second Rome, Constantinople, was smitten,... but this church of Third Rome—of Thy sovereign dominion—the Holy Catholic Apostolic Church, shines over the whole universe brighter than the sun."[8]

With this sense of divine authority, the Russian State began expansion. Although its power in Europe suffered many reversals, advance into Asia was steadily maintained. When Ivan the Terrible conquered the Tatars of Kazan in 1552, the way to the East was open. The Moslem ruler of Western Siberia became a Russian vassal in 1555, and in 1581 the trading enterprises of the Stroganov family began to spread their posts over Siberia. Government officials followed, and by their harsh rule and fiscal exactions helped to drive off and otherwise reduce the already sparse population of Northern Asia.

By the mid-seventeenth century, Russian settlements had been made on the shores of Lake Baikal and the Sea of Okhotsk, a great arm of the Pacific Ocean; by the end of the century, the Kamchatka Peninsula was reached. Subjugation of the Tatars of Southern Russia and the Crimea took longer; after a century of effort, they were fairly well subdued by 1783, but remained restive. In the Caucasus region, the formidable mountain ranges which serrate the land between the Black Sea and the Caspian had harbored many distinct ethnic groups. Some of these—the Georgians and Armenians—had enjoyed highly developed nationhood and Christianity longer than Russia itself. But this made no difference; by 1828 they had been annexed to the expanding empire, as were the Azerbaijanians and other peoples of the Caucasus.

The Russian advance in Siberia, the Aleutians, and mainland Alaska entailed hard fighting in some places, such as the Kamchatka Peninsula of Siberia. As with other European take-overs, Russian expansion often meant seizing land from the original users. Sometimes, as in parts of Kamchatka and the entire Outer Aleutian Islands, the land passed automatically to the newcomers after they had exterminated or deported all the local people. In other cases, such as the Kazakh area and the northern Caucasus, the best lands were expropriated by European newcomers. Throughout the growing empire, from the Caucasus to Alaska, it was a common practice to levy tribute by exacting heavy "taxes" in kind, such as furs, and compel the local people to work as virtual slaves for the Russian masters. Failure to turn over the "taxes" brought massacre to many a community. There was also much wanton abuse, not to mention dreadful repressions of native resistance. On Unalaska Island in the Aleutians, for example, Aleuts were lined up single-file so that projectiles could be fired into the foremost victim, thence passing through the other victims in turn —a matter of ballistic testing, some Russians said. Three thousand Aleuts died in this massacre, even though, to the Russians' disappointment, many of the bullets penetrated only two bodies.

Fedor Soloviev, who conducted these "tests", has been described as "a sadist with a scientific turn of mind and a dictator's instinctive knowledge of the social significance of terror."[9] (This description would fit some twentieth century totalitarian leaders as well.) Less sensational, but more broadly destructive, were the cultural dislocations and demoralization, and the ravages of newly brought diseases and alcohol. All in all, the population of Eastern Siberia and the Aleutians was reduced to about one-third of its pre-Russian size.[10]

Farther south, Russian pressures on China produced one gain after another for the Czar, and a great succession of losses for China. In the late 1600's, the Russians attempted to extend their power into Southeastern Siberia as far as the Amur River, and became involved in armed clashes with the Chinese, who claimed much territory north of the Amur. The altercation was settled by the Treaty of Nerchinsk in 1689, whereby the Russians were allowed to keep only a portion of the territory they had been occupying. The Treaty of Kiakhta, in 1727, took from China the remaining territory between Russian Siberia and Outer Mongolia. In 1858, when China was simultaneously embroiled with France, Britain, and Russia, the Czar's envoys were able to secure from China the Treaty of Aigun, by which all territory north of the Amur became Russian. In 1860, Russia against profited from China's acute quarrels with the Western powers, acquiring the "Maritime Province" from China. This includes the great port of Vladivostok and the territory east of Manchuria and south of the Amur.

Meanwhile, Russia got from Japan, by the Treaty of Shimoda of 1855, the northern half of the Kurile Islands chain, while the two countries agreed to joint occupation of another, larger island, Sakhalin. In 1875, however, a new Russo-Japanese treaty determined that Japan should have the Kuriles and Russia should have Sakhalin.

Russia's armies were also pressing deep into Central Asia, into the khanates to the east of the Caspian Sea. In 1864, Russia's Foreign Minister Gorchakov sent the other powers a circular in which he said that Russia's expansion in Central Asia was necessary in order to make her frontiers secure. Gorchakov made it clear that he was aware of similar moves by the United States on its western frontiers and the French in Algeria to make their frontiers secure by constantly advancing.

In 1880, the Russian General Skobelev, with about 7,000 men, besieged the Turkmen fortress of Gok Tepe. Although there were as many as 25,000 defenders, the Russians blasted a section of the fortress' walls in January, 1881, and took the citadel. The General ordered his troops to pursue the defenders, who fled from the fortress on the side opposite from where the Russians had entered it. The fleeing soldiers and inhabitants were massacred, by the General's orders, regardless of age or sex. About 8,000 perished. Within the fortress the Russians murdered all males, but spared most of the women and children.

General Skobelev explained honestly why he ordered such massacres of a defeated foe and of helpless women and children. He said, "I hold it as a principle that in Asia the duration of peace is in direct proportion to the slaughter you inflict upon the enemy. The harder you hit them, the longer they will be quiet afterwards."

The Russian take-over in Central Asia can scarcely be justified by any general moves to introduce even the degree of orderly administration and humanitarian penal codes which the Russians themselves enjoyed. On the contrary, the Emir of Bokhara and the Khan of Khiva were allowed to continue ruling their principalities after having been conquered by the Russians. In internal affairs, some inhumane local practices remained in effect. For example, criminals were flogged to death or had their hands or feet cut off, as had been the custom before the Russian victory. Slavery was forbidden only in theory; it continued in practice.[11]

When the Russian administration eventually supplanted that of the original inhabitants, it frequently proved to be an inefficient form of government. There was, for one thing, confusion and conflict between military and civilian Russian officials. It also turned out that many of those who conducted Russia's military administration in Central Asia were discards from positions in more desirable portions of the empire. Having been sent to Central Asia because of inadequacies or irregularities, they were far from satisfactory administrators in their new assignments. Furthermore, the great distance between them and their supervisors in the next higher echelon made corruption and abuse all too common.

The Russian imperialistic drive into Asia was encouraged by Germany, especially by the last Kaiser, William II, who repeatedly took up with his cousin, Czar Nicholas II, the theme of Russia's destiny in Asia. He did this partly as a diversion, of course. Russian aspirations in Europe were leading to enmity between the Czar's Government and Austria-Hungary. Germany regretted this enmity because, from the 1870's onward, the watchword of her brilliant Chancellor, Bismarck, had been stability. The German victory in the Franco-Prussian War had given the conquerors a larger, well-unified realm. Bismarck's Reich could best be safeguarded by preventing France and Russia from forming a strong alliance which could make war against Germany and Austria-Hungary.

Clearly, Russian aggression in Europe would menace vital German interests, so the German statesmen tried to direct Russia's aggressive drives eastward. Added to these European rivalries was a distinct anti-orientalism, fear of the "yellow peril," and sometimes scorn of the "inferior races" of Asia. The Russians, who had from 1240 to 1480 lived under the yoke of Mongol conquerors, could easily conceive of a "yellow peril." In the 1880's, Russian armies had been very successful in subjugating the amirs and khans of Central Asia.

When the Kaiser wrote to the Czar in 1895 that "the great task of the future for Russia is to cultivate the Asian continent and defend Europe from the inroads of the Great Yellow race,"[12] his words would be sympathetically received in Russia. The Kaiser implied that he would guard Russia's European interests while the Czar crusaded in Asia.

As the twentieth century opened, the Kaiser found other occasions to refer in glowing terms to his Russian cousin's destiny in the East. In a ceremonial seagoing encounter, William sent a telegram from his ship to the Czar's yacht, "The Grand Admiral of the Atlantic salutes the Grand Admiral of the Pacific." Nicholas' reply was less than enthusiastic. His telegram read, in its entirety, "Pleasant voyage."

The Sino-Japanese War of 1895–1896 had ended with a badly

defeated China forced to make extensive concessions to Japan. Russia, supported by her French ally and Germany, pressed Japan to yield some of her gains. In return, the "grateful" Chinese were obliged, in 1898, to lease to Russia for 25 years the strategic Liaotung Peninsula (one of the prizes Japan had thought to gain from her victorious war).

While the Boxer Rebellion was being suppressed by the European powers, Russia utilized the occasion to take all of Manchuria from the disorganized Chinese. Across Manchuria, in the shape of a gigantic "T," a Russian railway system was built. The horizontal line extended from Chita in Siberia eastward to Vladivostok in Russia's Maritime Province; the vertical line reached southward through Mukden to Port Arthur at the tip of the Liaotung Peninsula.

In 1871, when the non-Chinese inhabitants of Chinese Turkestan rebelled against Peking, the Russians occupied the Ili Valley, claiming that they merely wanted to help maintain the authority of the Chinese Government there. They withdrew from most of this area a decade later, after the collapse of the rebels had removed the "justification" for Russian presence. However, by the Treaty of St. Petersburg in that year, China permitted its Russian friends to keep a portion of the area. There were subsequent Russian efforts to dominate the rest of Chinese Turkestan, but in Russia's 1907 agreements with Great Britain the signatories agreed to leave Peking's rule in this area undisturbed.

Such American imperialists as Senator Albert J. Beveridge were inclined to believe that Russian expansion was beneficial for Asian lands which the Czar favored with his occupation. In his book of 1904, *The Russian Advance*, Beveridge expressed pleasure that Russia had taken Manchuria "in her firm, masterful, intelligent grasp." Beveridge traveled extensively in Russian-held Asia, and concluded that the Czar's Government had brought law, order, and justice for all to territories which, under Chinese control, had suffered ceaselessly from "murder and outrage." "If the Russian is uncivilized," said Beveridge, "at least in Manchuria he is erecting precisely those very things which, in America, we look upon as the results and proofs of civilization." Beveridge particularly admired the Cossack as an inheritor of the "instinct of the frontier," a sort of equivalent to the American frontiersman or cowboy.[13]

The Russian method of dealing with Asian resistance also seemed admirable to Beveridge. Skobelev's deliberate frightfulness at Gok Tepe was justifiable, thought Beveridge, because if war "must be it should be thorough, that it may be brief and not fruitless." The Senator observed the peaceable disposition of the Chinese in Russian-occupied Manchuria. A few months earlier, during the Boxer Rebellion, these same men had been real demons, said our traveler, and the great improvement in their nature had been wrought by the sensible "war of blood" waged by the Russians when they swept through Manchuria in pursuit of the Boxers. Most significantly, Beveridge viewed Russia as the standard bearer of the white race in its struggle with the Asiatics for mastery of the world. In the Russo-Japanese rivalry of 1896–1904, he therefore discerned with fascination "the staying powers of the flower of the people of the Orient, against . . . the most tenacious and most unexhausted race of the Occident."[14]

AUSTRALIA AND THE PACIFIC ISLANDS

WHEN THE first white settlements in Australia were begun in 1788, aboriginal inhabitants of Australia and Tasmania together numbered only about 250,000. This was a sparse population for such a vast area, and the inhabitants were exceptionally primitive, so white occupation of this continent met no major opposition. But even though settlement here involved no horrendous complications, white take-over was similar, in spirit and cruel practice, to the European advance on the other continents.

The British habitually used convicts as colonizers, but the earliest settlements created no conflict because the natives quietly withdrew into the interior. However, the land-hungry settlers soon began moving inland, taking over grazing lands for their flocks of sheep. The aborigines, having no sense of property, saw nothing wrong with killing sheep when they needed food, and the settlers reacted by counterattacking, as one might against any marauder.

That was bad enough; it set in motion series of reprisals and counterreprisals, and the invaders thought nothing of exacting a dozen or more native lives at a clip. It did not matter if the provocation had been merely a quarrel over a white man's relationship with an aboriginal woman; the point, said the settlers, was to teach the natives a lesson.

In South Australia, settlers sometimes distributed poisoned flour to the aborigines; they did not hesitate to shoot them on sight, sometimes murdering entire tribes.[15] There were cases, verified by Reverend Lang in his written accounts dated 1847, where arsenic was systematically given to the inhabitants in wheaten cakes, porridge, and other foods.[16]

Along with all this murder, many aborigines perished because their hunting grounds were preempted by whites, leaving no source of food. The interlopers were indifferent to the fate of the natives and seemingly thought of them as animals, bereft of all property, legal rights, and claim to compassion. The perpetrators of this savagery nearly achieved their aim of getting rid of the aborigines. From 250,000 in 1788, the native population shrank by 1958 to 42,451 full-blooded aborigines, plus 31,346 of mixed blood.

When Tasmania was first colonized, its aborigines consisted of between 2,500 and 7,000 Paleolithic men, but armed conflicts soon reduced their numbers. Darwin tells us that the culmination came in a grand hunt by the colonists, at the end of which the remaining natives gave themselves up; by then there were only 120. These were subsequently transported, in 1832, to Flinders Island, 40 miles long and 12 to 18 miles broad, situated between Tasmania and Australia. Though Darwin tells us that this was a healthy environment and the natives were well treated, he concedes that they suffered greatly in health. By 1835 they numbered only 100.

Apparently they and the colonizers agreed that they might survive better if moved elsewhere, so in 1847 they were transferred to Oyster Cove in Southern Tasmania. By then there were only 14 men, 22 women, and 10 children. Darwin is interested in the problematical infertility of the women of this sad and dwindling group. He notes the opinion of observers that the low birth rate and high rate of mortality were probably due to attempts to civilize the natives; if left to roam as they wished, they might have reared more children. He is also interested in similar population declines among the black aborigines in Australia, and the Maoris of New Zealand. However, the plight of the Tasmanians was the most drastic, and by 1864 only one man and three elderly women survived. Unfortunately, the Tasmanians—the very last Paleolithic men on earth—died out completely, an annihilation accompanied by more inhumanity than Darwin cared to mention. British settlers had been putting out poisoned meat for them, torturing and maiming them, roasting them alive, or shooting them on sight.[17]

What is the interpretation of these tragic events within Australia? The *Current Affairs Bulletin* of the University of Sydney provided the figures given above, and commented that "criticisms made against Australia for its treatment of the aboriginal people are usually met with embarrassed or indifferent silence by most Australians."[18]

The best repressed secret of all is that the surviving aboriginal minority often live in squalor, and undergo much the same discrimination that American Negroes have suffered—segregation in public accommodations, housing, and recreational facilities, and relegation to jobs as simple laborers. In 1965, a busload of student "Freedom Riders" caused great distress to white citizens of New South Wales by touring small towns to call attention to this discrimination. The students were pelted with gravel and pushed about by white crowds. Their first bus driver quit because he found the job too dangerous. Let us hope that such conditions, reminiscent of the American South, are far from universal in Australia.

In the Pacific there were a great many islands, virtually all of which came under European or American rule. To name a few typical acquisitions, the British took New Zealand in 1840, the Fiji Islands in 1874, and the British Solomon Islands in 1893. France undertook joint control of the New Hebrides Islands in cooperation with Great Britain. On her own she added such Pacific islands as New Caledonia, the Marquesas, and the Society group. These many annexations naturally involved some filching of native real estate and some violence, most notably the rebellions of New Zealand's native Maoris.

EAST ASIANS AND THE WHITE MAN

FOR THOUSANDS OF YEARS, the Chinese Empire had enjoyed over-whelming power and prestige in East Asia. China and its culture were also regarded with immense respect in Europe, at least until about 1840. Until the nineteenth century, China was quite capable of ignoring foreign demands and repulsing foreign efforts to invade her vast territories. The Chinese were able to limit foreign trade exactly as they pleased, confining oceanborne foreign trade to one port of entry, Canton. The Chinese Government compelled foreign merchants to deal only with an authorized guild of merchants known as the Co-Hong. Thus, the Chinese characteristically kept foreigners at arm's length, requiring them to make all arrangements through duly designated merchants without the benefit of regular contact with officials of the Chinese Government. Chinese authorities also were successful in limiting the foreign visitors to small, specified portions of land, and keeping the merchants' dependents from living there.

When foreign individuals killed Chinese subjects or otherwise transgressed against Chinese law or custom, the Celestial Kingdom could exact the full penalties of its laws. More than once, personnel of American and British ships had to be turned over to Chinese authorities for execution, since the only alternative would have been to give up the lucrative China trade. This trade was, of course, very important to the British, and in the early nineteenth century trade with China was a leading segment of the foreign commerce of the United States.

There was an unsatisfactory financial aspect to this trade with China. European and American traders had very few goods for sale which the China market would accept. The balance between goods procured by them in China and the small amount of goods sold to China had to be made up by turning over silver bullion. In the seven decades after American independence, almost $200,000,000 worth of silver was turned over to China by foreign merchants. Of course, a good deal of this could be earned by judicious trading en route to and from China. American and European traders made many of these en route trades all around the African, South Asian, and Latin American coasts, thus reducing the net drainage of silver from their homelands. Nevertheless, there was a strong temptation to find a product which the Chinese would buy; this commodity proved to be opium. The British were producing this under advantageous circumstances in India, where they compelled certain farmers to grow it under a forced-quota arrangement. American and other foreign traders soon got around to supplying this handy, low-bulk, high-value commodity, procuring it from Turkey and a variety of sources. The Chinese Government realized before long that the balance of trade was being reversed.

Opium importations had become so extensive in the 1830's that Chinese silver had to be exported in compensation for the "valuable" product being furnished the Chinese by Western nations. Not only did Chinese authorities view this unfavorable balance of trade with concern, but we also know that they deplored the physical and moral weakening of so many of their people caused by addiction to the drug.

In 1839, Lin Tse-hsu was sent by Imperial authorities to Canton. With the status of special Imperial Commissioner, he undertook to compel all incoming ships to turn their opium cargoes over to him for destruction. Although American merchants complied, the British Government decided to defy this Chinese attempt at seizure. There ensued the so-called "Opium War" between China and England, a conflict which did not end until 1842.

By the 1830's, unfortunately for China, the ships and guns of the Western powers were so superior that the outcome of this war could only be disaster for China. The British easily occupied the port city of Canton. Local Chinese issued the most violent written protests imaginable, but nothing would dislodge the British force. Farther north on the China coast, British naval units moved into the Yangtze River, and the Chinese Government was faced with an extensive invasion of its central territories. Under these circumstances, there was little China could do except negotiate. Commissioner Lin, meanwhile, wrote a communication to Queen

Victoria of England in which he remonstrated with her in a style that is a little ridiculous in Western eyes, yet very damning to the West. It is impossible to ignore the fact that, in taking the Queen to task for the vicious opium trade of her subjects, Lin was right. While lecturing the English Queen as if he were the representative of a civilized power clarifying the principles of righteous conduct for a barbarian, Lin actually had the facts on his side.

In the Treaty of Nanking, which ended the Opium War, the Chinese were obliged to allow the British full freedom to trade with any Chinese, and to offer whatever merchandise they wished. China also lost the right to impose tariffs at her own discretion— a necessary corollary if unrestricted importations were to go ahead, since power to tax and levy tariffs would have been used by the Chinese to make the opium trade impossible. The treaty did not take up the issue of opium importation as such, but made it impossible for the Chinese to limit it.

The Western apologist could say, regarding such agreements as the Treaty of Nanking of 1842, that the Chinese had been insufferably arrogant and would not trade with foreigners on an equal basis. Even foreign envoys had repeatedly been treated as mere supplicant inferiors when they approached the Imperial Court of Peking. The Emperor of China had sent away George III's envoy, Lord Macartney, with an arrogant letter for the barbarian ruler of England in which the Celestial Monarch declared that he had no need for any English article of export, but that from motives of generosity he would permit the barbarians to obtain in trade those Chinese products of which they had need.

While such condescension was irritating, it would appear that, within the territory of China, the Chinese Government possessed the right to receive or not to receive foreign envoys or merchants at its discretion. When foreigners desired entry, it would have to be granted on Chinese terms. The remedy for complaints and dissatisfactions could usually be stated very simply—withdraw or not enter China at all. The Western powers did not choose to observe any such restraint, no doubt chiefly because their superior force made it easy to impose themselves upon China, as they imposed their presence, or even rule, in many parts of the world.

The Treaty of Nanking was historically important as a precedent for other treaties between the Chinese and various European and American powers. Treaty after treaty was forced upon the Chinese, a common provision of these "unequal treaties" being that numerous ports or coastal areas became foreign preserves under the occupation and legal jurisdiction of various foreign powers. The device of extraterritoriality freed citizens of the principal foreign powers from jurisdiction of Chinese courts, under most circumstances.

In addition to foreign abuses within the Celestial Kingdom itself, the mid-nineteenth century brought a demand for the cheap labor of Chinese coolies in many parts of the world. The handling of these coolies was only a little better than that of slave exportees from Africa in past centuries. There was wholesale kidnapping or other pressuring of Chinese laborers to embark for various parts of the world, often accomplished with the connivance of local merchants and officials, just as the African slave trade had always depended upon local collaboration. Thousands of these miserable laborers were thus shipped, in European and American vessels, to the North and South American coasts, Australia, Malaya, and even the West Indies. Mortality was high aboard ship, as it had been with the Negro slaves. In 1855, one ship, the *Waverley*, carrying coolies to South America, lost 260 by suffocation. When the Chinese arrived in new lands, they were subjected to all manner of discrimination and indignities. They were exploited economically, living under conditions of extreme want. In Peru and Cuba they were virtual chattels of plantation owners, under contracts that bound them to many years of indentured service. Asians were also thoroughly ghettoized and kept separate from the local populations.

Of course, an unknown number of these poor emigrants may have gone abroad in a voluntary or quasi-voluntary way to seek improvement of a condition which was already wretched in China. We should also concede that their ghettoization in foreign lands was in large part by their own choice. Certainly, however, they were received with scarcely a particle of cordiality or Christian sympathy by the Europeans and Americans they encountered.

Meanwhile, the foreign powers acted, in the period 1856–1860, to obtain longer term, even more advantageous treaties from the Chinese Government. Minor incidents of violence sufficed as pretexts for extensive action by French, British, Russians, and Americans. The Tientsin Treaties of 1858 opened the Yangtze River valley to foreign trade, and stipulated that 11 more ports were to be treaty ports—in effect, new foreign enclaves of power and privilege. The Chinese Government was also required to admit permanent foreign diplomatic missions to the capital city of Peking. These treaties formally recognized and legalized importations of opium. Throughout the 1800's, opium remained a mainstay of the China trade. Only in 1906 were the Chinese able to arrive at an agreement with Britain whereby that power's opium sales were to be reduced from 48,530 boxes in 1907 to 4,136 in 1915. Along with other Western powers, the United States let its merchants participate for half a century in sale of opium to the Chinese.

In 1859, the British and French Governments were determined to secure ratification of the Treaties of Tientsin with China. The documents stipulated that such ratification should have taken place at Peking by this time, but the Chinese Government would not even allow British and French Ministers to approach the capital. Therefore, Britain and France felt compelled to send an expedition of ground forces to effect ratification of the treaties. Eleven thousand British soldiers and 6,700 French were assigned to this effort, accompanied by the British envoy, Lord Elgin, and the French plenipotentiary, Gros.

In August of 1860 the expeditionary force landed and advanced to Tientsin, where a high-ranking Chinese contacted the envoys. To develop this contact, Elgin sent a small advance party of English and French, under a flag of truce, to meet at a town called Tungchow near Peking.

The main body of the expeditionary force ran into a large number of Chinese troops, and some fighting broke out. Possibly in indignant reaction to this fighting, the Chinese violated the truce under which the Europeans in Tungchow had been working, and took the Europeans to Peking. The two leaders of the advance party were put in chains, while the others were taken to the Summer Palace and kept for three days on their knees in a courtyard, tightly bound, and subjected to all sorts of abuse.

The expeditionary force soon reached Peking, and the Imperial Court fled from the city. The Emperor's representative undertook to resume negotiations, and ordered the Tungchow captives released. Naturally, Lord Elgin reacted with great indignation when he learned that 13 of the British prisoners and 14 French were dead because of maltreatment during their captivity. Thus, the British and French were disposed to drastic measures to chastise the Chinese Government before beginning negotiations again.

Elgin wanted whatever chastisement he might adopt to weigh heavily upon the Emperor and his officials, not upon the Chinese people as a whole; therefore, the best penalty seemed to be a dramatic apology or other punishment of the top men responsible. However, most steps of this sort were not within Elgin's power to carry out promptly. The Summer Palace, on the other hand, was immediately accessible, and was an object of revenge that would naturally suggest itself to Elgin. It was, furthermore, the actual site of much of the mistreatment inflicted upon the personnel of Elgin's mission.

On October 18, 1860, the British force began destruction. The Summer Palace complex actually included more than 3,000 structures, including a great many palaces, halls, store rooms, and temples. The circumference of the Summer Palace was more than ten miles. Not all of the buildings were destroyed, but so much was burned that a real atmosphere of disaster was created. A pall of smoke hung over the area where burning was in progress, and embers drifted through the air to the nearby capital city of Peking. One observer, Colonel Wolseley, reported that "the light was so subdued by the overhanging clouds of smoke, that it seemed as if the sun was undergoing a lengthened eclipse."[19]

Destruction of this assemblage of countless and wondrous Chinese art objects and antiquities was a classic case of Western imperialism at its worst. The cultural significance and wantonness of the destruction enable the historian to rank it on a par with the worst deeds of Hulagu Khan in Mesopotamia, Attila the Hun in Europe, or the destruction of library materials in Alexandria, Egypt. Yet the tragedy is made more poignant by the fact that

Lord Elgin, who presided over it, was in many respects an enlightened, educated European who did not relish barbarity and destruction. Elgin seems to have viewed himself as being painted
into a corner. He felt that he had no choice but to order this dreadful, history-making destruction, an event that was both China's
and Europe's tragedy. The destruction was not a punishment of the
Imperial House alone, because the Chinese people were—not surprisingly—taxed to pay for the rebuilding and replacement of
those elements which could be replaced.

A Chinese patriot put his reaction this way: "I only hope
that my countrymen try to be intelligent and strong, so that some
day we may also march towards Paris and London to set fire on
everything there." Another stated it more moderately: "The
English and French soldiers became angry because of the bad treatment of the prisoners, but their looting and destruction will make
thousands and thousands of Chinese angry in the future
generations."[20] The burning of the Belgian University of Louvain
by the Germans in 1914 in revenge for the "murderous resistance"
offered by Louvain's inhabitants was described by a British prime
minister as "the greatest crime committed against civilization and
culture since the Thirty Years' War—a shameless holocaust of
irreparable treasures lit up by blind barbarian vengeance." Con-
veniently, the complaint excluded Chinese culture as a part of
"civilization."[21]

In 1860, this unpleasantness was finally brought to a temporary
end by the Conventions of Peking, which increased the indemni-
ties exacted from China by the previous treaties. Tientsin was
opened to trade, and the British obtained Kowloon as an addition
to their Hong Kong settlement. Unrestricted entry of missionaries
was now required, and the presence of these missionaries was causing even more altercations between foreign powers and China.

American diplomat Anson Burlingame was so well regarded
by the Chinese Government that in 1867–1868 it made him a high-
ranking Chinese official and sent him to the United States and
Europe as a Chinese envoy. The most successful aspect of
Burlingame's mission was the so-called Burlingame Treaty, concluded in 1868 between China and the United States. Had this

treaty been honorably observed by the United States, it could be regarded as a very fair agreement, since it provided for reciprocal rights of residence and travel by citizens of either country within the other nation. Chinese laborers were given the right to immigrate freely into the United States, and Chinese subjects residing within the United States were promised the same treatment as citizens of other countries. This was, in effect, the "most favored nation" feature often used by foreign powers in obtaining special treatment for their nationals within China; that is, the Chinese had been obliged to promise that they would give to the signatory all privileges they might give to other favored nations in other treaties. Not only did the Burlingame Treaty give this privilege to Chinese entering the United States, it also renounced any right to interfere in Chinese affairs.

After obtaining this excellent treaty from the American Government, Burlingame proceeded to Europe, where he tried to get similar treaties with other powers. From Britain he did obtain a declaration that the United Kingdom would not require China to make concessions inconsistent with China's independence. The British also undertook to deal directly with the Central Government of China, not with regional authorities. In other European capitals Burlingame did not even obtain this degree of satisfaction, and his mission ended prematurely when he died in the Russian capital.

America's equitable treaty with China was worse than useless; it was soon to appear as a fraud to the Chinese, because the people of America would not conform to its standards. In 1868, the very year the Burlingame Treaty was concluded, James G. Blaine, leading statesman, politician, and aspirant to the presidency, wrote: "The prejudice on the Pacific Coast against Chinamen is fearful and all measures looking to the encouragement of their importation or immigration are frowned upon if not openly resisted."

Chinese immigration into the United States had really begun with the Gold Rush, which brought Chinese to California along with the many thousands of others. Toward the end of the 1850's, several thousand Chinese were working on construction of the Central Pacific Railroad, while as late as 1861 about 20,000 Chinese were still mining gold. Others had found employment in laundering, domestic service, and farming. In San Francisco in 1870, one-fifth of the city's domestic servants were Chinese. The California Bureau of Labor claimed in 1886 that seven-eighths of the agricultural laborers in the state were Chinese—probably an exaggerated figure. Nevertheless, Chinese were then doing most of the handwork, such as hoeing and weeding, where intensive farming was carried on. The census of 1870 showed that 14 per cent of the Californians engaged in gainful occupations were Chinese.[22]

Hostility to Chinese immigrants had been seen in the mining camps as early as 1852, and discrimination began with the collection of a miner's license tax from Chinese only. When the Chinese entered such trades as cigar-making in San Francisco, they met further opposition. Non-Chinese workingmen resented being undercut by Chinese willingness to work under less advantageous terms than other workers could expect. Indeed, workingmen felt that employment of Chinese was just one more example of heartless exploitation by employers, so anti-Chinese agitation had both a racial and a class-antagonism aspect. Organized labor promoted anti-oriental legislation, just as for years it encouraged anti-Negro discrimination in employment practices.

The judiciary were not guiltless, either. They were prone to back up the predominant sentiment with whatever tortuous legalisms they could devise. The Supreme Court of California decided in 1854 that Chinese persons could not testify in court cases involving white persons. Significantly, the decision noted that Indians were not allowed to so testify, and since Indians had originally come from China, the law forbidding Indian testimony applied to the Chinese as well![23]

Aside from organized or official acts, there were public demonstrations and disorders on many occasions in San Francisco, other California towns, and even such far-flung locations as Tacoma, Washington, and Rock Springs, Wyoming.

By 1876, the platforms of America's two large political parties contained planks opposing immigration of Chinese. This high-level anti-orientalism was not soon to disappear. Much later,

Presidents Theodore Roosevelt and Woodrow Wilson followed similar lines. Wilson, during his 1916 campaign for the presidency, wrote endorsements of oriental exclusion. "I stand for the national policy of exclusion," he said.

Anti-oriental sentiment is usually grounded on fear of competition from the "teeming Asian millions" or of attack by the "yellow peril." However, there are also racists who believe in Asian inferiority. White supremacists have said that the Negro cannot progress in knowledge or brain power beyond a rudimentary point due to physiological factors; the same idea was applied to the Chinese by Henry George.[24] George was a curious recruit to the anti-Asiatic school, since his own single-tax theories were partially derived from Chinese thought, and found an exceptionally appreciative audience in twentieth century China.

Because of strong antipathy to the Chinese, the American Government found it expedient to nullify the effects of the Burlingame Treaty. In 1880, American diplomats were able to secure agreement from the Chinese Government that entry of Chinese workingmen into the United States could be "regulated, limited, or suspended" by the American Government. Two years afterward, Congress enacted a law suspending Chinese laborers' immigration for ten years. (By this time, the number of Chinese in the country had reached about 132,000.) In 1888, the Scott Act made it illegal for Chinese laborers to return to the United States if they had gone back to China for a visit, even in cases where reentry permits had been issued.

The unpleasant handling of Chinese residents seems to have produced part of the effect the exclusionists desired, in that the 1900 United States census showed considerable reduction in the number of Chinese in the country. Not only had they decreased, but many were apparently a transient or short-term population, as evidenced by the fact that 88,758 were males and only 4,525 were females.[25] Laws prohibiting Chinese immigration were regularly renewed for decades. What was more, even commercial visitors and students who were allowed to enter the United States experienced frequent delays and humiliations during the process of entry.

Within the United States, oriental persons did not receive equal protection of the law. Besides riots, there were such police actions as the surrounding of Boston's Chinatown in 1903 by officers of the law, who arrested hundreds of residents in order to catch a few dozen persons who had illegally entered the country. In 1906, the City of San Francisco segregated its schools with respect to Asiatics.

Japanese immigrants aroused much the same resentment the Chinese had faced, and there were powerful pressures to exclude them also. Faced with this problem, the Japanese Government agreed with the Government of the United States in 1907 that Japan would not issue passports to workers who desired to come to the United States. This "Gentlemen's Agreement" spared Japan the humiliation of having its people overtly excluded. Tragically, the immigration law enacted by the American Congress in 1924 excluded all Japanese. To avoid this gross affront to Asian sensibilities, it would have been necessary only to apply the same formula that was applied to European immigrants. This formula, fixed in 1924, provided that the number of immigrants from a given country to be allowed each year should not exceed 2 per cent of the number of persons of that nationality residing in the United States in 1890. This would have enabled only 100 to 150 Japanese to immigrate annually—an insignificant number. Asian observers consequently inferred that the reason for total exclusion was dislike or prejudice. Reaction in Japan to the act of 1924 was of wounded pride and indignation which would simmer for decades. This multitude of efforts by American authorities at the national, state, and local levels to exclude Asiatics and deny equal rights to orientals in the United States left many Asian persons persuaded that Americans disliked them, and that America did not honor her treaty commitments.

Meanwhile, the Chinese at home began the twentieth century with their Empire in a dishearteningly weak and dependent condition. The fate of China now depended upon the consensus of the foreign powers. Some of China's richest cities were European concessions or leaseholds; whole provinces of the Empire were designated as spheres of influence for some foreign nation. China had lost the right to regulate its foreign trade, determine its own tariffs, or operate its own customs houses. In desperation, many patriotic Chinese began to support the madly anti-foreign Boxer Society, and in 1901 the Society's fighters launched an all-out attack against the foreign legation quarter in Peking. While the Boxers besieged the legations, the European powers, Japan, and the United States sent a force to the rescue.

The commander of this international force was German Field Marshal Count von Waldersee, who was ordered by his Kaiser to be utterly ruthless in China. Not surprisingly, the foreign force reached Peking, relieved the legations, and put an end to this desperate Chinese effort to eject all foreigners. The "relief of Peking" was accompanied by a great burst of massacre, looting, and destruction by the foreigners. The Chinese Government, once again at the mercy of foreign governments, had to accept the "Boxer Protocol" imposed in 1901.

To chastise China for the violence inflicted upon foreigners during the Rebellion, the powers imposed many punishments in this Protocol. The indemnity provisions are perhaps the most important; certainly, they show the broad foreign participation in this belaboring of China by treaty. The following Western powers shared in the $330,000,000 indemnity, the shares allotted in the following descending order of magnitude: Russia, Germany, France, Britain, the United States, Italy, Belgium, Austria-Hungary, the Netherlands, Spain, Portugal, and Sweden. The indemnity was to be paid in 39 annual installments with an interest rate of 4 per cent on the unpaid principal. The obligation was secured by the receipts of maritime customs, domestic customs, and salt tax.

Other provisions of this Protocol were of more limited character, but included a number of serious humiliations. These requirements included: An apology by China for the murder of the German Minister, and erection of an expiatory monument to him; punishment by China of officials guilty of complicity in the Rebellion; suspension of Chinese Civil Service examinations for five years in towns where foreigners had been mistreated; construction of expiatory monuments in the Christian cemeteries which had been desecrated by the Boxers; prohibition of importation of any arms by the Chinese Government for a minimum of two years; reservation of a section of Peking as the "Legation Quarter" in which foreign authority would prevail, and foreign military units be stationed; designation of points on the route from Peking to the sea at which foreign soldiers would be stationed to safeguard the route; and issuance by the Chinese Government of edicts forbidding anti-foreign activities. Perhaps this last provision was the most unrealistic, because it was far beyond the power of any Chinese Government to prevent hatred of foreigners at this stage of China's relationship with Europe, the United States, and Japan.

Japan itself knew how it felt to be compelled to trade with foreign powers. Beginning in the 1850's, Japan's traditional isolation had been forcibly broken with threats and occasional bombardments by Western powers. Japan, like China, had known the imposition of extraterritoriality and the enforced designation of foreign concession areas. But in Japan these had been limited in scope and of brief duration. Before the end of the nineteenth century, Japan had industrialized, modernized, and strengthened herself, and had been able to put an end to such Western impositions.

Elsewhere in East Asia, the French extended their control, step by step, over Cochin China, Annam, and Tonkin—the areas occupied by the two Viet Nams today. Together with the kingdoms of Laos and Cambodia, these were thrown together under the colonial designation "French Indo-China." These acquisitions began as a series of diplomatic and military actions purporting to protect Christian missionaries. Eventually, the French had complete control, though they typically allowed indigenous rulers to continue on their thrones as puppets.

To conquer Indo-China, the French had to fight Chinese armies as well as local forces, because China has for thousands of years tried to keep much of Indo-China under her rule. By the late 1880's, however, it was clear that neither China nor local potentates could effectively resist the French power. Indo-China became a tightly organized and highly profitable colony. The French profited from their monopoly on salt and opium, while Government controlled distilleries produced most of the rice alcohol. By 1933, the opium monopoly was producing an income of about 200,000,000 francs per year, which was actually *ten times* the profit per annum from the distilleries. From 1900 to 1940, Indo-China was clearly yielding a profit to France, even when allowance is made for military and administrative costs.

French rule left much routine or local administration to indigenous persons, but virtually all important decisions were made by French officials. There was no pretense of cultural or economic equality. French firms profited from the building of railroads, often on routes where they were not needed. (The canals and rivers of Indo-China already provided excellent transportation for most areas.) The primary object of the railroad building was frequently to line the pockets of colonial officials and entrepreneurs. Forced labor was freely imposed by colonialists to provide manpower for the building of roads, railroads, and other projects.

The inhabitants of Indo-China were subjected to unconcealed scorn and discrimination by the Frenchmen in residence there, who called the natives *macaques* (baboons). The Vietnamese language, according to colonialists, was actually obscene in its phonetic characteristics, and of course quite unsuitable for use by civilized people. The French did establish a number of good schools where French language and culture were dispensed.

Far to the south, the British had taken control of the Malay peninsula, while the Dutch continued rule of the Indonesian islands. The demands of modern industry began to make these areas more profitable than ever as sources of rubber, tin, and oil.

Dutch economic exploitation was ruthless, but was usually carried out in the 1800's through Chinese or Indonesian intermediaries who milked the villages of revenue and passed on a goodly share to the Dutch. Forced labor was a part of the colonial system here, too. In 1860, the horrors of the system in Indonesia were exposed in a book by Edouard Douwes Dekker entitled *Max Havelaar*, but known in Holland as the "Uncle Tom's Cabin of Indonesia"—a good indication that oppression of non-whites by whites was recognized in its global identity. After 1890, the poll tax replaced involuntary servitude for the most part, but as late as

1916 the Dutch were still exacting some forced labor. Expoitation of Indonesia was indubitably profitable to the Netherlands; one analyst estimates the net annual profit of the Dutch at about $150,000,000.[26]

Concerning such humanitarian responsibilities as education, the Dutch in Indonesia had in 1854 recognized that, in principle, the inhabitants should receive some education. However, even by 1941 education was neither free nor compulsory, and only 5 per cent of Indonesians were literate.

After 1900, the Dutch administration relied less upon non-Dutch, intermediary agents, and Indonesian awareness of Dutch rule became keener. There were more Dutch administrative personnel who carried out reforms, raised taxes, and in many ways made their presence obvious and disquieting. There was a gradual increase in spontaneous peasant protests and passive resistance, until in 1914 disturbances required use of the armed forces to restore order. The peasantry resented the poll tax and other levies; many refused to pay taxes or perform compulsory labor as ordered by the authorities.[27]

AMERICA ACQUIRES AN EMPIRE

MOST AMERICAN possessions overseas were acquired during or soon after the Spanish-American War, although the American people had not thought of their crusade against Spain as an acquisitive enterprise. The War was idealistic, however misguidedly, but it came at a time when imperial expansion was in vogue among Western powers. President McKinley thought of the war against Spain as a matter of high moral obligation. "We took up arms only in obedience to the dictates of humanity and in the fulfillment of high public and moral obligations, said the President.[28] He denied that territorial ambitions were involved, and felt that excessive demands after the war was won might dim the shining reputation of the United States.

American opponents of annexation might have made a more

effective campaign if they had really felt that the Philippine Islands were capable of independent political life. Actually, even anti-annexationists had doubts about this. After all, they too had heard the recurrent theme of American newspapers at the turn of the century that the Philippine Islands contained diverse groups incapable of getting along with one another. This being the case, some foreign power must rule, said the annexationists, and it would be inhumane and a cowardly disregard of national responsibility to let Spain keep the Islands or give them to another power.

In truth, the Filipinos did have sufficient unity and concept of nationality to get by without foreign rule. The Philippines were one of many countries which had acquired nationalism, as we usually understand the term, through the work of early colonialist organizers. The Spanish conquerors created the unified Philippine nation. During more than 300 years of rule in the archipelago, they developed national spirit among these diverse peoples by providing such things as homogeneous laws, one central government, and a common Christian religion—with the exception of the Mohammedans of Mindanao. They also provided a common object for the people's resentment—Spain. Numerous revolts against Spanish overlordship during the nineteenth century were a clear symptom of this resentment on an archipelago-wide level. The uprisings also give evidence of development of a somewhat modern, enlightened Filipino leadership desiring a Philippine nation both independent and equipped with the political institutions of the West.

The expansionists won the argument to the extent of convincing the President that the United States should annex not only the Port of Manila, but all of Luzon, the island on which Manila was located. Expert strategists said that Manila alone would be useless in event of war. The expansionists also felt that the islands of the archipelago were so close to one another that it was similarly undesirable to take only Luzon—they wanted the entire archipelago.

Uncertainty in President McKinley's mind regarding the islands was probably being resolved under the influence of the religious fervor he had absorbed throughout his early life. His final decision was best described by him, more than a year after he made it, in an interview with a missionary committee of the Methodist Church:

> I walked the floor of the White House night after night until midnight, and I am not ashamed to tell you, gentlemen, that I went down on my knees and prayed Almighty God for light and guidance more than one night. And one night late it came to me this way —I don't know how it was, but it came ... that there was nothing left for us to do but to take them all and to educate the Filipinos, and uplift them, and civilize and Christianize them, and by God's grace do the very best we could by them, as our fellow men for whom Christ also died. And then I went to bed, and went to sleep, and slept soundly, and the next morning I sent for the chief engineer of the War Department (our map-maker) and I told him to put the Philippines on the map of the United States, and there they are, and there they will stay while I am President!

Of course, as the American policy of annexation became known to the Filipinos, there was a marked increase in their ill-will. American military commanders had been misled by an exceptionally friendly minority in the city of Manila, where many property holders felt that American rule might be less harmful than rule by Aguinaldo's insurgents. However, the typical Filipino was annoyed, under expanding American occupation, by insults or slights offered by some members of American forces in the Islands.

Filipinos or Americans who concerned themselves with misapplications of American political theory to the Philippine occupation would have been interested in a resolution which reached the American Senate in January, 1899. The proposed resolution stated that the Government of the United States did not have constitutional power to acquire territory and govern it as a colony. Annexationists did not agree; they said that the Constitution did not apply by its own force to new possessions like the Philippines or Puerto Rico. These, the expansionists said, were dependencies, not an integral part of the United States. Therefore, Federal authority could not be limited by such guarantees as the first ten amendments to the American Constitution, nor could local inhabitants claim rights granted to Americans under that Constitution. The expansionists did a nice job of summing up and interrelating the previous record of the United States in denying rights to some of its peoples. They reviewed our handling of Indian and Negro minorities as examples of non-application of Constitutional rights.[29]

The treaty of peace with Spain was finally accepted by the Senate with one vote to spare. The ensuing action on annexation was endorsed by a still badly divided Senate, with the Vice-President casting the deciding vote.

There still remained the problem of native Filipino independence forces under Aguinaldo. Supported by the populace, they would not give up, but fought a stubborn guerrilla-type war of resistance. It took more than three years of hard fighting by 60,000 American soldiers to make the Filipinos receptive to the program of "uplift and Christianization" that President McKinley had vowed to accomplish.

If the Afro-Asian nations have been considering themselves joint victims of a collective sort of Western imperialism, it is reasonable to expect that a nation under imperialist attack—the Philippines in this case—would receive support from other Asian nations. Was any such support forthcoming? The Japanese gave some thought to intervention, but very little was done. Japan did not recognize the insurgents as an independent government or as belligerents, nor did Japan give money or armed help to the Filipinos. It is true that several Japanese officers assisted Aguinaldo's insurgents as training officers, and Japan allowed the revolutionary forces to purchase two shiploads of armaments.

Even this very minor Japanese action involved indications of graver future developments. The Vice-Chief of the Japanese Army's General Staff said at the time that Japan could not really aid the Filipinos, but that action might be taken 50 to 100 years later. Aguinaldo and his fellow revolutionaries were so annoyed at subjugation by America in the wake of Spanish rule that Aguinaldo declared, "To oppose the white man and gain freedom and independence, the colonial races must join together."

In addition to limited Japanese support of the early Filipino independence movement, support came from Chinese revolutionary leader Sun Yat-sen, who gave the Filipinos his moral backing in the expectation that they would later aid China in a spirit of Asian solidarity. Speaking at Kobe in 1924, Sun was still saying that "all Asiatic peoples [must] unite and stand as one" if they were to gain independence. Sun also said on this occasion that the independence of Japan was a fine example for the rest of Asia, and that all Asians, like the Japanese, must secure their independence "with some use of the Western 'rule of might.' "[30]

In spite of the bitter and prolonged Filipino resistance to American occupation, there were positive sides to the American take-over. The American objective was, as repeatedly described by Americans from President McKinley on down, a program of uplift, Christianization, and other benevolences. Despite the condescension in all this, there were positive implications, such as firm assurance of eventual independence. From the very outset of American occupation, there was a more than token use of Filipinos as members of the administrative staffs of the Islands. Beginning in 1901, the Philippine Commission contained three Filipino members as well as five Americans.

The American Government made a great effort to educate the Filipinos, as God had instructed President McKinley, but the new program caused dissatisfaction. Some Filipinos resented imposition of a totally American education system upon the Islands. A form of racism, or at least contempt for the Filipino people, appears even in the words of the American General Superintendent of Education for the Philippine Islands, Dr. David P. Barrows, who declared in 1903, "The race lends itself naturally and without protest to the blind leadership and cruel oppression of its aristocracy."[31]

The texts and classroom materials prescribed for use in the schools were materials prepared by American writers for American children, such as: Newsom's *First Reader*, Arnold's *First Reader*, Gibb's *Lessons in English*, Lamb's *Tales from Shakespeare*, Stevenson's *Treasure Island*, Cooper's *Last of the Mohicans*, and Thomas' *History of the United States*. American songs were sung in these classrooms, and the walls decorated with American heroes' portraits. Equally bad was the complete absence of Filipino books and materials, an absence hardly consistent with the professed

intention of the United States to prepare the new Filipino generation for self-government.

Official Filipino cognizance of this abuse was restrained, of
course, but was not entirely lacking. A generation after the
American take-over, Manual Roxas was to claim that the schools
were training Filipinos to become American citizens. He said, "I
tell you, gentlemen of the Commission, that the present system of
public education is carrying on a subtle propaganda to kill the
nationalistic sentiment of the people of the Philippines."[32] However, we must grant that the American organizers of this school
system were almost forced to make English the language of the
schools because of the presence of many competing languages in the
Philippines.

Certainly the years of American administration saw impressive improvements in the Philippine economy, with such features as
a fivefold increase in value of exports from the country. The
United States Government and entrepreneurs could claim much of
the credit for such improvements; on the other hand, benefits from
such developments *within the Philippines* were poorly distributed.
Francis B. Sayre, the American High Commissioner, once acknowledged that most of the newly created income had gone to the
Government, cities, and landlords, and had done very little to relieve the poverty of the almost feudal peasantry and tenantry. The
Filipino farmer typically had a very small land holding of less
than five acres, and all too often his land was held in tenantry from
a landlord to whom he had to pay half of his crop in a
sharecropping arrangement. The landlord often took advantage of
the sharecropper, commonly extending loans (required by the
tenant to get along until the next harvest) at an annual interest
rate of 200 per cent.[33] Here were problems which the occupying
power might have dealt with to good effect, but it did not attempt
to do so.

Puerto Rico, like the Philippines, was taken from Spain by
the United States. Here also the new government did not manage
to bring immediate justice and economic opportunity to the
islanders. Senator R. F. Pettigrew reported in 1921 that the
English, French, and Spanish owners of large Puerto Rican planta-

tions managed to reinstitute under American rule the same abuses from which they had profited under Spanish rule. "Groups of foreign highwaymen," as Pettigrew called them, obtained the necessary legislation and influence over the government of the island to wreak with impunity all sorts of injustices. They canceled the leases of peasant farmers, after which these poor people had no choice but to work for wages on the landowners' plantations. Wages were scandalously low, so that real suffering and semi-starvation were common. When the laborers tried to organize and strike against the landowners, the police intervened, shooting some strikers and jailing many.

Pettigrew noted that his charges are thoroughly borne out by a report Joseph Marcus wrote for the United States Department of Labor, entitled *Labor Conditions in Puerto Rico*. Among other revealing data from this report, we may single out the fact that 14 per cent of the wealth of Puerto Rico in 1919 was held by actual Puerto Rican natives. The rest was in the hands of foreigners or of Americans.[34]

Even after 43 years of American rule, the condition of Puerto Rico was summarized by an American observer, John Gunther, as "in short, misery, disease, squalor, filth." He found that 350,000 to 400,000 children, 56 per cent of the school-age children, were not attending school because of lack of schoolroom space. Infant mortality was the highest in the world, four times greater than that of the mainland United States, while in some villages the entire population had malaria. The public water system was run so frugally that the water was unsafe. Some differences between Puerto Rico and its independent neighbor, the Dominican Republic, 45 miles away, were scarcely a credit to American rule. Gunther found that meat cost 30 cents per pound in Puerto Rico, but only six cents per pound in the Dominican Republic.[35] Of course there has been much improvement in recent years. The United States Government has spent large sums of money for the benefit of the Puerto Rican people.

What of Alaska? Evils of Russian rule there have been discussed, but did the American purchase of Alaska in 1867 bring prompt relief to that Territory? Best able to answer that question is Ernest Gruening, who was Governor of Alaska from 1937 to 1953, and more recently a Senator from Alaska. He characterizes the United States' Administration of Alaska as "total neglect" until 1884, "flagrant neglect" until 1898, "mild but unenlightened interest, 1898–1912," "indifference and unconcern, 1912–1933," and "growing awareness" since 1933.[36]

An American can be slightly reassured at seeing "neglect" as the charge here. At least this is less grave than the common and well-supported charge of "exploitation" against Western operations in Asia and Africa. However, the Eskimo minority in Alaska has been at some pains to recover vast areas of land guaranteed the Eskimos by the treaty of 1867. Sam Taalak, President of the Arctic Slope Native Association, protested in 1966 that all the money "dug out of the land" had left Alaska without helping the Eskimos. An Eskimo State Senator from Point Barrow, Ebau Hopson, complained that in his town, the most prosperous of all Eskimo settlements, there were only five native houses with running water—out of a total of 300 such houses. Asking for Federal help, Senator Hopson commented, "Compared to what the Government is putting into Vietnam, it isn't much." There was some discussion of coordination among the groups representing Alaska's 27,000 Eskimos, 17,000 Indians, 6,000 Aleuts, and the surprisingly large Negro minority, of whom there are 4,000 in the city of Anchorage alone.[37]

:: VI ::

Imperialism, Racism, and Totalitarianism: A Review of their Interrelationships

THE RATIONALE OF IMPERIALISM

IT IS NOT hard to discern greed as an important reason behind the wicked uses of power for which we have been indicting the white man. Especially with regard to imperialism, greed is an obvious fact. The economic motives of imperialism—the search for markets, raw materials, and places where surplus capital could be invested —have long been discussed by scholars; their real importance varied greatly from one situation to another. But the propagandists of imperialism often told their own people about vast profits to be made overseas when the actual economic facts did not bear out such promises. Profitability was, in such cases, a device to which these propagandists resorted. Like their kindred, the apostles of racism and totalitarianism, they found it expedient to offer concrete benefits to complement their ideological persuasions.

A typical and highly vocal spokesman of American expansionism, Senator Albert J. Beveridge, offered primarily commercial justifications for imperial growth, yet ideological reasons underlay his talk of economic development. He believed that the people of the United States had a duty to mankind and a responsibility to the God who had endowed them uniquely with gifts. God had prepared English-speaking and Teutonic peoples to function as the "master organizers of the world." The United States must not neglect its opportunities in the Orient, said Beveridge, urging that we move forward, thanking God "that He has marked us as His chosen people, henceforth to lead in the regeneration of the world."

Aside from these responsibilities to God, Beveridge stressed the economic profits of expansion. The *Congressional Record* for 1900 was loaded with his long-winded speeches about great resources awaiting the United States in the Philippines and Cuba:

> I have gold dust washed out by crude processes of careless natives from the sands of a Philippine stream, indicating great deposits. . . . The mineral wealth is but a small fraction of the agricultural wealth of these islands. . . . And the wood, hemp, copra, and other products of the Philippines supply what we need and can not ourselves produce. And the markets they will themselves afford will be immense.
>
> The Filipino is the South Sea Malay, put through a process of three hundred years of superstition in religion, dishonesty in dealing, disorder in habits of industry, and cruelty, caprice, and corruption in government. . . . They are not even good agriculturists. Their waste of cane is inexcusable. Their destruction of hemp fiber is childish. They are incurably indolent. They have no continuity or thoroughness of industry.

Beveridge claimed that the commerce of such lands would be increased "as much as American energy is greater than Spanish sloth." He claimed that the trade of these islands, and of Puerto Rico and Hawaii, would, when properly developed, "set every reaper in the Republic singing, every furnace spouting the flames of industry." In a totalitarian flourish, Beveridge alleged that God's purposes were revealed by the progress of the American flag, "which surpasses the intentions of Congresses and Cabinets, and leads us, like a holier pillar of cloud by day and pillar of fire by night."[1]

In spite of Beveridge's extravagant claims, the preemptive value of colonies as sources of raw materials was not always clear. Most Western powers were able to purchase materials from one another's colonies. As markets, however, the colonies could be sheltered by one power from the competition of another through preferential customs duties and regulations. Similarly, the nation in control of a possession often reserved local investment opportunities to benefit its own financiers.

Lenin made a cardinal tenet of Communism the belief that the collapse of capitalism was postponed only by availability in the nineteenth century of colonies as new markets for the surplus production of capitalists' factories. Lenin's analysis of imperialism was very nearly shared by French expansionist Jules Ferry, who wrote in 1890 that because of the saturation of the European consumer market, "unless we prepare in the dawn of the twentieth century for the liquidation of our society by revolution, new consumer markets will have to be created in all parts of the world."[2]

Partition of tropical Africa can be interpreted as economically superficial on grounds that little was done before 1900 to administer and use the region. Because commercial exploitation and occupation came after the parcelling out of this territory, it can be argued that the economic value of tropical Africa was an afterthought to expansion. If this argument is accepted, only strategic and ideological motives remain, and it would follow that, when Britain liberated India and Egypt, her principal reasons for holding tropical Africa disappeared. (In fact, British withdrawal from Africa was completed within 15 years after liberation of India and Pakistan.)

Some analysts of imperialism have found the economic motive paramount in German acquisition of colonies, in that the prime movers were trading and shipping firms and banking houses, working through Government officials, politicians, and publicists. Leonard Woolf, in his *Empire and Commerce in Africa*, tells how carefully Bismarck consulted the German mercantile communities before embarking upon aggressive colonization. Bismarck told the Reichstag, in 1884, "Our purpose is therefore to found not provinces but commercial enterprises." Detracting from this economic view are other facts. Fewer than 25,000 Germans lived in the German colonies, and the trade of Germany with her colonies was usually less than 1 per cent of total German foreign trade.

The "bureaucratic motive" attributed to imperialism by Hobson is really just a special form of desire for profits, received in this instance through creation of much-desired jobs for citizens of the imperial power. To be sure, if the colonies were not economically profitable, the salaries paid job-holders became a charge on the mother country. Nevertheless, as seen by the office-holder, these positions were lucrative or desirable.

Hobson mentions the armed services of European powers, to which imperial acquisitions brought larger allowances of personnel and more glorious opportunities for distinction and advancement. He believes that abolition of the purchase of officers' commissions in the British forces in the nineteenth century made the acquisitive impulse stronger, by peopling the British Officer Corps with middle class persons who had to rely on promotion within the services as their only avenue to distinction or riches.

Hobson also notes that the civil services—the British Indian Civil Service and many other administrative arms of empire—provided a great many jobs for would-be bureaucrats. He quotes one high Indian official as remarking, when Britain considered moving into Siam, "The real question was . . . how we could make the most of them, so as to find fresh markets for our goods and also employment for those superfluous articles of the present day, our boys."[3] Some indication of the privileged nature of the posts Europe's sons enjoyed in overseas empires may be found in reports on the Indian Civil Service of 1944, when 8,000 English members were receiving aggregate salaries of 70,000,000 pounds, while 130,000 Indian officials received only 16,500,000 pounds.[4] Hardly a "burden for the white man" or an equitable remuneration for the Indian !

When Americans first spun out their plans for commercial expansion across the Pacific Ocean to Asia, the profit motive was combined with the idea of being God's agent. Politician and statesman Thomas Hart Benton expected that America would compete with England for the rich Asian trade, at the same time offering modern science and "true religion" to the peoples of Asia. President Jackson's friend William Gilpin, first Governor of the Colorado Territory, foresaw American expansion westward to China to regenerate the superannuated masses of Asia, "to absolve the curse that weighs down humanity, and to shed blessings round the world."[5] Here, indeed, was the redemptive Messiah ! Even in Walt

Whitman's poem, "Years of the Unperformed," we have the same glorification of expansion toward Asia:

> His daring foot is on land and sea everywhere—
> he colonizes the Pacific, the archipelagoes;
> With the steam-ship, the electric telegraph, the
> newspaper, the wholesale engines of war,
> With these, and the world-spreading factories, he
> interlinks all geography, all lands.

Thus, American's concept of a "manifest destiny" to control her own continent was extended to an obligation of expansion in the Pacific, at least to the extent of profiting and doing good works there. Americans and their European colleagues did not fail to do good deeds in Asia; there was a great deal of humanitarian and evangelical activity. A good index to the actual extent of this benevolent activity is found in the church-sponsored schools and hospitals in China. Protestant churches alone were by 1925 operating 301 hospitals (more than half directly operated by American missions), 496 dispensaries, 333 middle schools, and 16 colleges.[6]

The French could be benevolent, too. They proclaimed their "civilizing mission," and indeed their cultural contributions in Afro-Asia were immense. The British ideal of service to mankind was epitomized in Kipling's poem, "The White Man's Burden." The Germans offered their superior *Kultur* to the world; the Russians, even to the present day, delight in labelling their opponents as *nekul'turnyi* (uncultured).

The Messianic white man also had his negative, offensive side. We can surmise that behind this lay what psychologists call the "mastery drive." As historian William Langer wrote: "It is now fairly clear, I think, that the Neo-Marxian critics have paid far too little attention to the imponderable, psychological ingredients of imperialism. The movement may, without much exaggeration, be interpreted not only as an atavism, . . . but also as an aberration, to be classed with the extravagances of nationalism." Apart from Marxian economics, Langer saw the interrelatedness of Europe's round-the-world troublemaking and the times of troubles within twentieth century Europe itself. He believed that great domestic crises and outbursts of expansion usually follow one another in history. In calling imperialism a throwback or atavism, he had support from Schumpeter, who applied the same words, and Hobson, who called it "a sociological atavism, a remnant of the roving instinct."[7]

Hobson believed that people have a strong, inbred impulse to rove and master which helped generate imperialism. He noted that the Anglo-Saxon had modified his need for adventure and conflict into an indulgence in various sports which satisfy the need for roaming, hunting, and fighting. However, because sports are not always adequate outlets for these drives, the aggressive imperialist betook himself to colonial lands where he could have a fuller measure of violence.[8]

Certainly the seizing of territories, subduing of resistance, and even overcoming of economic competition are all, in a real sense, acts of mastery. Perhaps the German Treitschke comes closest to this explanation of white aggression with his remark that "Every virile nation has established colonial power." But if you would speak of nothing more complicated than pure, overweening ambition, arch-imperialist Cecil Rhodes says it best: "The world is nearly all parcelled out, and what there is left of it is being divided up, conquered and colonized. To think of these stars that you see overhead at night, these vast worlds which we can never reach. I would annex the planets if I could; I often think of that. It makes me sad to see them so clear and yet so far."[9]

The theories of biologist Charles Darwin were one of the cardinal ideological pillars of imperialism and racism. Though he himself did not plan it in such a way, Darwin strengthened and supplemented the corollary to Calvinism which viewed those who prevailed or became most strong as "God's elect." Darwin did consciously build on the foundation laid by the famous student of population problems, Malthus. From Malthus, Darwin acquired the concept that, when any given animal has multiplied and grown so numerous in a region that the food supply there will not sustain all the offspring produced, there ensues a mortal competition for that limited food supply. Darwin's extensive and scientific field observations of various animal forms around the world showed that the victory in this struggle for food went to those animals which were strongest or most effective in dealing with local environmental conditions. Consequently, the survivors became the parents of succeeding generations of their kind.

Closely related to the fight for food was the fight for an essentially limited supply of mates. Again, the stronger or more effective of the species preempted the females through whom their strain would proliferate. Genetic mutations, Darwin pointed out, also led to such proliferation if the characteristic produced by the mutation proved more effective in the given environment.

Darwin reveals a clear belief in national superiority in his work *The Descent of Man.* One is tempted to call it racism; although in this book Darwin denies that "pure races" exist, his belief in Anglo-Saxon superiority comes close to being a superman doctrine :

> There is apparently much credit in the belief that the wonderful progress of the United States, as well as the character of the people, are the results of natural selection; for the more energetic, restless, and courageous men from all parts of Europe have emigrated during the last ten or twelve generations to that great country, and have there succeeded best. Looking to the distant future, I do not think that the Reverend Mr. Zincke takes an exaggerated view when he says: "All other series of events—as that which resulted in the culture of mind in Greece, and that which resulted in the empire of Rome—only appear to have purpose and value when viewed in connection with, or rather as subsidiary to... the great stream of Anglo-Saxon emigration to the West." Obscure as is the problem of the advance of civilization we can at least see that a nation which produced during a lengthened period the greatest number of highly intellectual, energetic, brave, patriotic, and benevolent men, would generally prevail over less favored nations.

In the same book, Darwin approvingly quotes a Mr. Greg as follows: "Given a land originally peopled by a thousand Saxons and a thousand Celts, and in a dozen generations, five-sixths of the population would be Celts, but five-sixths of the property, of the power, of the intellect, would belong to the one-sixth Saxons that remained."[10]

Darwinism was very acceptable in the nineteenth century to Europeans who were nationalistically or imperialistically minded.

A corollary to Darwinism justified nationalism within Europe on the ground that the strongest, most effective nation should survive. The nation was thought of—wrongly, I think—as a sort of organism, having a life and evolution of its own. Thus one could argue that it, too, would follow Darwinian patterns of evolution.

Going one step farther, Darwinism contributed to the Marxian idea of a global struggle between entire classes of society, and reinforced the socialists' expectation that old, ineffectual socio-economic orders would be displaced by better ones. A little more than a year after the appearance of Darwin's *Origin of Species*, Karl Marx said, in a letter to Ferdinand La Salle, that the book developed "a basis in natural science for the class struggle in history." A decade later, Marx told Darwin that he would like to dedicate *Das Kapital* to him. However, even though Darwin seems to have thought highly of the book, he feared that dedication to him of such an "atheistic" book would offend his family, and so declined the honor.

Prussian General Friedrich von Bernhardi applied Darwin's "struggle for existence" and "survival of the fittest" to his own theories of war and nationalism. Like many European nationalists of the post-Darwinian century, the General concluded that "War is a biological necessity; . . . it gives a biologically just decision." This was in 1912. In 1942, the English Lord Elton could still write, "War, however much we may hate it, is still the supreme agent of the evolutionary process, . . . the one test mankind has yet contrived of a nation's fitness to survive."[11]

American Admiral Alfred T. Mahan borrowed parts of his doctrine on domination through seapower from the Darwinists, it would seem, when he wrote of "the struggle of life" and "the race of life." Conversely, that arch-expansionist Reverend Josiah Strong, while relying primarily on God Himself to sanction American empire-building, did not miss occasionally exchanging views with seapower advocate Mahan.[12] The Reverend Strong prepared his book *Our Country* for the American Home Missionary Society in an effort to prove the case for worldwide evangelization, but really succeeded in laying bare the racism and expansionism congenial to so many Americans.

He, too, glorified the Anglo-Saxons, both ancient and modern, for their superior political life, love of liberty, and "pure spiritual Christianity." All mankind must share these great blessings, and so the Anglo-Saxon was divinely commissioned to be his brother's keeper. Strong actually expected that population trends would bring his Anglo-Saxons, before the end of the twentieth century, to the point of outnumbering all other civilized races of the world. The might of numbers and the strength of super-civilization would elevate the Anglo-Saxons to global rule.[13]

American expansionists were able to get the American public's assent to their program because that public was already conditioned, by its handling of the Negro and Indian minorities in the United States, to regard non-whites as lesser breeds who need help or enlightened supervision. From the 1870's there was also the domestic American precedent of anti-Chinese sentiment. *Atlantic Monthly's* review of Galton's *Inquiries into Human Faculty and its Development* in 1883 agreed that "Chinese, Indians, and Negroes should be excluded from the earth, and the sooner the better."

One further factor which helped produce imperialism was nationalism itself. Most vicious was a nationalism accompanied by an authoritarian government. The tide of nationalism in nineteenth century Europe was so strong, and the spirit of national expansion so omnipresent, that all sorts of events produced the same result—further expansion. For example, the Franco-Prussian War of 1870–1871 brought Germany a great victory which she followed by aggressive projects of colonization. The same war left France in abject defeat, and the Third Republic proceeded to build a colonial empire to demonstrate that France was still great.

The ways in which totalitarianism produces expansion and warfare are so well known that very little needs to be said here. We all know how a central government, when in trouble domestically, often shifts public attention abroad by emitting a cloud of alarmist or imperialistic propaganda. Indeed, it is difficult for a highly centralized government to dispense with militarism or menacing entities in foreign lands.

SOME INTERLINKAGES

THE FOLLOWING factors have been noted as contributory to imperialism, racism, and totalitarianism · the promise of profit, Messianism, the elemental mastery drive, Darwinism, and nationalism. The interworkings of nationalism and totalitarianism require a closer look at this point so that later European horrors of Nazism and Stalinism can be seen in full relationship to the abuses of Western power this volume has already surveyed. In addition to external aggression and imperialism, Europe's militant nationalists indulged in another form of aggression based on what Freud calls "the narcissism of minor differences." This stresses the hatred of neighbors or political factions which in reality differ very little from the aggressive majority. By directing rage and scorn toward this minority, the pride and unity of the majority is enhanced, at least temporarily, and the leaders avoid the danger of becoming targets for some of their followers' aggressiveness.[14]

Modern nationalist fervor has often fed on this "narcissism of minor differences," and twentieth century totalitarianisms have made good use of similar tactics. The National Socialists of Germany conducted their first drastic purges—massacres, really—against divergent cohorts of the Nazi Party, while the *bêtes noires* of the Bolsheviks were for years the Menshevik and Trotskyite wings of their own Communist Party.

These "minor differences" should not obscure for us the many features Europe's various revolutionary movements shared in spite of their quarrels with each other. After the revolutions of the 1917–1933 period, the nationalism of Russia, Italy, and Germany remained very much alive. The same factors that produced Europe's earlier nationalisms would inspire their Bolshevik, Fascist, and Nazi heirs.

The nationalism which developed in both Russia and Germany in the nineteenth century was indebted to Herder's idea that each European people should gain new inspiration through proper study and cultivation of its cultural heritage, literature, language, and so on. When Hitler took Herder's mild, tolerant concept of nationalism and made it a building block of his monstrous national socialism, the Herder philosophy was simply undergoing a deterioration comparable to what happened elsewhere in Europe to other moderate or idealistic doctrines of nationalism—as Peter Viereck puts it, "from Herder to Hitler in Germany, from Mazzini to Mussolini in Italy, from Wordsworth to Kipling in England." Richard Wagner, from whom Hitler later drew part of his philosophy, also partook a great deal of socialism. For example, the revolution of 1849 in the capital of Saxony had three anticapitalist leaders who tried, unsuccessfully, to convert the bourgeois uprising into a socialist revolution. These were none other than Wagner, a journalist named Röckel, and Russian anarchist Bakunin. At this time Wagner wanted not only German unity but also general abolition of class distinctions and property. He wished to wipe out poverty and reduce everyone's working day to just a few hours. Wagner wanted the aristocracy to surrender voluntarily, lest it face a long, bloody conflict. As a step toward elimination of all class distinctions, he wished to replace the regular army with a mass army of the people—a harbinger, perhaps, of the S.S. of Hitler's day.[15]

Wagner was recognized by his Nazi heirs as a *revolutionist*, a leader of revolt against many nineteenth century institutions uncongenial to Nazis and Bolsheviks alike. In evidence of this, Viereck notes a Nazi eulogy of this hero under the title *Richard Wagner, The Revolutionist Against the Nineteenth Century.* Wagner, in calling for abolition of money, property, and capitalism, considered himself a socialist in the tradition of Bakunin and Proudhon, not in the image of Karl Marx, whom he professed to detest as a Jew. Hitler likewise espoused a form of socialism. He originally planned to call his Nazi Party the "Social Revolutionary Party." borrowing the name of a Russian party which had helped to overthrow the Czar's regime but was opposed to the Bolsheviks.[16]

Western Messianic movements, despite their individual variations, have all shared a conviction of progress toward a great historic objective. The goal might be building God's kingdom on earth through conversion of the heathen, perfecting man through enlightenment or reason, the evolution of a super-race, or achievement of an equitable, socialist state. In all these forms, Western Messianism contrasts sharply with movements that occurred in Asia's long history. In the latter, there was little emphasis on historical evolution, little sense of Messianic leadership toward an ultimate goal. (Such a sense has come recently to Asia, but as an importation from the West.)

In contrast to the exalted claims of Messianic movements, we have to look at a strange and disreputable feature of most Western abuses of power. This is the common role of criminals, riffraff, or, in some cases, just rootless persons. A precursor of twentieth century totalitarianism is seen by Hannah Arendt in the nineteenth century colonial society where gentleman and de facto criminal learned to work together cordially, united by common race as well as common anticipation of profit. At home in Europe there were already ties between the socially eminent and criminals —indeed, such ties might occur at any time in history—but the colonial situation helped such alliances to flourish.[17] Of course, the thug-like activities through which imperialism and totalitarianism gain power and profit would call for criminal participants.

The thugs were seldom lacking. The British systematically sent them to colonies, often as penal colony inmates or indentured laborers for a time, and subsequently as free or quasi-free residents. This occurred in Australia, Tasmania, and America, to mention a few places. France had her penal colony in French Guiana—Devil's Island. The French Foreign Legion, used in so many colonial areas, was notoriously composed, in part, of escapees and parolees from Europe's jails. As for Russia, her territories in Asia were to a large extent developed and settled by exiled persons; some were political offenders, but many were ordinary criminals.

In racism and totalitarianism, as with imperialism, we find rootless, even criminal elements working with the ruling powers. The dictator or white supremacist will frequently encourage or condone illegal violence to supplement his repertory of overt or legal coercion. Thus, Imperial Russia had its "Black Hundred" mobs inflicting pogroms on the Jews; the British had their Jameson

Raid on the Boers' Transvaal, and their "loyalist reprisals" against the Sinn Fein independence movement; the Nazis had their "Crystal Night," and innumerable other unofficial acts against non-Germans, while Mussolini's goons were loosed against his adversaries from time to time.

The Colonial Contribution to Racism and Totalitarianism

WHEN COLONIALISM attained new heights in the nineteenth century, it was not surprising that racism flourished, too. There is no way to prove that the former led to the latter, but we have already seen that kindred elements were involved in what the white man did overseas and what he did to victims of his régimes at home.

For example, the imperialist powers all developed, back in their homelands, a newly invigorated anti-Semitism. Why? Hatred of Jews appealed to the same human traits that led to colonialist abuses. The racist derivations of Darwinism and various pseudo-scientific theories of race superiority were applied not just to races outside Europe, but also to scapegoats within Europe.

Two of the most famous racist works of nineteenth century Europe were the *Essay on the Inequality of Human Races*, by the French Count Arthur de Gobineau, and *Foundations of the Nineteenth Century*, by Houston Stewart Chamberlain, an Englishman who had become a German citizen. Both books were popular in Europe and the United States. There was considerable American interest in the books and all too great a degree of acceptance and approval. One interesting reaction to Chamberlain came from Theodore Roosevelt, who disliked Chamberlain's "violent partiality" but said "much that he says . . . is emphatically worth considering."[18]

It was de Gobineau's book that popularized the concept of blond, blue-eyed Aryans as a super-race. Chamberlain stressed the debased, objectionable quality of the Jewish race. Like his famous father-in-law, Richard Wagner, Chamberlain influenced considerably the thinking of Adolf Hitler. Anti-Semitism has commonly embodied more than the intrinsic ugliness of its prejudice or the immediate violence of its crimes. Often in European history it has been fostered by the authorities, or power seeking movements, to lend color and dynamism to their ideologies or distract the populace from other, more legitimate concerns.

The Czarist tyranny was benefiting from anti-Semitism as this century began. The leading "theologian" of Nazism, Alfred Rosenberg, conceded that he esteemed anti-Semitism not just for its own aims, but also as "the unifying element of the reconstruction of Germany."[19]

The Messianic quality of modern totalitarianism disposed its prophets to worry about rival Messianic movements, even the purely religious claim of the Jews to be God's chosen people according to the Scripture. In the following Nazi tirade, we see an anxiety that the German "master race," determined to be the only "chosen people," should not be upstaged by any *other claim* to chosenness: "Boys and girls, even if they say that the Jews were once the chosen people, do not believe it, but believe us when we say that the Jews are not a chosen people. Because it cannot be that a chosen people should act among the peoples as the Jews do today."[20]

The Dutch in South Africa may have similarly disliked the Jews as rival claimants to the honor of being God's elect. Boer hostilities were projected against Jewish immigrants, and especially against the alleged international financial connections of the Jews.

The South African racists, you will recall, derived their important tenet of racial inequality from the Scripture. When Transvaal's President Kruger met with Indians who objected to the discriminatory laws of the Transvaal, he quickly lost patience and said "You are the descendants of Ishmael, and therefore from your very birth you are bound to slavery. As you are the descendants of Esau and Ishmael, we cannot admit you to rights placing you on an equality with ourselves."[21]

In March, 1964, it was clear that anti-Semitism was still vigorous in South Africa. (An outburst of it came, curiously, at the same time as a violent attack on Jews in Russia's Ukraine.) Renewed hostility was partly due to the expressed opposition of some Jews to the Government's cherished apartheid program, opposition which may have extended to the furnishing of money to Africans campaigning against segregation. The 110,000 Jews of South Africa were assailed as subversives who wanted to go to Israel anyway. Some did think of going, but because of public hostility, not "internationalism" or foreign financial ties. There was, in fact, no legal way to take one's money out of South Africa due to strict laws against remitting money abroad.

France, in 1894, furnished a most dramatic case of anti-Semitism when Army Captain Dreyfus was wrongfully convicted of espionage and sent to Devil's Island Penal Colony. Although clear evidence of his innocence was presented, it was not until 1906 that reversal of judgment could be secured. Significant in our present analysis is that it was the advocates of French imperial expansion—the champions of "God, gold, and glory"—who resisted granting justice to Dreyfus.

The subject of racism in Russia will be covered more fully in Chapter Eight. Let us say here only that Russian anti-Semitism has remained strong, with scarcely a pause in the 1800's and 1900's. It was very noticeable in the 1948–1965 period, when a chief complaint against Jews in the U.S.S.R. was their "cosmopolitanism"— their ties abroad and interest in emigrating to Israel. In 1953, when the Soviet press was pillorying many Soviet Jews as "cosmopolitans," by a coincidence Prime Minister Churchill, in the House of Commons, accused opposition member Emmanuel Shinwell of "cosmopolitanism and internationalism."

The ties or influences among apostles of anti-Semitism in various Western nations are well exemplified by Henry Adams. Like many an American intellectual of the nineteenth century, Adams resided in Germany for a time, pursuing studies there. Being of a notable American family, he naturally made the acquaintance of prominent Germans. Adams viewed the Dreyfus case in France as a commendable action by the French Army to "... set its foot on the Jews." Even when Dreyfus' innocence was proven, Adams thought the affair no anti-Jewish conspiracy, just a "reasonable error." Adams repeatedly expressed his revulsion at the sight of Jews in public places, and especially dreaded the thought that his own *North American Review* might fall under Jewish control.[22]

More recently in the United States, one small remark by former President Harry S Truman in 1964 provides a hard-hitting summary of this problem. Anti-Semitism, said Mr. Truman, is "as grave a challenge to our sense of fairness and morality as the plight of the Negroes. It is a disease so virulent that each generation seems to be helplessly caught up in it."

Europe's experience with the non-white world facilitated development of modern European totalitarianism—its philosophy, bureaucracy, and methods. The operations of nineteenth century imperialism actually helped to develop modern bureaucratic standards and techniques. The colonial bureaucrat, reinforced by a well-developed European tradition of military discipline and enjoying power phenomenally swollen by Europe's domination of the world, could wield his authority with an impersonal detachment that he might call "selfless service of humanity," but which surely improved the art of report-shrouded, secrecy-encrusted, bureaucratic operations. These procedures, in a grim fusion of racism and twentieth century administrative efficiency a half century later would produce the grotesquely efficient Nazi death camps.

The aloofness of the bureaucracy, whether in Africa or Germany, and its great dedication to supposed higher goals which justified ruthless means in dealing with the governed make the abuse far worse than mere greedy tyranny would have been. Moreover, the "selfless" bureaucrat, being something of an automaton, does not presume to reflect about intricacies of morals or ideology when carrying out his instructions. Consequently, his acts are seldom mitigated by any liberal elements in the past traditions of his own people.

Even the laws themselves often failed to be a restraining force on the colonial bureaucrat. Similarly, if the totalitarian bureaucrat made use of laws, it was usually in the sense of decrees, or laws alterable in short order in whatever way the "cause" might seem to dictate. Russia's Stalin Constitution of 1936, for example, with its many fine guaranties of human rights, was ignored for decades.

In Europe and around the world, the oppressors enjoyed a power structure which, from the victims' standpoint, was monolithic. Their power was not counterbalanced and was subject to no effective appeal. This is most obvious in Russia and the rest of Eastern Europe, where balancing of power has seldom been a feature of society. In that region there has been scarcely any truly indigenous middle class which could influence or restrain the governing class. The Russian peasant traditionally felt that he could turn for relief only to God or that supposedly benevolent Father-image, the Czar; but the peasants of Imperial Russia also had a coolly realistic proverb which epitomizes the problem we are discussing here: "God is in heaven, and the Czar is far away."

Germany certainly had a middle class, but it was politically supine, confined to echoing the governmental ideology. The domestic officialdom in modern Germany was insulated from restraint by its own size and complexity and its traditionally sacrosanct role.

In the many lands where colonial impositions occurred, there was a lack of counterbalancing or checking power *on the scene*. The politicians far away in the homeland might be fine humanitarians, but the actual colonial rule was totalitarian. The policymaker back home was obliged to rely on his officials on the spot because he lacked the knowledge and close touch with the problems that could have emboldened him to impose his methods on administrators far away. Geography protected the colonial official.

Senator R. F. Pettigrew's book, *Triumphant Plutocracy*, published in 1921, expressed fear that American imperial expansion, subjection of distant races to arbitrary colonial administration, and concomitant enlargement of the apparatus of Government in Washington would generate a feedback of domestic authoritarian trends. As the Senator saw it, "The reflex of the conquest and of this tyrannical government will work its effect upon our own people, and free institutions will disappear from this land."

Were the philosophers of racism also totalitarian-minded? Conversely, did the prophets of the future Communist or Nazi movements indulge in racist views? In answer to the first question, consider American racists Madison Grant and Brooks Adams, as well as England's Rudyard Kipling. Grant, in his *The Passing of the Great Race*, advocated an "aristocratic" form of government, because this would be "government by the wisest and best, always a small minority in any population." Under a democratic system, he said, the genius of this minority is dissipated, and humanity can make very little progress.

Brooks Adams built into his prolific writings many of the trends we have been studying here. He espoused extreme forms of Darwinism, nationalism, and bureaucracy, and advocated rigorous training of the country's best minds for service in the national administration. This government was to be authoritarian; it would enforce comprehensive plans, leaving for the individual no freedom of social or economic action. Adams desired a bureaucracy as totalitarian as any the twentieth century has produced since his passing.[23]

As for Rudyard Kipling, the poet laureate of imperialism was not *just* an imperialist; he was in a general sense authoritarian, rather than liberal or permissive. He stressed not individualism, but what he called the *Law*. Kipling's *Law* consisted of the binding force of ethos, obligation, and social cohesion. This attitude was an understandable result of his residence in India, where only a few decades before the deeply shaking events of the Indian Mutiny had occurred. Even had there been no such Mutiny, the British community in India would presumably have felt the pangs of insecurity felt by exploiters everywhere—the fear that their victims hate them and may arise in revolt at any time. Kipling's brand of tightly ordered society was his remedy for the insecurities of his environment.

To answer the second question above, what more need we say about the racism of the Nazi prophets? We noted previously that Richard Wagner was at one and the same time a racist, a precursor of Nazism, and an authoritarian type of socialist. But what of Karl Marx, prophet of Communism? He was not, generally speaking, a racist, but his articles in the *New York Daily Tribune* do show a supercilious or derogatory view of some of Asia's greatest civilizations. Speaking of India, Marx said that the British had a civilization superior to that of the Hindus, although the English acted from selfish bourgeois motives. He rejoiced at the elimination of India's Oriental despotisms, and dismissed the Indian way of life as "stagnatory, undignified and vegetative." The Hindu culture, he said, evoked "wild, aimless, unbounded forces of destruction and rendered murder itself a religious rite in Hindostan." Marx wished, of course, that the regenerative, stimulating effect of British rule had been stronger.

Dehumanization

WORST OF ALL the white man's deeds, and most laden with ill portent for the future, has been his increasing inclination to dehumanize man, to treat his fellow creatures as *things*, not *men*. This he has done both to non-white victims and, somewhat later, to victims of his authoritarian machinery of government at home.

In America, one finds the origins of dehumanization in the fear of colonial slaveholders that conversion and baptism of their slaves might automatically free them, thus depriving the masters of their property. Consequently, the Negro became, in the colonial view, a special debased creature whose mental and spiritual being was on a lower plane than that of his masters. (The blackness of the Negro's skin somehow made these assumptions more readily acceptable.) Even such an anti-slavery writer as Morgan Godwyn carried this postulate to its ultimate conclusion, saying "Though in their Figure they carry some resemblance of Manhood, they are indeed no Men."[24]

Some pseudo-scientific justifications were found for this dehumanization. The early biological theory of the "Great Chain of Being" placed all creatures in a developmental series, from lowest to most highly developed. There remained only for Linnaeus, and later Darwin, to include human beings in this developmental hierarchy. The dehumanizer could extrapolate from the scientists' findings to declare that some races were more human or more ape-like than others. Even the enlightened, generous-spirited Thomas

Jefferson believed in this Negro-ape tie. Jefferson related that Negro men preferred white women to their own kind, even as orangutans preferred Negro women to their own females. So we see that there were outgrowths of research in evolution which contributed not just to racism and nationalism, but even to *dehumanization*.

The Calvinistic idea of "God's elect" was used as justification for all the malevolent crusades we have been discussing: crimes against the Indians, colonialism, the "super-race" ideologies, and enslavement. In early New England, some Congregational ministers rejected racism; others said with John Saffin that God had established "different degrees and orders of men, some to be High and Honourable, some to be low and despicable ... some to be born Slaves."[25] In a similar spirit, when the white man went to live in Africa his pride, dignity, or greed would not allow him to accept as fellow-men the dark-skinned multitudes around him. From this arose brutal exploitation, and often massacre— condonable, supposedly, since it did not involve destruction of one's fellow creatures at all.

This strange and terrible trick of dehumanization is probably a throw-back to primitive man, who often classified non-members of his group as "non-men." The actual name of many a tribal or national group carries to this day the literal meaning of "persons" or "the people." That is the translation of "Bantu" or "Hun," to name two examples. The corollary is that outsiders are not considered human. Often, in the primitive situation, the "non-person" was eligible to attend cannibalistic dinner parties, but as part of the meal, not as a guest.

Exaggerated nationalism often relates to membership in a group that speaks a common language. For instance, the word for "German" in Polish (*Nemec*) and Russian (*Nemets*) literally means "one who cannot talk," that is, a non-speaker of the in-group's language.

While literal cannibalization of "non-members" is rare in our day, the lack of human sympathy which it implies is very much with us. Russian newspapers have somehow picked up the anthropophagous analogy, and their propagandists often hang the label "cannibal" on anyone supposed to be exploiting or abusing mankind.

Actually, as von Mises points out, both the Russian Marxists and the Nazis were quick to label their adversaries and everything about them as "alien," "non-proletarian," or "non-Aryan." To many Nazis, "Jewish" really meant anything they disliked, particularly anything *not serving their ideology*. These "aliens," too, were to be treated as non-human, and their fate supposedly ceased to be a matter of human concern.

One of the most apt analyses of the Stalin era in Russia, George Orwell's *Animal Farm*, compared the dictator and his minions to animals who seized power on a farm in order to foster perfect equality. As the farm animals developed something more than simple equality, their original watchword, "All Animals are equal," was enlarged by the fateful addition, "But some are more equal than others."

The dehumanization effect has, of course, extended beyond straightforward matters of dictatorship or racism. Its more general effect may best be described, in Rollo May's words, as "the tendency to treat man as an object to be calculated and controlled, . . . the almost overwhelming tendencies in the Western world to make human beings into anonymous units to fit like robots into the vast industrial and political collectivisms of our day."[26]

:: VII ::

Twentieth Century Wars and
the Position of the White Man

GENERAL EFFECTS

IN THE twentieth century, the same aggressive impulses that had driven the white man to global dominion stampeded him into a number of wars. These wars, initiated by the white nations, were the beginning of the end of white overlordship.

The first important conflict came in the Far East when Russia, not content with control of Manchuria, infiltrated troops into Korea, which, still nominally independent, was earmarked for annexation by Japan. The Korean peninsula's nearness to Japan led the island empire to view as a serious threat any occupation of Korea by a competing power. Besides, Japan was still smarting from her ejection from the Manchuria-Liaotung region a few years earlier under Russian, German, and French pressure.

In 1904 the Japanese found that negotiations with the Czar's diplomats were getting them nowhere. Japan's armed forces were now strong and modern enough to have an outside chance of success in a war with Russia. Although the Russian Empire had vastly larger forces, it was hard to bring them fully to bear in East Asia at a distance of five or six thousand miles from the Czar's European domains. Japan chose to attack, and met greater success than most observers had expected. Japan's forces were well organized and led; those of Russia were not. On the Asian land mass, Japanese armies advanced slowly in the face of determined resistance. On the sea, the Japanese fleet scored brilliant victories, partly as the result of a series of incredible blunders by Imperial Russian leadership.

The war was concluded by a Russo-Japanese treaty negotiated at Portsmouth, New Hampshire, under the sponsorship of America's President Theodore Roosevelt. Japan got from Russia the southern half of Sakhalin Island as well as acknowledgment of her paramount position in Korea. Russia had to give up control of Manchuria, and Japan acquired the Russian-built railroads of Southern Manchuria. The lease on the Liaotung Peninsula was also transferred from Russia to Japan.

Although the Treaty was not altogether satisfying to the Japanese, their achievements were viewed by world opinion as a dramatic setback to white supremacy. Those who feared the "yellow peril" were alarmed. The multitude of colonial peoples, hoping someday to throw off white domination, were much encouraged by the Japanese victory. Indian poet Rabindranath Tagore said, "Japan's example has given heart to the rest of Asia." Overnight, the helpless despair of Asia and Africa was turned into hope.

As for the World Wars of 1914–1918 and 1939–1945, Europe could not afford *one* such conflict, let alone two. Even in 1913 Europe was fully extended in her global dominance, and was obliged somehow to adjust her political and economic order to accommodate new currents of industrialism and democracy. Thus she had no strength to spare for massive conflicts, and we can see why Europe's grip on the world was weakened by the strain of the World Wars.

World War I was a consummate disgrace to the dozens of "advanced Western nations" that initiated and fought it. Both in its origins and conduct it was a vast collection of foolish blunders, failures of understanding, cruelties, and futile operations. A great many statesmen, generals, and "thinking people" of Europe had desired either this war or national aggrandizements which were bound to produce war so long as all the powers retained their aggressive posture.

World War I featured new weapons which were cruel or of previously unknown destructive power. Most appalling were the poison gases used for the first time. They produced nearly a million casualties, including 79,000 deaths. Bombing of troops and civilian centers was also inaugurated, though on a much smaller scale than we were to see in World War II.

Worst of all, military operations on the Western Front were largely stalemated—entrenchments defended by the newly-developed machine guns were nearly impossible to capture. With fanatical determination, however, leaders of both sides launched offensive after costly offensive, hoping somehow to break through their opponents' lines. Terrible numbers of casualties resulted from desperate attacks against heavily fortified areas, attacks which were often prolonged for weeks or months. During half of 1916, the French-held fortress of Verdun was under German attack, an operation in which 500,000 men of the two armies perished. The Battle of the Somme, another prolonged engagement, cost the British Forces 600,000 casualties, and gained for the "victors" only a few hundred square miles of devastated territory. World War I produced as many as eight million military fatalities, plus millions of wounded and millions more of civilian casualties.

Not only did the people of Africa and Asia hear and read about this dreadful war of Europeans against Europeans; many colonial areas were required to send troops and labor battalions to Europe in support of the holocaust. India alone furnished more than a million men. Even China, though not a colony, sent thousands of laborers to work for the Allies in Europe and the Near East.

The Moslem world, all the way from Persia to Egypt, enjoyed direct experience with the War, thanks to Allied campaigns directed chiefly against the Turks. Here too, notably in the Mesopotamian campaign and the Gallipoli landing, the Afro-Asian observer saw impressive examples of how blundering and ineffectual a European Army could be.

Perhaps Marshal Lyautey, builder of France's Moroccan protectorate was quicker than most imperialists to see what the World

Wars would do to Europe's world hegemony. When in 1914 he learned that the War had begun, he remarked, "They're mad! A war between the Europeans is civil war! This is the greatest piece of stupidity the world has ever contrived!"[1] As if to confirm his fears of colonial disruptions, he was obliged to send a large part of his forces in Morocco to the Continent to fight the Germans, thus weakening his forces in Africa. The Germans and their Turkish allies also tried to stir up a Holy War of Moslems against the French in North Africa. The Turkish Sultan's position as spiritual head of a large portion of the Moslem religious community facilitated such agitation. Doubtless the agitation bore some later fruit of nationalism, but at the time the North Africans could not be stirred into action against the French.

World War I offered one prime example of complete destruction of the colonial empire of a major European power, Germany. Admittedly, most German colonies remained in the hands of other European powers for several more decades. In the Pacific area, however, Japan occupied three groups of German-held islands—the Carolines, Marianas, and Marshalls—as well as German areas of control in China's Shantung Province. Postwar arrangements left her in full control of the islands. Although, like most former German colonies, these theoretically came under League of Nations control, the League gave Japan a "Class C" Mandate to administer them, meaning that the mandatory power was authorized to administer the islands as integral portions of her Empire, "subject only to native welfare." Since Class C Mandates provided for no inspections by League officials, or even for reports by the mandatory power to the League, there was no limitation whatever on colonial power.

All of the following Mandates were also Class C: Nauru Island to Great Britain, German Samoa to New Zealand, and German Southwest Africa to the Union of South Africa, while Australia received German New Guinea, the Bismarck Archipelago, and the German Solomon Islands.

Class B Mandates imposed mild, flexible limitations on the mandatory power, as follows: The "open door" must be maintained for trade by all nations. Freedom of worship and free exercise of local customs was provided, "where consistent with the standards of Western Civilization." The slave trade, as well as trade in arms and liquor, was to be suppressed. Imposition of forced labor was forbidden, except for essential works. Military training was not allowed, except for police and defense, with a general exception for French Mandates. The exceptions, admittedly, would accommodate almost all the desires of a colonial power. At least there was to be a League of Nations Committee to supervise these limited Mandates.

Under Class B, Germany's Cameroons and Togoland colonies were parcelled out between France and Britain. The latter was to handle most of German East Africa, now "Tanganyika," while the portion known as Ruanda Urundi was mandated to Belgium, since this territory lay on the eastern border of the Belgian Congo. A small piece of German East Africa was handed over to Portugal to become part of that nation's Mozambique colony.

The peoples of Afro-Asia could enjoy the spectacle of one colonial empire being abolished, surely suggesting to some onlookers that the future might bring further demolition. After all, part of the ousting of Germans had been done very effectively by Japan, itself an Asian power. Germany now joined Russia as an example of a great European world power defeated by a non-Western power in the twentieth century.

World War I also began the economic liberation of Asia. The production capacities of the Allied powers were concentrated on the war effort, so little could be exported to Asia. Moreover, the Allies imported more goods from Asia to supply increased wartime requirements, so the factories of Japan, China, and India enjoyed heavy demands for their products. Asian entrepreneurs prospered, and were able to expand their factories.

The treaties imposed by the victors of World War I, especially the Treaty of Versailles with Germany and the Treaty of Sèvres with Turkey, constituted unreal and unsteady rearrangement of European colonial holdings. The domains of the losers were in large part added to the French and British Empires, whose proprietors were in a decline industrially, commercially, demographically, and perhaps morale-wise. In a world where Germany, Russia, America, and Japan were the rising centers of power and driving ambition, this settlement was eminently unstable, and probably hastened the end of colonialism.

Another by-product of World War I was generated within Europe itself. The dislocations and frustrations engendered by the war led to a wave of revolutions and installation of numerous dictatorships in Europe, including the unprecedentedly monstrous régimes of Hitler and Stalin. From these the whole world learned much that was new about totalitarian methods.

Then came the blood-bath of World War II—a more total war than the first in some ways, since the participants now knew more about the regimentation of their people and economies. Some idea of the death-toll suffered in this struggle by soldiers, partisans, and civilians, emerges from the following figures: The U.S.S.R. lost 15,000,000, Germany 3,750,000, and France 625,000, while Britain and the U.S.A. each lost one-third of a million.

The salient horror of warfare in the 1940's was the bombing of cities, especially when it became common practice on both sides to carry on massive bombings to ruin the morale of the enemy's populace, not for the destruction of specified objectives. Within Europe itself, the most indefensible of these gigantic "terror raids" was the bombing of Dresden, Germany, on February 13, 1945. This raid was strategically unwarranted, and came, as statesmen of the West knew, on the very eve of German collapse. The order to bomb Dresden was questioned by the military commanders who received it, but statesmen of the West then gathered at Yalta reaffirmed the order. The raid killed about 135,000; it was the largest single day's killing in all European history.[2]

Until the World Wars, the white nations could claim to be the world's peacemakers. They could remind their colored brethren that from 1815 to 1914 the "civilized countries" had fought no really extensive, catastrophic wars except the American Civil War. They could point to the peacemaking role of the white man in Africa, India, and other areas where European rule had almost eliminated inter-tribal and inter-regional warfare. However, in launching the World Wars, the West forfeited this proud claim, a loss of moral standing aggravated by the special nature of the World Wars.

Besides the European phase of World War II, there was fighting in Asia and the Pacific, initiated by Japan. Japan's war there was widely touted, and accepted, as an effort to expel white interlopers from Asia. To be sure, Western presence in Asia was unwelcome, but the effect of Japan's propaganda might have been weakened if the Western powers had agreed to liberate their Asian possessions after expulsion of the Japanese.

A few weeks before the United States was plunged into World War II, Mohandas Gandhi asked that the United States not extend aid to Britain unless definite assurances were tendered by the latter that human liberties would be accorded the colonial peoples. American aid was, as we know, given without any such assurances.

The following words of Mohandas Gandhi, written after America entered the war, illustrate how an Asian may view Western responsibility for colonial misdeeds as a joint affair; at the same time, you will see here the view that Nazis and Anglo-Saxon imperialists were not immensely different with respect to moral excellence: "Since America has become the predominant partner in the Allied cause, she is partner also in Britain's guilt. The Allies have no right to hold their cause to be morally superior to the Nazi cause, so long as they hold in custody one of the most ancient nations of the earth."[3]

In a letter to Franklin D. Roosevelt dated July 1, 1942, Gandhi said that the Allies' assertion that they were fighting for democracy and the freedom of the individual sounded "hollow, so long as India and for that matter Africa are exploited by Great Britain, and America has the Negro problem in her own home."[4]

Unfortunately, Winston Churchill made several clear re-affirmations of British supremacy, or white supremacy. When in August, 1941, Prime Minister Churchill and President Roosevelt enunciated the humanitarian principles of the Atlantic Charter from a ship at sea off North America, Deputy Prime Minister Attlee told a Negro gathering in London that the new Charter implied that no race would be denied freedom. On September 9, 1941, in a Parliamentary address, Churchill carefully corrected any impression this might have given that equal treatment would be extended to British subjects of all racial or national types. The Prime Minister said that the Charter's provision for "the right of all peoples to choose the form of government under which they will live" was made with a primary view to "the restoration of the sovereignty . . . of the states and nations of Europe now under the Nazi yoke . . . so that it is quite a separate problem from the progressive evolution of self-governing institutions in the regions and people [sic] who owe allegiance to the British Crown."[5] Later, in November, 1942, Churchill made England's position even clearer by declaring, "I have not become the King's first Minister in order to preside over the liquidation of the British Empire."

The United States did not accept Churchill's interpretation of the Atlantic Charter, as we see from Under Secretary of State Welles' statement in the spring of 1942 that the victory of the United Nations "must bring in its train the liberation of all peoples. . . . The age of imperialism is ended." Speaking out for the freedom of colonial peoples were many other Americans—Henry Wallace, Wendell Willkie, and President Roosevelt himself. In 1942, the President told Russia's Molotov that Chiang K'ai-shek had proposed international trusteeships for such territories as Indo-China, the Malay States, and the Dutch East Indies. Roosevelt observed that these colonies must eventually be liberated from their European owners, and implied that Chiang's idea was good.[6]

Notwithstanding good intentions, the postwar settlement in which the United States Government acquiesced left Southeast Asia and most other colonial areas unliberated. Liberation was not, therefore, a laudable by-product of the war; freedom for the colonies usually had to be wrung from the powers. Sometimes, notably with British possessions, independence was granted before wars of liberation broke out. Even in those fortunate cases, delays had been sufficient to leave a residue of bitterness.

Now let us consider the effects of the World Wars in particular colonial areas.

THE TWENTIETH CENTURY IN
AFRICA AND SOUTHWEST ASIA

THE TWENTIETH CENTURY ACQUISITION by Europeans of land in East Africa somewhat resembled the handling of North American Indians in earlier centuries. The newcomers grabbed the good land and farmed it, whereas in many colonial regions they were primarily administrators, merchants, or mining entrepreneurs.

In the Kenya Highlands, for example, the Europeans took land from its African users under what were often flimsy pretexts. Even when normal European legal documents were executed to sanction transfer of land, Kikuyu tribesmen misunderstood the documents, just as American Indians misunderstood transfers of title. They supposed that they were allowing white settlers to enjoy for a time the fruits of lands not then being used by the Kikuyu. Even more than most American Indian tribes, the Kikuyu possessed a deep religious attachment to their land, identifying it with venerated ancestors who had tilled it for generations. Thus, when the African inhabitants found that the land had been permanently taken away from them, they felt that they had been tricked in a terribly sacrilegious way.

During the twentieth century, appropriation of Kikuyu land, whether by individual purchase or designation of entire regions for "white landholders only," injected enormous bitterness into the European-African relationship. Setting aside the best land of the country, the highlands, for white owners only was naturally resented by the former inhabitants. Even as late as 1960, on the very eve of independence for Kenya, justice had only partially been done by making some highland territory available to Africans once again.

Until then, the common British solution resembled the dealings of the United States with its Indians in another respect—creation of reservations for natives, and recurrent whittling away of reservation lands under white pressure. In 1906, for example, reserves were established for several tribes, but it was legal to take land on the reserves from the natives whether they were occupying it or not, provided only that the governor obtained consent from the

Secretary of State. Eventually, in 1930, a Government ordinance declared the reserves to be tribal lands in perpetuity.

In 1906, the Indian minority in Kenya made an elaborate legal effort to obtain equitable rights of land acquisition in the highlands, and many Englishmen in responsible positions, including Undersecretary of State Winston Churchill, expressed doubt that they could properly be excluded from the highlands. The Secretary of State for the Colonies favored exclusion of Indians in 1906. Although by 1908 he admitted the legal right of Indians to acquire land, he said even then that, as a matter of administrative procedure, such land would be granted only to Europeans.[7]

Elsewhere in the eastern portion of Africa, peace between the two World Wars was disturbed by Italian invasion of Ethiopia. Italy's attempt to seize that country at the end of the nineteenth century had ended disastrously for Italian arms. She was more successful in this new attempt, even though there was no more legal or moral justification in 1935 than there had been in 1896. In October, 1935, Italy began invasion, and by May of 1936 Ethiopian resistance had been broken. Although public opinion of England, France, and the United States was quite sympathetic to Ethiopian independence, very little was done to help the Ethiopians. Certain sanctions were placed in effect to limit shipments of commodities to Italy, but were simply not decisive in nature. Italy proclaimed formal amalgamation of Ethiopia with the earlier Italian holdings, Eritrea and Italian Somaliland, calling the new entity Italian East Africa. By 1938 all pretense of opposition to this conquest was dropped by England and France, and they recognized the new Italian imperial creation.

When World War II began, East Africa was at first very little affected, except by the usual "voluntary contributions" to the motherland. The British colonial government in Tanganyika exhausted its reserve funds in 1940 to present 200,000 pounds to the home government as a contribution to the war effort.[8] In June, 1940, Italy declared war on France and Britain. Soon the British East African forces received reinforcements from Nigeria, South Africa, and the Gold Coast. Consequently, in 1941, Italian

Somaliland fell into the hands of the British, and as the war continued the Italians were dislodged from Ethiopia.

Japan's seizure of the Southeast Asian possessions of Britain, France, and the Netherlands in 1941-1942 caused East African authorities to be concerned lest Japan seize Madagascar and/or such strategic African mainland points as Mombasa. As Japan's Southeast Asian campaign had shown, there was no reason to expect local populations to aid the Europeans against Japanese attacks. To the contrary, the invaders might obtain considerable local support. Also dangerous was the continuing control of Madagascar by the Vichy French in 1942. Japan had taken Singapore and other major naval bases on the eastern end of the Indian Ocean. The British, retaining bases in India and Ceylon, still controlled the northern shores of that Ocean, but a Japanese jump to the Ocean's western shores did seem possible. Meanwhile, since 1940, all the countries on Africa's Mediterranean coast had been treated to large-scale displays of inter-European fighting. The summer of 1942 found German General Rommel's force in control of Libya and of Egypt as far as El Alamein, a desert point not far from Alexandria. The Germans' Vichy French collaborators remained dominant in Morocco, Algeria, and Tunisia. In November, 1942, an Anglo-American army attacked these French territories while British Commonwealth forces advanced westward from Egypt. By the following spring, the Axis forces in North Africa, were defeated.

Understandably, British East African forces were dispatched in 1942 to seize control of Madagascar from the Vichy French. Later, in 1944, East African troops participated in action against the Japanese in Burma.

As the war was being fought to a victorious conclusion by the Allies in Western and Southern Europe, there were many occasions for use of troops recruited in the African and South Asian possessions of Britain and France. Similar extensive use of colonial troops in Europe had occurred during World War I. Thus, there were many opportunities for Africans and Asians to witness global holocausts generated by their "civilized" European mentors. Troops from the French West African colonies were also used after World

War II in prolonged wars against local armies of liberation in French Indo-China and Algeria.

Looking at North African nationalist efforts in the period of the World Wars, we find that Moroccan nationalism was somewhat damaged by the rivalry of local political factions whose leaders worked against one another as well as against the French. However, the Moroccans were unified by a reasonably general devotion to their titular ruler, the Sultan. Morocco was blessed with a particularly effective leader in Sultan Mohammed V. In Spanish Morocco, nationalists gained some ground in the late 1930's because their contingents had rendered important help to General Franco during the Spanish Civil War.

In the days of Hitler's domination, the Vichy French Government had tried to issue anti-Jewish laws in Morocco. The Sultan, to his credit, refused to promulgate them, saying "Moroccan Jews are my subjects and my duty is to protect them against any aggression."[9]

The fall of France and the coming of British and American military forces to North Africa gave greater hope to the nationalists. Symbolic of this apparent encouragement was President Roosevelt's dinner meeting with the Sultan in 1943, during the Casablanca Conference then being held by Roosevelt and Churchill on Moroccan territory. Whether or not the encouragement was substantive, it was at least enough to motivate Moroccan nationalists to form their best-known political organization, the Istiqlal, or Independence Party, in December of 1943.

The first modern political party in Tunisia was organized in 1920 under the name of Destour, or Constitution Party, but moved too slowly and conservatively in the eyes of such young nationalists as Habib Bourguiba. He and his associates founded a new, progressive party, the Neo-Destour, in 1934. The new party was not altogether revolutionary, and worked for gradual development of autonomy designed eventually to produce Tunisian independence. Despite its evolutionary approach, the party was attacked by French authorities, and Bourguiba and other leaders imprisoned. In 1937, the French fired on a large protest demonstration the Neo-Destour organization had formed, killing about 200, and leading to the arrest of 3,000 members of the party. Such persecutions drove the party underground, and the outbreak of World War II found its leaders still in jail.

The nationalism of French-occupied Algeria differed significantly from that of Algeria's neighbors, Tunisia and Morocco. Europeans constituted a larger fraction of the population in Algeria than in those other two regions—10 per cent in 1954. In addition, many Algerian nationalists resided, or were present as students, in France, so some Algerian revolutionary organization and agitation took place in Paris itself.

Algeria's most serious problem as the effort toward independence matured was the European minority, which was well-organized and obdurate in resisting all efforts to make Moslem Algerians equal citizens. The colonial types did not even countenance giving full citizenship to Moslem Algerians who had served France in war. In fact, in 1914 there had been strong opposition to drafting Moslems into the French Army, for fear that military training would make them more dangerous as potential rebels. Richard M. Brace quotes Jean Daniel, who wrote in the weekly l'Express on June 4, 1955, that the French in Algeria "have more than one point in common with the southerners of the United States: courage, dynamism, narrowness of views, the sincere conviction that they are born to be masters as others are born to be slaves."[10] Brace also reports the horrifying view of some Algerian Frenchmen that they should have wiped out the Moslems in Algeria as the colonizers of North America did with their Indians. Also of special interest is Brace's suggestion that the Algerian Frenchman feared the Moslems because he had treated the Moslem as sub-human and now feared, as the threat of an independent Moslem Algeria emerged, that the Moslem might handle the French similarly.

In Egypt, World War I had put a stop to the pretense that the nation was independent. The British proclaimed their protectorate over Egypt, and deposed the Khedive because of his intrigues with Britain's Turkish adversaries. When World War I was won by the Allies, the Egyptians appeared quite tired of arbitrary wartime rule by British appointees, and much unrest ensued. In 1922 the protectorate was terminated, the British said, but substantive power there remained in English hands. After a variety of half-hearted British concessions, Egypt finally secured a treaty with England in August, 1936, by which British forces were to leave Egypt except for a small contingent along the Suez Canal and a naval base at Alexandria. For a time, Egypt was independent.

However, World War II caused a re-emergence of the dictatorial British hand. The exigencies of defending North Africa and the Near East against the Nazis, who were invading Egypt, gave the British a good excuse for high-handed conduct. A scene between King Farouk and the British representative at this critical point of the war represents the classic case of imperialism at work. The British had demanded that the King appoint as his Premier the British choice, Nahas Pasha. The King rejected the demand. Into the courtyard of the King's Abdin palace rolled British tanks, after which the demand was reiterated. In a summarily unpleasant way, Farouk acceded to the British demand, saying menacingly, "You will regret this day!" Whether regretted or not, this "tough-minded" action was one of the last of its kind in that part of the world, because the era of European Empire was ending.

The defeat of Turkey in World War I had brought independence very near for many of the Sultan's other Arab subjects. Saudi Arabia, occupying most of the Arabian peninsula, became an independent Arab kingdom. However, Turkey's Mesopotamian region—the valleys of the Tigris and Euphrates—became a British mandate called Iraq, which included the oil-rich Kurdish province of Mosul.

Mandating of territories from the League of Nations to colonialist powers was little more than a trick to deceive Western leaders, notably America's President Wilson, who advocated self-determination of all peoples. Eventual independence was forecast for the mandates, and did come to some in a decade or so, but the League of Nations had no stated powers or procedures for taking a mandate away from the recipient nation, or for terminating it, even if the mandatory power withdrew from the League.

Iraq, even as a mandated protectorate, had its own King, Feisal. He and his kinsman Abdullah, who reigned over the British mandate of Trans-Jordan, belonged to the family of that famous Sherif of Mecca who had collaborated with Lawrence to chase the Turks out of the Arabian peninsula.

Recurrent disorders in Iraq stemmed from the desires of its people to be independent. Regarding British suppression of these disorders by aerial bombardment, an English officer, Lt. Col. Arnold Wilson, spoke to the Royal Asian Society in 1932 concerning "the pertinacity with which (notwithstanding declarations at Geneva) the R.A.F. has been bombing the Kurdish population for the last ten years." Not only were villages devastated, but to insure a goodly toll among the inhabitants, delayed-action bombs were used. The villagers often fled as the planes approached, and the bombs were timed to explode after they came back to their homes. India's Nehru notes, with a bitterness that must have been widely felt among Afro-Asians, that when the powers conferred on disarmament in 1932, they passed a resolution calling for abolition of air attacks on civilian populations, but making an exception for attacks on "native villages."[11]

Iraq was designated an independent kingdom in 1932, but Britain reserved the characteristic rights to maintain forces in Iraq. As in Egypt, the nation's independence was disregarded under the pressures of World War II, when British forces intervened to prevent an alleged German puppet from seizing power. After World War II, Iraqi independence was fully restored.

Although the British mandate over Trans-Jordan ran smoothly enough between the two World Wars, the adjacent British mandate of Palestine stirred with much unrest. This, of course, was related to Jewish colonization and impending Zionist plans to make Palestine a national Jewish homeland.

Two other portions of the old Turkish Empire, Syria and the Lebanon, became French mandates, while a special twentieth century role was in store for protectorates along the coasts of the Arabian Peninsula. These little sheikdoms, originally dominated by the British in order to safeguard the route to India, became newly important in the mid-twentieth century because of rich oil deposits. Development and protection of the oil sources caused Western powers to maintain a keen, continuing interest in these areas after colonialism in the Near East had otherwise ended. At the southern end of the peninsula, the former Aden Crown Colony and Aden Protectorate received independence as the "People's Republic of South Yemen," effective January, 1968. The end of British control there did not mean the end of British military protection, however. Ships and planes were kept ready in the Indian Ocean to deter violent moves by dissident or subversive groups. Such threats were plausible, since the British had been plagued by terrorists in Aden and because the neighboring country of Yemen, though independent, was troubled by civil war.

Last of the Southwest Asian lands to be discussed here is Persia, usually called Iran today. This kingdom retained its titular independence throughout the age of European imperialism, but the Russians and British had for decades before World War I achieved partial domination of the country. World War I made Persia a helpless battleground of various European expeditionary units, German as well as Allied. Russian military occupation of Northern Persia was ended by the collapse of Russian power, 1917–1921. However, the Shah found it necessary to dispatch a delegation to the Paris Peace Conference to demand return of Persia's ancient territories in the Caucasus and along the Caspian coast, which had long ago fallen into the Czars' hands. The delegates also demanded abrogation of the entente between Britain and Russia which had divided the Shah's territories into three parcels, one for England in the south, one for Russia in the north, and one neutral zone in the middle. Abolition of the Europeans' extraterritorial rights was also requested.

British diplomats saw to it that this Persian delegation was not officially admitted to the Conference, and a vapid Anglo-Persian agreement was substituted for the steps sought by the Shah's Government. However, the Russian Revolution brought into power a government which gave up its extraterritorial privileges and turned over to the Shah many Russian-controlled transportation facilities within Persia. With defeat of the Turks and Germans, and the Russian withdrawal, the British lost the excuses which war and rivalry had provided for their presence in Persia. They began to withdraw their own troops in 1921.

World War II found Persia victimized again by rival moves of European powers. The German advance through Russia toward the Caucasus and the Axis victories in North Africa made Persia seem vulnerable again, and to "protect" her the Russians again entered their old preserve in Northern Persia; the British moved back into the southern portion. The Shah fell into line with the occupying powers and declared war on Germany. The powers, on their part, promised to preserve Iranian independence and to withdraw their troops after the end of hostilities. The British did leave in March, 1946, and the Russians grudgingly did so a little later. In the postwar years, the U.S.S.R. built up new influence in Iran by sponsoring a separatist movement in the northern provinces, but by 1949 these efforts had largely failed.

INDIA

WE HAVE NOTED previously that World War I slogans of the Allied Powers about bestowing democracy and freedom on all peoples led Afro-Asians to hope for some degree of freedom. During World War I, India's more determined nationalists demanded that genuine political freedom be given India as a prerequisite to full Indian participation in the war effort. However, no such concession was made. Indians were expected to support the war effort, and seem generally to have done so, hoping for postwar concessions.

Prominent Congress Party members supported the war by raising money and helping with recruitment. On the war fronts, 800,000 Indian soldiers served, while 400,000 Indian laborers were sent to the war zones. The people as a whole put up with food shortages, price increases, and rises in tax rates. To be sure, some Indian support was given under duress. Jawaharlal Nehru commented on the so-called "gift" of 100 million pounds which the Indians were made to contribute to the British war budget, saying that use of the word *gift* did "credit to the sense of humor of the British Government."[12]

Many Indians hoped for British gratitude after the war. Some supposed that this would extend to the gift of independence, while others anticipated liberalization of British rule. The World War I years had brought special restrictions upon the Indians, such as the Defence of India Act. This Act was intended to prevent treason, sabotage, and so on, during the war, and it was reasonable to anticipate its disappearance when the war ended.

Instead, in March of 1919 the hated Rowlatt Acts were enacted, continuing many of the wartime restrictions. They made it possible for police and civil authorities in India to arrest people arbitrarily, hold them in jail without trial, and proceed to trial when they chose, without giving the accused such rudimentary benefits as public trial, public records of trial, legal counsel, or jury trial. The charges and the basis of charges were left to the discretion of the authorities. Though the general object was repression of treason or revolt, almost any complaint or demonstration might bring a person under these arbitrary enactments. It is understandable that the Rowlatt Acts were met with much indignation by the Indian people.

Meanwhile, Mohandas Gandhi's programs of peaceful civil disobedience and non-violent resistance were beginning to give the people of India the kind of exercises in which the quest for freedom could be continued, even though the colonialists held a near monopoly of military might. In 1919, the *hartal* was a common tactic of non-violent resistance. This was a strike of all workers and merchants, intended as a demonstration or gesture of grievance. Hartals unavoidably involved occasional unplanned violence, such as between strikers and individuals who were unwilling to participate. There was considerable violence in many cities, but the unrest in Amritsar seems especially to have made an impression on British authorities. This city saw several riots and acts of arson. Efforts by military forces to stop the disorders by firing at the rioters simply added to popular indignation. The rioting crowds not only damaged property and attacked Indians; they proceeded to kill several inoffensive Englishmen in office buildings, and an English missionary, one Miss Sherwood, was attacked.

The episode which ensued, the Amritsar Massacre, occupies an important place in the history of European imperialism. This sad event had a great effect on the image of Europe in the minds of Afro-Asians. Let us sketch out the event itself, and then consider its consequences.

General Dyer, military commander of the area that included Amritsar, received a request from city officials for further military assistance. Accordingly, he proceeded to the afflicted city. We know that higher British authorities took a serious view of the disorders. The Provincial Governor of Punjab talked with Government of India authorities at Simla on the night of April 12, 1919, and was told that if troops were forced to fire at disorderly groups, "they should make an example."[13]

General Dyer clearly shared his superiors' drastic view of the situation. We can sympathize with him to the extent of noting that he had only a few hundred men with whom he was expected to pacify a city of 160,000. On the other hand, one can blame the British authorities for an overly suspicious and apprehensive attitude toward populations over which they ruled. They seem to have believed, in 1919, that there was an extensive conspiracy in India aimed at violent overthrow of British rule—a plot which really did not exist. It is, of course, understandable that British administrators and generals were aware that most Indians did not desire their presence in that country. The reliability of military and police units manned by Indians was also a matter of conjecture. As Nehru describes the mood of these English colonialists in April, 1919, "a sudden fear overwhelmed the authorities, made them see danger everywhere, a widespread uprising, a second mutiny with its frightful massacres, and in a blind, instinctive attempt at self-preservation at any cost led them to [acts of] frightfulness."[14]

General Dyer, certain that only drastic action would enable him to keep any semblance of order, issued two proclamations forbidding demonstrations, parades, and all public gatherings. He also imposed a curfew under which anyone going into the street at night was subject to being shot. The General took considerable care to inform the populace of his orders on the morning of April 13, by having them read at 19 prominent points in the city. Having done this, he felt that he could punish with any amount of violence whatever disobedience might ensue. However, many people did not get word of his decrees. The British Government's later investigation of the fateful incidents of April 13 were published as the "Hunter Report." This Report concludes, regarding General Dyer's proclamation against public gatherings, "It is evident that in many parts of the city the proclamation was not read."[15]

General Dyer learned, between noon and 1 P.M., that a gathering was to take place at an Amritsar location known as the Jallianwala Bagh. This was an open area of about eight acres, surrounded almost completely by buildings and walls. It was suitable for large assemblies, and about 25,000 persons gathered there on April 13. To assess properly the reprehensibility of events which ensued, note that the largest entrance to the Bagh was about seven and one-half feet wide (too narrow, incidentally, to permit entry of armored cars bearing machine guns, a fact which General Dyer regretted). There were about five other openings four feet in width, and a few fissures or holes through which people could crawl from the Bagh. An additional method of exit was to climb over one stretch of wall which was only five feet high.

The General's tactics were to proceed to the Bagh and take violent action against the people gathered there. He took 50 riflemen into this enclosed place and deployed them on either side of the main entrance. Without any attempt to order the crowd to disperse, the General passed the order for the riflemen to fire. Their first volley apparently went over the heads of the people, and at the urging of their officers the men proceeded to fire point blank at this very dense crowd, which could only escape very slowly. The General seems to have ordered the fire shifted in whatever direction would secure the best rate of casualties.

Tactically, this was very successful. A subsequent count of ammunition expended, made after the soldiers had returned to their barracks, showed that 1,650 shots were fired. This meant a ratio of nearly one casualty per bullet, because at least 379 persons were killed and 1,200 wounded by this fire. After about ten minutes of firing, the General ordered the riflemen to desist because he feared that ammunition was running low. Dyer felt that his results were quite commendable. In his own words, "I thought I would be doing a jolly lot of good."[16] The General thought that firing only a little would have been insufficient to cow the populace into proper submission. We must note that the wounded victims were given no assistance by the authorities. In fact, when night fell even private citizens scarcely dared visit their helpless wounded in the Bagh, because to do so meant violation of the British curfew.

If this massacre had not been followed by other acts of frightfulness, its effect on Indian and world opinion might not have been so immense. However, other drastic actions did occur thereafter. The Governor of the Punjab allowed bombing of villages and machine-gunning of people by aircraft. Applicable here are words from a speech made by Senator Robert F. Kennedy in 1965, within a different context, of course. The Senator said that when a government proceeds to "make war on its own people it abandons its reason for existence." Even when a government force is fired upon from a village, said Kennedy, "A government which attacks that village from the air . . . abandons the first duty of any government worthy of the name."

In Amritsar itself, a special rule was applied to the street where Miss Sherwood had been attacked. All Indian men entering it were compelled to proceed on all fours. This went down in history as the "Crawling Lane of Amritsar." Corporal punishment was freely imposed upon inhabitants for a variety of offenses, such as failure to bow to an officer, disrespect for a European, or violation of the curfew.

The subsequent status of the Amritsar affair would also have been less if the perpetrators of this reign of terror in the Punjab had been punished by higher British authority, or the Government had apologized for the unjust, totalitarian Rowlatt Acts which had done so much to bring on the tragedies of 1919 in India. To be sure, the Hunter Committee disapproved of General Dyer's actions; the British Government censured him for excessive severity, and there was much sentiment in the House of Commons for his punishment. Nevertheless, British Conservatives tended to back him up, and a large majority of the House of Lords approved of his course of action. He received a number of awards for having "saved India," including a sword and a purse of 20,000 pounds gathered through public contributions.[17] The Governor of the Punjab concluded that Dyer's action did a great deal of good, in that it soon became widely known throughout India and prevented further serious outbreaks.

Of course, the effect of those sad events in the Punjab was to inflame Indian public opinion and arouse the sort of resentment which lingers for many years. They must have done a great deal to hasten the end of British rule in India and shorten the life expectancy of European imperialism in more than one part of the world.

We know that the aftermath of this affair brought Gandhi and Nehru closer together in India. They and other Congress Party leaders were involved in their own inquiry to establish exactly what had happened in the Punjab. Nehru reports that at this time his faith in Gandhi's political insight grew. While he does not say much about his own feelings, he mentions those of his father, saying, "The Punjab happenings and the enquiry into them had a profound effect on father." Nehru also tells us that when he traveled from Amritsar to Delhi by train toward the end of 1919 he happened to share a sleeper car with General Dyer and other British officers. Nehru heard the General holding forth in a loud voice, telling how he had the whole city at his mercy and was tempted to reduce the rebellious city to ashes. Apparently the General had just returned from giving evidence before the Hunter Committee. Nehru concluded from this affair, "I was greatly shocked to hear his conversation and to observe his callous manner."[18]

Another example of the broad impact of this matter may be found in the case of writer Rabindranath Tagore, who gave up the knighthood he had received from the British Sovereign as a protest against the Amritsar events. This action was more impressive coming from a non-politician than it would have been coming from an Indian Congress Party leader. Tagore seldom left his ivory tower and purely cultural pursuits; only in a case like this, where he felt he could no longer tolerate a development, did he take such action.

Did Britain manage to compensate India for such abuses by promoting the welfare of the people and developing the economy?

Nehru's judgment was that "The British conception of ruling India was the police conception of the State. Government's job was to protect the State and leave the rest to others. . . . The cultural and other needs of the people, except for a tiny handful, were entirely neglected."[19]

So far as public administration was concerned, the Indian Civil Service, according to Nehru, held "practically absolute" power, "subject only in theory to a control by the British Parliament." Nehru asserted that this sort of administrative corps could be reconciled with only one type of state—the Fascist type.[20]

Industrial development had been slight before World War I because of the poverty of the land, and because of British policy. Under the pressure of war, the masters encouraged some development, subsidizing the iron and steel industry and allowing some protection of other new industries by tariffs. There was rapid progress for a time, but unfortunately the war boom ended; the brief postwar boom evaporated, and India felt some of the effects of the Western world's Great Depression. The sufferings of her people were severe, yet throughout these trying times the Government granted no reductions in tax payments or other charges levied on the peasantry. We cannot say that the last decades of British control brought notable improvements in sanitation and public health, either. Even in the twentieth century—after 150 years of English rule—five to six million Indians died annually from preventable diseases. Infant mortality rates were six times those of England; average life expectancy was 25 years.

Mohandas Gandhi reached the following verdict about British rule in India: "Why do I regard the British rule as a curse? It has impoverished the dumb millions by a system of progressive exploitation and by a ruinous expensive military and civil administration which the country can never afford. It has reduced us politically to serfdom. It has sapped the foundations of our culture."[21] Gandhi chose to object most bitterly and pointedly to the salt monopoly of the British Government. He protested imposition of taxes on the salt which every Indian workingman simply must have. Too much of the burden of taxation fell on the poor peasant, said Gandhi, and the alcohol and drug revenues exploited the poor, as well as sapping, through their commodities, the health and morals of the Indian people.

Gandhi corresponded with the British Viceroy, and notified the Government that if its overbearing exploitation were not relaxed, he would make a protest demonstration by publicly violating the Salt Laws. There was no stop to exploitation, and accordingly, in 1930, the Mahatma led his followers in a march to the sea. It was a 24-day walk which Gandhi actually performed without any transportation other than his legs. The march to the sea brought valuable grass-roots contact between the leaders and the villagers. The marchers passed through many villages, at each one of which the farmers were given an indelible impression of the firm determination of the new movement. Gandhi's frugality and simplicity naturally appealed to the Indian masses. Two or three times each day the march paused for meetings at which Gandhi and his colleagues explained the principles of their movement and urged the people to wear only homespun clothing, in order to shut out British textiles.

By the 1930's, independence was the fully acknowledged goal of the Indian National Congress. Public sentiment had matured sufficiently so that no enduring compromise short of independence could be adopted. Yet most English leaders still felt that they could, and must, hold India in their grasp for a long time. Winston Churchill said in 1931 that England would cease to be a great power if she lost control of India. In the *Daily Mail* of May 16, 1930, Lord Rothermere said, "Many authorities estimate that the proportion of the vital trading, banking, and shipping business of Britain directly dependent upon our connection with India is 20% .... If we lose India the Empire must collapse—first economically, then politically."

Consequently, the British would not grant independence, and the friction between Indian nationalists and British authorities continued on into the years of World War II. The Gandhian campaigns of non-violent resistance also continued, and their cumulative effect was very great indeed. The demonstrations, sit-ins, strikes, and various acts of civil disobedience had built up a massive public determination to secure freedom for India.

In spite of their troubles with tyranny in their own country, Indian leaders were mindful of the growing menace of the Nazi tyranny in Europe. The Indian National Congress passed resolution after resolution in the 1930's denouncing Nazi and Fascist aggressions, and criticizing the governments of Western Europe for acquiescing in these moves. A resolution of the 1938 Congress stated that Britain's foreign policy had consistently supported the Fascist power.

Finally, Britain and France began their war of opposition to Hitler, and their resistance on the Continent of Europe proved unexpectedly brief and ineffectual. When Jawaharlal Nehru heard of the collapse of the allied armies of Europe in 1940, he wondered what could account for that abject defeat, especially for the utter demoralization of France. He wondered if the imperialism of Britain and France, which had seemed to strengthen them, might really have weakened them. How could they fight for the same ideals of freedom which they were crushing in far-flung colonial areas? Nehru saw a certain logic in the events whereby imperialist France fell before Germany and became a Fascist nation.

When, in 1941, Japan launched one successful drive after another against America and the European powers in Asia and the Pacific, the Indian reaction was, as Nehru put it, "satisfaction at the collapse of old-established European colonial powers before the armed strength of an Asian power"—this despite a certain sympathy for China vis-à-vis Japan. Nor could Asians overlook the declaration of a highly placed Englishman that he wished the battleships *Prince of Wales* and *Repulse* had been sunk by Germans instead of the Japanese.[22]

Unfortunately, the war years meant a British crackdown on advocates of Indian freedom. From the Government's point of view, those who wished to eject the British might seek Japanese aid in doing so. Invasion of India by Japan seemed altogether possible. Indeed, Burma fell to their armies, as did part of India's easternmost province, Assam. All of Southeast Asia had fallen to the Japanese, and absence of any local popular will to resist Japan had been plainly observed. Gandhi, in India, did not desire the coming of the Japanese, being naturally disinclined to substitute their overlordship for that of the British. But he continued to insist that the British "Quit India." If the Japanese came, said Gandhi, he would offer against them the same non-violent resistance used against the British.

There was disagreement among the Japanese as to how far Japan should go in sponsoring Indian independence, invading India, or organizing an Indian army within the Japanese forces. Some generals felt that invasion of India would not work out well, so the invasion operation was kept too small and too much delayed to achieve its full potential. Eventually Japanese expansion in Southeast Asia led to organization of an "Indian National Army," under Japanese direction, to join in an invasion of India. The leader for the Japanese-Indian project was Subhas Chandra Bose, who had considerable popular backing in India, had been prominent in the Indian National Congress, and represented the true Indian leadership as far as many Indians within Southeast Asia were concerned. Bose worked in Southeast Asia to create a so-called Free Indian Government and to recruit an "Indian National Army."[23]

As it turned out, Japanese invasion of the Assam province of India was only an abortive campaign, and the Indian National Army was defeated along with the forces of Japan. Even so, the recruiting, fighting, and propaganda developed considerably more Indian patriotism and enthusiasm than had heretofore been evident. Since Bose did not live to make his full influence felt after World War II, this movement among Indians overseas in Southeast Asia was one of his final accomplishments. Within India, the movement at least achieved some recognition by leaders of the Congress Party.

In 1942, the best response the British would make to the Indian clamor for freedom was the "Cripps Plan" for dominion status, to come into effect after the war. Unacceptable to the Indian leadership was Cripps' provision that each province, and each of the many princely territories of India, must have the right to remain outside the proposed Indian nation. Thus, a truly free and viable India was not assured.

On August 8, 1942, the Indian Congress Party rejected the Cripps Plan and demanded that the British "Quit India." On

August 9, the British promptly moved to arrest Gandhi, Nehru, and other advocates of independence. The populace, reacting with spontaneous indignation, attacked or damaged many Government facilities. The Government itself reported 539 incidents where violence had to be used against crowds, and official reports acknowledged 1,028 casualties among "native terrorists," although Nehru estimated his people's casualties at ten times that figure. In December 1942 alone, 60,000 arrests were made, and many of the victims were detained until 1945.[24]

At the end of the war it was clear to many observers, though some British leaders still did not realize it, that the Indian people were indeed ready to eject the British at any cost. Fortunately, the postwar Labour Government knew that this was no time for gradualism. Plans were quickly made for British departure from India in mid-1948, but even that proved not quite fast enough. The British, now properly concerned, were happy to liberate the sub-continent in 1947; there were no delaying tactics at this stage of the crisis.

Although the grant of freedom came quickly, there were tragedies and difficulties in 1947 and the years that followed. These arose from partition of the sub-continent into a Hindu India and a Moslem Pakistan, the latter composed of two widely separated portions. Although this partition enabled most Hindus and Moslems to be in a nation where they were members of the dominant religion, large minorities were trapped in the wrong country —and for many this entailed immediate persecution, even murder, followed by waves of riots in reprisal, and counter-murders. Not only did Hindus and Moslems fight each other; 1948 also brought the murder of Mohandas Gandhi, apostle of non-violence and father of Indian freedom, at the hands of a fellow Hindu who considered Gandhi a traitor to Hinduism.

These birth-pangs of Indian and Pakistani independence were not in any clearly demonstrable way the fault of the now departed colonialists. Moreover, apologists of imperialism were able to cite the rioting as proof that the colonial powers had been, in truth, peacemakers when they bore the white man's burden.

What of our criticism that imperialist rule stunted the economic and cultural growth of colonies? Do recent statistics show enough dramatic post-liberation improvement to support this charge? Here are a few figures comparing India's status in the years 1950–1951 and 1962–1963. Life expectancy went up from 32.5 years to 42, and electric power capacity increased from 2,300,000 kilowatts to 7,750,000. Steel production rose from 1,500,000 ingot tons to 5,4000,000, and the value of machine tool production increased from $700,000 to $23,600,000. If India is at all characteristic of liberated colonial territories, the answer to the preceding question should be affirmative.

Elsewhere in Asia and the Pacific

IN DISCUSSING effects of the Russo-Japanese War and World War I on the position of the white man in Asia, we saw how the Western relationship with China and Japan evolved in the early twentieth century. After World War I, East Asia was powerfully stirred up by the gospel of Marxist revolution. In the 1920's, Communist parties were founded by revolution-minded *and* independence-minded citizens of all the East Asian countries, including nearly all the colonial lands of Southeast Asia. Only in China, however, did the revolutionary movement achieve impressive successes. In the mid-1920's, a wave of violent nationalistic, anti-foreign feeling swept over China and for a time threatened to engulf the foreign concessions and treaty ports.

Sun Yat-sen's Kuomintang ("National People's Party") made common cause with the Chinese Communists, and Red Russian advisers arrived to assist in a program of political and military reorganization and training. In 1927, under Chiang K'ai-shek's leadership, the Kuomintang turned against its Communist comrades. The Communists of China, expelled from the Kuomintang, began a 30-year period of defensive, guerrilla-type resistance against Chiang's anti-Red campaigns. Only after World War II would the Communists be able to prevail in China.

As for Chiang K'ai-shek, anti-Red though he was, he remained anti-Western as well. His book, *China's Destiny*, made it amply clear that he, like all Chinese, had not forgotten the unfair treatment of his country. He proposed to terminate the unequal treaties, concessions, and other foreign impositions on China. Some foreign concessions were returned early in Chiang's career, and others were brought to an end by the Japanese invasion. (The foreign powers voluntarily agreed, during World War II, that these special territories would revert to China.)

It was, of course, Japan that did the most to wipe out the white man's privileged position in East Asia. After four years of war with China, the Japanese enlarged their struggle in 1941, proclaiming the "Greater East Asian War" to expel Western powers from Asia. The island empire aspired to be the creator, protector, and leader of a "Greater East Asia Co-Prosperity Sphere," welding the economic resources of the region into one smoothly integrated system in which Europe and America would be shorn of influence.

In 1941 and 1942 the world saw the Japanese dream brought to fruition, at least temporarily. All white forces in East Asia went down in unexpectedly rapid defeat before the Japanese onslaught. Only the French in Indo-China, who took the precaution of surrendering, escaped dramatic defeats in battle. From the Philippines to Northern Australia, from India to Hawaii, the world saw astonishing evidence of Japanese power and Western weakness.

Meanwhile, the United States began to have panicky thoughts of Japanese invasion supported by America's own population of Japanese descent. Consequently, in 1942, 110,000 of the 127,000 persons of Japanese descent in the West Coast states were moved from their homes to concentration centers far inland. This deportation, with all its financial losses and privations, was applied both to Japanese citizens and American citizens alike. Wartime dangers at the time seemed to justify these violations of citizens' rights. To many Afro-Asians, however, these measures underscored the racial nature of the war in the Pacific. After all, no massive internment was applied to American citizens of German or Italian descent!

Of course the war in Asia was not just a racial struggle. The Western allies were aiding Chiang K'ai-shek's Government in

Western China. In Southeast Asia, however, the abject defeat of the colonial powers made their return to those colonies difficult or impossible, despite the complete military defeat of Japan.

Although Japanese occupation of many regions of Southeast Asia brought hardships and resentments, there was also a positive response to the Japanese which should not be overlooked. The Japanese attempted, not without success, to build a feeling of Asian solidarity, increase the feelings of resentment toward former imperial powers, and show themselves as deliverers and "elder brothers" among Asians. One specific acceptance of the line espoused by Japan came at the end of the war when Justice Pal, the member of the International Military Tribunal for the Far East from India, found Japan to be not guilty of aggression because he considered her warlike acts a natural response to the prior aggressions and impositions of the West.[25]

It may be worthwhile to explain that the Southeast Asians did not resent Japanese occupation in the way that many Westerners expected. There were, of course, Japanese brutalities and exactions, but these were not unlike experiences Southeast Asians had had with their own rulers or Western colonialists, and which, for that matter, the Japanese clearly inflicted on their fellow Japanese.

The people of Southeast Asia also accepted the general propaganda line of the Japanese that Japan was not actually fighting their countries or occupying them in a hostile manner, but was rather maintaining an armed presence because of Japan's war against the former colonial powers. One could hardly have expected former colonial subjects of the Dutch, British, and French to feel that they were part of those nations merely because those nations had been colonial proprietors in their respective areas. What is more, Southeast Asians were so accustomed to knuckling under to European overlords that it was not a particularly difficult adjustment to submit to Japanese occupation, and even to cooperate with the Japanese in much the same way they had cooperated with the European colonialists.

The importance of effective leaders and dramatic personal symbols of nationalism in Southeast Asia cannot be stressed too much.

The lack of a public sufficiently educated to follow debates on such things as national goals and national programs made the role of the heroic national leader especially important. Subhas Chandra Bose was such a man for the Indians in Southeast Asia, as was Emilio Aguinaldo for the Filipinos. The Japanese, appreciating this fact, planned to bring key leaders from Southeast Asia to Japan for special indoctrination, after which they would be used to promote Japanese interests in Southeast Asia. The Japanese Total War Research Institute planned, in fact, for control of the intellectual class in all Southeast Asian lands.

(This is essentially the same policy being followed with such success by Communist China in the 1960's. The Red Chinese have made African leaders their special target; by judicious use of money and other support, they have secured the cooperation of a disconcerting number of leaders in sub-Saharan Africa.)

The Japanese did not overlook the possibilities of mobilizing mass opinion through informational programs directed toward the broader public through newspapers and radio broadcasts. They gave much attention to this, greatly increasing the publications and broadcasts in the native languages of the Southeast Asian peoples. While this was intended to serve Japanese interests, it gave nationalist leaders, for the first time, a modern means of communicating with their people.[26] The leaders of Southeast Asia were not slow to take advantage of this.

Having considered the general effects of the Greater East Asia War in Southeast Asia, let us look at each region there to see how its nationalism developed during these years.

Although Siam, or Thailand, was not wholly taken over by a foreign power, there were reasons for Siamese resentment against France. In the 40-year period ending in 1907, France had seized five portions of Thai territory. Since the Siamese thus lost some parts of their territory and population, it was natural that these deprivations were retained in Thai memory and that Thailand took advantage of Japanese occupation of Southeast Asia in 1941 to regain portions of Cambodia and Laos. There had also been an uncertain boundary to Thai territory and/or influence in the

Malay peninsula, and so in 1943 Thailand took (or regained) four states which had been made part of British Malaya.

In spite of these indications of unfriendly feeling toward the West on the part of some Siamese, aggressive expression of these feelings was limited to the special occasions of World War II days. Although the Thai Government must have been at least annoyed when Allied victory in World War II made it necessary to return the territories so recently regained, there has certainly been very little overt, anti-foreign feeling in recent decades. One supposes that this is because Central Thailand was neither colonized nor subjected to such semi-colonial régimes as flourished in the foreign concessions of China.

As with so many Southeast Asian countries, anti-Western resentment has had to compete with Thailanders' hostility toward their large Chinese minority. This minority constitutes 20 per cent of the population, and predominates in the commercial and industrial life of the country. It nearly monopolizes retail trade, controls the milling and sale of rice, and is conspicuously more prosperous than the other inhabitants.

Chinese minorities in Southeast Asia had a certain nationalism all their own; that is, the continuing loyalty to the Chinese homeland which overseas Chinese feel wherever they are. While this loyalty may have been mostly a matter of cultural, commercial, and family ties, the Revolution of 1911–1912 in China sharpened it. Establishment of the Chinese Republic made the overseas Chinese, like their compatriots within China, more mindful of political innovations. After the Revolution there was a greater flow of students returning to China for education, and this movement in turn sharpened the nationalism of overseas Chinese. In recent years, the Red Chinese Government and the Nationalist Government on Taiwan competed actively for the allegiance of the overseas Chinese. This meant that more attention was paid to the Chinese in Southeast Asia, resulting in an even greater sense of Pan-Chinese solidarity.

In the case of Burma, nationalism was much influenced by the Buddhist religious community. Buddhist monks were very active politically. The victory of Japan over Russia in 1904–1905 seems to have accelerated the growth of a group of Burmese organizations known as the Young Men's Buddhist Associations. These associations soon became politically influential, and after World War I were consolidated as the General Council of Buddhist Associations. The Council was modeled after the National Congress in India, and like the Indian patriots endeavored to refuse cooperation with the British in every way.

In Burma, as in Malaya, the whole matter of nationalism has been muddled by the polyglot nature of the land. One-quarter of the native inhabitants are, in fact, not Burmese at all, but belong to a variety of minority groups. Substantial numbers of Indians and Chinese also entered the country. The million or so Indians tended for many years to dominate Burmese business and landholding. The Burmese resented the overly prominent role of Indian landowners and money lenders, a resentment made especially bitter by economic pressures of the Great Depression. Such grievances helped to generate a rural revolt in the years 1930–1931 which was both anti-Indian and anti-British, and enjoyed considerable support from the influential Buddhist clergy of Burma.

The British at least acknowledged that the rebellion was genuine, and designated a Commission to investigate its causes. The Commission decided that the causes were primarily economic, related to the declining price of rice. However, Burmese who conferred with the Commission at this time were critical of British rule. Their spokesman, U Su, declared that exploitation had ruined the economic system and frustrated the aspirations of his people while an indifferent government looked on.

In 1937, a new constitution for Burma was put into effect by Britain, but it fell far short of the independence desired by the Burmese, since the important controls over foreign affairs, finance, and defense remained in the governor's hands, and since Article 139 allowed the governor to assume any powers if he considered the authority of his government to be imperiled.

In 1941, as Japanese invaders approached, Premier U Saw offered to cooperate with the British if they would promise to grant Burma a dominion status soon. He got nowhere with the British, and subsequently he and other leaders were arrested on charges of collaboration with the Japanese. The new invaders did give Burma a form of independence in 1943, but as with other Southeast Asian countries the Japanese were primarily using Burma as an accessory in the war effort.

After the defeat of Japan, the British returned to Burma. Many Englishmen rather felt that the Burmese would be happy to see them back after the rigors of Japanese dominance. They were wrong, however, because Japanese control had also meant at least a token form of independence. Many Burmese were allowed the dignity of senior government positions (albeit as figureheads), a concession which the British had not allowed.

The Burmese, especially those led by the Anti-Fascist People's Freedom League, resisted the newly-returned British Governor, and the League had the support not only of its own guerrilla forces but of many factory workers and police as well. Confronted with this uncordial reception and many demonstrations and strikes, the British concluded that true independence must be made available to the Burmese. Therefore, in 1947, the British permitted a Constituent Assembly to be elected in Burma to determine whether Burma should remain in the British Commonwealth or be completely on its own. By June of that year, the Assembly had decided to sever all ties with the Commonwealth.[27] One further complication was that, as a by-product of World War II, quantities of arms fell into the hands of the local people, who could thus engage in protest, riot, revolt, or robbery in a well-armed fashion. When Burmese independence finally came, the fledgling Burmese Government found the country seething with well-armed dissident movements.

Ceylon's independence movement was brought to life by the slogans of World War I. The Wilsonian principle of self-determination of peoples inspired the people of Ceylon to greater efforts toward independence after the War. Nationalist feeling also grew when indiscriminate arrests were carried out by panicky colonial authorities in the face of various public disorders. Consequently, in 1919 the Ceylon National Congress was formed, uniting the major ethnic groups of the island. Thereafter, until independence came in 1948, the island's political trends were reasonably orderly, both in the evolution of political autonomy and in working constructively with British authorities.

Malaya owed to British rule its birth as a political unity, so it is not surprising that dynamic nationalism did not reach the Malays until World War II. Before that War their loyalties lay with regional potentates, or more generally with the Islamic faith and the Malay culture.

A special form of nationalism appeared in Singapore, where the Malay Union was founded in 1926. In Singapore, of course, numerous successful Chinese settlers had competed very effectively with the local Malays, so it was natural that a racist sort of nationalism would begin in Singapore. Later the Malay Union founded branches in the other states of the Malay Federation.

When the Japanese took over Malaya, still another form of nationalism was encouraged, one might almost say forced. The Japanese were determined to develop anti-European feeling and present themselves as an Asian people who would give their fellow-Asian Malays full self-government. They did give the top jobs of local administration to Malays, who previously were not allowed to have these prime positions. It was soon clear that the Japanese themselves would make top policy decisions and might deal with the Malays as figureheads. Even so, when the British returned after the war and resumed control of top administrative positions, the Malays resented it. Particularly disenchanted were local individuals who *were* in some degree loyal to the British during the Japanese occupation, or had at any rate suffered from the Japanese occupation. When they found the British, upon their return, unwilling to give them special favors or recognition, such people became particularly bitter and inclined to see imperial rule in terms of racism.

Another cause for adverse reactions was that the landing of the British forces on their return to the peninsula was almost as a continuation of the military campaign against the Japanese, which had ended rather suddenly. The British had planned invasion of Malaya to wrest it from the Japanese, so when they did land they behaved rather like a hostile, conquering force, much to the annoyance of the local population. An orderly, friendly re-occupation would have served the British better.

The Netherlands East Indies, as Indonesia was called during the colonial period, had its freedom fighters in the early 1900's, but their lot was hard. The Dutch were uncompromising, thorough, and militarily so strong that a fight for freedom was virtually hopeless. Even so, minor revolts continued intermittently up to the very year of Japanese invasion, including several rebellions on Java and Sumatra, 1926–1927, which were sternly repressed by the Dutch.

The coming of the Japanese in 1942 eliminated the Dutch quickly enough, but the new overlords were reluctant to let the islanders have a government of their own. Indonesian leaders tried steadfastly to get the Japanese to grant independence, but it was not until 1944, when defeats in war had weakened the Japanese armed forces, that the Empire's military leaders began to change their minds on this point. Finally, in July, 1945, Japanese authorities proclaimed an independent Indonesian Republic.

Even as the Republic of Indonesia came into existence, the surrender of Japan was near. Indonesian leaders hoped for full independence after the Japanese departure, while the Dutch hoped to regain the islands for themselves. In July, the great powers conferring at Potsdam had determined that Java should be British-occupied, but the United Kingdom was ill-prepared when the Japanese surrender ensued. The forces available for this occupation were limited in number and thoroughly tired of warfare. Many of the units brought in by the British were in fact Indian, and could hardly be expected to welcome an anti-Indonesian campaign in support of the Dutch. Various skirmishes occurred between the new occupying forces and the Indonesians; at one juncture, the British had to order some recently surrendered Japanese units to fight the Javanese—a step which weakened the claim that the war had been fought to "liberate" such areas from Japan.

After lengthy and difficult negotiations, a conference at The Hague produced agreements in 1949. These included a Charter which gave independence to the so-called Republic of the United States of Indonesia. Western New Guinea was to remain part of the Netherlands pending the outcome of future negotiations between the Dutch and their former colony. A "Statute of the Union" agreement provided for Dutch-Indonesian cooperation in foreign affairs, defense, and finance.

The federated form of the Indonesian Republic was superseded by a centralized government in 1950, and the Statute of the Union was cast aside in 1954. The issue of Western New Guinea remained unsettled until 1961, when that territory was transferred from the Netherlands to Indonesia.

There was an inconsistency about the arrangements the Japanese made with the French regarding Indo-China in 1940 and 1941. The Japanese agreement to leave the French officially in control of that area hardly seemed consistent with the professed Japanese desire to free all of Southeast Asia. Unfortunately for the leaders of independence movements in Indo-China, the paramount consideration for the Japanese was to take over this region promptly and efficiently and get on with the rest of Japan's program of war and expansion. To avoid delays, the Japanese were willing to leave the French in charge in Indo-China, and it was not until 1945 that the Japanese relieved the French of all administrative control in Indo-China.

The fact that American and European powers had been defeated by the Japanese, and their control in Southeast Asia had lapsed, operated powerfully to encourage local people in defying the Western forces when efforts were made to return those forces after World War II. Notable as an example of this contempt for the once-defeated imperialists is the following statement made by Vietnamese independence leaders on August 18, 1945: "Do not keep the air of the conqueror, you have lost all the battles. And if you are authorized to remain here, it is as the vanquished that you must bear yourself and act."[28]

Western leaders were by no means unanimous in desiring resumption of French colonial rule in Indo-China. President Franklin D. Roosevelt had hoped to avoid this; he wanted at least to provide international supervision of the region. However, Prime Minister Churchill had consistently backed France, so nothing was done to provide for early liberation of Indo-China. The death of President Roosevelt in April, 1945, meant that there was no Western statesman powerful and smart enough to prevent renewal of French control.

For more than a year after the end of World War II, the mode of Government in French Indo-China remained unclear. The summer of 1946 saw the French once more in occupation of Indo-China. The usual puppet monarchs continued to reign in Laos and Cambodia, while the French tried to keep Viet Nam in a similarly docile state of submission. Unfortunately for them, the Viet Nam liberation movement was now spearheaded by the "Viet Nam Independence League," or "Viet Minh," led by Communist cadres under Ho Chi Minh. The Viet Minh were not willing to become mere puppets of the French; when French forces moved in the winter of 1946–1947 to extirpate the recalcitrant Viet Minh-led Government, a prolonged guerrilla-type war of resistance ensued.

The Viet Minh were well organized and superlatively led by Ho Chi Minh and his brilliant general, Vo Nguyen Giap. They were quite well equipped, because the Japanese surrender had enabled them to acquire quantities of former French and Japanese weapons. The people of Viet Nam were largely sympathetic to the Viet Minh; they had experienced more than enough rule by colonial administrators. The French resuscitated the hereditary Emperor of Annam, Bao Dai, and declared him the ruler of an independent Viet Nam. However, this grant of independence was not sufficiently genuine and substantial to appease Viet Nam.

Meanwhile, a Communist Government had come to power in China, and France had another enemy on the northern border of Indo-China. Across that frontier in the 1950's came an increasing flow of aid and support for the Viet Minh. In consequence, a prolonged war ensued. Both the French and the people of Viet Nam suffered immense losses. For nine long years after the end of World War II, the French continued their hopeless and costly struggle. During all this time very little was done in the councils of Western statesmen to terminate the war. In Washington and the capitals of Western Europe, all attention was focussed on defense against the aggressive designs of the Soviet Union in Europe, and on the struggle with North Korea and Red China on the war-torn Korean Peninsula. Indo-China was simply a French affair, said the statesmen; to interfere therein might detract from French participation in the carefully planned defense of Western Europe.

The territorial settlement in the Pacific after World War II should be summarized here. Although Japan's aggressive conduct seemed to justify fragmentation of her Empire in 1945, it is significant that, except for Korea, the parts taken from the Empire fell into Western hands. The Western powers agreed that the U.S.S.R. should get the Kurile Islands and Southern Sakhalin. The United States took over the Mariana, Caroline, and Marshall Islands as trust territories under United Nations supervision. Japan's Ryukyu Islands, including Okinawa, were U.S.-occupied, and continued to be held after the four Japanese "home islands" were released from occupation by the Allied Powers in 1951. These acquisitions or occupations seemed appropriate enough in the first two postwar decades, but one wonders if longer-term historical perspective may show these acts as late incidents in the domination of the world by the West.

One other long-lasting aftereffect of World War II has been the scar left on the white conscience by the dropping of two atomic bombs on Japanese cities. The first atomic bomb was dropped on Hiroshima, August 6, 1945. About 78,000 inhabitants perished on that day; 20,000 were seriously injured, and more have died each year thereafter as a result of injuries or radiation suffered at the time. On August 9, a second bomb was dropped on the city of Nagasaki. It was a more powerful plutonium-using bomb, but did not kill so many persons as its predecessor because no "firestorm" occurred in its aftermath. This time, the dead numbered only 36,000.

The numbers of deaths alone would not render these acts so monumental. Consider the two largest B-29 incendiary raids on Tokyo: 125,000 were killed in the first and 100,000 in the second. What were the special evils of the atomic attacks?

For one thing, there was genetic damage, the extent of which is still uncertain. Use of the bomb was also a most sinister precedent; it may be more readily used again because of that precedent. To

Afro-Asians, furthermore, it is significant that the bombs were used against cities when plenty of primarily military targets were available, and *against Asians, in Asia, by white forces.* The non-white person remembers that no such devices were used in the European phase of World War II. He can be told that no atomic bombs were ready in time for use against Germany, but he wonders: If they had been ready, would they have been used against European cities?

What of the circumstances of the bombing? Did it save count-less casualties, both Japanese and American, by stopping the war? Perhaps; no one can be sure. Ever since February, 1945, important elements in the Japanese power-structure had been trying to arrange a surrender, but because of the strength of the militarist faction, it appeared that the surrender could not be *unconditional.*

On July 26, the Western leaders' declaration at Potsdam had, for the first time, allowed certain conditions in a Japanese surrender: Japan would not be destroyed as a nation, said the declaration. Japan could maintain industrial plants, except "those which would allow her to re-arm for war." Also, very im-portantly, occupying forces of the Allies were to be withdrawn as soon as the Allies' objectives in Japan had been achieved.

Once this declaration was announced, peacemakers in Japan began to make progress against the "Never surrender" doctrine of the militarists. Tragically, they were given few days' time before the atomic bombs fell. Would it not have been helpful to give Japan some idea of the sort of occupation which would be carried out? Admittedly, the statesmen may not have had time to think much about it, but certainly the occupation *as it did occur* would have been an attractive prospect to the Japanese nation in July, 1945. One has to conclude, therefore, that the bombs were dropped hastily. Steps which could have been taken to achieve Japanese surrender were omitted or given insufficient time to produce results.

Since World War II, the world has seen constant development of better and better atomic and hydrogen bombs by the United States and the Soviet Union; in recent years these two powers have been joined by Britain, France, and other nations as developers of atomic devices. Finally, in 1964, China became the first Afro-Asian nation to detonate an atomic explosion. By that time, however, the world had formed a long-lasting image of the great Western powers as *the* developers and users of atomic weapons. The impression left by Hiroshima and Nagasaki was reinforced by testing operations, particularly in cases where the tests claimed new victims. This occurred most dramatically in 1954 when the Japanese fishing ship, the *Fortunate Dragon*, was showered with fallout from American tests at Bikini, causing radiation sickness and the subsequent death of a crew member. It is understandable that the Japanese reacted adversely to this "third exposure" of their compatriots to atomic bombs.

In the Marshall Islands, where several such tests were carried on, the people of certain islands had to be transferred to other islands to escape radiation hazards, and this also caused complaints. World opinion viewed these procedures as falling short of optimum handling of a territory held in trust from the United Nations. Furthermore, people everywhere became aware that atomic testing by the U.S.A. and the U.S.S.R. was generating radioactive fallout throughout the Northern Hemisphere. Some of this radioactive material would persist for many years, and such material as strontium 90 would contaminate the milk consumed in most countries.

No one knows the full or exact damage being caused by the rising levels of radioactivity, either as a cause of cancer or a source of genetic damage—harmful changes in the hereditary characteristics of human beings. For leukemia alone, a conservative estimate was that the testing, 1945–1963, would be the cause of a thousand or more cases during the remainder of the twentieth century. That is very few cases as global populations go, but even those few might be hard to condone if they were unnecessary.

Annually, at Hiroshima, people from all countries have gathered to observe the anniversary of the first atomic bombing, and all around the world the testing escapades have been loudly denounced. Some of the criticism was, to be sure, self-serving propaganda; many critics, however, spoke sincerely, and addressed themselves to valid matters of hazard or injury.

When the U.S.A. and the U.S.S.R. reached an agreement in

1963 to cease atomic testing in the open air, an accord to which most other nations soon subscribed, world opinion was much relieved. But the Russians and Americans were still subject to criticism for taking 18 years, 1945–1963, to bring this testing to a halt. Were these powers erecting citadels of nuclear strength and knowhow which no Afro-Asian nation was supposed to challenge with open-air testing programs of its own?

:: VIII ::

The Totalitarian Régimes of
Twentieth Century Europe

THE LEGACY OF THE GREAT DICTATORSHIPS

THE WELL-KNOWN totalitarian governments produced by European man in modern times have been monumentally dreadful. The twentieth-century wars ruined the white man's record as keeper of the peace, but it was the dictatorships of Hitler and Stalin that detracted most grievously from the white nations' claim that freedom and justice flourished in their European homelands.

World War I had helped to create the régimes of Russian Communism, then Italian Fascism, and lastly German Nazism. Naturally these dictatorships borrowed much from the old governments of Czar and Kaiser, which had their own forms of intra-European empire-building and bureaucratic callousness. Each of these three postwar revolutionary governments stimulated the next, and each learned useful techniques from the earlier one—the one-party system, secret police, glorification of "The Leader," as well as the arts of totalitarian propaganda and persuasion.

The Communist, Fascist, and Nazi movements were related to one another in many ways. They were all partial heirs of socialism, they were messianic, and they declared that the higher ends they served justified use of any means. Each partook of the idea that it was the heir of ancient Rome. The notion of "Moscow the Third

Rome" had been built into Russian ideology since the fifteenth century. We have noted previously that Constantinople was understood to have been the Second Rome, and the fall of Byzantium to the Turks in 1453 supposedly left the Muscovite ruler as standard bearer of Orthodox Christendom. The historical record shows an unbroken succession of later Czars and Commissars who treated Moscow as the proper source of guidance for all men—or at least for all "true believers."

In Fascist Italy, Mussolini made no secret of his aspirations to recreate the glories of ancient Rome. In fact, his aggressive ventures in Spain, Southern France, North Africa, and the Eastern shores of the Adriatic were geographically consistent with the shape of the old empire. (Mussolini's Ethiopian conquest, admittedly, was not.) As for Hitler, his very phrase, "Third Reich," implied a succession to the *Holy Roman Empire* of the Hapsburgs.

Rather than discussing the many smaller-scale imitations of the great twentieth century tyrannies, let us consider chiefly Russia and Germany, while acknowledging that most European countries had similar governments during parts of the twentieth century. Moreover, Africa and Asia have had admirers of Hitler, and on those continents are still some reasonable facsimiles of the great dictators. In a sense, that may be a mitigation of the European record, but it is also an aggravation: Hitlerian or Stalinist methods are surely an evil legacy for Europe to bequeath to Afro-Asia.

The legacy includes wicked *acts* which have been imitated and misleading *doctrines* which have been borrowed. Barbara Ward is deeply concerned by the outmodedness and consequent unreality of Marxist dogmas as applied to late twentieth century affairs. She says, "It is a sobering thought that . . . men like Khrushchev and Chou En-lai may well be alienated from reality to a degree which would probably consign them, in private society, to a mental asylum."[1]

THE ROOTS OF TOTALITARIANISM IN RUSSIA

HOW WAS IT that Stalin's Russia made such a tremendous contribution to the development of totalitarianism? Russia's heritage included most of the predispositions to imperialism and authoritarian rule mentioned throughout this volume, including the messianic concept of Moscow as the Third Rome and the authoritarian influence of Muscovy's neighbors, the Byzantine and Mongol tyrants. Furthermore, Russia shared with that early agent of European expansion, Spain, a passion for spreading the Christian faith and a tendency to expand her power over a vast domain.

What of the basic psychological roots of the Russian drive for power? We recall that Carl Jung places the psychological problem of Western man "in the context of historically discordant symbols —the pre-Christian paganism, the Græco-Hebrew religiosity, the militant Protestant intensity," and that he finds in the resulting tension "a source of the inner turbulence that has come to the surface in recent years."[2]

The context just described is applicable to eastern as well as western Europe. Russia, too, had the pre-Christian paganism and Græco-Hebrew religiosity. Although Russia did not have precisely a "militant Protestant intensity," the conflict in seventeenth century Russia between the "Old Believers" and the dominant majority in the Orthodox Church shares most of the elements of Western Europe's Protestant-Catholic strife.

The chief difference between the two situations was that, in Russia, the innovators dominated the established church, so that the Old Believer members, in resisting liturgical changes, and so on, became the persecuted minority. The Orthodox majority partook more of the renaissance-type renewal of interest in original Greek texts of the New Testament, and a generally closer study and reasoned application of all scriptural texts.

From the Old Testament, the Russians drew the familiar identification of themselves with God's Chosen People, an idea closely associated with the "Third Rome" concept. It became ingrained in Russian thought and was a major determinant of attitudes in the nineteenth and twentieth centuries. The Chosen People, according to the Russian view, need not take the offensive; the heathen will bring disaster on themselves when they attack. The Russian Zion, the unique possessor of truth and righteousness, is bound to win in the end by virtue of its moral strength.

The War of 1812 was the culmination of a series of victories in defensive wars fought on Russian soil: Expulsion of the Mongols, ejection of the Polish invaders from Moscow in 1612, and defeat of the Swedes in the Ukraine in 1709. The important, military contribution of Russia to the defeat of Napoleon, and the appearance of her units as conquering, occupying forces in extensive areas of Germany and France made a profound impression on all concerned. The Russians' *amour-propre* was further encouraged by the key role played by Czar Alexander I in the councils of post-Napoleonic Europe. It was obvious that the Bourbon House, for one, owed much to the Emperor's firm defense of traditional authoritarian governments. Whenever a democratic upsurge threatened an established régime, Alexander worked through his "Holy Alliance" with Europe's other autocrats to crush that threat. His successor similarly came to the rescue of the Hapsburg Emperor in 1848, when the Hungarians tried to free themselves from their Austrian overlords.

Besides political interests, the Russians developed a racial motive for "being their brothers' keeper." Imitating the Germans' claim to be a super-race, the Czar's subjects began to believe that *Russians* were superior. Going a step further, they proclaimed the superiority of all Slavic peoples, of which the Russians were the mightiest.

The Russians had a strong brotherly interest in their fellow Slavs of the Balkans, who were in the process of freeing themselves from Turkish rule, and in those Slavic peoples living under Austrian rule. "Panslavism"—a powerful force in nineteenth and twentieth century Russia—was really a special form of nationalism and messianic expansionism which revealed a sacred duty to "liberate and protect" (actually to rule) fellow Slavs.

Along with expansionism, the Czars maintained their tradition of authoritarian government until 1917, so these traditions were, in effect, handed intact to the revolutionists of that year. The Empire had developed no strong middle class or any other group which could share, balance, or curb the power of the Government. The nobility, military officers, and officials of the Government were all members of the same in-group, a tightly knit establishment which *was* the Government of Russia.

The Revolutionists of 1917 tried to inaugurate a liberal or democratic form of government, and succeeded in removing from office those who had been ruling in Russia. However, the new Government was faced with acute dangers and immense tasks: A counter-revolutionary movement led to civil war and intervention by foreign powers. The armed forces of Britain, France, the United States, and Japan occupied numerous points in Russia, attempting to return the anti-Communists to power. This foreign intervention was not completely ended until 1925, when the Red régime could at last call all Russia its own. Meanwhile, a Russo-Polish War threatened the new Government for a time, and rivalries among several factions of Communists and Socialists kept the pot of crisis bubbling. If that were not enough to inhibit development of a free, democratic nation, there were critical economic emergencies. World War I had greatly impoverished Russia, and the Civil War added further to the sufferings of the people. Furthermore, the new rulers nationalized all industry and most of the agriculture and commerce, and all the attendant reorganization caused more shortages and stringencies. The Bolshevik leaders were determined to build new, larger industrial plants. To do so, they had to deprive their people of much-needed consumer goods; the entire Russian economy was for decades obliged to carry this burden of plant expansion, even though millions of citizens went hungry.

Joseph Stalin saw clearly that all these problems and tasks called for highly centralized, totalitarian rule using much the same bureaucratic mechanisms that had long been part of the Russian tradition. Accumulating power gradually, Stalin patiently collected the ultimate levers of appointive power for the Communist Party and Government. By the mid-1930's, he was in a position to silence all opposition and liquidate persons who challenged his policies, or who *might threaten* his position in the future.

Dostoevsky had warned an earlier generation of Russians that the "crystal palace of socialism" might in just this way become a regimented "anthill." In his novel *The Possessed* the revolutionary conspirator Shigalev finally admitted, "I lost myself in my own arguments. . . . Beginning with unlimited freedom, I end with unlimited despotism."

STALIN'S PURGES

THE GREAT PURGES carried out by Joseph Stalin from 1935 to 1938 are in themselves a monument in the history of modern Western totalitarianism. They are impressive in both numbers of victims and the fact that the victims included hundreds of the most highly placed men in Soviet leadership. The purges feature almost invariably procurement from the accused victims of abject, often fantastic confessions of their own guilt. The Stalin leadership had an obsession with wringing of admissions from prospective victims. Using both torture and other prolonged, more or less non-violent processes, interrogators of the Soviet Secret Police conditioned these victims in such a way that those appearing for public trial confessed fully and freely in open court. The substance of the confessions—often extending to admission of operations as a Japanese or German agent—was such that most rational persons would regard this evidence with skepticism. There were occasional breaks in the smooth-running juridical machinery, as when an accused would recant. When this happened, proceedings were suspended and the accused returned to further processing by the authorities. Before very long he would be back in court confessing his sins more systematically.

Conditioning the responses of helpless prisoners to make their behavior very different from what they would normally have intended has given birth to many properly horrible dramatic works or fictional pieces by Western writers, such as Koestler's *Darkness at Noon* and George Orwell's *1984*. To dispel any doubt as to the dreadful reality of these Purge processes, there came in 1956 Nikita

Khrushchev's exposé before the Central Committee of his Party, denouncing the tyrannies, tortures, and manifold abuses of the Stalin régime.

The assassination of Sergei Kirov, boss of the Leningrad Party machine, was probably arranged at the behest of Stalin himself, yet the assassination was officially treated by the Government as an act of terrorists. The Government moved against these "terrorists," arresting such top leaders as Zinoviev and Kamenev. At first these two topflight victims were given jail terms; later their cases received further processing, and they were executed. Other leading persons who perished in the Purges included Karl Radek, Alexei Rykov, Nikolai Bukharin, Henry Yagoda, and a host of others. It is curious to see how the organs of destruction directed by Stalin often sentenced these people to imprisonment, then became more confident and moved on to execute them.

Besides eminent Communist Party leaders, government officials, and industrial executives, an especially impressive number of Soviet army leaders were purged. According to one report which Merle Fainsod describes as "sober," three of the five marshals of the Soviet Union were purged, 13 of the 15 army commanders, 30 of the 58 corps commanders, and 110 of the 195 divisional commanders. Of the 406 regimental commanders, only 195 escaped arrest.[3] One special characteristic of the Stalin Purges remains to be noted: Several heads of the Secret Police itself became, one after another, victims of the very activity they had directed for Stalin. This was presumably part of the totalitarian leader's efforts to remove all his most capable, prospective competitors. Stalin also doubtless found it expedient to liquidate those at the top who knew the most about his foulest deeds. If we credit Khrushchev's 1956 charge that Stalin's inquisitors even tortured children in order to elicit confessions from their parents, such concealment would be only natural.

Khrushchev defended the Purge victims as follows:

Many party, Soviet and economic activists, who were branded in 1937–1938 as "enemies," were actually never enemies, spies, wreckers, etc., but were always honest Communists; they were only so stigmatized and, often no longer able to bear barbaric tortures, they

charged themselves with all kinds of grave and unlikely crimes. . . .
Of the 139 members and candidates of the party's Central Committee
who were elected [in 1934] 98 persons, i.e. seventy per cent, were
arrested and shot (mostly in 1937–1938).[4]

In addition to the millions who suffered arrest or more drastic
fates during the years of the Stalin Purges, the approach of war
between Stalin's Russia and Hitler's Reich brought special types
of repression. When Stalin and Hitler partitioned Poland, the
Russian Secret Police made wholesale arrests throughout the
Russian portion of Poland, arresting entire categories of people
whose class, social position, or intellectual standing supposedly
made them potential enemies of the Soviets. Most celebrated of these
"preventive" measures was the massacre of about 12,000 Polish
officers who fell into Russian hands. At Katyn, near Smolensk, these
hapless victims were shot to death en masse, after which the Soviet
Government attempted to persuade the world that the Nazis had
done the deed. The Nazis were fully capable of it, but virtually all
scholars agree that this was a Soviet program of execution. The
only extenuation is that Stalin and some of his top lieutenants
may have been unaware that the Secret Police actually murdered
all these prisoners; it is possible that misinterpretation of certain
remarks by Stalin caused the mass executions.

The purges of Poles were paralleled by similar programs in
Estonia, Latvia, Lithuania, and the other countries of Central and
Eastern Europe occupied by the U.S.S.R. In 1940 and 1941, Soviet
authorities deported 600,000 of the 5,500,000 total inhabitants of
Lithuania, Latvia, and Estonia. After World War II, having dislodged German occupiers from these lands, the Russians deported
about 200,000 more. An uncertain but large number of these persons remained in permanent banishment or in penal servitude in
Siberia, where many perished.[5]

Concerning Hungary, a Polish statesman once mentioned the
"Hungarian problem" to Stalin. Marshal Stalin said that Hungary
was not really a problem, just a matter of assembling enough trucks
to haul away all Hungarians who failed to fit in well with his
régime there.

The Stalin repressions set a record in Europe for systematic inhumanity which was surpassed only by the genocidal Nazis. Premier Khrushchev's indictment of Stalin concluded that the dictator had done his horrid deeds in the sincere belief that he was acting in the best interests of the Russian people. In this, said Khrushchev, lay the greatest tragedy of all. Perhaps Dostoevsky, anticipating the evils of totalitarianism far in advance, described the danger best in his religious terms: "Conscience without God becomes monstrous, and can lead man to the greatest crimes."

ANTI-SEMITISM IN THE U.S.S.R.

I WOULD LIKE to give special attention to Soviet anti-Semitism and other racism in the U.S.S.R., because this helps demonstrate the resemblance of Stalinists to Nazis, and serves once against to show the close relation of racism to totalitarianism. Persecutions of Jews, like other totalitarian practices in modern Europe, are events *within* the white community; even so, they are meaningful in the present context as blotches on the white record, and burdens on the white conscience.

Anti-Semitism had a long history in Russia, as in most European countries. This hatred became increasingly virulent during the reigns of the last two czars, taking the form of bloody pogroms —mob actions against Jews—in several Russian cities. Governmental regulations implemented the prejudice by restricting travel, limiting areas where Jews might live, and so on.

The Soviet Russian Government claimed fervently that anti-Semitism and all other racial prejudice would be stamped out, being incompatible with the new Communist order. The Soviet Union established the Birobidjan Jewish Autonomous Region, a dreary, unattractive area in Eastern Siberia. This step toward Jewish autonomy was a very incomplete measure; it received only a small fraction of Russia's Jewish population. Unfortunately, despite all the benevolent talk and plans for autonomy, it was soon obvious that virulent anti-Semitism was coexisting with Russian Communism. Indeed, it was being aggravated by acts of government officials.

The mid-1920's brought a strong wave of anti-Semitism in Russia. Authorities chose to say that peasants and other persons with rural backgrounds were chiefly responsible for this harassment and denunciation of Jews. However, even official reports contained acknowledgments that the racists included many Party members, Communist Youth cadres, trade unionists, and officials. The Soviet officials could outdo their Czarist predecessors in harassment of Jews, because this totalitarian Government controlled virtually all jobs and buildings. Thus the victim of racism had almost nowhere to turn. The highest officials in the early years of the Soviet Government tried to fight anti-Semitism, but widespread local approval of the racists made it hard to substantiate a victim's complaint—if he dared submit a complaint at all.

During the Great Purges there was also some degree of anti-Semitism. Many of the leading victims were Jewish, and the Stalin leadership subtly called this to the attention of the public by coupling the better-known assumed names of such "wicked" figures with their original Jewish names, e.g., "Trotsky (Bronstein)."

Even when much of Russia suffered Nazi occupation after the invasion of 1941, guerrilla untis seldom admitted Jews to their ranks, nor did they, or the local peasants, show much interest in saving Jewish refugees. Solomon Schwartz concludes from his study of numerous war documents that "Most partisan units were either blatantly or covertly antisemitic."[6]

The Jewish population of the U.S.S.R. was 3,100,000 in January, 1939. The Soviet annexations of 1939–1940, when the Nazis and Communists divided the spoils of Eastern Europe, added to the Jewish minority, bringing it up to about 5,000,000. By the end of World War II, scarcely more than 1,800,000 of these five million survived. Accordingly, some reduction in the portion of official posts held by Jews might have been natural. Indeed, by 1950 Jews were very scarce in both chambers of the Supreme Soviet, amounting to four-tenths of 1 per cent—compared with 4.1 per cent in 1937.[7]

After World War II, Jews in the Soviet Union were subjected to considerable discrimination in such matters as university admissions and practice of certain professions. Jewish participation in intellectual and scientific pursuits continued, however. Top Party posts seem no longer to have been occupied by Jewish persons, with the exception of Lazar Kaganovich.

Establishment of the independent nation of Israel appears to have contributed in a sense to Russian anti-Semitism. Since there now existed a separate nation to which Soviet Jews supposedly attached their loyalty or part of their loyalty, allegations of disloyalty against Russian Jews became easier. By 1952 the persecutions went so far that most outstanding Jewish cultural leaders were executed, and deportation of Jews en masse was possibly in the works.

Of particular interest was the Government's handling of the "doctors' plot" in 1952–1953. The Soviet press announced that a group of terrorist doctors had been discovered, and that these villains had confessed the murder of Andrei Zhdanov. The doctors were also supposed to have plotted to injure or murder some leading generals. Among these nine distinguished medical men were seven Jews. Allegedly, the accused had been agents of American intelligence, having made contact with it through a Jewish philanthropic organization. Inevitably, the Jews confessed to all this, but after Stalin's death the press announced the release of these doctors, conceding that their confessions had been obtained by torture. The abuse of the men under arrest must have been drastic, because when they were finally declared innocent, two were already dead.[8]

After Stalin's death, most Soviet citizens were able to enjoy the cessation of drastic police-state operations. Even the Jews of Russia were relieved of the threat that a massive campaign against them was imminent. It soon became clear, however, that Khrushchev, like Stalin, viewed his Jews as prone to disloyalty. He acknowledged this in an interview with a Canadian Communist delegation. Khrushchev also admonished the Central Committee of the Polish Communist Party that the leading ranks of that Party contained "too many Abramoviches," a condition unnecessarily offensive to Polish public opinion. In 1958 he told a French journalist that Jews "do not like collective work [or] group discipline. They are individualists . . . and end up by having profoundly different opinions."⁹

The newspaper *Minskaya Pravda* is published in the Byelorussian Soviet Socialist Republic, where many of Russia's Jews live. In 1961 it denounced Jews, both collectively and by individual names, carping at the "tricky and dishonest" means by which synagogue leaders gather funds. The paper treated even contributions from visiting foreign Jews and kosher slaughtering fees as instances of shady practices, and implied that synagogue "ruffians" dishonestly kept for themselves part of the money contributed by gullible congregations.¹⁰

A decade after Stalin's death it appeared that Jewish persecutions were not abating, but instead were gaining momentum in the U.S.S.R. Some patterns could be seen; there were at least 102 Jews among the 198 persons executed in the U.S.S.R. for "economic crimes" during the period 1961–1964. In April, 1964, a conference convened in Washington, D.C., by 24 major Jewish organizations attempted to get world opinion alerted to these persecutions. United States Senator Abraham Ribicoff told the conference that "all of us in the West—Jews and gentiles alike—owe a debt of shame" for our failure to do more to save Hitler's Jewish victims. "We owe it to the dead to save the living now," said Ribicoff.

In response to such interest within foreign countries, the Soviet Government has made occasional concessions. A *Pravda* editorial which was widely reprinted in regional newspapers of the U.S.S.R. in September, 1965, indicated that the top leaders were fighting anti-Semitism. This editorial quoted Lenin's call for "tireless struggle" against anti-Semitism. *Pravda*'s readers were reminded that newly developing nations look to relations among Russia's peoples as a "model" of relations among diverse ethnic groups.

At other times, persecutions seem to be renewed. On February 2, 1965, for example, the newspaper *Zviaza*, in the capital of the Byelorussian Soviet Republic, published a long denunciation of Judaism as "the enemy of human culture." *Zviaza* said that Judaism was not just an accumulation of harmful prejudices, but actually "a form of culture; not dead superstition, but living words."

No one can say what the future course of Russian anti-Semitism will be, but the record thus far has been enough to reinforce the suspicions of Afro-Asians that the Soviet Government is not the consistent opponent of racial discrimination it has so often claimed to be.

OTHER SOVIET-STYLE RACISM

THE GOVERNMENT of the Soviet Union inherited from the Czars' Empire a well-established tradition of harsh treatment for Asian minority groups. This tradition was maintained even during World War I, when the Imperial Government was tottering to its fall.

There had been a great many grievances and episodes of violence during Imperial Russia's rule of her Central Asian provinces. These grievances also applied to the provinces of the Caucasus, where large non-Russian populations lived. One of the most notable occurrences was an epidemic of unrest in 1916, when Russian Central Asia was deeply disturbed by the draft of its citizenry for laboring tasks. This program, occasioned by Russian participation in the war in Europe, was neither understood nor approved by the local inhabitants, who rioted extensively and began to speak of independence. The worst of the numerous disorders and fights occurred in the region around Dzhizak, where a thousand or more natives were killed in skirmishes and many others were executed.

The resistance lasted four months and was bitter for several reasons: The Kazakh and Kirghiz people did not want Russian overlordship at all; much less would they tolerate a manpower draft, especially when it began at harvest time. As many as 150,000 may have perished in the skirmishes, in the Russian Army's bloody repressions, and from privations engendered by the conflict.[11]

The measures taken by Russian authorities also included decrees prohibiting public gatherings and requiring all natives to bow to any Russian officer or official they met. (These same rules were applied by the British in India during the Amritsar episode of 1919.) Native hostages were taken, and natives forbidden use of post, telegraph, and railroad facilities unless the Russian Commandant of the area authorized it.

Aside from the rough estimates of casualty figures above, we have data on reductions in the population of Russian Turkestan which show in a general way how grave the conflicts were. A Soviet demographer estimated that this population declined by 1,230,000 persons, or 17 per cent, between 1914 and 1917, largely as a result, he thinks, of the events of 1916. Other sources simply try to measure the number who fled to China, and estimate that 300,000 natives did so.[12]

In 1903, the Communist Prophet Lenin had espoused the principle of self-determination for non-Russian national groups within the Czar's Empire. Although for some time Lenin was not agreeable to the secession and independence of such groups, he did admit even of this in 1913. However, when the Bolsheviks' assumption of power presented Lenin with the job of keeping his nation together, he managed, with twisted logic, to endorse self-determination of peoples while rejecting separatist efforts by non-Russian minorities. He negated his acknowledgment of a nation's right to self-determination by saying that the authorities must rule on the *expediency* of the self-determination in each case.[13]

In the period 1918–1921, the new Soviet Government crushed separatist movements in its Caucasian and Central Asian territories. Everywhere there were arrests, executions, and stern repressive measures. However, it is really not possible to distinguish repressions on an ethnic basis during those years from the nationwide effort to wipe out anti-Bolshevik movements. Frequently we cannot tell whether the unrest was anti-Bolshevik or a matter of nationalism among the non-Russian populations.

Because the early Soviet régime faced horrendous problems and extensive opposition, both at home and abroad, its early dealings with the peoples of Soviet Central Asia were often mild as a matter of expediency—so long as the inhabitants were docile and loyal. For some time the Moslem faith, institutions, and customs were left virtually undisturbed. Moslem scriptures continued to be standard in the schools of Central Asia, and the Moslem way of life, including such things as seclusion and veiling of women, continued as before. Even Moslém ecclesiastical courts kept on handing out their accustomed decisions and penalties. Finally, in 1927, the Soviet régime felt strong enough to make some efforts to free the women of Central Asia from the limitations of the Moslem mode of life. Women were encouraged to put the veil aside and participate in public life in the same manner as men. The purchase of wives was declared illegal. However, in the early 1930's Soviet efforts in this direction had borne very little fruit. Women who attempted to disregard the time-honored customs were likely to be ostracized and disciplined within the family, or even condemned before a Moslem ecclesiastical court to death by stoning.

In the early 1930's, Hans Kohn investigated conditions in Soviet Central Asia and seems to have concurred with Stalin's report of 1930 that nationalism in the region was growing. (Stalin also said that *Pan-Russian* chauvinism was increasing.) Kohn found that the Pan-Turk and Pan-Islamic movements were gaining strength, and that there was a strong urge toward independence. He noted that Soviet authorities were "kept busy by a series of armed risings in Central Asia."

Lenin had made a number of candid and illuminating remarks concerning the need for careful handling of Asian minorities in his speech to the Eighth Congress of the Russian Communist Party in 1919. Lenin said that the Bashkirs distrusted the Russians because the Russians "used their civilization to rob the Bashkirs. Consequently in these remote districts the name Russian means oppressor to the Bashkirs. . . . Above all such a nation as the Russians, who have excited a wild hatred in all other nations, must be particularly cautious." Lenin went on to denounce "Pan-Russian chauvinists," who would limit education to Russian language and Russian culture alone. Lenin acknowledged, "This tendency still exists in many of us, and we must wrestle with it."[14]

In the early Soviet Government, Joseph Stalin was Commissar of Nationalities. A Georgian himself, he was bound to take a special interest in the non-Russian peoples of the U.S.S.R.—but it was not a kindly, forbearing interest. Lenin himself felt that Stalin's methods for stamping out dissidents in Georgia were excessively brutal.

Nevertheless, we should concede that Stalin, even as dictator, maintained the political and administrative identity of the Soviet Union's many non-Russian republics and regions. He also allowed cultural autonomy to most of his Asian subjects, including governmental encouragement of the respective local languages, literature, and indigenous arts. Of course, there are sizable groups of ethnic Russians living in the Asian republics and various autonomous regions of the U.S.S.R. Separate schools are maintained for their children so that they may pursue their studies in the Russian language. At any rate, that is the reason given in the Soviet Union, and it may be valid. However, such visitors to Russia as U.S. Supreme Court Justice Douglas have wondered if this was not essentially a system of segregated and not entirely equal schools.

It has also been suggested that the Soviet régime was not just bestowing regional autonomy when it created five separate Central Asian Republics—the Kazakh, Uzbek, Tadzhik, Kirghiz, and Turkmen S.S.R.'s. This fivefold division served to drive administrative wedges between peoples who were ethnically similar to one another, had a common Moslem religious and cultural heritage, and who, except for the Tadzhiks, really spoke the same native language. The boundaries of one such republic do not and could not include, for example, "Kirghiz only." In 1956 the population of the Kirghiz S.S.R. was 11 per cent Uzbek, the Tadzhik S.S.R. was 18 per cent Uzbek, and the Turkmen S.S.R. was 10 per cent Uzbek.[15]

Another problem which lurks behind the façade of autonomy is the common subordination of non-Russian administrators to "men from Moscow." Local comrades who acquire a good education and are given high public office in the republics and autonomous regions often find themselves treated as puppets. Decision-making is reserved to men from European Russia. If the local men complain, they are frequently charged with "bourgeois-nationalist deviationism," losing their offices and even incurring drastic punishment. Merle Fainsod calls this a "counterpart to the difficulties encountered by Western imperial powers in dealing with the native intelligentsia in their colonies."[16]

As for Stalin himself, Georgian though he was, his integration into the Bolshevik movement and subsequent high position in the Russian Government seem to have made him a thoroughgoing Russian nationalist. He had a clear disdain for the Asian people of the U.S.S.R., as we see in his remark, "There are so few intellectuals, so few thinking people, even so few literate people generally in the Eastern republics and regions that one can count them on one's fingers." Stalin also deplored the nationalism of the minority races of Russia, saying that "under cover of nationalism various kinds of bourgeois, including Menshevik, influences penetrate into our organizations in the border regions."[17] In 1934, Stalin charged that "The deviation towards nationalism reflects the attempts of 'one's own national' bourgeoisie to undermine the Soviet system and to restore capitalism."[18]

The people of the Kazakh Republic had the most extensive farming and animal husbandry enterprises in all of Russian Central Asia, so they incurred the most noticeable economic regimentation. In Kazakhstan the Bolshevik planners added to the long-standing burdens of a stern overlordship the new strain of collectivization —that is, abolition of private ownership of farms and herds. Between 100,000 and 200,000 Kazakhs fled into China at the end of the 1920's.

In the years 1935–1938, when the Stalin Purges brought death and imprisonment to so many Russians, we suspect that some of the purgees in Central Asia were actually non-Russian men desirous of real autonomy or freedom for their region. Certainly those charged with "bourgeois nationalism" fall into this category.

In the Soviet Census of 1939, the Kazakh population was 21.9 per cent less than it had been in 1926. The population of the U.S.S.R. as a whole grew by 15.9 per cent during this period, despite major famines in Southern Russia. Thus there was an aggregate loss of one-third of the population—really a matter of genocide.[19]

The Stalin Purges in the Caucasus area—chiefly the Armenian, Azerbaijanian and Georgian Republics—were directed especially toward officials and intelligentsia, and in that sense were not ethnic in their antagonism. But if we accept the estimate of 422,000 carried off to Siberia or shot out of a population of 11,000,000,[20] we have a proportionately far heavier toll than the Purges exacted in European Russia.

Beyond the borders of the U.S.S.R., control of China's mineral-rich northwestern province of Sinkiang became an aim of the men in the Kremlin, just as it had attracted the Czars' Government. It was not until 1932 that Russia could reassert control of this region. The U.S.S.R. gained influence by assisting the Chinese Governor in suppressing renewed revolts by the Uighur inhabitants. Soviet advisers and military personnel virtually dominated Sinkiang, while the Russians developed and controlled many mines, oil wells, and other industries. Finally, when the Nazi invasion left Russia no strength, the Chinese reasserted their control and expelled the Russian personnel.

Farther east in Siberia, in the border lands where Russian territory met Japanese-controlled Manchuria, there was occasional intensive border fighting between Russian and Japanese forces from 1936 to 1939. This also meant grief for Asian minorities in the area. Soviet authorities organized wholesale deportations of the Koreans who lived in the U.S.S.R. near the Manchurian and Korean borders. These people were relocated in the Uzbek Republic, far away in Soviet Central Asia.

When, at the end of World War II, the hordes of Adolf Hitler were finally obliged to retreat from Eastern Europe, Soviet authorities indulged in further repressions which take on something of a racist character, in that many, though not all, of the victims were members of distinct, small, non-Russian minorities. These minority groups had allegedly collaborated with the Nazi occupation forces. Perhaps some of them had collaborated, as had numerous Russians. At any rate, the political entities known as the Kalmyk and Chechen-Ingush Republics, and the Autonomous Republic of Kabards and Bolkars, all ceased to exist, and many of their inhabitants were executed or imprisoned. Soviet police boss Ivan Serov was famous for his massive liquidations of the Tartars of the Crimea, who had allegedly collaborated with the Nazis.

Such persecutions of a racist complexion were doubtless facilitated, as is racism in its worst forms anywhere, by the easy identifiability of minority-group victims. Their non-Russian appearance, distinctive geographic grouping, and unusual personal names made it tragically easy to liquidate almost all of them.

Moscow's approach to the problems of Negroes in the United States and the Union of South Africa gives us some further clarification of the Russian record in race relations. Recurrently from 1928 to 1941, and again after World War II, the authorities in Moscow required the Communist Party in the United States to espouse a "Black Republic" or "Southern Negro Autonomy" program. Apparently the Russians believed that the American Negroes could be grouped together geographically, like Russia's own ethnic minorities. Some of the latter are so concentrated in geographic areas that "autonomous governments" are feasible, a condition less prevalent in the United States. The Russian comrades also chose to overlook the Negro consensus, which opposed such programs. With great persistence, Party leadership has allotted to this scheme as much as half of the propaganda directed to American Negroes.

Such suggestions for geographic separation of racial groups bear a strong resemblance to plans entertained by the Black Moslems in the United States in recent years, with the endorsement of the American Nazi Party. Also similar were projects of some Southern white leaders in the nineteenth century to resettle American Negroes on various islands of the West Indies, or in Africa.

Not only did Communist leadership in Moscow require the American Communist Party to espouse the "Black Republic" plan in the 1920's; the same approach was required of South African Communists. The "Black Republic" tactic was a blunder; in South Africa, as in America, it interfered with cooperation between white and Negro Communists or potential Communists. In general, the tactic weakened the forces which might have opposed discrimination and segregation.

Another indication of the shortcomings of Stalin's type of Communism in interracial relationships comes from a Negro former Communist, who characterized the American Party of the 1930's as "dominated by foreignborn elements [who] had the mistaken idea that colored people . . . needed somebody to take care of them.

Running through their whole attitude was an offensive paternalism."[21]

Right in the thick of this conflict between Moscow's ideals and practices was a well-known Negro organizer for the Communist International, George Padmore. Comrade Padmore originally came from Trinidad, British West Indies, but gained his interracial experience from an amazing variety of sources. He encountered racism within British possessions and in the United States, where he lived and received a goodly part of his education. Padmore also seems to have gained inspiration from the Chinese Revolution of 1911. He was particularly influenced by one Eugene Chen, who had been born in Trinidad of Chinese-Negro parentage and returned to China to become an official in Sun Yat-sen's revolutionary government.

The Russian Communists recruited Padmore, who worked for them in Moscow and South Africa trying to organize Negroes in Moscow's behalf. When in the 1930's Russia found it expedient to conciliate Britain and France in the face of the Nazi German menace, Moscow ceased to consider any racial grievances which might detract from Anglo-Franco-Russian cordiality. Padmore concluded that the Red Government had been interested in Negroes only as a means of building its worldwide influence, but when he objected to this cavalier treatment of the Negro revolutionaries he was labelled a "black nationalist" by the Moscow leadership. He managed to leave Russia and actually tried to operate from Berlin, no longer as a Communist, of course. However, the Nazis didn't care for his anti-racist operations, so he was jailed and deported to England.[22]

During the Italo-Ethiopian War, the Communist apparatus tried to reinforce its appeal to American Negroes by claiming that the U.S.S.R. was Ethiopia's best friend, but recurrently in 1935 and 1936 *The New York Times* reported that Russia was continuing its shipments of supplies to Italy, including war material. This tended to show up the Communists' pro-Negro line as mere opportunism. Later, after World War II began, Soviet opportunism was revealed again, in that the Communists strongly supported Negro rights movements until Russia was attacked by Nazi

Germany in 1941. After that, and particularly after America entered the fray later that year, the Red line was "Win the war; cease agitation for Negro rights."[23]

The Communist Party in the United States often had occasion, through the years, to discipline Party members for "white chauvinism," but on several occasions in 1947 the *Daily Worker* disregarded this position, and actually complained that the jury for the trial of top U.S. Communist Gerhart Eisler was composed of seven Negroes and only five whites. Similarly, it complained that the jury hearing the Marzani-State Department case included nine Negroes.[24]

To conclude this analysis of Russian totalitarianism and racism, one can only say that its crimes have been immense, and the gap between ideals and practice in Russia has been wide. In one way, however, the Soviet record has been far better than that of Nazi Germany: The Nazis solemnly believed that their wretched practices were right; the U.S.S.R. has always proclaimed the evils of racism and exploitation of human beings.

NAZIS AND FASCISTS

THE ORIGINS of Nazi totalitarianism and racism have already been partially explained. It should suffice here to recapitulate the factors which helped make Nazism what it was. Many are the same elements that led to Stalinism in Russia, or are directly comparable to the latter. The list includes nationalism—the overweening nationalism so characteristic of modern Europe; the racist pride and expansionism which we call Pan-Germanism, but which the Russians adopted with minor changes as Pan-Slavism; and neo-paganism—exaltation of the alleged old Germanic heritage of war-lust, myths, and deities. Then there were a multitude of grievances: Resentment against the rich, anti-intellectualism, impoverishment of the middle class, and sufferings or injustices brought about by World War I.

As a remedy for all these troubles, the Germans followed the typical prescriptions of nineteenth century Europe: The national government must rectify all the injustices, and in doing so could expect the unquestioning support of the individual citizen. In fact, Germans had become so disturbed by their grievances that the wild oratory of a Hitler could draw forth their fullest enthusiasm; whatever the Leader ordered would be done.

Italian dictator Benito Mussolini, explaining his "Fascist conception of history," expressed this recession of individualism in more philosophical terms when he said: "Outside history man is a nonentity. Fascism is therefore opposed to all individualistic abstractions based on eighteenth century materialism. . . . Anti-individualistic, the Fascist conception of life stresses the importance of the State and accepts the individual only in so far as his interests coincide with those of the State."[25]

Along with their emotional and authoritarian appeal, the Nazis were careful to offer genuine rectifications of many grievances; they fostered full employment, and undertook to give the worker a better deal—not just income, but pride as well. Hitler's Party had as its complete title "National Socialist German Workers' Party"; the Nazis were borrowing from Marx, as well as from Hegel, Nietzsche, and Wagner.

Hitler himself acknowledged his debt to Marxism in discussions reported by Hermann Rauschning. He had learned a lot from the Marxists' methods. The whole of National Socialism was based on Marxism, said Hitler: "National Socialism is what Marxism might have been if it could have broken its absurd and artificial ties with a democratic order. . . . I am not only the conqueror, but also the executor of Marxism—of that part of it that is essential and justified." Hitler did not consider that his Government need take formal title to banks and factories. Ownership is not the vital thing, he said: "We socialize human beings." Hitler's feeling of kinship with Communism also appears in the following words: "There is more that binds us to Bolshevism than separates us from it. There is, above all, genuine revolutionary feeling. . . . I have always made allowance for this circumstance and given orders that former communists are to be admitted to the party at once. The petit-bourgeois Social Democrat and the trade-union boss will never make a National Socialist, but the Communist always will."[26]

The Bolsheviks and Nazis possessed some common orientations which were more apparent *before* Hitler came to power and *after* the Nazi defeat than they were during the heyday of Hitlerian power. The early Nazi party had its Strasser wing, a faction Hitler liquidated in 1934, which strongly emphasized the "Socialist" part of the Nazi Party's title. It was anti-capitalist, and seems to have contemplated thoroughgoing confiscation of capitalist property. Peter Viereck points out that Hitler's prime collaborators, Goebbels and Himmler, were originally Gregor Strasser's private secretaries, and their original orientation was toward his faction, not precisely toward Hitler. Viereck appears to suspect that these two men, who were especially prominent in the last days of the Third Reich, might have reverted to their early factional type if the Nazi debacle had not stopped them.

The theory of common ground between Nazis and Communists also derives some confirmation from the behavior of the East German Government, set up under Russian Communist tutelage after World War II. This régime, and its Socialist Unity Party, have remained under a substantial measure of Russian influence. Even so, the puppet Government has gone out of its way to welcome former Nazis and SS officers into its fold, and to install ex-Nazis of considerable standing in important East German jobs. For example, Leo Lange, a former Gestapo official, was put in charge of East German radio and press activities, while SS Obersturmführer Adelbert Baumler became head of Russian political counterintelligence for West Germany. (Similiarly, the Red Hungarian Government staffed its Secret Police with many men who had previously served the pro-Nazi Government in comparable jobs.) The 1960 report of the International Committee of Free Jurists listed 75 Nazi criminals in high office in East Germany. Of these, a significant figure for our present argument was Kurt Lange, an East German Secret Police official who had in 1944 personally conducted the interrogation and torture of anti-Hitler revolt plotters. Lange's victims of 1944 were precisely the men most inclined to resist *left-wing* Nazism—or Communism.[27]

By the 1960's, both East and West Germany had elevated ex-

Nazis to be their heads of government—Willi Stoph and Kurt Kiesinger, respectively. Both were supposedly nice Nazis or reformed Nazis of the *past only.*

Hitler's antipathy to capitalists and industrialists was recognized by the Nuremberg Tribunal in connection with the prosecution of certain I. G. Farben Corporation executives. The defendants claimed they had been very much on the defensive against Nazi leadership, and the Tribunal concluded that "there was credible evidence that Hitler would have welcomed the opportunity to make an example of a Farben leader."[28]

We should not conclude that Hitler's Germany and Stalin's Russia were just alike, but rather that Europe's dictatorships could be sized up by observers outside Europe as being part of an over-all authoritarian trend in the West. Thus from Asia Nehru could say that the best parallel to the absolute rule of the British Administration in India was the Hitler régime.[29]

At the end of World War II, the victorious powers held numerous war crimes trials in a history-making attempt to prosecute the vanquished leaders in a systematic, legal manner. It was hoped that the wrongful practices of these leaders would be clearly labelled as criminal, constituting a warning for future offenders and erecting some sort of legal precedent for such international prosecutions. Best known of the trials were the prosecutions of top Nazi leaders before the International Military Tribunal at Nuremberg. These defendants were charged with crimes against the peace, war crimes, and crimes against humanity. The trials of the 22 accused leaders were consummately thorough, requiring almost one year; records of trial covered 17,000 pages. Nineteen of the accused were convicted, and 11 were sentenced to death.

The voluminous records of these trials provide a far more complete record than is available for the many other offenses of Western nations discussed in this book. This, and the unprecedented nature of most of the crimes, makes it worthwhile to summarize the offenses here.

The planning and waging of aggressive war requires no discussion here. Serious though it is, the offense is not at all new. Nor will we discuss charges of conducting cruel air raids against helpless civilians. All of the planners of the Nuremberg trials avoided specifying, among the offenses charged, infliction of deaths through air raids carried on by the Germans against non-military targets.

Prosecution of German airmen on such counts had been planned in 1918, as the zeppelin raids on London in World War I were considered highly uncivilized. Even then the idea of such prosecution was dropped. Records of the 1945 Conference in London, which worked out the Nuremberg trial plans, omit all indications that the air raid issue was discussed. However, Justice Jackson acknowledged, many years later, that the issue had been taken up and shelved because the Germans' opponents had themselves committed extensive acts of this sort.[30]

Genocide is the grave and uniquely modern charge that received the most attention in the Nuremberg proceedings. Extensive and varied programs were carried out by Nazi administrators with the common aim of literally "depopulating" vast regions of Europe, supposedly strengthening Germany by making the depopulated regions available for further German settlement and development. Depopulation had many aspects: About 5,700,000 Jews (more than half the Jews of Europe) were the best-known murder victims; such Eastern European nationalities as Poles and Russians constituted another large group; prisoners of war and hostages, as well as aged, infirm, and insane persons, also became the victims of depopulation.

The Nuremburg trial produced massive evidence of all these targets of inhuman treatment and massacre. The methods of liquidation varied, of course. Least violent, but deadly, was the method proposed in a Nazi document of May, 1941, entitled "Economic-political directives for economic organization East, agricultural group," which dealt with allocation of foodstuffs within Eastern Europe. The recommendation was that in areas of the occupied Soviet Union where food surpluses were generated, such foodstuffs must be tatken to Germany. The document conceded frankly that the result would be to starve the populations of important industrial centers of Russia. The conclusion of this document was simply, "many tens of millions of people in these areas are superfluous and will die or have to emigrate to Siberia."

The above approach to the handling of helpless populations is in effect what was often done with superfluous prisoners of war as well. The Nazis contemplated with equanimity the possible death of most of their 3,600,000 Russian P.O.W.s' Leading Nazi Alfred Rosenberg told Marshal Keitel in 1942 that only a few hundred thousand of these P.O.W.s were still strong enough to do useful work. Many did indeed die because little or no food and shelter was provided for them.

A more positive form of violence was inflicted upon *hostages*. These were most often persons in German-occupied countries who were not even allegedly guilty of a crime. They were shot simply because partisans or resistance agents had attacked German personnel or damaged German property. Often the Nazis applied a ratio of 50 executions of hostages for one German death. The Germans shot 29,660 hostages in France alone.

Still another monumental form of Nazi brutality may be found in the annals of Nazi slave labor programs. The Reich's plenopotentiary general for the allocation of labor, Fritz Saukel, was found guilty at Nuremberg of being principal architect of "a program which involved the deportation of more than five million people for the purpose of forced labor, which subjected many of them to terrible cruelty and suffering." The evidence showed that Sauckel declared openly on March 1, 1944, that "of the five million foreign workers who have come to Germany, less than 200,000 have come voluntarily."[31]

The International Military Tribunal indictment charged that in Eastern Europe:

> The Nazi conspirators mercilessly killed even children. They killed them with their parents, in groups, and alone. They killed them in children's homes and hospitals, burying the living in the graves, throwing them into flames, stabbing them with bayonets, poisoning them, conducting experiments upon them, extracting their blood for the use of the German Army, throwing them into prison and Gestapo torture chambers and concentration camps, where the children died from hunger, torture, and epidemic diseases.[32]

In all the sad history of imperialism, racism and totalitarianism in modern times, the most eminent monument of all may be the

Hitlerian effort to exterminate the Jews of Europe. This campaign embraced some important aspects of all three of the categories of Western abuses we are discussing in this book. It was a gigantic exploit of totalitarian bureaucracy, a racist exploit of great magnitude, and at the same time the product of the same rampant European nationalism and expansion which had produced imperialism.

This anti-Semitic exploit was also of unprecedented magnitude in the history of human violence and brutality. As Raul Hilberg wrote in 1960, in his preface to *The Destruction of the European Jews*, such unprecedented occurrences "are accepted academically only when they are studied as tests of existing conceptions about force, about relations between cultures, about society as a whole." Hilberg feels that the immensity and horror of this destruction has interfered with its absorption by the Western mind, preventing its full recognition as an historical fact. It is the very extremeness of the Hitlerian anti-Semitic campaign which necessitates special effort to study it.

Extermination of the Jews had been pondered by many Nazis for a long time, but it appears that the beginning of definitive action came with the Wannsee Conference on January 20, 1942. This conference, convened and presided over by the infamous Reinhard Heydrich, was attended by a large number of senior Nazi officials, and it reached the conclusion that the emigration or banishment of Europe's Jewish population to such a place as Madagascar was no longer to be pursued. Instead, the Jews were to be evacuated to the East. The conferees considered the fate of 11 million Jews all told, including even one-third of a million Jews in England, then certainly not immediately available for murder by the Nazis. The verdict of the conference appears in its most ominous form in the concluding words: "valuable experience has already been gained, and will be of considerable importance in view of the imminent final solution of the Jewish problem."

Even these leading Nazis seemed to have recoiled from overt mention of extermination as such. Certainly they did not recoil from carrying it out, but they preferred, even in official documents, roundabout descriptions of the extermination program. The term "final solution" was a subject of much argument between prosecutors and defense counsels at Nuremberg; undoubtedly, however, it did indeed mean "extermination."

Heydrich instructed the conferees that Jews were to be taken to the East and subjected to forced labor, from which a large proportion would die. Again shrinking from the use of honest words, Heydrich told his officials that the survivors of the labor program, "since they undoubtedly represent the most resilient ones, must be handled accordingly." What "accordingly" meant became clear within two months after this fateful conference when in March, 1942, the gas chambers and the killers of the mobile murder groups began their work.[33]

Later, when some Nazi quarters were ready to release a portion of their Jewish victims to the Allies in exchange for war material, the Allies themselves found such a proposal inexpedient. The State Department considered the plan objectionable in many respects, and the British Foreign Office consistently opposed all plans to rescue large numbers of Jews from Eastern Europe. The objection most often cited was that there were not enough ships or other means of transportation available to get hundreds of thousands of people out of Eastern Europe.

In May, 1944, Nazi official Adolf Eichmann contacted the Jewish negotiator, Brand, to offer liberation of one million Jews in return for 10,000 new trucks. There ensued frustrating efforts at negotiation by officials of the Jewish Agency. British and American leaders were at this time either unwilling to be contacted or difficult to contact. Brand relates that during his detention in Cairo he met a man who may have been Lord Moyne, the ranking British official there, and that this gentleman said to him, regarding the offer to free a million Jews, "But Mr. Brand, what shall I do with those million Jews? Where shall I put them?"[34] This being the attitude of the Western Allies, even the ransoming of the Jews was not to be. Anti-Semitism came to the grimmest possible end of its road, and undertook complete annihilation of its victims —a step which, a generation before, would have appeared impossible.

The early Nazi handling of Jews had resembled the discrimination, riots, and other sporadic anti-Jewish actions which had so long been found in most European countries. As Nazi anti-Semitism matured, however, it exhibited increasingly the hallmarks of a bureaucratic totalitarian operation. The totalitarian administrator instinctively disliked unpredicted, random acts by the populace or by minor, local officials. The Nazi policy, therefore, became one of systematic, methodical handling of the Jews in accordance with duly issued directives from high authority.

In its totalitarian form, this very modern anti-Semitism could proceed through the logical phases of (1) identifying Jews, (2) expropriating their property, (3) gathering the unfortunate victims into concentration camps, and (4) murdering the victims. Hilberg makes the significant point that even identifying or defining "Jews" was a complex undertaking which involved in some way *most* organs of the German Government, Army, and Nazi Party. He feels that the "machinery of destruction" in charge of the liquidation process was really the *German Government itself*, not a few special organizations thereof. The Civil Service ground out the voluminous procedural directives which enabled "Jews" to be identified and moved from place to place. Officialdom also planned and conducted the expropriation of Jewish property, while the diplomats of Germany arranged for the Europe-wide destruction arrangements which involved all the countries of Nazi-dominated Europe during World War II.

The contributions of the Army, Police, and National Socialist Party action groups in arousing anti-Semitic feeling, and in doing the actual killing, are painfully obvious; nor should one forget the operators of industry, both high and low, who were much involved in the forced labor system and the handling of former Jewish property.[35]

Hilberg notes that "in many countries, bureaucracies have launched the opening phases of a destruction process." However, in the Nazi epic, the process was not stopped or mitigated by any of the psychological or circumstantial factors which had usually done so in previous history. Thus it could show its full, elemental ferocity, destroying not only Jews but all individuals who might be objectionable to the State or deserving of death in terms of Nazi ideological criteria. The diverse victims caught up in this juggernaut of death included many European nationalities—the Gypsies were sentenced to death as a people, while such categories as tubercular Poles and various other physical or mental defectives were nominated for destruction. In another latter-day bizarrity of Nazi officialdom, a conference in 1944 brought the conclusion that inmates of prisons who were physically ugly should also be liquidated, because they "hardly deserve the designation human." This was not just racism, but totalitarianism running rampant. The wrath of the bureaucracy was also turned against that natural target of the official, the person not connected with an organization or otherwise closely involved in society's better coordinated routines. Thus, the anti-Gypsy decree included certain non-Gypsies, "persons who wandered around in a 'Gypsy-like' manner."[36]

A special feature of the Nazi genocide was the screen of painstaking concealment which kept most of Hitler's people from getting a clear idea of what was going on. The phenomenon of suppression of facts by totalitarians is analyzed by Hilberg as including five phases, which apply to most forms of imperialism, racism, and totalitarianism. First, the perpetrators naturally prefer to conceal their unsavory deeds from as many people as possible, and want to avoid the weakening or undue distraction of themselves and their confederates which would surely result if much attention were given to dreadful programs of violence and coercion. Nazi censorship was most thorough in concealing the ultimate aim of the anti-Jewish campaign from everyone who did not need to know.

Second, a corollary to this "need-to-know" restriction was that those who *did know* should be personally, morally if you will, involved in what occurred. They were to be fully-acknowledged and self-confessed executioners' accomplices. A third phase of repression was prohibition of criticism of the liquidation operations by anyone at all. The Party Chancellery instructed its underlings that, after all, people who did not understand the full dreadfulness of the Bolshevik terror could not comprehend adequately the need for the liquidation campaign. The fourth and fifth phases of suppression lay in elimination of references to the destruction process in conversation and official correspondence. The latter form of censoring included vague or deceptive words for the process and for equipment used in the mass murders, such as the general term, "special installations."[37]

When Germany had been defeated, the victorious powers began to prosecute the persons responsible for the Nazi crimes. The prosecution involved an immense amount of field investigation, research, court procedures, and publicity. This long process, which lasted more than two decades, served as a gigantic "collective psychoanalysis" for the German people and others who shared the guilt. For two decades, Europe lay, so to speak, on the psychoanalyst's couch. The Americans, British, and French sentenced 5,025 persons, of whom 486 were put to death. The U.S.S.R. handed out about 10,000 sentences to Nazi offenders, while 4,000 more were convicted in various countries. In addition, West Germany itself regained its independence, and had by 1962 tried 12,846 war criminals or genocidal offenders. Of these, over 5,000 were convicted.

Impressive though all these prosecutions were, it appears that he "psychoanalyst's therapy" did not achieve a complete cure. There was much reluctance among Germans to pursue vigorously the prosecution of wartime offenders. In 1964 and 1965 there was a prolonged debate in the German parliament and in the press, ending in a rather weak consensus that the legal statutes of limitations were to be extended in order that the hundreds of still-unprocessed offenders might be brought to justice.

Another indication that the totalitarian spirit had survived Germany's "cure" appeared in the revival of German authoritarian political parties. These are quite small, but one recall's that Hitler's Party was very small for years. The overtly fascist parties revived, for the most part in about 1949–1950, as splinter groups of such postwar, non-Nazi nationalist parties as the National Right Party and the German Conservative Party. (Both of these, Richard Cromwell tells us, closely resembled the old German National People's Party.)

Such groups as the Socialist Reich Party (which seceded in 1949 from the German Right Party) desired a "leadership democracy," with a "national chief" as ruler, a totalitarianism, really, buttressed like all totalitarianisms by popular election proceedings.

When this Party won 366,700 out of 3,330,000 votes in the Lower Saxony state elections of 1951, it was considered dangerously successful and outlawed.

The U.S.S.R., recognizing the potential for collaboration with these small but growing organizations of neo-Nazis, has tried hard to work with them.[38] The prosperity of West Germany and its dependence upon Western Europe and the United States have thus far helped to keep neo-totalitarianism at a low level. However, the Führer's ghost was not being evoked merely by right-wing crackpots or fanatical anti-Germans. A major statesman of West Germany, former Defense Minister Franz Josef Strauss, declared in 1965 that a new Führer might arise if Germany continued to be subjected to "military discrimination." By this he meant that Germany must participate in the multinational "European Nuclear Force." Denial of this right to Germany would be reminiscent of the unfair restrictions imposed on her by the Versailles Treaty of 1919, said Strauss. He also objected to the United States' proposals at the Geneva Disarmament Conference that powers not yet possessing nuclear weapons be barred from developing or acquiring them.

Aside from Germany, the Western world was tending toward Cæsarism in the long, tense decades of the Cold War. There was anxiety in Paris, London, and Washington regarding the "Russian menace," and anxiety in Moscow about "encirclement" by the North Atlantic Treaty Organization. Inevitably, this bred a crisis mentality, a "garrison-state" outlook which enabled the central governments of several NATO powers to enlarge their authority, budgets, and staffs. In Russia, at least until the 1960's, the Stalinists were able to stave off some promising democratic trends, and the Red Army's phalanx of bemedalled marshals held on grimly to their cherished large military budgets.

:: IX ::

The Flood Tide of
Independence in Afro-Asia

SMOOTH ROADS TO INDEPENDENCE

INDEPENDENCE came in the 1950's and 1960's to practically every remaining colonial area large enough to be organized as a sovereign nation. The searing effects of the World Wars and the great European dictatorships had brought the white nations to a point where they could not easily carry on the imperialist role. The colonial peoples were stirred in their own ways by these same events, and were emboldened to seek their freedom.

For those countries to which freedom did not come as an immediate result of World War II, the important distinction is: Did sovereignty come smoothly and easily, or was it conveyed with reluctance, warfare, and bitterness? This distinction affects the gravity of the future burden on the white conscience, and also determines the quality of resentment which former colonials may bear against their former overlords.

The magnitude and rapidity of the liberation process is shown by the fact that the United Nations now has more than twice the number of members it had in 1947; that is, more than half of the members are former possessions of the Western powers. The time a colony became a U.N. member is often a good indicator of its *real* independence, and such dates will be cited occasionally to avoid confusion with the fictitious or partial independence which colonial powers have often been pleased to bestow. Rarely, if ever, has an Afro-Asian nation become a U.N. member without possessing full political independence.

The loss or abandonment of colonial empires was doubtless speeded up by the fact that the white population in most colonies was only a tiny fraction of the total number of inhabitants. In 1921, for example, there were 156,637 Europeans in India. Of those, only 45,000 were women, a clear indication that the foreign white persons were largely transients, not settlers. In Malaya, there were in 1931 17,768 British, only 0.4 per cent of the population, while the Netherlands East Indies' population of 60,727,233 included, in 1930, only 240,417 white persons.[1]

Looking first at North Africa, we find one country to which independence came without great difficulty. Libya had been liberated from its Italian colonial rulers during World War II, after which it was under British administration until 1952. The long delay after the war years was naturally resented by the Arabs, but the transition to freedom took place fairly smoothly. Other North African lands must be reserved for the second part of this chapter, where protracted wars of liberation and post-liberation conflicts are treated. Even Egypt, though the war's end left her free, had to regain that part of her country through which the Suez Canal ran.

We have already seen how World War II brought rapid liberation everywhere in South and Southeast Asia except French Indo-China and Malaya. Real independence for the Philippines had been envisaged by the Tydings-McDuffie Act of 1934. This Act not only set up the Philippine Commonwealth, with important self-government features, but also firmly promised independence within a decade. Of course World War II continued beyond 1944, but the promise was fulfilled in a substantially honorable manner on July 4, 1946, after the struggle with Japan had been concluded. It is true that the United States attached some strings to her grant of independence. The grant was contingent upon concession of bases in the Philippines for American armed forces, and another requirement was that the Republic of the Philippines adopt a constitutional amendment to ensure that American investors would receive equal treatment with Filipino investors.

The Government of the Philippines, in arranging for these amendments, violated its own Constitution, doubtless because of a feeling that even if legislative support for the amendments might not be obtainable, they must be pushed through at all costs in order to get independence. The Constitution of the Philippines required a vote of three-fourths of all members of the Senate and the House of Representatives for approval of an amendment, but the "parity" amendment did not get this support. Furthermore, the Senate had kept three members from entering the chamber for this vote, and the House had excluded four members.

In these rather arbitrary proceedings to protect American investors through enforced amendment of the Constitution of the Philippines, one cannot avoid discerning strong American commercial interests which exercised a lot of influence upon the United States Government. Nevertheless, the Philippines thus became independent. The fact that from 1949 to 1955 the Republic had to fight its own rebellious "Huk" guerrillas does not constitute a reproach to the United States, although in some quarters the Huk rebellion would be described as an outgrowth of failure during the years of American rule to protect the Filipino peasants from exploitation by their landlords.

American military bases still exist in the Philippines, and inevitably there is friction between local citizens and foreign personnel generated by individual disputes and the occasional shooting of a local person who attempts to enter an American base by stealth. From 1952 to 1964, 30 Filipinos were killed by U.S. sentries at Clark Field alone.

On the Asian mainland, the end of World War II was supposed to mean the end of foreign concessions and extraterritoriality in China. However, the Russian Army that had attacked Japanese-held Manchuria in 1945 did not withdraw until the U.S.S.R. had accomplished systematic looting of Manchuria's industrial plants. All machinery and equipment was removed to Russia—quite a deprivation to China, since Manchuria's industries had developed considerably under the Japanese occupation.

In the immediate postwar years, several North China ports, such as Tsingtao, were used as bases by U.S. forces, largely in connection with American efforts to support Chiang K'ai-shek's Nationalists in North China. By 1949 the Nationalists were defeated; the Americans left, and a Communist government ruled in China. Then, however, Russian military units were installed in bases on Chinese soil. The Soviets also retained their interest in the Chinese Eastern Railway and the extensive mines and lands which belonged to that Railway in Manchuria.

The Red Chinese Government pressed determinedly for Russian abandonment of the Railway and its properties, and finally achieved this in 1952. It was not until May, 1955, after various Russian delays, that Soviet Forces finally gave up their Port Arthur base on China's Liaotung Peninsula. Meanwhile, the Nationalist Chinese Government had taken refuge on the island of Taiwan, where from 1950 its independence was maintained under the protective supervision of the United States. After 1955, therefore, we may say that the only foreign bases on Chinese territory were American military facilities on Taiwan. Russian military and civilian personnel were present on the Chinese mainland in considerable numbers until at least 1960; it is not clear what they enjoyed in the way of de facto freedom from Chinese authority. The British retained possession of Hong Kong and the Portuguese held on to Macao, but the Chinese have not been trying recently to regain these bits of land.

What of the British record during all this dismantling of the white empires? One may say that the English withdrawals were delayed too long. Professor Stewart Easton, in *The Twilight of European Colonialism*, opines: "From Gandhi and Nehru to Mboya and Banda, all the nationalists have been opposed, treated with condescension and contempt, and their motives have been impugned; only when their power has grown so strong that it can no longer be resisted have the British . . . come to terms with it."

However, the British retreat was orderly; local administrations were trained to assume self-rule without great confusion, and only Kenya and Malaya saw extensive military conflicts as the time of withdrawal approached. In other words, the departure was not so long delayed as to cause bitter wars of liberation. Nigeria, Tanganyika, Zambia, Malawi, and other possessions were freed in such a manner. In the 1960's Basutoland, Swaziland, and Bechuanaland began the transition toward freedom, though one wondered how they would solve their problem of being surrounded or partly surrounded by territories of the white-supremacist Union of South Africa.

The remaining British (and Australian) possessions or dependencies are not being retained as a matter of traditional imperialism. If they are still struggling on the road to freedom, it is usually because their people are so backward that they will not be a viable nation until much more work is done (as in the case of Australian New Guinea).

Numerous island possessions of various white nations are so small that full independence seems irreconcilable with their security or welfare. Similar problems affected the last few United Nations trust territories: New Zealand was able in 1962 to liberate its Western Samoan trusteeship, where the population was about 116,000, but how could Australia's Nauru Island trusteeship be put on its own with a population of just a few thousand and only one industry, phosphate production? (Even these phosphate deposits will be exhausted in a short time.) For better or worse, Nauru received its independence effective January 31, 1968. The wiser solution for tiny islands is federation with other small, nearby territories. If that is not workable because of geographic or ethnic problems, it is possible to grant local self-government, with a larger nation retaining the responsibilities of foreign relations, defense, and economic assistance.

Demolition of the French colonial empire had its stormy aspects, but the liberation of French West Africa and Equatorial Africa was smoothly accomplished. While we may worry about the future development of new nations there—Niger, Chad, Mali, Mauritania—their relations with France have been largely cordial since liberation, with advisory and financial assistance continuing to flow from the former proprietary country.

PROTRACTED WARS OF LIBERATION AND POST-LIBERATION CONFLICTS

FOR MANY YEARS after the end of World War II, the French stood pat in their North African colonies, and the independence movements had a very difficult time. In Morocco, Sultan Mohammed V offered the little resistance he could by refusing to sign certain French-sponsored decrees. As of 1953, the French were pressing the Sultan to comply with their policies and sign decrees which would actually have reduced his power instead of moving toward greater autonomy. Typically, the French applied the old "divide and rule" maxim, enlisting the Berber hill people under Pasha Al-Glawi in moves against the Sultan. Armed Berber contingents assisted French soldiers in disarming Mohammed's Palace Guard, and the royal family was sent into exile. Mohammed was replaced by his uncle, a pliable French puppet.

By 1955 Moroccan unrest was so pronounced that the French found it necessary to restore the ousted Sultan Mohammed to his throne. After this, independence for Morocco came quickly; it was formulated in 1955 and implemented in 1956. At the same time, the Spanish portion of Morocco was returned to the Sultan's Government, although enclaves in the cities of Ceuta and Melilla remained in Spanish hands. The internationally administered city of Tangier also reverted to Moroccan control.

In Tunisia, despite decades of French repressions, Habib Bourguiba's nationalists retained an evolutionary approach to independence for some years after World War II. In the early 1950's, there was divergence among the French themselves on Tunisian policy. Enlightened French officials had programs for increasing local autonomy, while the European minority of Tunisia managed repeatedly to abort these projects. As in so many colonial areas, the vested interest of European settlers worked against development of local democratic institutions, doubtless fearing that the non-European majority would make short work of the Europeans if it gained substantive power. By 1952, the resulting frustration of Tunisian independence aspirations had caused some local leaders to substitute terrorism for peaceful negotiation.

When in March, 1956, the Tunisians saw Morocco being given its independence, their negotiators pressed the French with renewed vigor, and before the month was over they also obtained independence. The three Northwest African countries intricately affected one another's destiny. Rebellion in Algeria accelerated Moroccan and Tunisian freedom. Conversely, extrication of France from the latter two countries enabled her to struggle longer and harder against the liberation of Algeria.

The Algerians, like their North African neighbors, desired more than tokens of autonomy in the aftermath of World War II. Richard M. Brace considers an event at Sétif in May, 1945, the turning point from peaceful evolution to militant reaction in Algeria. In this incident, a Moslem victory parade led to gunfire, and 30 persons were killed. In reaction, Moslems destroyed considerably property and killed about 100 Europeans. The French pursued their characteristic policy of utterly crushing all dissidence —or so they hoped—by sending aircraft to attack Arab residential areas and dispatching troops to kill, abuse, and destroy on a great scale. The French have admitted the death of 1,500 Moslems in this operation, while Algerian nationalists claim that 45,000 were killed. Wholesale arrests were also carried out, in the usual arbitrary fashion.[2]

Algerian efforts toward independence received much encouragement and help not only from her neighbors, Tunisia and Morocco, but also from Egypt, a nation which had entered a period of revitalized nationalism in the 1950's. When Gamal Abdel Nasser became top man in the Egyptian revolutionary government in 1954, the nations of Northwest Africa benefited from his willingness to offer whatever support he could, whether material aid, diplomatic support, or training and advice.

In November, 1954, a full-scale armed rebellion began in Algeria and continued until independence was gained in 1962. In addition to support from the other North African nations referred to above, Algeria received certain assistance from the Communist Bloc. For one thing, many North African Moslems had taken part in the long, fruitless war of the French in Indo-China. They had been exposed to Vietnamese independence literature, and those who fell into Viet Minh hands were usually thoroughly indoctrinated in the Communist revolutionary approach during their captivity. The Vietnamese war had come to an end in 1954, the same year in which the Algerian rebellion broke out. Former prisoners of the Viet Minh were reappearing at about this time in their North African homelands, where they constituted a strong force for resolute opposition to the French, not to mention the new knowledge of revolutionary techniques and guerrilla warfare methods which some had acquired under Viet Minh auspices.

In listing the special assistance received by North African rebels, one should also note that some efforts were made by Communist China and the Soviet Union to render a modest degree of assistance. The Communist Bloc offered plenty of moral support and back-up propaganda. The anti-French propaganda effort was also given quite a boost by the French themselves. French forces and security police were, as usual, inclined to use torture in the processing of rebel prisoners or suspected rebels. These cruelties were extensive enough to become well-known in France and in other world capitals. By 1957, letters and petitions from eminent Frenchmen to the President of France asked that these interrogations under torture be stopped.

It is most interesting that several conferences of African powers were held in 1957, at which not only the North African Arab nations, but also Ghana, Ethiopia, Liberia, and the Sudan joined in something of an early Pan-African effort to support the Algerian Revolution morally or with material aid.[3]

Finally, in March, 1962, the French Government entered negotiations in earnest for Algerian independence. Despite last-ditch efforts by the "Secret Army Organization," sponsored by Algerian Frenchmen and military personnel to head off independence, an accord was reached, and by the summer of 1962 Algeria was free.

The Belgian Congo was particularly important to the United States in the decade following World War II because of its huge uranium deposits. These were considered vital for atomic bomb development, and the U.S. enjoyed a virtual monopoly of the uranium produced there. The importance decreased as many other uranium sources were developed and technology progressed. Aside from the slight public notice occasioned by the uranium factor, most Westerners heard nothing about the Belgian Congo until its abrupt liberation in 1960. Thenceforth, the violent crises of the Congo made it inescapably clear that something had gone wrong.

Economically, the Congo had been better off than most colonies in the twentieth century, but the Belgians had not translated its rich resources into anything like modernization or preparation for autonomy. They had not expected to liberate this colony for many years, and only did so when the threat of revolt became great. The new nation could boast of only 17 citizens with college educations. There was not one Congolese doctor, and only one engineer, though 542 Belgian engineers were present. The Belgians had accorded commissioned rank to no Congolese in the Congo's Army; in the civil administration, Belgians had monopolized all the senior positions in a nation of 13,559,000 people !

Just two weeks after independence came, the Army revolted, the administration broke down, and the economy began to collapse. The Congo Government asked the United Nations to send troops and other assistance. The U.N. sent 18,000 soldiers, and essential services were improvised by staffs from such organs as the International Telecommunication Union, the International Civil Aviation Organization, the World Meteorological Organization, and the World Health Organization. Walter Lippmann called this "the most sophisticated example of international cooperation in history." However, there still ensued numerous episodes of secession attempts and revolts in various regions of the Congo, some encouraged by European elements, others by Chinese Communist agents. In 1964 the Congo Government was so hard pressed by Communist-sponsored rebels that it hired European and South African soldiers of fortune to fight the insurgents. This helped precipitate massacres of many helpless white residents of the Congo, though the Western press all but overlooked the fact that far greater numbers of Congolese victims were killed by the insurgents.

Another rough transition to independence occurred in Britain's colony of Kenya, where European settlers' preemption of the best lands had made Negro inhabitants exceedingly bitter. This bitterness was not duplicated in the neighbor colonies of Tanganyika or

Uganda, where interracial competition for land was not acute. The public mood in Tanganyika was of satisfaction, because after World War II the British placed this former League of Nations mandate under United Nations trusteeship. This was not an empty gesture, because there were regular visitations and administrative recommendations by representatives of the U.N.'s Trusteeship Council.

In Kenya, however, violent programs were aimed at expelling the Europeans when leaders of the Kikuyu and other tribes formed the Mau Mau terrorist organization in 1947. Kenneth Ingham has defined Mau Mau as "a Kikuyu movement of resistance against alien forces which appeared to treat men as being less than human beings and which deprived them of their land and made them labourers on other men's farms."[4] Serious violence against Europeans began in 1952, and British military retaliation only seemed to cause thousands of young Kenyans to join the rebel guerrillas. The most critical phase of the war ended in 1955, but the state of emergency could not be officially terminated until 1960. Three years after that, Kenya became independent.

The gravest problem in all Africa is doubtless that of the Union of South Africa, where over three million whites confront 11 million Africans and a half million Asians. Instead of easing their white supremacy measures, the dominant minority has become more unreasonable since 1948, and African resentment has continued to build up.

In 1948, the white minority of South Africa was exceedingly well unified under a militant Nationalist government in which the restraining influence of English inhabitants ceased to be effective. The English, considerably outnumbered by their fellow-whites of Dutch Afrikaner origin, were not enlightened liberals, to be sure. They were most notably mine operators, financiers, or at least well-established members of the middle class, and did not need to stress the whiteness of their skin as a reason for their differentiation from the poor Negro Africans. The Afrikaners, on the other hand, included many poor people and people of very modest means to whom the racist appeal was strong.

White laborers in the American West of the late nineteenth

century had vented their resentment in two directions at once—against the employers and financiers, and against the Chinese and Japanese who competed for their jobs. In exactly the same way, the white workers of South Africa resented both their employers and the non-white competition. This accounts for the warrant enjoyed by the South African Government in recent decades to take the most extreme measures against the non-white population.

The *apartheid* (segregation) measures taken after 1948 created a comprehensive system restricting non-Europeans as to residence, nature of employment or trade, legal status, marriage, and movement. This system of laws resembles the Black Codes enacted in Southern states of the U.S. after the Civil War, and also the legal defenses which these states attempted to erect against integration in the 1950's and 1960's. The resemblance lies notably in the complexity of the laws and regulations, and in the unconcealed intent of the legislators to erect as many barriers as might be necessary to achieve a desired condition of separateness.

The analogy with America is incomplete in one sense, of course: The National Government of South Africa after 1948 could not be overruled or checked by any separate or higher authority, but such checks and vetoes were always potentially available in the United States. South Africa's Criminal Law Amendment Act of 1953 also constitutes a notable difference between American and South African conditions. The penalties of this statute are extremely severe and of wide application, in that it became a criminal offense to break *any given law* in order to protest against *any other law*. Since the penalties included a fine of 500 pounds, five years' imprisonment, and a whipping of ten strokes, non-violent resistance and demonstrations were greatly discouraged. The penalties were, after all, too severe to be faced by massive numbers of people. Another tough law passed in 1953 was the Public Safety Act, which allowed the Government to declare states of emergency at its pleasure, and then override any other laws in order to by-pass the regular courts and impose whatever penalties it might desire.[5]

The divide and rule tactics of the dominant white minority further weakened resistance against discrimination. Colored persons of mixed blood in South Africa were given a special, distinct status before the law. They suffered discrimination, but of varying kinds and degrees. In 1936, to ensure that the Negro majority in South Africa would not acquire political power through even the most gradual socio-political progress, laws were enacted to prevent Negro representation in Parliament, except through a small number of European surrogates. The white minority intended that Negro autonomy would develop, but only within the isolated spheres and segregated political organs prescribed by the ruling minority. The spheres for Negro political development resemble somewhat the reservations set up for America's Indians, except that the Bantu preserves seem to be allowed a more sophisticated political life of their own.

South African racists were still seemingly confident, as late as 1960, that God was on their side. In that year, an assassin shot at Prime Minister Verwoerd; the bullet entered his head, but did not reach the brain. The newspaper *Die Burger* commented, "In this miraculous escape all the faithful will see the hand of God."[6] The murder of Verwoerd in 1966 required, presumably, some new interpretation of God's plans.

At about the same time as the first assassination attempt, a demonstration was organized by the Pan-African Congress to protest the law requiring Negroes to carry "pass" documents at all times. About 10,000 people at Sharpeville discarded their passes and went to the police station, seeking arrest as pass law violators. Some threw stones, and the police became panicky in the face of such a large, unfriendly crowd—though there is no clear evidence that the crowd made an organized attack. Most witnesses report that no order to disperse was given, nor were warning shots fired. Instead, in the style of India's Amritsar Massacre, the police fired volley after volley of shots and sten gun bursts into the crowd. About 67 were killed, and some 186 injured. The indiscriminate slaughter included women and children as well as male demonstrators. Of the police, three were hit by stones![7]

The vitality of the American civil rights movement in the 1960's did not go unnoticed in South Africa. Just as Hitler's actions had encouraged South Africa's white supremacists, the movement for interracial equality in America encouraged the advocates of justice in South Africa. The American civil rights hymn, "We Shall Overcome," became popular in South Africa, especially among folk singers.

Most dramatically, the hymn was sung on April 1, 1965, by a condemned man on the gallows at Pretoria Central Prison just before he was executed for planting a bomb in the Johannesburg railway station. The security police were persuaded beyond any doubt that the song had connotations of treason. They visited numerous record shops, seizing some recordings of "We Shall Overcome." In effect, they banned the record, although not through the legally prescribed method of listing the banned object in the Government Gazette. Here again we see the characteristic totalitarian readiness to violate the Government's own laws, substituting violence, threats, or chicanery for legal process.

There is also plenty of formal legal procedure against Negro citizens of the Union. *The New York Times* reported in July, 1965, that 918 persons had been arrested in the eastern part of the Cape Province alone for supporting African nationalist causes. Those arrested began to come to trial in 1963, producing 452 sentences aggregating 2,339 years in jail. Only 19 acquittals occurred, and most of the acquitted were soon arrested again. One would suspect from these figures that a real spirit of justice seldom prevails in these courts. In fact, the courts fall short in such elements of fairness as providing adequate defense counsel to the accused. Most of the accused are city residents, but are taken for trial to remote villages to which a lawyer can hardly afford to travel. Many lawyers are reportedly afraid to handle such cases. The testimony against these offenders is often memorized word-for-word by the Government's witnesses in a style reminiscent of Stalin's Purge trials.

These relatively elaborate trials are complemented by the very swift trials of simple offenders against the Union's routine laws of regimentation—non-white persons who are caught in "whites only" areas without properly validated pass documents. These trials do their job of "keeping the Negroes in line" with small expenditure of time or legal attention. Court A of the Bantu Affairs Court in Johannesburg has managed to complete as many as 57 cases in an 80-minute period—cases which produce jail sentences of one to eight weeks.

Such "justice" is obviously weirdly inconsistent with testimony being given to the International Court of Justice in The Hague while the South African courts were handing out these sentences. Ethiopia and Liberia had brought to the International Court a complaint that the Union of South Africa was failing to fulfill the terms of the League of Nations mandate through which she acquired the former German Southwest Africa. The complainants charged that the Union violated its commitment to "promote to the utmost the material and moral well-being and social progress of the inhabitants of the territory." Not so, said a witness for the Union; his Government was just trying to develop an authoritative voice for its non-white people. "You want to build up their personalities and then you can talk to them," said the witness. He assured the International Court that the Government was very fair, and added somewhat furtively, "We are an open society and injustice is brought to light somehow."[8]

It would be gratifying to relate that the International Court did something in behalf of the people of Southwest Africa, if nothing more than a legal finding that the Union of South Africa had violated its commitment. However, when in 1966 the Court got around to issuing its decision, the finding was merely evasive, alleging that the complainant nations could not properly bring this complaint to the Court.

Another neighbor to the Union of South Africa is Rhodesia (formerly Southern Rhodesia), which Britain retained as a colony in the 1960's because Rhodesia's 230,000 whites wished to impose their own white-supremacist régime on the 4,000,000 Negro inhabitants. As of 1965, local authorities had given evidence of these designs by arresting thousands of Africans for nationalist agitation. Late 1965 brought a unilateral declaration of independence by the white Rhodesian Government. Britain and the United States made clear that they disapproved. Some economic pressure was exerted upon the Rhodesian Government, but sterner measures were rejected in London and Washington. A United Nations report in

May, 1967, pointed to one possible reason for this indecisiveness: Investors in Britain and the United States led the world in their financial commitments within the Union of South Africa. Britain's stake was nearly three billion dollars out of a total investment abroad of $4,800,000,000. The United Kingdom's earnings in dividends from that country increased sharply from $81,000,000 in 1960 to $173,000,000 in 1964, helping considerably to relieve Britain's recurrent and acute balance of payments problem. These financial considerations were relevant to the Rhodesian problem because decisive action against Rhodesia would probably include a full embargo on trade and a blockade which would have to extend to Rhodesia's sympathetic neighbor, the Union of South Africa.

Those who defended the restraint shown by London and Washington could point out that a readiness to take unfriendly action against foreign nations constitutes an aggressive, war-breeding habit, even though the governments in question are unjust. Nevertheless, during the late 1960's, the halls of the U.N. rang with cries from Afro-Asian delegates for U.N. action to liberate the people of Rhodesia and Southwest Africa. But now, leaving these simmering cauldrons of South Africa, let us see what difficulties and grievances arose when Europe completed liberation of the Moslem countries of the Near East.

British authorities in Palestine after World War II were unable to settle conflicting claims of Zionists and Arabs, so in the fall of 1947 they declared their intention of abandoning their Palestine mandate after six months. This would have the effect of letting Arab and Jewish inhabitants of the region settle their own dispute. There followed hostilities involving the establishers of Israel with Arab opponents, not only within Palestine but emanating from neighboring Arab lands as well. Finally, hostilities among these groups were largely terminated during the first half of 1949 by several armistices.

Thus a new ingredient was added to Arab nationalism. The desire for independence had long been present. Anti-Western resentments caused by colonization or other forms of domination were also strong and of long standing. Now added was the special resentment derived from establishment of Israel by persons the Arabs regarded as European interlopers, as well as resentment at the support of these interlopers by the United States and other Westerners. These resentments facilitated the birth of new revolutionary movements in several Arab lands during the 1950's and 1960's. In such countries as Syria, Iraq, and Egypt, the new leadership came primarily from officers of the army. The army was actually doing far more than just exploiting the resentments. It was trying commendably, in several cases, to fill a power void, not to mention a great void of popular understanding and interest. The army leaders were not typical totalitarian dictators, but were trying to reform their countries, keep them free, or expand the nation's influence.

The most dynamic form of Arab nationalism and Pan-Arab unity began in the mid-1950's with the Egyptian revolution. In 1953 King Farouk was deposed, and a republic was proclaimed with General Naguib as head of state. His most active collaborator, Gamal Abdul Nasser, wielded considerable power behind the scenes, and a year later Nasser took charge of the government.

For the British, the years during which Nasser took charge and consolidated his government were a fortunate extension of their apparently strong position in Egypt, or at least at the Suez Canal. Once Nasser's position was firm, however, the British were obliged to withdraw their troops from Egypt, the last finally leaving in May, 1956. Next the British, Americans, and French went through a phase of increasing worry about Egypt. The Americans worried that Russia might assume some sort of protectorate over Egypt, or at least hold excessive influence there. The French had reason to be annoyed with Nasser's government because of the aid and comfort it rendered to the rebels fighting French forces in Algeria. The British became concerned about the Suez Canal and the Pan-Arab program Nasser promoted. Would this program unseat the British from their oil-rich protectorates of the Persian Gulf Coast?

The Western nations' suspicions were sharpened in July, 1956, when Nasser attended a meeting with Marshal Tito of Yugoslavia and Nehru of India, joining them in a declaration of "positive neutrality." The American Secretary of State, Mr. Dulles, decided at this point that a proper check on Egyptian ambitions would be withdrawal of American financial backing for the Aswan High Dam, which the United States had provisionally granted and which Egypt had fully expected to receive. This move was characterized by *Time* magazine as brilliant. *Time* opined that "Chessmaster Dulles had his opponents in check." But the chess game was not over. Nasser's next move was to nationalize the Suez Canal, with the claim that Egypt could use the Canal revenues to build the dam.

This, of course, alarmed the British and French even more. Not only did it seem to be a financial deprivation and an aggressive Egyptian move; it was striking at the very point—the Canal— which had long been important to both countries as a life-line to their holdings in Asia. Even though the British Empire in India was now gone, the Canal was still an important route by which petroleum products reached Western Europe. Although much of the Iraqi oil moved by pipelines to the Mediterranean Coast (in Syria and Israel), this portion of the oil supply could be cut off by political disorders in Iraq, Syria, or Israel.

Nasser was careful to observe the provisions of the old Suez Canal Convention of 1888 insofar as freedom of passage through the Canal was concerned. Right of passage had been denied to Israeli ships for years, even before the fall of the Egyptian monarchy, and no other restriction on traffic was imposed in 1956. Nasser's officials managed the mechanics of keeping the Canal in operation, although the French and British tried to tie it up by withdrawing their men who did the vital job of piloting ships through its waters. This tactic simply did not work; the Egyptians found new pilots by a variety of means. In fact, recruiting of replacement pilots provided just one more occasion to demonstrate Afro-Asian solidarity, because pilot volunteers were offered by the Chinese and other friendly nations. Navigation through the Canal continued with very little difficulty.

The final deterioration of the situation between the French and British on one hand, and Egypt on the other, came with another move of Arab consolidation. Egypt, Syria, and Jordan announced that their armed forces would be grouped in a joint command, with an Egyptian commander-in-chief. At this point the Israelis feared a joint attack on them by the three Arab countries, and therefore made plans to attack Egypt with a movement toward the Canal. The French had information about the Israeli attack in advance, and gave their support to the forces of Israel. The British may not have known of the attack in advance, but when it came they seem to have decided to occupy the Suez Canal Zone once again, justifying their move by the alleged need to protect the Canal and safeguard passage through it as provided by the Suez Canal Convention of 1888.

The British and French issued an ultimatum to the Egyptian Government requiring withdrawal of the Egyptians to a line ten kilometers distant from the Suez Canal. When the ultimatum expired without compliance by the Egyptians, the British and French proceeded to strafe Egyptian airfields and then to reoccupy the Canal Zone.

There was very little excuse for this invasion of what had become sovereign Egyptian territory. Nationalization of the Canal by the Egyptian Government was not truly different from numerous other nationalizations of foreign enterprises by sovereign governments which had been occurring in the twentieth century. The Anglo French move did immense damage to the prestige of those two countries; for one thing, it eventually led to nothing more than ignominious withdrawal of their forces. By its arbitrariness, however, and by the Kiplingesque atmosphere in which it was carried on, it dissipated whatever good will for the British had been remaining in the Near East. Whether rightly or wrongly, the Arabs were inclined to take the whole affair as proof that old-time British and French imperialism was still alive; while these two West European powers were weaker, their malevolence and greed were as great as ever. The pattern of the attacks tended to convince the Arabs that the Western powers were friends of Israel and enemies of the Arab nations.

The position of the British and French before world opinion was devastatingly confirmed by a United Nations Assembly resolution, passed by a vote of 64 to 5, condemning the Anglo-French action. The United States alone of the Western powers salvaged something by voting for the resolution. American pressure had also helped to prevail upon Israel to withdraw from the operation.

However, it was obvious to the entire Afro-Asian bloc during the 1950's that the United States was a very important friend to Britain and France, and that those two nations received an immense share of American foreign aid. Therefore, American gestures in support of the Egyptian position may have left a weaker impression than the more flamboyant gestures of Egypt's Russian and Chinese friends.

The British position in Southwest Asia had become infirm when India and the Suez Canal were lost by Britain. The Western-sponsored Baghdad Pact and "Central Asian Treaty Organization" consequently had very little real strength to back them up. The American President, Eisenhower, attempted to compensate for the weak Western position in the Persian Gulf area with his message to Congress in January, 1957. He underlined the importance of the Middle East, requested funds for the economic development of Middle Eastern nations, and asked authorization to use American forces in that region if Communist aggression occurred. Nevertheless, the strength of Pan-Arab sentiment and the force of anti-Western resentment were shown in 1958 by two events. First was the union of Egypt and Syria into one nation called the United Arab Republic. Though this union certainly had its ups and downs, being dissolved and renewed as the years went by, it was an impressive demonstration of Arab collaboration. The second event, very upsetting to the West, was a revolution in Iraq. This coup demolished a régime which had worked fairly smoothly with Western diplomats, and raised the specter of a Communist seizure of power in a country whose oil resources were essential for Europe's economy !

Because Britain and the other West European nations depended so heavily on Southwest Asia for oil, their active diplomatic interest in the region was understandable, even after the nations of that region were largely independent. The United States did not have a vital interest in that oil so far as its own energy sources were concerned, but we should note that Americans dominated oil production in Saudi Arabia, and their interest in Iranian oil production was augmented by U.S. participation in the troubled affairs of Iran. A serious crisis had arisen in 1951 when the Iranian

Government headed by Premier Mossadegh expropriated the Anglo-Iranian Oil Company. The British withdrew their technicians, and the Iranian Government had great difficulty in operating the expropriated fields and marketing the product of those fields. Those difficulties helped bring about the overthrow of Mossadegh, though the actual coup d'état was planned by the American Central Intelligence Agency. The Shah took the reins of government from his fallen Premier, and His Majesty permitted Western entrepreneurs to resume operation of the oil industry. (Formal title to the fields remained in the hands of the Iranian Government.) As a reward for the effective cloak and dagger work of the C.I.A., the oil companies of the United States got a 40 per cent share in Iranian production under this new dispensation.

In the 1960's, the British Government has still been willing to intervene with military forces in order to maintain stability in such a Persian Gulf sheikhdom as Kuwait. The sheikhdoms are largely independent in their internal affairs, and largely under British guidance with regard to foreign affairs and defense problems. The strongest reason why West European powers cannot entirely bow out of Southwest Asia is their requirements for fuels. The situation in this regard is much changed since even as recent a year as 1938. In that year, the West European nations consumed 710,000 barrels of petroleum products daily, most of which came from the western hemisphere; by 1955 they consumed 2,570,000 barrels, 75 per cent of which came from the Near East and Iran.[9]

Europe's conversion from coal to oil also made the problem more acute: Between 1957 and 1967 European consumption of oil increased three-fold, and this fuel came to supply 50 per cent of Europe's energy requirements. Stepped-up production of oil in Libya and Algeria diversified the oil sources somewhat, and these two sources could not be disrupted by closing the Suez Canal or blocking international pipelines. On the other hand, Libya and Algeria were staunchly Moslem nations, often inclined to collaborate with their fellow-Arabs of the Near East. One more summary statistic might be useful here: As of 1967, oil fields in the Moslem belt from Algeria to Iran supplied three-quarters of Western Europe's oil.

Consequently, we have seen, and may continue to see, exertion of pressure on the governments of Southwest Asia and North Africa by the West European governments and their ally, the United States. The Soviet Union has similarly had, and will probably continue to have, a strong interest in the region. Whether interference by any of these governments results from interest in oil, interest in Israel, or from some form of opportunism, nations which are targets of the interference may be expected to resent it as they have resented it in the past. Even those Afro-Asian nations not directly concerned are naturally inclined to regard all such acts of pressure as further demonstrations of European or American villainy.

In the 1960's, the United States made sophisticated weapons systems available to Israel, while the Soviet Government furnished quantities of military equipment and economic aid to Egypt and other Arab nations opposing Israel. The armed forces of Egypt, particularly, grew so strong that a crushing blow against Israel seemed feasible. However, when this was attempted in 1967, the Arab side suffered impressive defeats, and considerable territory of Egypt, Syria, and Jordan was seized by Israeli forces. The Soviet Union gave its sympathy to the Arab side but did not venture to intervene actively, fearing counter-intervention by the United States in behalf of Israel. The Arab nations blamed the United States for its alleged support of Israel. The Saudi Arabian envoy to the United Nations, commenting on the Johnson-Kosygin conference in Glassboro in June, 1967, said simply that Israel is a manifestation of colonialism.

From East Asia came strident denunciations of all Western parties to this affair. The People's Republic of China indicated that the U.S.A., U.S.S.R., and Israel were conspiring against the Arab nations. Most intelligent Arabs probably did not believe that the U.S.S.R. was "in league with Wall Street," since the Soviet Union continued to give non-belligerent aid and support to the Moslem nations. Some segments of world opinion may have believed Peking's charges that the U.S.S.R. was a "paper tiger"—or should we say "paper bear"? For example, the Cuban Government declared, "It is painful to the peoples of the world that the United

States manifests its joy at what it obviously considers a political, diplomatic, and military victory for imperialism." A Brazilian delegate to the United Nations, who according to *The New York Times* reflected a view widely held by Latin American diplomats, called the Soviets' position of restraint "a complete capitulation."[10]

Other U.N. delegates said that China was trying to replace Russia as the Arabs' leading ally. It was true that the Peking Government offered to relieve Egypt's crisis at the war's end by providing 150,000 tons of wheat and $10,000,000 in cash. It was also conceivable that China might offer atomic weapons to the Arabs in some crisis.[11] Perhaps some Soviet leaders are worried about this Chinese role, but China does not have the economic or military resources to maintain a strong position of influence in Southwest Asia. Not only is this region remote from China, but it is the center of such intense political and diplomatic pressures that Peking's influence must be rather vague or tenuous.

In *Southeast* Asia, the most troublesome transitions from colonial rule to independence developed in Malaya and Viet Nam. On the Malay Peninsula itself, ethnic Malays were more numerous than Chinese; on the island of Singapore, at the southern end of the peninsula, Chinese outnumbered the Malays. While the British and Malays pondered the problem of making these territories into a nation without creating a Chinese predominance, there erupted a prolonged guerrilla war. The guerrilla organization had an anti-foreign, anti-capitalist, pro-Chinese orientation. It had enough popular backing, especially from Chinese villagers of the peninsula, to hold out against intensive British counter-guerrilla warfare from 1948 to 1958.

Meanwhile, English statecraft began to move toward a grant of independence, a sensible means of contributing to the pacification of the country. In 1957 Malaya became independent. A few years later, Singapore was also freed, but in adding this Chinese metropolis to Malaya the outgoing colonialists took care to also add their former possessions of Sarawak and Sabah on the island of Borneo. Enlarged in this way, Malaya could resist Chinese domination. In 1965, Singapore left the Malay Federation, becoming independent with the apparent blessing of the Malay Government.

In Viet Nam, withdrawal of the French masters came in 1954 as a result of the French defeat at Dien Bien Phu. There, in the interior of North Viet Nam, a European force equal in size to about two divisions was surrounded, besieged, and compelled to surrender to the forces of the Viet Minh. The French, who had been bled of so much manpower and wealth during nearly a decade of war with the guerrillas, were now so convinced that their position was hopeless that they agreed, in conference with the Red Chinese and Viet Minh at Geneva, to leave Indo-China. The conferees agreed that Cambodia and Laos were to be neutralized, not dominated by either China or the West. North Viet Nam was given to the Viet Minh, and South Viet Nam was placed under a non-Communist but fully independent government. Viet Minh forces in South Viet Nam were to be deactivated or moved to North Viet Nam.

The Geneva Agreement did not produce lasting peace in these former French colonies. The Viet Minh, who had fought the colonialists for so many years, enjoyed great prestige and had become consummately clever revolutionaries. With Chinese backing, the Government of North Viet Nam was able to mount a campaign of guerrilla warfare and terrorism against the South Viet Nam Government, a campaign which was scarcely noticeable in 1958, but which by 1962–1965 threatened to overwhelm the Government in Saigon. The American Government therefore considered it necessary to enter the war to assist the southern régime, and eventually the U.S. committed hundreds of thousands of men to the war.

Leaders in Washington were convinced in 1963 that the southern régime would be strengthened by the downfall of its President, Ngo Dinh Diem, whose administration was manifestly undemocratic. Diem's overthrow was accomplished in that year with the assistance of American agents and diplomacy. The coup d'état did not, however, strengthen South Viet Nam; it became weaker. The United States was charged with interference in the affairs of an Asian nation which it had recognized as a sovereign state. Further controversy swirled around American recourse to massive bombings, use of napalm and other incendiaries, and destruction of villages. The American position in Viet Nam was even more problematical than its Korean War had ever been, because the U.S. was, despite its honorable intentions, taking upon itself the horrendous confusions and welter of hatreds which French imperialism had accumulated during its century of exploitation in Indo-China.

An American President, like the leaders of other nations, has to shape his major policies in accordance with whatever popular consensus he can muster. So it was with policy on Viet Nam, where the national consensus arose from fragmented public opinion. One fragment opposed the American war effort and advocated with-drawal of U.S. forces. This faction was not strong enough to have its way, but was strong enough to restrain a second group which advocated aggressive pressure on North Viet Nam and China to end the war. Either of these segments of public opinion could severely endanger the political future of a president or party which followed the opposing segment. Therefore a negative consensus emerged, resting on a middle-of-the-road policy which was dreadful indeed : To continue the war in a highly destructive but indecisive way for an indefinite period. For this the American people bear some sort of collective responsibility—however quarrelsome they were about it, this was the national consensus.

Planners in Washington spoke freely of prolongation of hos-tilities far into the 1970's. Was there an element of racism in this willingness to prolong the ordeal of conflict which, in Viet Nam, had never ended since 1946? What of the American readiness to carp at the Vietnamese governments and people for their demorali-zation or lack of democracy? Isn't it probable that Americans, or any other people, would be severely demoralized after such a long period of warfare?

We might consider whether the Vietnamese war is part of the over-all, lengthy, global process of white assertiveness chronicled in this book. A large part of world opinion—the most clearly heard part, anyway—sees the war in that light. Most Americans probably do not. In 1967, however, there were interesting affirmations in America of this interrelatedness. Dr. Martin Luther King called on Negroes and "all whites of good will" to boycott the war, both be-cause it represented a wrongful "national arrogance" and because it was a stumbling block to the civil rights movement in the United States.

Such militant Negro leaders as Floyd McKissick of the Congress of Racial Equality and Stokely Carmichael of the Student Non-Violent Coordinating Committee had already linked their civil rights objectives with an anti-war stand, but the views of King, a moderate leader, made a deeper public impression. Dr. Ralph Bunche and other prominent Negroes objected to King's linkage of the war issue to the civil rights program. Bunche said this was "a very serious tactical error which could do much harm to the civil rights struggle." On May 10, 1967, Dr. King reiterated his opposition to the war and to racial injustice, saying, "From a content point of view, the two issues are tied together and I'm going to keep them together." He went on to attack "the three evils of racism, economic exploitation and militarism."

Dr. King also said that the testing of new U.S. weapons against the peasants of Viet Nam was "reminiscent" of Nazi actions during World War II. (A few weeks after this speech, Pastor Martin Niemoller addressed a gathering of former Dachau Concentration Camp inmates at the old camp site. The Pastor, a famous anti-Nazi and a Dachau veteran, also compared the events in Viet Nam to those in Hitler's Germany.)

Another unpalatable tie-in with the war issue came with an offer from Rhodesian Prime Minister Ian Smith and his cabinet to send 5,000 troops to assist the United States in Viet Nam. The offer was announced by South Carolina Senator Strom Thurmond at a "peace with Rhodesia" banquet in May, 1967. Of course there was no serious possibility that the United States Government would accept such an offer. However, would world opinion reject all these debatable analogies between the bad actors of history and the well-intentioned American leadership?

:: X ::

Reactions and
Afterthoughts

PSYCHOLOGY OF THE PERPETRATORS

PREVIOUS CHAPTERS of this book have examined the underlying psychology of imperialists, racists, and totalitarian-minded persons, and we have noted the responses of their victims on various occasions. Now it seems advisable to see what universal or very common reactions have occurred among the perpetrators or among the victims. These reactions-in-common may provide indications of encouraging or troublesome factors in the relations between the Western powers and their Afro-Asian brethren.

The wielders of Western power have all defended their actions by claiming that the benefits of their overlordship far exceeded the negative aspects. These claims have always been partially correct: The slaveholder *did* organize, train, and maintain his slaves; the colonial régimes and the totalitarian régimes in Europe *did* improve their economies in various ways, and contributed impressive scientific or cultural developments. The hallmarks of modern Western power everywhere included better administration and a high standard of orderliness.

Another common strand running through the justifications of Western authoritarianism has been the argument of *unavoidability*. Sometimes it was a claim of destiny, fate, or divine mission.

America had its manifest destiny, while Englishmen, Frenchmen, Germans, and Russians supposed themselves to be bearers of a sacred trust, endowed with a superior form of civilization.

Governments have also claimed to be the prisoners of circumstances. They were "unable to avoid" annexing areas which were "ungoverned" or "poorly governed." Furthermore, when the first colonies or stations were planted in America, Africa, Australia, or India, each addition to these initial holdings was "essential" to make the preceding one secure. Sometimes the governments "could not control" their military representatives, or "could not keep their eager settlers at home." Some conquests were described as "occurring in a fit of absentmindedness."

Another form of this apology is that man cannot resist his innate drive to master others, or that an organization of human beings cannot resist imposing its views, methods, or standards upon others. Here we should mention the supposedly natural "law of the jungle," or "law of tooth and claw," which was so often used to justify aggressive nationalism, racism, and imperialism. The German interpreter of history, Spengler, said, "War is the primeval policy of all living things. . . . When the will to fight is extinguished, so is life itself." Gestapo Chief Heinrich Himmler likewise stressed this theory of general combat in his exhortations to mobile killing unit personnel.[1]

Individual offenders often declare that their governments were irresistible, however wrong or cruel their dictates might be. The individual carried out all the commands of his government because disobedience meant severe punishment for him. The participant in Western crimes often said that he could not do a thing to change the system, whether the "system" was the American slavocracy, racial discrimination, or the Nazi genocide program. "If I hadn't done it, someone else would have," was another common form of this defense. Lastly, some offenders lacked the brains, knowledge, or resourcefulness to avoid doing their evil deeds. In 1965, a German judge acquitted 14 participants in Hitler's genocide operations because he believed that "They were automatic robots, simple-minded persons who lacked the ability to realize the illegality of their doings." A proper inference is that ignorance, unthinking obedience, and too much loyalty to organizations or communities has caused much grief.

The perpetrator of aggressive acts also rationalized that what he himself did was less crucial or serious than the acts of certain others. The "others" might be men in the apologist's own group who did worse things, or they might be the opposing side—even the victimized group itself. The Japanese supposedly treat their minority groups of *Eta* pariahs far worse than Europe treats its minorities; the Chinese are more imperialistic than the Russians; the Hindus and Moslems abuse each other more than the British ever hurt either group in India, and so forth. Two scholarly analysts of colonialism have said, "With all our faults, we of the West cleave closer to the human norm than do our adversaries. We cannot and will not match them in rage and self-righteousness."[2]

Most ridiculous of all the alibis, and yet quite widely used, is the claim that the victims didn't object or care. In 1763, a British East India Company representative, Luke Scrafton, elaborated this claim in his *Reflections on the Condition of Hindustan.* He said that the Indian people were by nature a servile lot, and that even the ruling classes of India had become servile because of the Indian climate—allegedly a debilitating influence which eroded character and dignity.

Scrafton also believed that the Hindus were "by nature" long-suffering, and if only left to cultivate the soil and procreate at will would gladly leave the tasks of government to others. It is unclear whether Scrafton treated Hindus as a religious group or as a race. He assumed a great deal about the innate or inbred character of the groups he discussed. Of course he also felt that the Hindu rulers were chiefly concerned with leisure and enjoyment of their "take" from the masses, and that the rulers were almost as servile as their subjects. Scrafton made another foolish assumption—that the Hindus are endowed with such an ancient sense of culture that they cannot take the initiative in matters of action. He was by no means the only European to produce these observations. Clive and Verelst, and others in later generations, voiced similar ideas.

Verelst said that the Indians were docile and subservient races who desired only to be left alone with their caste system, subsistence agriculture, primitive economy, and so on. As Dr. Barun De points out, Verelst is implying, among other things, that government by fraud and deceit would be all right with these passive, primitive people.[3]

The problem of repression of guilt has been analyzed in an earlier chapter and requires no further discussion here, other than to say again that it is a general reaction. The opposite reaction, admission of error, can also be found here and there among all the offending groups. In British India long ago, a merchant serving the East India Company, William Bolts, indicted the British rule in his *Considerations on Indian Affairs*, spelling out clearly the charge that British power in India was based on fraud and force, dignified only by the most arbitrary treaties.

There were always many Americans and Europeans who proclaimed the wrongfulness of their countries' systems of involuntary servitude, and there are plenty of conscientious Americans in the present who attack the evils of race prejudice. There are even signs that the unconscious forms of racism are being modified. In recent American literature, suggests Leslie Fiedler, a common type of new, white leading character is acting out the violent behavior traits and evil desires which earlier literature and folklore frequently projected upon non-white characters. In the recent *One Flew over the Cuckoo's Nest* by Ken Kesey, we find an Indian and a white character as allies and fellow victims of the authoritarian figure of "Big Nurse," who lobotomizes [in effect, de-individualizes] her victims.[4]

Looking back at Nazi totalitarianism, even one of Hitler's prime leaders, Baldur von Schirach, former Gauleiter of Vienna, has avowed that he is sorry that he helped train the young people of Germany to obey Hitler.[5] As for the German hatred of Jews, it has shown signs of abating. Whereas in 1952 a survey found one German in three felt it was better for Germany to have no Jews, by 1959 only one out of five made this response to the survey.[6]

The war crimes trials in Germany have aroused much awareness of past Nazi misdeeds and new totalitarian hazards in Europe. Arthur Miller remarked, after attending these trials in Frankfurt in 1964, that the question in the courtroom "spreads out beyond the defendants and spirals round the world and into the heart of every man." Miller thinks the trials teach a lesson about authoritarianism, because the German dilemma is "actually an unresolved problem for all mankind." The warning for the future is, he thinks, that "With the atomic bomb in so many different hands now it might be well to take a good look at the ordinariness of most of the defendants in Frankfurt."[7]

PSYCHOLOGY OF THE VICTIMS

GLOBAL EXPANSION of Western power and influence inflicted a great shock upon the previously dominant cultures. In its most drastic form this meant destruction of the old way of life. An example would be the crushing of the Aztec civilization by Cortes in Mexico. Much more commonly, the old order remained partially alive, but was disrupted or modified. The disruption might come through acts of the occupiers' army and officials—as often happened to the American Indians—and might arise from the local people's realization that their way of life no longer produced the results it once had, or that its results were far less satisfactory than those which the newcomers' ways could produce. This was the dilemma of China in the nineteenth century, a dilemma made all the more acute by reluctance to break with China's age-old traditions. Arnold Toynbee says that when the "culture-ray of a radioactive civilization hits a foreign body social, the assaulted foreign body's resistance diffracts the culture-ray into its component strands." Some of these "strands" can penetrate better than others. Professor Toynbee thinks of Western nationalism as just such a penetrating strand of culture. Switching to a different analogy, he suggests that while the West is accustomed to this nationalism, elsewhere in the world it will be as deadly as a "bacillus" in a host which has no immunity to it.[8] Thus Prime Minister Nehru warned the Lucknow Conference of the Institute of Pacific Relations in

1951 that, when a colony is liberated, its nationalism often becomes unhealthy, reactionary, or expansionist.

Nationalism was not the only Western importation that left the non-European world confused. In many regions it was not conquest or economic exploitation that shattered the native culture; trouble arose from the energy with which the white man condemned the beliefs and customs by which these people lived. Sometimes the colonizers' power or prestige made it easy to supersede the old way of life, but it was *not* easy to "root" the new Western ways. The danger was that the indigenous people would be suspended in a limbo between new and old cultures; the prestige of the old was gone, but they felt ill-at-ease or inferior vis-à-vis the new. As Aimé Césaire told the Paris Conference of Negro-African Writers and Artists in 1956, a "régime which destroys the self-determination of a people also destroys the creative power of that people." Nor could the interlopers give people a culture, said Césaire; they must make that for themselves.[9]

Even Japan, though not colonized, suffered the anguish of suspension between two cultures, and it is possible that the trauma of Japanese rootlessness helped drive Japan into its ill-starred wars of 1932–1945. If this is so, the future may bring unexpected violence from other traumatized peoples.

In a psychological sense, it is a grave matter to tamper with the religion or rites of a people. The rites commonly function, in the realm of the mind, as dams or conduits to handle the hazards of the unconscious, thus keeping the conscious mind strong and intact. In some cases the people's own rites have been forbidden by the conqueror's decree, as when United States authorities forbade the plains Indians to perform the Sun Dance ritual. In other cases, their religious foundation has been weakened by the vigorous missionary work of the newcomers' clergy, while in many instances the prestige of the new rulers detracted from the strength of old cults and their symbols.

In all such cases, the result may be demoralization of the victimized society, or perhaps a violent reaction bringing war or other catastrophe. Carl Jung thought of all this when the religious leader of the Taos Indian pueblo complained to him, "The Americans should stop meddling with our religion, for when it dies and we can no longer help the sun our Father to cross the sky, the Americans and the whole world will learn something in ten years' time."[10]

This cultural limbo also seems to afflict some of the best-known Afro-Asian leaders. Colin Turnbull, in his personal encounters with Nkrumah of Ghana and Nehru of India, found confirmation of the gap between these western-educated leaders and their own people. He reports that Kwame Nkrumah expressed his admiration for Mahatma Gandhi, revealing "something of the same wistful admiration that Nehru had for the Mahatma." This wistfulness, Turnbull suggests, rests on Gandhi's feat of being western-educated, yet thoroughly rooted in India's own culture, and in full rapport with the common man in India.[11]

Aside from problems of culture, a common reaction of the victim of Western power has been straightforward inferiority. As Nehru said of the Indian response to colonialism: "We developed the mentality of a good country-house servant.... Greater than any victory of arms or diplomacy was this psychological triumph of the British in India. The slave began to think as a slave."[12]

A poignant example of this acceptance of inferiority was the case of a Negro boy, about eight years old, who confronted "Bull" Connor just after that gentleman had succeeded in subduing a civil rights demonstration in Birmingham, Alabama. Connor's victory had been won by attacking the demonstrators with the bruising, surging waters of powerful fire hoses. As the sodden victims of the hoses watched "Bull" Connor stride by, the little boy could not contain his indignation; he shouted right in the big man's face, "You nigger!"

There appears to be one more way to aggravate the sense of inferiority imposed by the white man. This aggravation has occurred when the victims felt not only disruption but *abandonment* as well. A good example of this reaction was discernible among the people of France's Madagascar colony. The Malagasy people resembled other colonized peoples in their transference, or attempted transference, of old habits of dependence (as upon the tribe or upon ancestors) to a new relation wherein the European became the venerable all-providing father figure. This is more personalized than the paternalism of the totalitarian state in Europe.

Under French rule, a Malagasy would address a French superior by the term *Ray aman' d Reny*, meaning "father and mother." The coupling of the two parental titles seemed to imply hope that the authority thus addressed would be both stern father and protective mother; the native was thus positively seeking *dependence*. Dominique Mannoni's observations in Madagascar indicated that when this dependence was not accepted by the European, or "abandonment" seemed to occur, the Malagasies felt betrayed, unbearably inferior (apparently dependence was *not* inferiority in their familial view), and proceeded to react with violence.[13] Certainly the Malagasy revolt of 1947, an abrupt and murderous movement among normally gentle people, exemplified this conversion of "abandonment feeling" into hostile acts.

One can think of several forms which "abandonment" took among colonial subjects. One, as noted above, was the failure of European dignitaries to be "fatherly and motherly." Often Europeans in the colonial situation were altogether too stern and not at all protective. The feeling of rejection also came from failure to obtain positions in the white man's establishments, especially if the applicant was well qualified for a job but was rejected on racial grounds. Lastly, the often abrupt departure of European rulers in the precipitous liberation of some colonies probably led to the "abandonment" reaction—however welcome the European withdrawal was. This last reaction is inconsistent, but the mind is often inconsistent.

One has to consider, at this juncture, the Afro-Asian reaction to Christian missionary efforts. Surely the missionaries were "father figures" in many positive senses of the word—benevolent, self-sacrificing, often offering such parental contributions as education or medical care. Yet an important facet of anti-European reaction is the frequent rejection of Christianity in Asia and Africa. The ministrations of missionaries were surely among the noble, philanthropic aspects of the white man's global activity. Why then did a century or more of persistent mission work produce so few converts, in China for example? Why was a hostile reaction fairly common?

To answer these questions, let us begin by underscoring the fact that the staffs and installations of missionary organizations were a very important form of the European presence in Asia and Africa. Many areas had more missionaries than European officials, and these clergy had a longer-term, more intimate contact with the people of Africa than did the governmental representatives.

The chief factor which militated against the Christian mission effort in Africa and Asia was that the missionaries inevitably reflected the cultural, political, and economic patterns of their homelands. Thus, they seemed to be agents or accomplices of the politico-economic drive of imperialism itself. For example, in attempting to raise the educational level of the local people, the missionary almost unavoidably used his own country's language and cultural methods. This made him a "cultural infiltrator," even though that was not his intention. The clergyman could not help being a citizen of the country from which he had come, and church hierarchies reflected a sort of ecclesiastical nationalism, at least in the Afro-Asian view. Economically, the missionary was also the prisoner of his origins. If he ate, dressed, and lived in his habitual manner, he appeared to the indigenous folk as a rich profiteer in league with the more obvious oppressors of the local people.

Another strike against Christianity in the Afro-Asian mind was its frequent intolerance or exclusiveness. This was particularly painful in such cultural areas as China and Japan, countries which throughout much of their long history had enjoyed a religious eclecticism. This had permitted them to participate concurrently in several religions or philosophies without any feeling of disloyalty.

From time to time there were clergy who saw Christianity as a new and better mode for the expression of traditional local beliefs. Conversely, such early Jesuit missionaries as Fathers Ricci and von Schall tried valiantly to persuade their ecclesiastical superiors that Christianity could be imparted to the Chinese only if China's vital Confucian rites were accepted as compatible with Christianity. However, the dominant authorities of most Christian churches held out for acceptance of their faith as a total and exclusive way of life, making them seem much more demanding and intolerant than any local religion. One could also note that the Christian scriptures, with their vehement teaching of the brotherhood of man under the fatherhood of God, conflicted with the political philosophy and practice of the chief imperialists, who were clearly not practicing this. The serious charge of hypocrisy could be brought against such clergy as appeared in Afro-Asian eyes to be associates of the colonizers.

Even for the fully-converted native, Christianity was likely to mean really painful wrenches. In Central Africa, for example, the native Christian could no longer participate in the life of his village. The Bantu tribes' vital social or economic communal activities were so involved with the traditional religious system that the Christian convert must also be divorced from all these, an almost impossible dilemma for him.

In contrast with most Christian denominations, the Islamic faith required fewer painful adjustments of its converts. It interfered less with tribal practices; for example, it allowed polygamy and did not choose to extirpate pre-Islamic religious practices. Since 1800 there have been in Africa twice as many converts to Islam as to the Christian faith.[14]

We have seen the ways in which the victims of the West were *disrupted*. What purposeful actions could these people take to deal with the disruptive influences? What common elements can we find in these actions? The aggrieved culture may often produce what anthropologist Anthony Wallace calls a "revitalization movement," under the direction of a new local leader or "prophet." The movement can be "nativistic," trying to wipe out alien persons (as in the Chinese Boxer Rebellion) or expunge foreign customs (as in Japan during World War II). In other instances, the movement may incorporate foreign ideas, such as Christianity or Communism, into its program. The revitalization emphasizes an austere morality and "mobilizes moral strength." Dr. Wallace finds many close parallels among widely separated revitalization movements of the nineteenth century—for example, those of China's "Tai P'ing Kingdom" and America's Seneca Indians.[15]

MORAL FORCE AGAINST BULLETS

REVITALIZATION movements have often used tactics which belong to an especially significant grouping, that is, use of moral force in lieu of armed force or as a special supplement to grossly inadequate military resources. I say that these tactics are especially significant because in several ways they have offered new hope for the future. They have clearly helped to gain freedom for India and Pakistan and to secure just treatment of Negroes in America. Furthermore, non-violent resistance could be a very attractive alternative to violence in our new age of nuclear, biological, and chemical weapons—weapons so widely destructive that their use may be impracticable in future situations. Last, the threat of totalitarianism is augmented now by new resources in the hands of the world's major governments. These include amazing electronic, opinion molding, and data-handling technology. Governmental capability to watch citizens, control them, and influence them is so overpowering that people in all lands should begin to consider ways and means of restoring freedom in the face of new totalitarian usurpations. Non-violent methods may provide solutions. Let us therefore look at the many usages to which moral force has already been put in the face of the white man's superior military power.

When revitalization movements have involved armed conflict with superior European or American forces, a remarkably widespread reaction of the hard-pressed, outgunned victims has been to devise "cults of invulnerability." For example, almost everywhere in the American Great Plains region the warriors' shields were supposed to acquire mystic powers to keep weapons off the warriors' bodies if the shields were prepared or decorated in accordance with instructions received in visions.

In the 1880's, the Plains Indians had been repeatedly defeated and massacred by forces of the United States. In their acute demoralization, they were much interested in the revelations of a Paiute Indian, Wovoka, who had been receiving special instructions during trances. The spirits had told Wovoka how a new dance, the "ghost dance," was to be performed, accompanied by a certain chant. The result of this procedure, said the spirits, would be eventual disappearance of the white man, leaving only Indians (and abundant buffalo herds) in America. Wovoka also devised the "ghost shirt," a sacred garment which reputedly gave protection from the white man's bullets.

In another part of the world, the T'ai P'ing Rebellion was a powerful challenge to the Manchu rulers of China in the 1850's. It was a mixture of reactions to various foreign influences. The Manchu dynasty of China was itself foreign, and this rebellion aimed at its overthrow. The rebels were also given impetus by the government's abject inability to resist European pressure—especially by the complete British victory in the Opium War.

Hung Hsiu-ch'uan, the rebellion's leader, proposed to set all things aright with a new theocratic government. His new order borrowed many foreign Christian concepts. Hung, who had learned of Christianity from evangelists' tracts, had been gravely ill and in a prolonged coma. He recovered, and later announced that during this coma he had met God the Father and Jesus His Son. Hung learned that he was the younger brother of Jesus. The régime which he subsequently conducted was called the "Heavenly Kingdom of Great Peace." (T'ai P'ing is a short Chinese form of this term.) Beginning their rebellion against the decadent Manchu régime in 1848, Hung's forces achieved considerable success, seizing the southern metropolis of Nanking and ruling numerous provinces from 1850 to 1865.

Regardless of the T'ai P'ings' borrowings from Christianity, foreign merchants viewed them as a threat, if only because their revolt disrupted normal, peacetime trade. With foreign support, the Manchu Government was finally able to defeat the T'ai P'ings. Hung, who believed that he could die only by a silver bullet, had put aside such a bullet for his final departure from earthly power. He did indeed exit by suicide, shortly before the final collapse of this "Kingdom."

The idea of immunity to injury from anything but a silver bullet also occurred to a revitalization movement's leader in another part of the world. In 1790, the Negro and mulatto inhabitants of the West Indies island of Espanola (on which the modern nations of Haiti and the Dominican Republic are located) began a long struggle against slavery and colonial oppression. The colored leaders Toussaint L'Ouverture and Jean Dessalines were able by 1804 to eject the French administration from the entire island. In the eastern portion thereof, European authority was restored by a series of campaigns conducted from 1806 to 1814. At about the same time, Negro king Henri Christophe ruled over Northern Haiti, where he built immense fortifications, held an elaborate court after the European model, and created an army which emulated the best European military organizations of the day. Henri Christophe, like Hung Hsiu-ch'uan, professed to be vulnerable only to silver bullets. When his career ended in defeat by his rivals, he did contrive to end his life by just such a bullet.

A few decades later in China, a more severely nativistic antiforeign movement developed. In North China, the "Society of the Righteous and Harmonious Fists" was able, by the end of the nineteenth century, to demand the expulsion or annihilation of all Europeans and Americans, not to mention the liquidation of Chinese Christians. This society was commonly known as the "Boxers," a reflection of the supposedly magical boxing exercises performed by its members. The Boxers believed that when properly trained they were immune to bullets. The society may have existed as early as 1727, but became most important after 1898 because it stood for traditional Chinese culture and for the Buddhist faith, and denounced all things foreign. China had been repeatedly overwhelmed in the nineteenth century by European military forces. Large areas of the nation were dominated by European powers as "spheres of influence." China had lost the right to regulate foreign trade, determine tariffs, or operate her own customs houses. In the foreign "concessions," which included the best port areas, foreign law was the rule.

Under these desperate circumstances, the Boxers even got the support of some high officials and some members of the Imperial Family. Other officials regarded them with skepticism, noting that ". . . they had neither effective guns nor cannon, nor had they any training on the battlefield." The governors of the South China provinces managed to suppress the Boxers despite the favor the sect enjoyed at the Imperial Court. One Governor in the South, receiving a Boxer delegation, said that their immunity to Western bullets had to be confirmed by public demonstration, and accordingly had them shot by his soldiers—with Western bullets.

In Peking, however, the Boxers' violent nativism prevailed completely. Their proclamations announced that all the spirits of heaven had come down to Earth ". . . to teach our young men their magic boxing so they can . . . extinguish the foreigners, and enforce right principles on behalf of heaven."[16] Their altars were installed even in the homes of princes and high officials. Their mobs massacred Chinese Christians and many foreigners, including the German Minister to China. The foreign legation quarter of Peking was besieged, and barely escaped a general massacre during the summer of 1900. Finally, 16,000 soldiers sent by six European nations, the United States, and Japan fought their way to Peking in the summer of 1900 to relieve the legations.

The most extensive anti-Western struggle waged in modern times was Japan's Greater East Asia War—seen by many Westerners as the Asian phase of World War II, but viewed by Japan as her ultimate effort to expel all European and American power from East Asia and the Western Pacific. This great struggle was also the most monumental anti-Western "suicide effort." We should understand, as so many Japanese leaders did at the time, that it was a desperate war fought against immense material odds, where only the utmost moral strength and self-sacrifice could provide even a slight chance of ultimate success. Edwin Reischauer concludes that the Japanese miscalculated in 1941 ". . . not so much on geographic, economic, or military as on human factors. They counted heavily on their own moral superiority."[17]

Their desperation is understandable, because after July, 1941, all oil and gas shipments to Japan were stopped by the United States, Britain, and the Netherlands East Indies. Lacking other sources of supply, Japan either had to watch her petroleum stocks dwindle to the point of immobilizing her war machine, or she had to restore the imports, whether by diplomacy or by war.

In an Imperial Conference, September 6, 1941, Admiral Nagano, Chief of the General Staff, agreed to the Pearl Harbor attack plan, commenting, "It is agreed that if we do not fight now, our nation will perish. But it may well perish even if we do fight. It must be understood that national ruin without resistance would be ignominy.... Then, even if we lose, posterity will have the heritage of our loyal spirit to inspire them in turn to the defense of our country." In the later years of this war, an official Japanese slogan, *Ikki, waki, soteki* (meaning "single-minded, all-out effort in the Japanese tradition"), reflected the nature of the struggle as Japan saw it. The spirit of discipline and self-sacrifice had always been strong in Japan, but the "banzai charges" of Japanese troops in this war often demonstrated a willingness to die to the last man.

Most impressive of all were the "kamikaze" aerial attack groups activated under Vice-Admiral Ohnishi after the war had entered its final, crucial stages. The "kamikaze" plane was piloted all the way to its target—usually a ship of the U.S. Forces. More than other methods of bombardment, this offered excellent prospects of achieving a damaging hit. The pilot was sure to perish, but he and his plane would not be completely wasted. "Kamikaze" means "divine wind," a reference to winds which scattered a Mongol Armada off Japan in the thirteenth century, thus sparing the island kingdom from Mongol invasion. Revival of the word in the extremities of World War II seems to reflect hope for a comparable modern rescue by divine providence. Captain Inoguchi and Commander Nakajima believe that never before in history was such a suicide-attack program carried out so systematically, extensively, and over such a period of time.[18]

Marginal instances of faith as a major supplement to physical force are discernible in several parts of the Moslem world. The dervishes of the Sudan and the "juramentado"[19] Moslems of the Philippine Insurrection were perhaps nothing more than devout patriots whose religious ecstasy motivated them to persevere in desperate attacks.

On March 29, 1947, the French colonial régime of Madagascar was hit by a full-scale revolt sponsored by the "Malagasy Democratic Renewal Movement." The M.D.R.M. was to a large extent created by young local intellectuals, with some support from the French Communist Party. Their revolt was, however, not judiciously planned. It was a desperate step with little chance of long-term success, because the rebels had only old flintlocks and spears with which to fight the well-armed French. The revolutionaries did enjoy temporary successes thanks to the element of complete surprise. Hundreds of Frenchmen were killed in this phase, and it took 18 months before order could be restored by the French colonial forces.

When the Malagasy fighters faced the superior weaponry of the French side, they were much encouraged by prophecies that the French bullets would be converted into water in mid-trajectory if the Malagasies intoned the words "rana, rana," meaning "water, water," at the right moment. With courageous resistance by the population, and a colonialist tactic of "repression by blood bath," 12,000 persons died before the revolt was stamped out.[20]

In the Congo warfare of 1964–1965, the Central Government at Leopoldville was contending with rebels of at least two kinds: those under Gbenye, aided by Russia, and those under Mulele and Kanza, sponsored by Red China. While most of this fighting has been between native Africans, several aspects of imperialism or racism were involved. There were reflections of the Sino-Soviet rivalry—an important, long-term feud of Communist coalitions which was also a conflict of Europe versus Asia. In addition, the Leopoldville Government was repeatedly accused of being a stooge of the Belgians or Americans, accusations especially heaped upon its Premier Tshombe. Undoubtedly this Premier did call in white mercenaries to help him in 1964—Belgians, South Africans, and others—and this brought down upon him the wrath of almost all African leaders. Involved in these actions was the attempt of the mercenaries to rescue some hundreds of white persons held by the rebels. Belgian paratroopers and U.S. Air Force units also joined in this rescue. Although many of the captives did perish miserably at rebel hands, the Africans generally viewed the coming of Europeans as a revival, however brief, of white imperialist occupation.

Under these confused and desperate circumstances, the rebels' tactics were quite varied. Pierre Mulele had been trained in Chinese guerrilla methods for six months at a Chinese school near Peking. Among other things, he had learned to improvise.

The result of this improvisation was a weirdly varied display of expedients drawn from China, the West, and African witch-doctors. The witch-doctors provided Pierre Mulele's forces in the Eastern Congo with protective amulets and special witchcraft medicine. With these and the aid of preliminary ritual dances, the Mulelists were assured that they could not be hurt in combat. This confidence was further buttressed by administration of the hemp drug, with pep pills and tranquilizers sometimes brought into play.

The rebels' regular army men, as another token of confidence and courage, called themselves "simbas," or "lions." Some members of the rebel "youth force" wore war bonnets of feathers and monkey skin which were believed to have the magic power to turn bullets into water.

A leading witch-doctor was Mama Onema, a member of the late Patrice Lumumba's Batetela Tribe. So great was the reputation of her magic that in the summer of 1964 she was made chief witch-doctor under rebel leader Nicolas Olenga. Captured by the Leopoldville forces, Mama Onema reportedly confessed that she had baptized hundreds of rebel soldiers with "Mulele water," a fluid which supposedly protected them against bullets.[21]

Congo rebels also made efforts to compensate magically for a lack of anti-aircraft guns. In November, 1964, there were reports of rebels who would point a finger at hostile planes overhead, believing that this destroyed the aircraft, or at least drove it away. In the same month, an officer of the rebels sent an urgent message to his headquarters requesting that all bridges in his area be given applications of protective medicine, lest they be damaged by air attack.

To summarize, the powers claimed by various practitioners included: (1) Protection of the person from injury and death; (2) protection of sites (the most specific claim was for protection of bridges from bombardment); (3) protection from hostile aircraft by the ability to "shoot them down" with the finger. If these superstitious practices were the work only of benighted village medicine men and crackpots, they could be quickly forgotten. Yet some of the leaders who made the claims, or caused them to be made, have been very capable, enlightened leaders of large political or military organizations. What benefits did they expect to derive from such nonsense?

The leaders have all been "revitalizers" of weak, poorly equipped, and demoralized peoples. Such practices eliminate fear, develop scorn of the adversary, and strengthen morale. The magical procedures therefore enable the fighting force to attack (or defend) determinedly, even against superior weapons.

Putting aside all jokes about "overcoming the opponent by sheer force of will," we should consider Salvador de Madariaga's dictum that all armed force is in the last analysis moral force, i.e., the readiness and willingness to use the weapons as they could best be used. The readiness of Europe's opponents, in so many times and places, to rely heavily upon such extraordinary forms of moral force testifies eloquently to their exacerbated feelings and their desperate determination.

The moral position of Europe and America in the world is similarly illuminated by the successful use in modern times of non-violent demonstrations and civil disobedience as means of exerting moral force. With non-violent techniques, as with the immunity cults, we find that related remedies have worked against related abuses—for the relief of oppressed minorities in South Africa and the United States, as well as for the liberation of British India.

In the early 1800's, advocates of freedom for the slaves in the United States began to consider non-violent means whereby they could press for abolition of slavery. Inspired by the Biblical injunction, "Resist not evil," these non-violent abolitionists were most influential in the 1830's and early 1840's. Their best-known spokesman, William Lloyd Garrison, in his newspaper The Liberator, told the slaves, "Not by the sword shall your deliverance be." He believed that through dissemination of "light and truth" the evil of slavery could be overthrown.[22]

Another American, H. D. Thoreau, contributed ideas of civil disobedience—such non-violent acts as non-cooperation with governmental authorities, non-compliance with laws, and non-payment of taxes.

It was Mohandas Gandhi who demonstrated extensively that

moral force alone could be a most potent weapon. He synthesized
the ideas cited above with those of Tolstoy. Tolstoy's belief in the
power of the moral individual and the efficacy of civil disobedience
is perhaps best shown in his words, "The position of governments
in the presence of men who profess Christianity is so precarious
that very little is needed to shake their power to pieces."[23]

Gandhi corresponded with Tolstoy from 1900 to 1910, and in
honor of this contributor to his philosophy and method the
Mahatma established "Tolstoy Farm" near Johannesburg, South
Africa. It was a simple hermitage for him and his followers, and
from it went out directions for the Indians' campaign of non-
violent resistance to the white supremacists of South Africa.

The special power of Gandhi's methods lies in the fact that they
are programs of positive action. As we noted in Chapter Seven,
Gandhi avoided recourse to force, which might be answered with
hopelessly superior armed might. Yet the Gandhian approach can
draw an oppressed people out of a slough of inaction and despair.
Best of all, it enables them to project their rectitude, confidence,
and just complaints directly into the awareness of the people
acquiescing in their ill treatment. It is not surprising that this
form of "force without bullets" has had powerful effects, not only
in Gandhi's own campaigns, but in the campaigns of American
Negroes to gain equitable civil rights.

A number of American Negro leaders visited Gandhi, including
Dr. Channing Tobias, Director of the Phelps-Stokes Fund, and Dr.
Benjamin Mays, President of Morehouse College. These men discussed non-violence with the Mahatma in 1937. (It was only three
years later that Gandhian techniques were applied to racial problems in Chicago.) Gandhi expressed his regret that the Ethiopians
had not met the Italian invasion of the mid-thirties with non-
violence; however, he viewed the violent successes of Hitler and
Mussolini as transitory. He explained at some length how effective
a non-violent minority could be against a powerful majority, provided only that the former was well disciplined and prepared to
suffer.[24]

In 1936, Dr. and Mrs. Howard Thurman visited Gandhi. Dr.
Thurman, a Negro minister and writer, asked Gandhi to come to

America in behalf of the Negro minority there, which he said was prepared to use Gandhian techniques. The Mahatma said he must first finish his work in India, but added in parting, "It may be through the Negroes that the unadulterated message of non-violence will be delivered to the world."[25] Gandhi promised that the American Negroes would have a bright future if they would employ non-violent methods.

Gandhian methods became the guiding light of the American civil rights movement when such events as the Montgomery, Alabama, bus boycott of 1955 underlined their efficacy. In 1958, Chester Bowles, for some time American Ambassador to India, wrote an article for the *Saturday Evening Post* telling "What Negroes Can Learn from Gandhi." The year 1960 brought many demonstrations of the usefulness of "sit-in" tactics for the integration of restaurants and other public places.

Of course the immunity practices which we discussed previously differ from non-violent demonstrations in one important respect. The former are coupled with some use of physical force; the latter are not. Both are, however, the deeds of seriously aggrieved people whose morale is being revitalized, and who furthermore have poor prospects for success through use of conventional violence.

In conclusion, we have found exceptional forms of moral confidence and intensity of feeling among many of the peoples who have been under white domination. What could be more portentous than the modes in which this feeling will make itself felt in the future?

If you regard the immunity cults and banzai charges as merely cases of group-suicide by fanatics, think what may happen in future recurrences of those desperate actions. Now that nuclear weaponry is becoming available to more and more nations, the result could extend virtually to global destruction. In times to come, we must expect that the victims of the West will overcome the abject inferiority of armament which previously hampered them. What then?

We can find some tentative encouragement regarding avoidance of all-out violence in the future when we consider the findings

of Konrad Lorenz and Robert Ardrey in the field of animal behavior. Their respective books, *On Aggression* and *The Territorial
Imperative*, both published in 1966, have led me to think that non-
violent tactics may not be irreconcilable with common animal
behavior. Lorenz describes the ritualization of combat by many
species, including some higher mammals. Quite commonly, fights
to the point of serious injury or death are avoided by a gesture of
submission from the weaker combatant. When the conventional,
symbolic act of submission occurs, the prospective victor instinctively stops fighting. Of course the practitioner of non-violence
is personally stronger than his opponents. Even so, may not his
gesture of non-resistance help to save *homo sapiens* from self-
destruction, just as the instinctual restraint described above has
kept other species alive?

Another somewhat encouraging discovery from the animal
world is the pattern of "territorial defense." Defense of an animal's
territory—its customary feeding ground—increases in violence
and determination when the invader is nearer to the heart of that
territory. On the outer perimeter, or beyond the perimeter, the
occupant fights more casually and often abandons the fight.

This may help to explain the desperate behavior of the "in-
vulnerable fighters" and suicide fighters described herein. Usually
they were defending the heart of their territory or making a last-
ditch stand of some kind. The same principle might also help to
account for the rapid withdrawal of European governments from
remote colonies where, if military strength alone was considered,
they could still prevail. Careful international planning may therefore have a hitherto unformulated asset—human beings can be
pacified more easily if they are campaigning far away from home.

All of these considerations are, so far as we can tell, equally
applicable to all groupings of our species. Neither the instinctual
causes of aggression nor these palliatives for it belong more to one
continent than to another. These matters are nevertheless relevant
to the present study, because resistance to white power has so often
involved a force which differed from conventional violence .

:: X I ::

The Past Meets
the Future

AFRO-ASIAN SOLIDARITY AS A FORCE
IN WORLD AFFAIRS

COLONIALISM has actually come to an end, except for a small number of minor possessions of the white nations and the Russian control of Central and Northeastern Asia. However, the Afro-Asian resentment of colonialism is not oriented only toward the past, but demonstrates a real fear of it as a present and future danger. Indian writer Sripati Chandra-sekhar warns Americans and Europeans not to be surprised that in Asian eyes colonialism still appears to offer greater threats of misery and unhappiness than Communism. "Asia has not had time to forget her wounds," he says.[1]

In the United Nations, a resolution passed on December 14, 1960, declared in part that the General Assembly,

> Convinced that the continued existence of colonialism prevents the development of international economic cooperation, impedes the social, cultural and economic development of dependent peoples and militates against the United Nations ideal of universal peace...
> Believing that the process of liberation is irresistible and irreversible and that, in order to avoid serious crises, an end must be put

to colonialism and all practices of segregation and discrimination associated therewith . . .

Solemnly proclaims the necessity of bringing to a speedy and un-conditional end colonialism in all its forms and manifestations.

This intense consciousness of colonialism in the 1960's seems to be due to three factors: (1) The "anti-imperialist" propaganda of the Russian- and Chinese-led groups of countries; (2) the very real and immense military power in the hands of the United States and the European powers which makes them appear to be a great potential menace, a factor reinforced by the racist and totalitarian proclivities which, as we have seen, remain very much alive in many Western countries; and (3) the economic problems and tribulations of the Afro-Asian nations, whose governments often use the Western powers as scapegoats for these troubles.

C. L. Sulzberger wrote in *The New York Times*, July 1, 1960, the day after the Belgian Congo became independent, that the West "must fight a legacy of prejudice and exploitation which is not simply erased by grants of sovereignty." However, Afro-Asian solidarity involves more than the negative attitude of anti-colonialism. It is more than the joint pursuit of a vendetta against former colonial powers of the West. Perhaps the fairest and clearest explanation was given during the Asian-African Conference at Bandung, Indonesia. This meeting in 1955 was a great early mile-stone in Afro-Asian solidarity. A pro-Western member of the Con-ference explained that the conclave was "an effort for these coun-tries to regain their personality and international dignity and was an assertion of their personality vis-à-vis the West."[2]

Bandung was not the first conclave of Asian or African dele-gates. There had been Pan-African conferences in the 1920's and 1940's too, but the coming of independence made such delibera-tions much more important. Besides general political gatherings, there are the common-sense activities of regional coordination— especially economic—which should develop on any continent. (Consider the European Economic Community or the Pan-American Union.) These coordinative efforts also generate soli-darity, largely in a positive, constructive sense of the term.

It was natural for many of France's former colonies to enter the African and Malagasy Union to maintain some of the coordinative arrangements which had been provided by the French imperial system. Even when this body deteriorated, ten of its members regrouped in the so-called African and Malagasy Union for Economic Cooperation.

The Organization of African Unity was formed in 1963, with 31 nations adhering to its Charter in that year. It proved to be the broadest based, most successful African continental body, but it did not eliminate the need for more specialized bodies to coordinate marketing arrangements for African commodities. Many of the recently freed Afro-Asian lands were formed quite artificially by the deals and démarches of their former European proprietors. These small units could not flourish without close cooperation. The Senegal River Valley project, for example, requires the cooperation of Mauritania, Senegal, Mali, and Guinea. To be sure, there are equally tiny, strangely configured nations in Europe, but Africa hopes to accomplish in a few decades the industrialization that took two centuries in Europe. This generates an urgency which may promote quite surprising projects for unification.

Ethnic influences are another unifying factor; there is Moslem unity, Black African solidarity, and sometimes even a unity of major tribes that live in more than one nation. For instance, the Bakongo people are located in the two Congo Republics and in Angola. The common cultural heritage derived from former membership in, for example, the British Commonwealth is another influence that can lead to closer cooperation.

The Buddhist heritage is shared by Asians, all the way from India through China and Southeast Asia to Japan. Though most Indians and Chinese do not adhere to the Buddhist faith, its modes of thought are still influential. Another group of joint heirs, partially congruent with the preceding one, comprises the inheritors of Confucianism—China, Viet Nam, Korea, and Japan.

Such common backgrounds, however, lend themselves to regional solidarity, not to complete Afro-Asian unanimity. The latter may be almost impossible to achieve in any thorough, lasting way; there are just too many points of difference within these two continents. Still, some degree of cohesion has resulted from the existence of problems common to all Afro-Asians. They were all victims of European impositions, and observed the cohesiveness of Westerners vis-à-vis non-Europeans.

In recent decades, the competition of blocs led by the U.S. and the U.S.S.R. produced among Afro-Asians a strong "plague on both your houses" reaction. The newly independent nations resisted pressures from either bloc to enlist them on its side. They disliked any plan to lead them in a crusade against capitalism or Communism; they had already been led too long by the white man. A third World War was an unattractive prospect, with the fantastically destructive weaponry brandished by the Soviet Union and America; perhaps the statesmanship of a strong bloc of neutrals could head off such a war. When the first conference of non-aligned nations was held at Belgrade in 1961, the central concept of the conferees was that their countries—mostly Afro-Asian nations—should be a cohesive, third coalition or force, free of the blocs led by the U.S.S.R. and the U.S.

On some occasions, Afro-Asian cohesiveness has had its negative and irresponsible side. Demonstrations against American, British, and other European Embassies are commonplace. The American-Belgian mission in 1964 to rescue white hostages of the Congolese rebels provoked violent indignation and hostile acts throughout the former colonial areas.

In the United Nations, over 60 members of the African-Asian caucus have wielded more and more influence. This caucus, when it manages to act in unison, controls more than half of the vote in the General Assembly. There is a tendency, however, toward separate meetings by more than 40 African members. Their strength lies especially in their numerous votes at the U.N. The Asian members, on the other hand, represents the greater portion of the world's population, and they too have begun to meet apart from the two-continent caucus (while also still taking part in it). The new African delegations ceased following the lead of such seasoned Asian diplomats as the Indian delegates when the Sino-Indian border disputes began. It is also possible that animosity has been generated between Moslem members and representatives of Sub-Saharan Africa during the long guerrilla warfare between the

Arab rulers of the Sudan and the Negro populace of the Southern Sudan. Nor should the Red Chinese contributions to this uprising be overlooked.

Despite all this, a move back toward Afro-Asian coordination came in 1965 when the Foreign Minister of Pakistan suggested the foundation of an organization similar to the Organization of African Unity, but including both continents. The Foreign Minister said that all these nations must build up traditions of equal and just relationships among themselves to insure that Western colonialism would not be superseded by local imperialism.

THE SINO-SOVIET QUARRELS

FROM THE 1920's, when Communism began its development in Asia, until at least 1959, hardly anyone in Europe or America acknowledged the possibility of discord among Communist nations on racial lines. The Red parties themselves were loath to acknowledge it; their creed rejected racism, and their movement aspired to rise above ethnic barriers, healing old animosities through the power of ideology. All workers of the world were understood to have identical interests, like their proper adversaries, the capitalists of the world.

The anti-Communists of the West likewise believed in the indivisibility of Communism. Regarding it as the essence of evil, they could not visualize it in a subdivided form. Even when Titoism in Yugoslavia had shown that Communist schisms or heresies were possible, a decade passed before a Sino-Soviet split was recognized by experts in Washington. Perhaps one reason for this was that the Western inclination to "go crusading" was still powerful, and a crusade proceeds more smoothly if all the heathen are homogeneously evil. Furthermore, the crusade against Communism—-the Cold War—created vested interests, military-industrial-governmental complexes which could flourish only if the crusade continued. The Soviet bloc has had its crusade, too— against "capitalistic imperialism"—and there are vested interests in Soviet military and governmental circles which have found this crusade most useful.

These out-of-date views of Communism as a monolithic unity remained popular in Russia and other Western countries, even though China and Russia developed quite different forms of Communism. In China, a special indigenous Communism stressed the revolutionary role of the peasantry, while European Marxism stressed the role of the industrial proletariat. Stalinism in Russia was, of course, far from being true Marxism. It was evil, but in its own special way.

The Russian Party under Stalin was so poorly attuned to China's special problems that Moscow repeatedly gave ineffectual guidance to the Chinese comrades. "Work with the Chinese Nationalists," said Stalin in the 1920's, contributing to the near-demolition of the Party in China at Chiang K'ai-shek's hands in 1927. When World War II ended, Stalin advised his Chinese comrades to refrain from full-scale civil war against the Nationalists. Mao Tse-tung disregarded the Russian advice, and triumphed.

In preceding chapters we have noted Sino-Russian altercations after World War II concerning the factories, railroads, and military bases of Manchuria. Other debates centered around Soviet programs of aid to China. This aid helped to push Sino-Soviet trade to its peak in 1958–1959, when half of China's total trade was with the U.S.S.R. That commerce fell off heavily in 1960–1962, when the U.S.S.R. insisted on full payment for its goods and required prompt remittance of all interest due on China's sizable past debts.

It is important to remember that the Soviet economy has a less ample base than the economy of the U.S., so that greater allocations of resources to major programs can only mean painful cutbacks elsewhere. The Soviet foreign aid programs, though far smaller than American ones, make unwelcome demands on the national economy. In this sense alone, the cutback and virtual termination of loans and aid programs for China was, without a doubt, welcome to Soviet economic and financial planners.[3] Some authorities believe that the Sino-Soviet conflict was caused primarily by the Soviet Government's refusal to allot huge resources to develop Chinese industry—because the people of Russia could not and would not tolerate a gigantic aid-to-China program.[4]

Chinese bitterness was also aggravated by Soviet refusals to share atomic bomb data with the Peking Government. On top of that came the dramatic Soviet achievement of launching the world's first artificial satellite in 1957. This, and subsequent Russian feats in missilery and space exploration, showed China that her Russian "partner" possessed amazing resources, but, as Peking saw it, these resources were not "fully committed to the struggle against imperialism." That is, the Russians seemed too reluctant to challenge the United States. A Russo-American entente was entirely possible, suspected Peking. Accordingly, every gesture of cordiality between Khrushchev and the American Presidents was taken by the Chinese as confirmation of such an understanding. The Russian retort to these allegations was simply that nuclear warfare was not to be courted.

By 1960, the Sino-Soviet feud was so obvious that an objective observer could not write it off as superficial. The Party conferences at Bucharest and Moscow in 1960 and the Twenty-second Party Congress in 1961 were increasingly violent demonstrations of·deep differences between the two Red giants, with Moscow rejecting the Chinese view that violent world revolution and war against the "imperialists" was both inevitable and desirable.

These conferences were more than mere oratorical competition, of course. Both Chinese and Russians used them as a platform for trying to convince other Red bloc members and Communist Parties in both neutralist and Western bloc nations that they were right, and that their respective programs offered more for the future of Communism. More important still, they were appealing to latent opposition in the rival country. The Russians were thinking, for one thing, of Chinese military leadership, which had everything to gain in terms of modern equipment and technical support by a rapprochement with the Russians. The Chinese could appeal to Stalinist, doctrinaire Russians on grounds of Marxist dogma, as well as to the Soviet marshals, whose quest for military appropriations often made them allies of those who preached aggressive tactics.

The Bucharest Conference of Communist Parties met in June, 1960. From the fifth to the ninth of June, the General Council of the World Federation of Trade Unions was in session at Peking, and was used as a forum for a strong indictment of Khrushchev's view that world wars were to be avoided, delivered by the Chinese Vice President of the WFTU. He also attacked Khrushchev's belief in the possibility of peaceful coexistence with the capitalist world, and the possibility of disarmament as a corollary to peaceful existence.

This clear challenge to the Soviet Premier must have strengthened the Premier's resolve to have it out with the Chinese at Bucharest. There he told the Chinese representative that Mao was an ultra-dogmatist with the same narrow viewpoint that Stalin had, and that the Chinese were ignorant of the potential of nuclear weapons in modern warfare. The Chinese replied with similar bitterness. Back in Russia, the Premier appears to have enlisted the aid of influential Party members to acquaint the Soviet Party with the dispute, and to prepare both Party leadership and public opinion for the confrontation that was to come at the Moscow conference of all the Communist Parties in November, 1960.

At this Moscow conference, the Chinese were so uncompromising, careless about inter-Party harmony except on their own terms, and brutally inclined to accept or even welcome a nuclear war which might—as they themselves put it—kill 50 per cent of the populations involved, that they lost much of the support their theories had previously enjoyed in the Russian and other Communist Parties. At the Twenty-second Party Congress, in October, 1961, the U.S.S.R. delegation made a pretense of focussing its attack on Albania, while the Chinese, conversely, emphasized defense of Albania. On later occasions, the Chinese press quoted Albanian criticisms of Khrushchev, instead of making an overtly Chinese attack on the Soviet Premier. The adversaries thus avoided attacking one another directly. However, the real importance of the noisy Albanian defiance was that it could serve as a rallying point for anti-Russian actions around the Communist world.

Concerning the nationalistic aspect of the Russian side of the dispute with China, Adlai Stevenson found that most Russian officials with whom he talked about China were worried about the burgeoning Chinese population, its aggressive government, and their long common border. Soviet nervousness must have been heightened by General Charles de Gaulle's view that China is destined eventually to detach Asiatic Russia from Muscovite control.

Border incidents were a matter involving, from the Russian point of view, simple national defense. Their anxiety about the border was given substance by Peking's claim that territories Russia had gained by the Treaty of Peking of 1860 should be returned, and Chinese maps which persistently showed parts of the Sino-Soviet border and much of the Sino-Mongolian border as "undemarcated." Also, the official Chinese maps up to the Communist period always showed the Pamir region of Soviet Central Asia as Chinese. Although the Mao régime withdrew those, the Chinese rights there are historically as valid as claims on the Indian frontier.

Substantial border flareups occurred in 1962, though only in 1963 did Peking bring them to light with a broadcast charging that Russia coerced tens of thousands of Chinese citizens into entering the U.S.S.R. China also charged that the U.S.S.R. tried to overthrow the local government in the Ili district of Sinkiang Province. The most sweeping charge came in 1963 with a Soviet statement that the Peking Government tried "to appropriate individual sections of Soviet territory," and that the Chinese violated the border 5,000 times in 1962 alone.

Khrushchev found it expedient to say that Sino-Soviet arguments were only a quarrel between friends, and his government moved toward another conference with the Chinese, held finally in Moscow in July, 1963. Whereas in April Khrushchev had called for worldwide Communist unity and curbs against "war-minded imperialist madmen," by July the atmosphere was different. The Sino-Russian conference began with strict secrecy, but it was soon evident that Soviet leaders were unable or unwilling to reach agreement with the Chinese. Peking Radio accused the Soviet Government of trying to poison the relations of the two countries.

It was not even possible to quiet down the discord in which the meeting ended. The U.S.S.R. moved again to friendliness with the West and talk of disarmament and peace. Khrushchev continued to call for worldwide Communist unity and curbs against "war-minded imperialist madmen," but Sino-Russian differences had become too great to reconcile so easily.

Mikhail Suslov, a top official of the Russian Communist Party, complained to the Central Committee in 1964: "The scheme of the Chinese Communist Party leadership amounts to an intention to foist their adventurist conceptions and methods onto the peoples of Asia, Africa, and Latin America, to set peoples against one another according to racial distinctions."

Mao had the last word in his dispute with Khrushchev, who was dislodged from office in late 1964, partly because of this feud. However, the new leadership of Brezhnev and Kosygin could do nothing about the dispute, and Peking continued to denounce the "revisionist Russian clique and its collaborators the American imperialists." Peking complained in 1965 that Moscow was abetting Indian aggression against Pakistan while failing to support Vietnamese patriots in their resistance against American aggression. Worse still, said the Chinese press, the U.S. and U.S.S.R. were controlling the United Nations in a joint attempt to dominate the world.

Chinese turmoil at home during Mao Tse-tung's cultural revolution of 1966–1967 inspired a continuing barrage of insults and threats between Peking and Moscow. Both countries complained that the other Red giant was mistreating its citizens. Europeans may have recalled those insulting signs in the foreign-controlled parks of Shanghai before World War II, which read "No Chinese or dogs allowed," when the restaurants of Mao's Peking put up signs in 1967 to proclaim, "Out of bounds for Russian revisionist swine and dogs."

COMPETITION FOR INFLUENCE IN
AFRO-ASIA

TO THE recently liberated nations of Afro-Asia, the Sino-Soviet dispute has appeared as competition for their favor. The competition has sometimes become multilateral when these two competitors vied with the United States and the nations of Western Europe. All offered gifts and assistance to the new nations, but their gifts were sometimes Trojan horses, bringing unwelcome intrigue, pressures, and coups d'état to the recipient.

From the end of World War II until the death of Stalin, Russia was somehow inhibited from developing rapport with the non-Communist, "just plain nationalist" leadership of many newly emerging nations. Little or no effort was made to establish close ties with such states, or to assist their economic development. Soviet spokesmen charged the new "bourgeois nationalist leaders" with being exploiters of the people," in the Western capitalist tradition.

After 1953, Russian policy makers did not let ideological differences keep them from working with nationalist régimes. In 1956, the Russians acknowledged that new nations of a capitalist type could be clearly distinguished from West European and American capitalist powers, provided the new nation was a neutralist in the Cold War and strove for real economic independence from the great capitalist powers.

Red Chinese leaders naturally objected when the U.S.S.R. tendered economic aid to new nations of the above sort. The aid was substantial, equaling billions of dollars, applied to dozens of non-Communist countries. China, with a desperate need for economic assistance in her abortive "Great Leap Forward" of the late 1950's, considered that more of this Soviet aid should have come to her.

In regard to Marxist doctrine, moreover, the Chinese found aid to capitalist nations unjustifiable. How, the Chinese asked, did such nations fit into any proper Marxist plan of development? How would they make the transition to socialism? To answer, in 1960 the "Moscow Statement of Eighty-one Communist and Workers' Parties" declared that a country qualified as a national democracy if it was free, independent, and anti-imperialist, and progressive, with agrarian reforms and other social improvements. As an example of how these features could lead to socialism, a Russian writer pointed to Cuba.[5]

One suspects that China's selection of recipients for her own aid was based on the same criteria Russia used. Chinese aid from 1956 to 1965 went to ten countries in Asia and nine in Africa. The grand total of these commitments has been the equivalent of about three-quarters of a billion dollars, although in some cases the commitment was not implemented fully. Though the aggregate amount is far smaller than the U.S. or U.S.S.R. programs, nearly half of the assistance went to Africa, and most of the rest to Asia. Of course, most of this aid was given to non-Communist countries, lands where true Marxism could not materialize in the near future.

If one compares the foreign aid policies of Red and anti-Red countries, it is noteworthy that African countries received 30 per cent of the $1,500,000,000 in Sino-Soviet distributions outside the Red blocs, 1954–1963. During the same period, only 6 per cent of U.S. aid went to Africa.[6] The newly developing countries can complain of the distribution of U.S. aid (military and economic) over the longer period, 1945–1962. To state it in billions of dollars, Europe received 45, the Far East 22, the Middle East and South Asia 18, Latin America 7, and Africa 2.[7] Though the absolute amounts are larger than the aid from China or Russia, the relative amounts show great emphasis on helping Europe, not the populous and needy Afro-Asian countries.

The traditional role of Moscow as headquarters of world Communism, a role dear to Russian hearts, has been challenged very effectively by Peking in recent years. The Chinese can do this because of their "non-white" status and their clear record as a past, and allegedly present, victim of European and American imperialism. In their economic problems, too, they have much in common with the poor, industrially primitive areas of the world. As Dr. Walt Rostow would put it, the Russians have reached "technological maturity," while the Chinese are far from doing so. Relatively crude Chinese expedients for industrialization, and the Chinese programs in general, may seem applicable to visitors from less developed countries, while Russian demonstration of a fully automated, highly intricate, costly industrial plant may seem impressive but irrelevant to a nation which lacks the capital to set up such a plant and the technology to support it.

The Chinese, as conscious of prestige and world position as the Russians, began in earnest to offer a worldwide challenge in early 1960, when they created the Committee for the Support of Afro-Asian Emancipation Movements and the Chinese-African Friendship Society. While the latter worked on cultural and economic exchanges, Peking proceeded in 1961 to establish the Chinese People's Committee for the Aid of African Countries against Aggression, a propaganda organ, and the Institute for African Affairs, for training African members of the Party. At the Afro-Asian Solidarity Conference of 1960, the Chinese challenge to Russia was manifested by the largeness of Peking's delegation, and its opposition to proposals of the Soviet delegation.

At exhibitions and trade fairs, the Chinese have gone to much expense to show what they can offer the newly emergent nations. Chinese trade and economic aid can hardly be huge in quantity, but it has been carefully placed to supplement ideological infiltration. The terms of Chinese aid have at times been more attractive than Soviet terms—with the offering of interest-free loans, for example. In trade agreements, it has not been difficult to rival Soviet terms; the U.S.S.R. is often a notoriously hard bargainer.

The U.S.S.R. authorities seem to have tried hard to cultivate the newly emergent nations; extensive acceptance of Afro-Asian students at Russian universities has been one program. As of 1963, there were 2,000 Africans studying at Patrice Lumumba Friendship University in Moscow and 1,000 more studying elsewhere in Russia, as compared with 5,000 in the United States. These 3,000 have been carefully handled by the authorities, but there still have been interracial incidents and complaints, as well as dissatisfaction with curricula.

Other troubles for the Soviets came at the Afro-Asian Solidarity Conference at Moshi, Tanganyika, where the Chinese representatives were far better received, while President Nyerere of Tanganyika implied that the Russians were just a new type of white exploiters who wished to colonize Africa. As one Russian observer at the conference, Vladimir Kudryavtsev, put it: "Some of the more chauvinistically inclined leaders would like to direct the solidarity movement, not against imperialism and colonialism and its agents, but against all white people."

The prominent Russian specialist on Africa, Professor Potekhin, had foreseen the exploitation of Pan-Africanism by China. He said that Pan-Africanism could "give rise to extreme forms of nationalism, and may be used by opponents of the peaceful coexistence of peoples to set the black and white race in opposition."[8]

In Asia, Chinese influence could be seen in the Japanese Communist Party, and there was nothing surprising about Chinese influence in the North Korean and North Viet Nam satellites; but an interesting conflict came into the open in 1963 concerning the Mongolian People's Republic, when the First Secretary of that country's Party addressed a special ideological conference in Ulan Bator. He declared that Peking had busily built factions in almost every Communist Party and had irresponsibly sown discord everywhere. He accused the Chinese of using the ideology of nationalism as a weapon, while disguising this nationalism as ultra-revolutionary. The conference denounced the pro-Chinese nationalist faction of D. Tumur-Ochir, former Mongolian Party Secretary and Politburo member. The importance to the U.S.S.R. of the Sino-Soviet tug-of-war over Mongolia was underscored by prominent mention of large-scale Soviet economic aid to the Mongols, and the arrival of a special Soviet delegation to this conference, headed by a top-flight Soviet official.

In discussing the Sino-Soviet rivalry in various nations, we have considered mainly the effort to dominate the parties of Communist faithful. In addition, the two powers must be concerned with their appeal to socialists of many types.

The result of Peking's belligerence has been to leave these promising fields to the Russians. Moderate socialists have been alienated by China's aggressive moves, particularly the socialists of such Chinese neighbors as India or Japan. For example, the Indian Socialist magazine, *Link*, which had for years described the Chinese Communist Government as peace-loving and progressive, issued an article after the 1962 invasion, strongly denouncing it as a chauvinistic government of Chinese mandarins in Marxist disguise. *Link* noted that Mao Tse-tung had declared in 1939, in a pamphlet called "Chinese Revolution and the Chinese Communist Party," that China must regain her territories seized by the imperialists, including Korea, Viet Nam, Burma, Bhutan, and Nepal.[9]

In South and Southeast Asia, the inter-bloc rivalries take many forms. Chinese influence is in the ascendancy in Viet Nam, but the counterweight of Soviet competition gives the Vietnamese Communists a little freedom of action with respect to their powerful neighbor. Burma also has a common border with China, whose expansionism would worry any neighbor. On the other hand, even Burma, remote as it is from the U.S.S.R., has had its worries with the Soviets too. There were cargoes of cement delivered to open Burmese wharves by Soviet ships at monsoon time, with predictably sad results; this was the quid pro quo for Burma in a barter deal with Russia! There was also the fight put up by Soviet agents at the Rangoon airport in defiance of national authorities, so that an unwilling Soviet citizen could be put on a Russia-bound plane.

Indonesia, the most powerful Southeast Asian nation, has accepted the blandishments and gifts of all blocs. After taking more than a half billion dollars worth of aid from the U.S.S.R., and close to $700,000,000 from the U.S., Indonesia's leader, Sukarno, decided that more benefits would accrue from a close relationship with China. With Peking's support, Indonesia might dominate much of Southeast Asia. After the Chinese had successfully tested a nuclear device, Sukarno's Government apparently requested Chinese assistance for an Indonesian atomic bomb program. In return for Peking's favors, Indonesia's diplomatic establishments helped to maintain China's global network of activities. For example, Sukarno's Consulate in Calcutta handled disbursements to pro-Chinese Indians.[10] However, in 1965 the Indonesian Communists went too far by attempting a coup d'état, with Chinese encouragement. Indonesian Army leadership resisted this coup and struck shattering blows to the Red organization in Indonesia. Cordial relations with Peking were broken off.

India itself, once very friendly with Red China, became inimical when Sino-Indian border warfare broke out repeatedly in the 1960's. The Indians resented the Chinese invasion of territory claimed by India, and a settlement of the border disputes was not achieved. Add to this the humiliation felt by the Indians because of military defeats in the border skirmishes, and the hostility toward China is understandable.

As a rule, the neutralist nations of Afro-Asia have reaffirmed their freedom of action by taking jabs at all great powers. The second conference of non-aligned Afro-Asian nations at Cairo in 1964, with 47 countries participating, produced thrusts in every direction. One of its resolutions called for a U.N. investigation of alleged U.S. abuses of Puerto Rico; another demanded that the Union of South Africa be blockaded to make it desist from its white supremacy program. The conferees called for cessation of all nuclear weapons development and production, yet Indonesian delegates managed to defeat an Indian motion that China be urged to abstain from nuclear weapons development. The conference also passed an Indonesian resolution that "Peaceful coexistence cannot fully materialize through the world without the abolition of imperialism, colonialism, and neo-colonialism."

Although much of these proceedings sounded favorable to the militant Communist line, there was an even greater feeling of actual neutralism. This was clarified by the host to that conference, Egypt's President Nasser, who declared in February, 1965, "Our differences with Communism are radical. We believe in religion and we reject the dictatorship of any class. We look forward to national unity [meaning probably *Arab* unity]."

The relation of the United States to non-aligned nations is compounded of generous foreign aid programs on one hand, and on the other hand an American failing, best formulated by Chester Bowles: "We Americans have one peculiar national habit: We tend to act much better than we sound. Thus we argue that the time has come to grant our Negro citizens first-class citizenship, not because they have been waiting 180 years since the Declaration of Independence asserted that 'all men are created equal,' but because the colored majority of mankind in Asia and Africa is said to be breathing down our necks."[11]

The world should not speak of American *imperialism* today, but rather of American *messianism*, a continuing world-view which the late House Speaker Sam Rayburn epitomized in a speech of April 3, 1961: "A world that the United States does not lead, if there ever is such a world, will be a world that is not free." That these views still flourish in U.S. Government circles was affirmed by a memorandum written by Senator Henry Jackson's Subcommittee on National Security in May, 1965. "The idea of manifest destiny still survives," said the memorandum. "Officials make sweeping declarations of our world mission, and often verbally commit the nation to policies and programs far beyond our capabilities."

Unfortunately, freedom and American-style democracy do not have the intense appeal for Afro-Asians that Americans expect. It is *independence*, non-interference from abroad, that means so much to victims of the colonial experience. They may even adopt modes of totalitarian government that seemed hateful when practiced by Europeans, but can appear useful to a new nation faced with urgent problems.

What orientation have the little Communist Parties of Sub-Saharan Africa taken in the Sino-Soviet dispute? In 1964, the magazine *Communist Affairs* found that none of the formally organized parties were pro-Chinese. In three countries, Basutoland, Senegal, and South Africa, the Communist Parties were believed to be following the Russian Party line. (However, the Basutoland Congress Party apparently gets most of its election campaign funds from China.) There were Communist-related political groups whose orientation was unclear, including movements in the former Belgian Congo and Swaziland. Similarly uncertain were the Malagasy Communist Party and the tiny Communist Party of Nigeria. The Malagasy Party is more likely to follow the Peking line, because there is a Chinese minority on Madagascar and the island is receiving particular attention from China's propagandists.

So far as competition on the air waves is concerned, in 1964 Moscow and the radio stations of its satellites were broadcasting a total of 247 hours per week to Sub-Saharan Africa, while Peking broadcast 62 hours weekly.[12] Chinese propaganda in printed form has been including maps of Asia and Africa on which little red torches mark areas where "just wars of liberation" are supposed to be going on against white colonialists. The torches appear on all the Central Asian republics of the U.S.S.R.!

Chinese money has been used judiciously to assist local leaders in widening their power, or even in dislodging governments which were too moderate or too much under European influence. Kenya's Home Minister, Oginga Odinga, was reported in 1964 to have taken over $250,000 in backing from the Chinese to gain control of the Luo tribe. In Africa, where political power continued to rest on tribal influence, this was especially important because the money enabled Odinga to take control of this large tribe from another, much better known Luo, Tom Mboya.

Certainly African advocates of daring tactics were turning more to Peking at this time. Even some moderate men with long-standing Western ties found that they could retain their influence only if they jumped on the bandwagon of militant neutralism. This neutralism implied rejection of the West, and the best way to demonstrate that one was free of Western influence was to work with Peking. Dr. Eduardo Mondlane, leader of the liberation movement in Portuguese Mozambique, had lived in the United States for a decade, earning an American Ph.D., acquiring an American wife, and teaching in an American university. Under heavy pressure from other leaders to move aggressively against the Portuguese, Dr. Mondlane journeyed to Peking at the end of 1963, securing an interview with Chinese leader Mao Tse-tung.

At the same time, the leader of Portuguese-held Angola's liberation movement, Holden Roberto, declared that he would welcome any Communist assistance. Had he not done so, there were rival leaders eager to unseat him. He would also have found it hard to get much-needed support from his fellow Africans—the African Nations Solidarity Fund, for example—if he failed to accept offers of aid from Peking or Moscow.[13] Roberto's background of visits and governmental contacts in Western countries really made it *all the more essential* for him to follow a militant revolutionary line.

In other countries where moderation was superseded by a mood

of militant independence, the French could still exercise a stabiliz-
ing influence. Gabon's President Mba called in French paratroopers
to quell a revolt. The former French Congo ejected Fulbert Youlou,
its moderate chief-of-state. Within 18 months the country was
following the Chinese line, and several distinguished moderate
statesmen were murdered. However, the Chinese were unlikely to
throw the French out, because Peking would not care to take over
the burden of subsidies paid by France.

A big event in China's drive for influence in Africa was Premier
Chou En-lai's African tour in December, 1963, and January, 1964.
His long itinerary included Egypt, Algeria, Morocco, Mali, Sudan,
Ethiopia, Guinea, Ghana, and Somalia; the objects were public
relations and a careful assessment of China's new position in Africa.

Stopping first in Egypt, Chou told cheering crowds that Afro-
Asian countries working together can outstrip the West. Egyptian
President Nasser gave Chou a banquet and a medal, but kept meetings with him to a minimum. Egypt had more to gain from Soviet
aid than from China. Both in Egypt and Algeria Chou was cordially received, but there were indications that China's warlike talk
—and such deeds as her border warfare with India or her genocide
in Tibet—had somewhat alienated the neutral nations.

Chou was well received in the former French colonies. When
Mali's President Keita met Chou En-lai, he managed in one sen-
tence to echo the "Africans and Chinese are brothers" line and to
reproach the West (especially Russia, one gathers) for its inadequate support of African aspirations. He told Chou, "You have
understood that we are in a hurry and you have avoided the mis-
take of those who are trying to conquer space before completing
the liberation of man on earth." However, France's continuing
aid to her former possessions was a concrete thing that Chou's
diplomacy could not hope to match. In Guinea the Red influence
was strong, but President Sekou Touré had discovered that Russian
intrigue could be a threat to his own position; before long he would
also find the Chinese troublesome. Somalia was happy with Chinese
offers of military equipment, but even that success was offset by
resentment of the gift in Somalia's neighbor, Kenya. Kenya itself
continued to get most of its military equipment and training from

the British Commonwealth, and Kenyan President Kenyatta seemed able to resist Red attempts to gain more influence. Africans wondered if the revolts of some military units in Kenya and Tanganyika at this time had been encouraged by the Chinese.

In Zanzibar, a government was formed in early 1964 which showed pro-Peking orientation. However, in April this gain would be canceled by a quick merger of Zanzibar with Tanganyika. In the new "Tanzanian" Government, Zanzibar leader Babu, who was in the pay of China, lost his power.

Behind these reversals for the Peking line was the alarm of established governments that the super-revolutionary line would mean their overthrow, too. One new nation, Burundi, was the scene of a defection by Red Chinese Assistant Cultural Attaché Tung Chi-ping. Tung, who received asylum in the United States, may have alarmed African readers with his statement that Mao Tse-tung viewed the Congo as China's gateway to dominion over all Africa. To the Burundi Government, a more immediately unsettling event was the assassination of its Premier Ngendandumwe in January, 1965, a few months after Tung's statement. The Premier was murdered two hours after he formed a Cabinet expected to take stronger measures to curtail Peking's operations. Malagasy President Tsiranana was worried about revolution in his island republic, where the large Chinese minority might help to hasten his overthrow. He announced in 1964 that his government would not recognize Peking. The Chad and Cameroon republics made similar announcements. Of the former French colonies below the Sahara, only Guinea, Congo, Mali, and Senegal extended recognition. Senegal, like Tunisia in North Africa, tried a "two-Chinas" approach, recognizing the Taiwan Government as well as mainland China, but exchanging diplomats with neither on grounds of avoiding embarrassment. Thus these two new countries could appease their own advocates of cooperation with Red China, yet avoid the subversive effects that might flow from installation of Chinese embassies in their capitals.

Peking's many difficulties in Africa had not prevented some impressive accomplishments. In 1964 alone, China extended grants and loans of $94,000,000 in Africa, where during the entire preceding decade these had totaled $138,000,000.[14] As of March, 1965, the Red Chinese Government was recognized by 18 African nations. (In 1961 only four had accorded recognition.) The Taiwan Government was recognized by 15 African states, and three recognized neither China. Peking did not do well in 1965–1966, however. When the United Nations General Assembly voted on admission of the Peking Government (in place of Nationalist China) on November 29, 1966, less than half of the African members backed this step (16 voted for it, 17 were opposed, and five abstained).

Meanwhile, the U.S.S.R. continued to have its troubles with militant independence sentiments. The Afro-Asian Solidarity Conference of March, 1964, was the scene of a rebuke to the Soviet delegate, Bobozhan Gafurov. (His name, incidentally, indicates that he was of Central Asian origin—a natural choice to support Russia's claim that she is Asian, too.) Gafurov condemned as gross slander the Chinese delegate's classification of the U.S.S.R. as an imperialist power plotting with the U.S. to dominate the world. He declared that many other delegates joined with him in condemning the Chinese view, whereupon the delegate of Tanganyika objected that the Soviet representative had no right to speak for other delegations. The Conference Chairman ruled that each delegation must speak only for itself. It appeared that the conferees would tolerate no vestige of a "big brotherly" role by European powers.

A few weeks after this, a meeting was held in Indonesia to make plans for a "Second Bandung Conference" of the Afro-Asian nations, to be held in 1965. The Chinese member of this planning session said that Russia should not be invited, since it was not an Asian nation. Moscow reacted by communicating directly to the Afro-Asian governments a warning that Peking was building a "Chinese wall between white, yellow, and black nations." The warning, published in the Soviet Government newspaper *Izvestia*, claimed that China's new racism was only a cover-up for Peking's "hegemonic aims toward the Afro-Asian countries." The message compared China to Nazi Germany by saying, "It is unnecessary to mention the names of those who tried to base their policy on such man-hating principles, and how they ended." During the ensuing year the U.S.S.R. tried to get invited, and the Chinese continued to object. The invitation issue became a cause célèbre, and there was every prospect that the "Second Bandung" meeting would be far less harmonious than the original Bandung Conference of 1955. Plans were made to hold the meeting in Algeria, but in June, 1965, the Conference was called off. Indications were that the host country and many prospective conferees were tired of efforts by Red China and the U.S.S.R. to use them as pawns in the Sino-Soviet dispute or anti-American strategy.

Chinese propaganda declared that the Conference postponement was the result of "imperialist intrigues." Actually, Peking's trumpetings about "ripeness for the inevitable revolutions" had perhaps become less congenial to established rulers of free African nations than they had sounded to men seeking release from colonial rule. This would not imply a lapse of Afro-Asian cohesiveness, but merely unwillingness to accept dictation from Peking.

We have been considering three interrelated points: The "developing nations" need help; they are vulnerable to intrigue or pressures by the great powers; they often resent bitterly any real or fancied attempts by foreigners to dictate to them. What can be done about these problems? The United Nations can and should help, but the U.N. cannot always do the job. Perhaps it is too much to expect all solutions to flow from one global organization vis-à-vis more than 100 highly varied national entities. We should therefore rely more on regional groupings of nations as intermediate organs.

Strong, regional, multi-national organizations can discourage intervention by foreign powers. More importantly, such organs are an excellent means for coordinating and improving the economy of a region. (An example is the Asian Development Bank, which in 1967 had 32 members and a capitalization of $1,000,000,000. Much of this capital, and most of the Bank's leadership, comes from the Asian nations themselves.) When it is necessary to import force to keep peace in an area, there will be less resentment if the enforcement is not always spearheaded by the same globally dominant powers. Stronger regional authority can do much to prevent rekindling of old grievances among the world's races or nations.

HAZARDS AND HOPES FOR THE FUTURE

THE HAZARDS our world faces in the late twentieth century are in large degree the result of the West's own creations—the imperialism, racism, and totalitarianism analyzed in this book. Will these creations turn against all the world's people, like Frankenstein monsters? In an era of stupendous scientific progress, with worldwide diffusion of technology, the West must be very careful that its new technology benefits mankind and does not lend itself to new epics of destruction and tyranny.

The most obvious hazard seems to be the nuclear bomb. In 1965, England's Prime Minister Harold Wilson warned that nations lacking nuclear weapons must have protection from China's fast-developing A-Bomb capability. Without some safeguards, he said, all the Asian nations will become nuclear powers. "Once this happens, world nuclear war is inevitable," declared Wilson. A black prediction indeed! Nor did nuclear scientist and Nobel Prize winner Harold Urey detract from Wilson's urgency when he predicted, at about the same time, that China would have hydrogen bombs and delivery systems for them by 1970. Perhaps China would show great restraint about using such weapons—but Adlai Stevenson had told the U.N. General Assembly on October 16, 1963, that the People's Republic of China was "the world's most warlike regime."[15]

What must we do to dispel the dangers of future imperialism and aggression? Warlike conditions will impend until the benefits of modern technology are shared by all people, at least to the extent of relieving poverty, disease, and ignorance. Western technology has been made available to the Afro-Asian peoples. Colonial powers usually created a network of roads, railways, and telephone lines. Truly marvelous knowledge has emanated from Western research and development. Industrialization is a dazzling prospect for the former colonial regions. In the imperialist days, however, the occupying powers usually discouraged industrialization.

Independence put a stop to that, but the almost insuperable problem remains of finding capital for industrial development in nations whose gross national product is very low. Foreign aid programs conducted by the United States, as well as by Japan, Taiwan, and several European nations, have provided assistance. Yet, as of 1964, the 29 nations of Sub-Saharan Africa had an average per capita annual income of less than $100. (Latin America, poor as it was, enjoyed an average of $295.)

Barbara Ward has suggested that one remedy for the 400 years of Western imperialism is a 50-year program of aid. She doubts that the Asian nations could absorb more than three billion dollars of new capital annually, but even a dependable annual Western contribution of one or two billion, given generously and intelligently, could, in her opinion, "finally wipe out the picture of western exploitation and imperialism, and, by doing so, . . . preserve liberal and freedom-loving ideals in Asia."[16] U.S. aid chief David E. Bell anticipated in 1965 that there would be a 10 to 25 year requirement for American assistance.

Western medical science and sanitation methods were passed on to the colonial regions. Smallpox immunization, antiseptic procedures, and suppression of the insects which spread yellow fever, malaria, and sleeping sickness illustrate some of the great benefits of this sort. All this has helped to increase life expectancy, and especially to increase the percentage of infants who live to reach adulthood, but in many Afro-Asian lands life expectancy remains far below that of the white countries. It averages, for example, 32 years in Indonesia and 30 in Pakistan, as compared with 67 in Australia and 70 in New Zealand.

Western education was made available to many colonial populations, but was usually of very limited extent and far inferior to the educational systems of the mother countries. Consequently, to cite just one area, the 29 nations of Sub-Saharan Africa now have an aggregate literacy rate of 10 per cent.

The West and non-West, working together, can relieve all these immense deficiencies, but progress will be impossible unless the burgeoning population of all countries can be stabilized. At the current rates of increase, the world's present population of over 3,000,000,000 will more than double in 50 years. While the new technology might provide ways to feed these people, it could not simultaneously make progress against the miseries and competitive pressures through which overpopulation will menace world peace.

The rate of population growth in the world's richer nations (Japan and the Western countries) has been lowered to about 1.1 per cent per year, but the poorer populations are increasing faster—about 2.5 per cent annually. Add to this the widening gap between individuals in the affluent and the poverty-stricken countries: Although per capita incomes in the latter are rising about 1.5 per cent each year, the former enjoy an annual rise of 3 per cent. That might not be serious if there were not already a ratio of 15 to 1 between incomes in the rich nations and the poor.[17]

Population control for peace was given added point by recent biological and behavioral research which showed that men and animals tend toward violence and other behavioral disorders under crowded conditions, even though ample nourishment is provided for all. British biologist W. M. S. Russell suggested to the British Association for the Advancement of Science that this tendency explains rising crime rates in crowded areas. Aggression on the national level may also stem from such factors. In fact, greater aggressiveness under crowded conditions—*not* always intrinsically *uncomfortable* conditions—may have originated as a "survival trait," a means by which evolution prepared our species to thin itself out when it became too thick on the land.[18] Of course this self-thinning through competition, however beneficial it may have been under primeval conditions, would be an unbearable hazard in our heavily armed world ! It is relevant that many of the crowded areas happen to be those same locations in which the misdeeds of white men have accumulated so many grievances: the heavily populated and poor nations of Afro-Asia and the densely packed ghettos of American cities.

With respect to honest effort toward stability of population, the conscience of the West is far from clear. Its politicians and religious leaders have too often been either confused, indifferent, or timidly silent. Greater public attention to this matter was forthcoming in the late 1960's, but the attention came tardily, and sometimes with bad grace. Frequently, when increases in population are bewailed by Western writers, they regret the excessive numbers of Indians or Chinese, suggesting that *these* people be controlled as to numbers. Needless to say, population control should mean a worldwide approach, equitable among all nations or races.

Even if we achieve some stabilization of population and are able to provide a decent *subsistence* for people everywhere, it is far from certain that imperialist-type aggression and racism will promptly disappear. We would still encounter the "revolution of rising expectations," as it has been called with regard to both American Negro goals and the goals of former colonial countries. Two sociologists, Lewis M. Killian and Alvin Seeman, have noted the new problems raised by this factor in America. Dr. Killian related the Negro riots in Los Angeles and other cities in 1965 to such rising expectations—great promises of political power, better jobs, and better living which never quite seemed to materialize. Dr. Seeman thought the riots centered on the idea, "we're not moving fast enough."[19]

Regarding worldwide "rising expectations," Indian writer Chandrasekhar calls for justice, not just aid. He suggests a redistribution of the world's real estate, especially farm land. He considers it uncondonable to leave vast empty spaces in the hands of nations which hardly need or use them, while elsewhere there is terrible crowding and resultant suffering. He notes, significantly, that the owners of surplus lands got them through "historical and political *accidents* involving no small amount of aggression." By clear implication, he and the Asian expansionists would, for example, invalidate Russia's title and moral claim with respect to that nation's Asian holdings.[20]

In this context, what are we to say about Theodore Roosevelt's argument that expansion into a country is proper when that land is lightly populated? He used this "greatest good for the greatest number" principle to defend seizure of the American Indians' territories. Should the same rule be applied in coming decades to enable the world's most crowded peoples to share less populated regions?

The foregoing problem is complex, and may foreshadow great conflicts; even so, it does seem possible to achieve equitable solutions and satisfy most of the "rising expectations"—again provided that the nations of the world stabilize their populations.

When and if all this has been accomplished, it is not too optimistic to expect virtual disappearance of the kinds of imperialism and racism in which white nations have excelled in modern times. Most of the preconditions of such aggressiveness would be gone if all regions possessed the same technology and enjoyed about the same level of well-being. Furthermore, cultural homogenization of the world through adoption of Western culture is even now quite far along, and new modes of communication should help in reducing antagonisms which have always occurred so easily between peoples who did not know one another.

How long would all these improvements and adjustments take? Easily three or four generations, one is inclined to say upon considering the timing of the past, when a century did not suffice, after American Negro emancipation, to secure that group equal treatment before the law. On the other hand, with developments tending to be more rapid, accelerating technical progress, and the hazards of modern weaponry as a special motivation for settlement of quarrels, the process may be more rapid than we think.

This sort of long-range optimism does not seem applicable however to the third aspect of Western misdeeds, totalitarianism. This may indeed be a Frankenstein monster turning on its creators. One may even predict that the imperialism of the recent past will be internalized—Stalin and Hitler have shown that it can happen.

We have seen that totalitarianism thrives on crises, and *plenty of them* can be expected to continue cropping up. We also noted trends toward centralization of power in the great nations of the West. As Erich Fromm says, both Communist and anti-Communist nations create bureaucracies which transform man into a thing. The alternative, as he sees it, is not between capitalism and Communism, but between bureaucratism and humanism.[21] Add to

this the governments' virtual monopoly of new devices for surveillance of all citizens and new techniques of insidious persuasion
—ranging from advertising methods to the starkest mind-molding
techniques of brain-washing—and one fears that the citizens of
any nation will be as helpless to resist tyranny as were the poorly
equipped peoples of Afro-Asia before the white advance.

We have noted that authoritarianism likes to justify its
measures as producing economic benefits which outweigh the coer-
cive burden. The future is surely full of critical economic pressures
which may seem to justify drastic and oppressive solutions. India's
Ambassador to the United States, B. K. Nehru, declared in 1966
that the gap between rich and poor nations is widening. He also
noted that the underdeveloped nations' share of world trade shrank
from 23 to 20 per cent between 1958 and 1963. This certainly
points toward economic emergencies for the world of the future.

Even *within* the United States, economic benefits are used to
justify infringement of individual freedoms and aggrandizement
of the national government's power. In 1966 Secretary of Labor
Wirtz unveiled his new "policy for youth," a Federal system to
channel all young persons into appropriate service, "meaningful
employment," or training, for a period of two years. Wirtz said
that such beneficial training and education would warrant "insistence on the obligation" to use the opportunities. Probably
Wirtz' carrot will be used before the stick. That is, benefits con-
sisting of government-financed education (including "G.I. Bill"-
type rewards after the period of national service) may be the
inducement that will secure public acceptance of such
regimentation.

Is totalitarianism the "wave of the future"? Even though we
recoil from it, must we concede that this is the "shape of things
to come"? Not necessarily, but the degree of danger can be discerned by application of the following test to events of our time:
Do trends and pressures which are intrinsically *opposite* to each
other contribute *alike* to diminution of democracy and aggrandizement of powers? In a number of respects, this has been happening.
For example, it is notorious that war or threat of war enhances
authoritarianism, but the threat of any extensive outbreak of peace

is also worrisome to the economic planners of Western nations. Prevention of depression in the face of peace would call for heroic measures of planning and control.

To cite another pair of opposites, nationalist-minded, military-minded groups, sometimes labelled as conservatives, call for anti-democratic measures to impose their standards of behavior on all the people, while many of their enemies in the so-called liberal camp have their own set of authoritarian proposals. The former group favors conscription "for defense," while the latter often advocate involuntary servitude as a feature of their programs. These latter types deplore the allegedly discriminatory drafting of Negroes for the war in Viet Nam, yet their own involuntary labor projects would in fact—though not in theory—impose discriminatory servitude on the same disadvantaged persons.

One last example of these opposites with similar effects is that of the traditional racists and their opponents. The anti-democratic qualities of the former are obvious, but the anti-racists, in their zeal to right long-standing, stubborn wrongs, are also inclined to augment the powers of national authorities in an impressive degree.

It is reassuring on the other hand to see that twentieth century opppression has often failed. Hitler, Stalin, and most of the imperialists are gone; they are more widely regretted than imitated. Modern oppression has been successfully resisted, especially in the cases of India and the American Negroes, through well-organized, non-violent action. Such action may be the best means for defending democracy within a nation, and these tactics may also take the place of destructive international conflicts. The latter application would be more practicable if a world police authority could be created. Even if that authority were somewhat limited, a local oppressor's violence might be tempered by legal restraints as well as the stirrings of his own conscience. Both of these factors have been necessary for the success of non-violence in modern America. I say *success*, because even those regrettable, recent violent operations by black nationalists in America would have been impracticable before Martin Luther King and his colleagues, using non-violent methods, made a deep moral impression on behalf of their people.

Let us hope that men will review the dreadful aspects of the white man's past record, and thus be better prepared to recognize and resist totalitarianisms of the future before they are fully developed. Professor Guenter Lewy has raised the momentous question, how do you recognize something like National Socialism in time to do anything about it?[22]

I hope that the detailed examination of the white conscience attempted in this volume will be helpful in two ways: First, having surveyed our legacy of the past, we can be more perceptive and less inclined to repression when we run into new manifestations of similar evils. Second, we Westerners, with a gradual clearing of our collective conscience, can face the rest of the world with an appropriate mixture of understanding, helpfulness, and self-confidence. We shall need more of all three qualities in the years to come.

Notes to the Text

CHAPTER I

[1] Wilfrid S. Blunt, *My Diaries: Being a Personal Narrative of Events, 1888–1914* (London: Martin Secker, 1919), I, 464.

[2] John A. Hobson, *Imperialism: A Study* (New York: James & Co., 1902), pp. 261, 271–272.

[3] William Stringfellow, *My People is the Enemy* (New York: Holt, Rinehart and Winston, Inc., 1964), p. 3.

[4] Thomas Mann, "Freud and the Future," in *Essays of Three Decades,* trans. H. T. Lowe-Porter (New York: Alfred A. Knopf, Inc., 1947), p. 416.

[5] Theodor Reik, *Myth and Guilt* (New York: George Braziller, Inc., 1957), pp. 3–4, 35–36.

[6] *Ibid.,* pp. 420–421, 428.

[7] Ashley Montagu, *Man's Most Dangerous Myth: The Fallacy of Race* (Cleveland: The World Publishing Co., 1964), p. 180.

[8] Carl G. Jung, *Modern Man in Search of a Soul* (New York: Harcourt, Brace and World, Inc., 1933), p. 246.

[9] Hobson, *op. cit.,* pp. 222–223.

[10] Gyorgy Paloczi-Horvath, "A Meeting of Two Young Men," *Irodalmi Ujsag* (Budapest: July 7, 1956), trans. and reprinted in *Bitter Harvest,* ed. Edmund Stillman (New York: Frederick A. Praeger, 1959), p. 89.

[11] Carl G. Jung, *Essays on Contemporary Events* (London: Routledge and Kegan Paul, Ltd., 1947), pp. 46–48, 50–51, 53–54, 56, 62–64, 86.

[12] Edmund Stillman and William Pfaff, *The Politics of Hysteria: The Sources of Twentieth-Century Conflict* (New York: Harper & Row, 1964), p. 17.

[13] Jawaharlal Nehru, *The Discovery of India* (Garden City, N.Y.: Doubleday and Co., 1960), p. 2.

[14] Jawaharlal Nehru, *Toward Freedom, The Autobiography of Jawaharlal Nehru* (New York: John Day Co., 1942), p. 15.

[15] Nehru, *The Discovery of India*, pp. 3–4.

[16] Jawaharlal Nehru, *Glimpses of World History* (Allahabad, India: Kitabistan, 1935), II, 1465, 1467.

[17] Albert J. Beveridge, *The Russian Advance* (New York: Harper & Row, 1904), pp. 96–97.

[18] Jung, *Modern Man in Search of a Soul*, loc. cit.

[19] Sigmund Freud, *Civilization and Its Discontents*, trans. James Strachey (New York: W. W. Norton Co., 1962), pp. 58–59.

[20] Letter from Dr. Jung to Rev. David Cox (September 25, 1957), quoted in H. L. Philp, *Jung and the Problem of Evil* (London: Rockliff, 1958), p. 245.

[21] Georges Sorel, *Reflections on Violence*, trans. T. E. Hulme and J. Roth (New York: Free Press of Glencoe, 1950), cited in Henry A. Murray, *Myth and Mythmaking* (New York: George Braziller, Inc., 1960), p. 359.

[22] Carl G. Jung, *The Archetypes and the Collective Unconscious*, trans. R. F. C. Hull, Vol. IX, Part I, Bollingen Series XX, *The Collected Works of C. G. Jung* (New York: Pantheon Books, 1959), pp. 29, 42, 44, 48.

CHAPTER II

[1] A. Grenfell Price, *The Western Invasions of the Pacific and its Continents* (Oxford: Clarenden Press, 1963), p. 71.

[2] *Ibid.*, p. 29.

[3] George F. Willison, *Saints and Strangers* (London: William Heinemann, 1946), p. 349.

[4] A. Hyatt Verrill, *The Real Americans* (New York: G. P. Putnam's Sons, 1954), p. 10.

[5] *Old South Leaflet No. 53* (Boston: Old South Association), pp. 5–8, cited in Wilcomb E. Washburn, *The Indian and the White Man* (Garden City, New York: Doubleday and Co., 1964), pp. 102–104.

[6] Willison, *op. cit.*, p. 341.

[7] Edmund S. Morgan, *The Puritan Dilemma. The Story of John Winthrop* (Boston: Little, Brown and Co., 1958), pp. 51–52, 70.

[8] Perry Miller, ed., *The American Puritans* (Garden City, New York: Doubleday and Co., 1956), pp. 64–65.

⁹ Perry Miller, *Errand into the Wilderness* (Cambridge, Massachusetts:
The Belknap Press of Harvard University Press, 1956), pp. 107, 119.
¹⁰ Walter P. Webb, *The Great Frontier* (Boston: Houghton Mifflin
Co., 1952), pp. 3, 13.
¹¹ L. C. A. Knowles, *The Economic Development of the British Empire*
(London: G. Routledge and Sons, 1924), p. 74.
¹² Brooks Adams, *The Law of Civilization and Decay* (New York: The
Macmillan Co., 1896), p. 313.
¹³ A. H. Stamp, *Other Nations' Colonies* (Tunbridge Wells, England:
Courier Press, 1957), pp. 464-466.

CHAPTER III

¹ John Bigelow, ed., *The Complete Works of Benjamin Franklin* (New
York: Letter-Press, 1887), II, 231, cited in *The Founders of the Republic
on Immigration, Naturalization and Aliens*, ed. Madison Grant and
Charles Davison (New York: Charles Scribner's Sons, 1928), pp. 26-27.
² Lecture by Professor Leslie Fiedler, "Indian and Negro Themes in
American Literature," Colorado College, May 10, 1965.
³ Andrew F. Rolle, in Introduction to Helen Hunt Jackson, *A Century
of Dishonor: The Early Crusade for Indian Reform* (New York: Harper
& Row, 1965), p. x.
⁴ Inez Hunt and Wanetta W. Draper, *To Colorado's Restless Ghosts*
(Denver, Colorado: Alan Swallow, 1960), pp. 42-43.
⁵ James D. Richardson, ed., *A Compilation of the Messages and Papers
of the Presidents, 1789-1908* (n.p., 1909), III, 294.
⁶ A. Hyatt Verrill, *The Real Americans* (New York: G. P. Putnam's
Sons, 1954), p. 34.
⁷ *Ibid.*, p. 36.
⁸ Theodore Roosevelt, *The Winning of the West* (4 vols.; New York:
G. P. Putnam's Sons, 1889-1896), I, 238, 331-335.
⁹ Wilcomb C. Washburn, *The Indian and the White Man* ("Documents
in American Civilization"; Garden City, N.Y.: Doubleday and Co.,
1964), pp. 400-401.
¹⁰ Basil Davidson, *Black Mother* (Boston: Little, Brown & Co., 1961),
pp. 59, 80.
¹¹ Herbert I. Priestley, *The Coming of the White Man, 1492-1848*,
Vol. I of *A History of American Life*, ed. Arthur M. Schlesinger and
Dixon R. Fox (12 vols.; New York: The Macmillan Co., 1929), pp.
324-325.
¹² Severn Duvall, "Uncle Tom's Cabin: The Sinister Side of the
Patriarchy," *New England Quarterly* (March 1963), 5.

[13] Horace M. Bond, *Negro Education in Alabama* (Washington, D.C.: Associated Publishers, 1939), pp. 159–163.

[14] Genevieve S. Brown, "An Analytical and Statistical Study of Higher Education for Negroes during the Period 1877–1900" (Master's Thesis, Howard University), cited in Rayford W. Logan, *The Negro in American Life and Thought* (New York: Dial Press, 1954), p. 327.

[15] Logan, *op. cit.*, pp. 174–175.

[16] C. Vann Woodward, *The Strange Career of Jim Crow* (New York: Oxford University Press, 1957), p. 81.

[17] Gilbert Thomas Stephenson, *Race Distinctions in American Law* (New York: Appleton-Century-Crofts, Inc., 1910), p. 164, cited in Thomas F. Gossett, *Race: The History of an Idea in America* (Dallas, Texas: Southern Methodist University Press, 1963), pp. 285–286.

[18] Rayford W. Logan, *The Negro in the United States* (Princeton, New Jersey: D. Van Nostrand Co., 1957), p. 65.

[19] Gossett, *op. cit.*, p. 374.

[20] Logan, *The Negro in the United States*, p. 75.

[21] Gossett, *op. cit.*, p. 452.

[22] *Ibid.*, pp 391, 395–397.

[23] Roi Ottley, *No Green Pastures: The Negro in Europe Today* (London: John Murray, 1952), pp. 19, 22–23, 31–32, 44.

[24] *The New York Times*, April 18, 1967, pp. 1, 17; April 28, 1967, p. 6.

[25] Ottley, *op. cit.*, pp. 152–154.

[26] *Ibid.*, pp. 160–161.

CHAPTER IV

[1] John A. Hobson, *Imperialism: A Study* (New York: James & Co., 1902), pp. 18, 21, 27.

[2] Richard M. Brace, *Morocco, Algeria, Tunisia* (Englewood Cliffs, N.J.: Prentice-Hall, Inc., 1964), pp. 48–49, 52.

[3] *Ibid.*, p. 55.

[4] Donald L. Wiedner, *A History of Africa South of the Sahara* (New York: Random House, Inc., 1964), pp. 77–78.

[5] Herbert Samuel, "The Congo State and the Commission of Inquiry," *The Contemporary Review* (July–December 1905), pp. 872–883.

[6] Mary E. Townsend, *European Colonial Expansion since 1871* (Chicago: J. B. Lippincott Co., 1941), pp. 196, 203.

[7] Leonard Woolf, *Empire and Commerce in Africa. A Study in Economic Imperialism* (London: George Allen and Unwin, 1920), p. 345–346.

[8] Edward Roux, *Time Longer than Rope* (Madison: University of Wisconsin Press, 1964), pp. 104–108.

[9] Carlton J. H. Hayes, *A Generation of Materialism, 1871–1900* (New York: Harper & Row, 1941), p. 338.

[10] Francis A. March, *History of the World War* (Philadelphia, Pennsylvania: United Publishers, 1919), p. 283.

CHAPTER V

[1] Maurice and Taya Zinkin, *Britain and India* (London: Chatto and Windus, 1964), p. 19.

[2] Penderel Moon, *Warren Hastings and British India* (London: English Universities Press, 1947), pp. 79–80.

[3] Jawaharlal Nehru, *The Discovery of India* (Garden City, N.Y.: Doubleday and Co., 1960), p. 212.

[4] John A. Hobson, *Imperialism: A Study* (New York: James & Co., 1902), p. 310; Kumar Goshal, *People in Colonies* (New York: Sheridan House, 1948), pp. 130, 148–149.

[5] T. Walter Wallbank, *A Short History of India and Pakistan* (New York: New American Library, 1962), pp. 82, 93–94.

[6] *Ibid.*, pp. 99–101, 105–107.

[7] Zinkin, *op. cit.*, pp. 36–39.

[8] Cyril Toumanoff, "Caesaropapism in Byzantium and Russia," *Theological Studies* (June 1946), 236.

[9] Murray Morgan, *Bridge to Russia* (New York: E. P. Dutton & Co., 1947), pp. 68–69.

[10] A. Grenfell Price, *The Western Invasions of the Pacific and its Continents* (Oxford: Clarenden Press, 1963), p. 65.

[11] Richard A. Pierce, *Russian Central Asia, 1867–1917. A Study in Colonial Rule* (Berkeley: University of California Press, 1960), pp. 20, 41–42, 45, 58.

[12] Hugh Seton-Watson, *The Decline of Imperial Russia, 1855–1914* (New York: Frederick A. Praeger, 1961), p. 202.

[13] Albert J. Beveridge, *The Russian Advance* (New York: Harper & Row, 1904), pp. 9–12, 21.

[14] *Ibid.*, pp. 29–30, 128.

[15] Douglas Pike, *Australia, the Quiet Continent* (Cambridge: Cambridge University Press, 1962), p. 36.

[16] Ernest Scott, *A Short History of Australia* (London: Humphrey Milford, 1930), p. 31.

[17] Charles Darwin, *The Descent of Man* (New York: Appleton-Century-Crofts, Inc., 1883), pp. 183–184; H. G. Wells, *The Outline of History* (Garden City, N.Y.: Garden City Publishing Company, 1930), p. 746.

[18] University of Sydney, "The Outback Aborigines," *Current Affairs Bulletin* (December 1, 1958).

[19] E. W. R. Lumby, "Lord Elgin and the Burning of the Summer Palace," *History Today* (July 1960), 485–487.

[20] Carroll B. Malone, *History of the Peking Summer Palaces under the Ch'ing Dynasty* (Urbana, Illinois: University of Illinois Press, 1934), pp. 191–192.

[21] Garner, *International Law and the World War*, I, 439, quoted in Malone, *op. cit.*, p. 190.

[22] U.S. Immigration Commission, *Abstracts of Report* (2 vols., 1911), extract in *Immigration and Naturalization*, ed. Philip Davis (Boston: Ginn and Co., 1920), pp. 192–194.

[23] People v. Hall (4 Cal. 399), October Term, 1854, cited in Thomas F. Gossett, *Race: The History of an Idea in America* (Dallas, Texas: Southern Methodist University Press, 1963), p. 290.

[24] *Report of the Joint Special Committee to Investigate Chinese Immigration*, Senate Report No. 689, 44th Congress 2d Session, 1876–1877, p. 289, cited in Gossett, *op. cit.*, pp. 290–291.

[25] Davis, *op. cit.*, p. 190.

[26] Goshal, *op. cit.*, pp. 120, 122; Jawaharlal Nehru, *Glimpses of World History* (Allahabad, India: Kitabistan, 1935), II, 737.

[27] George McT. Kahin, *Nationalism and Revolution in Indonesia* (Ithaca, New York: Cornell University Press, 1952), p. 43.

[28] Margaret Leech, *In the Days of McKinley* (New York: Harper & Row, 1959), p. 331.

[29] *Ibid.*, pp. 387, 353–354.

[30] Willard H. Elsbree, *Japan's Role in Southeast Asian Nationalist Movements* (Cambridge, Mass.: Harvard University Press, 1953), pp. 4, 6–7.

[31] Joseph R. Hayden, *The Philippines* (New York: The Macmillan Co., 1942), p. 518.

[32] William L. Holland, *Asian Nationalism and the West* (New York: The Macmillan Co., 1953), pp. 14–15.

[33] W. Macmahon Ball, *Nationalism and Communism in East Asia* (Carlton, Australia: Melbourne University Press, 1956), pp. 88, 93–94.

[34] R. F. Pettigrew, *Triumphant Plutocracy* (New York: Academy Press, 1921), *passim*. Pettigrew cites various U.S. Government reports.

[35] John Gunther, *Inside Latin America* (New York: Harper & Row, 1941), pp. 423–424.

[36] Ernest Gruening, *The State of Alaska* (New York: Random House, Inc., 1954), cited in Price, *op. cit.*, p. 80.

[37] *The New York Times*, August 1, 1966, p. 15.

CHAPTER VI

[1] Curti, Merle E., and Thorpe, Willard, *American Issues. The Social Record* (Chicago: J. B. Lippincott Co., 1960), pp. 915–916.

[2] Jules Ferry, *Le Tonkin et la Mère-patrie* (Paris: Victor-Havard, 1890), trans. Robin W. Winks in *Major Crises in Western Civilization*, ed. Richard W. Lyman and Lewis W. Spitz (New York: Harcourt, Brace and World, Inc., 1965), II, 147.

[3] John A. Hobson, *Imperialism: A Study* (New York: James & Co., 1902), pp. 50–51.

[4] Frances Gunther, *Revolution in India* (New York: Island Press, 1944), p. 107.

[5] Henry Nash Smith, *Virgin Land. The American West as Symbol and Myth* (New York: Vintage Books, 1957), pp. 28, 40.

[6] Kwang-ching Liu, *Americans and Chinese* (Cambridge, Massachusetts: Harvard University Press, 1963), pp. 17–18.

[7] William L. Langer, "A Critique of Imperialism," *Foreign Affairs*, XIV (October 1935), 110–111.

[8] Hobson, *op. cit.*, p. 213.

[9] Quoted in Kumar Goshal, *People in Colonies* (New York: Sheridan House, 1948), pp. 30–31.

[10] Charles Darwin, *The Descent of Man* (New York: Appleton-Century-Crofts, Inc., 1883), pp. 138, 142. Darwin quotes Mr. Zincke's remark from "Last Winter in the United States," 1868, p. 29.

[11] Friedrich von Bernhardi, *Germany and the Next War* (New York: Longmans, 1912) and Lord Elton, *Saint George or the Dragon* (London: Collins, 1942), both cited in Ashley Montagu, *Man's Most Dangerous Myth: The Fallacy of Race* (Cleveland: The World Publishing Co., 1964), pp. 252–255.

[12] Alfred T. Mahan, *The Interest of America in Seapower, Present and Future* (Boston: Little, Brown and Co., 1897), pp. 18, 267.

[13] Curti, Thorp, and Baker, *op. cit.*, pp. 894–896.

[14] Sigmund Freud, *Civilization and Its Discontents*, trans. James Strachey (New York: W. W. Norton Co., 1962), pp. 61–62.

[15] Peter Viereck, *Metapolitics. The Roots of the Nazi Mind* (New York: Capricorn Books, 1961), pp. 52, 99, 101–102.

[16] *Ibid.*, pp. 106, 120.

[17] Hannah Arendt, *The Origins of Totalitarianism* (Cleveland: World Publishing Co., 1958), p. 190.

[18] Review of *The Foundations of the Nineteenth Century*, *Outlook*, XCVIII (July 29, 1911), 728–731, cited in Thomas F. Gossett, *Race: The History of an Idea in America* (Dallas, Texas: Southern Methodist University Press, 1963), p. 352.

[19] Robert H. Jackson, *The Case Against the Nazi War Criminals* (New York: Alfred A. Knopf, 1946), p. 122.

[20] Speech by Jules Streicher, June 22, 1935, cited in Raul Hilberg, *The Destruction of the European Jews* (London: W. H. Allen, 1961), p. 12.

[21] Edward Roux, *Time Longer than Rope* (Madison, Wisconsin: University of Wisconsin Press, 1964), p. 102.

[22] Henry Adams, *Letters of Henry Adams* (New York: 1930), ed. Worthington C. Ford; letters of May 26, 1875, January 13, 1898, and September 25, 1899: I, 267, 114; II, 241; cited in Gossett, *op. cit.*, pp. 304–305.

[23] Perry Miller, *American Thought* (New York: Holt, Rinehart, and Winston, 1961), pp. xliii-xliv.

[24] Morgan Godwyn, *The Negro's and Indians Advocate* (London: 1680), p. 3, quoted in Milton Cantor, "The Image of the Negro in Colonial Literature," *New England Quarterly* (December 1963), 459.

[25] John Saffin, "A Brief and Candid Answer to a Late Printed Sheet Entitled The Selling of Joseph," quoted in Cantor, *op. cit.*, p. 471.

[26] Rollo May, "The Origins and Significance of the Existential Movement in Psychology," in *Existence. A New Dimension in Psychiatry and Psychology*, ed. Rollo May, Ernest Angel, and Henri F. Ellenberger (New York: Basic Books, Inc., 1958), p. 12.

CHAPTER VII

[1] André Maurois, *Lyautey* (New York: Appleton-Century-Crofts, Inc., 1939), p. 242.

[2] A very complete study of this raid is found in David Irving, *The Destruction of Dresden* (New York: Holt, Rinehart and Winston, 1964).

[3] Francis Gunther, *Revolution in India* (New York: Island Press, 1944), p. 66.

[4] Louis Fischer, *The Life of Mahatma Gandhi* (New York: Harper & Row, 1950), pp. 539-540.

[5] Roi Ottley, *No Green Pastures: The Negro in Europe Today* (London: John Murray, 1952), p. 51.

[6] *U.S. Department of State Bulletin*, May 30, 1942, p. 488; Robert E. Sherwood, *Roosevelt and Hopkins, An Intimate History* (New York: Harper & Row, 1948), p. 573.

[7] Kenneth Ingham, *A History of East Africa* (New York: Frederick A. Praeger, 1962), pp. 216–217, 357.

[8] *Ibid.*, p. 369.

[9] Richard M. Brace, *Morocco, Algeria, Tunisia* (Englewood Cliffs, N.J.: Prentice-Hall, Inc., 1964), pp. 79–81.

[10] *Ibid.*, pp. 65, 101–102.

[11] Jawaharlal Nehru, *Glimpses of World History* (Allahabad, India: Kitabistan, 1935), II, 1215, 1218.

[12] Kumar Goshal, *The People of India* (New York: Sheridan House, 1944), p. 171.

[13] Rupert Furneaux, *Massacre at Amritsar* (London: George Allen and Unwin, 1963), p. 46. In its subsequent pages, this recent study gives an account of the Massacre which is authoritative and interesting, and a helpful source for details of the events at Amritsar.

[14] Jawaharlal Nehru, *Toward Freedom, The Autobiography of Jawaharlal Nehru* (New York: John Day Co., 1942), p. 70.

[15] Government of India, *East India. Report of the Committee Appointed by the Government of India to Investigate the Disturbances in the Punjab* (London: His Majesty's Stationery Office, 1920), pp. 61 ff.

[16] Louis Fischer, *Gandhi* (New York: New American Library, 1962), p. 67.

[17] Goshal, *op. cit.*, p. 178; T. Walter Wallbank, *A Short History of India and Pakistan* (New York: New American Library, 1962), p. 146.

[18] Jawaharlal Nehru, *Toward Freedom*, p. 50.

[19] Jawaharlal Nehru, *The Discovery of India* (Garden City, N.Y.: Doubleday and Co., 1960), p. 277.

[20] *Ibid.*, pp. 282, 284.

[21] Fischer, *Gandhi*, p. 96.

[22] Jawaharlal Nehru, *The Discovery of India*, pp. 360, 370.

[23] Willard H. Elsbree, *Japan's Role in Southeast Asian Nationalist Movements* (Cambridge, Massachusetts: Harvard University Press, 1953), pp. 33, 35–36.

[24] Jan Romein, *The Asian Century: A History of Modern Nationalism in Asia*, trans. R. T. Clark (Berkeley: University of California Press, 1963), pp. 297–298.

[25] W. Macmahon Ball, *Nationalism and Communism in East Asia* (Carlton, Australia: Melbourne University Press, 1956), p. 15.

[26] Elsbree, *op. cit.*, p. 38.

[27] Ball, *op. cit.*, pp. 122–125.

[28] Elsbree, *op. cit.*, p. 101.

CHAPTER VIII

[1] Barbara Ward, *Five Ideas That Change the World* (New York: W. W. Norton Co., 1959), p. 138.

[2] Ira Progoff, *Jung's Social Concepts and Their Significance* (New York: The Julian Press, 1953), pp. 200–201.

[3] Merle Fainsod, *How Russia is Ruled* (Cambridge, Massachusetts: Harvard University Press, 1959), p. 372.

[4] Nikita S. Khrushchev, *The Crimes of the Stalin Era. Special Report to the Twentieth Congress of the Communist Party of the Soviet Union* (New York: The New Leader, 1962), p. S 20.

[5] Robert Strausz-Hupé and Harry W. Hazard, eds., *The Idea of Colonialism* (New York: Frederick A. Praeger, 1958), p. 324.

[6] Solomon M. Schwarz, *The Jews in the Soviet Union* (Syracuse, N.Y.: Syracuse University Press, 1951), p. 326.

[7] *Ibid.*, p. 364.

[8] Leonard Schapiro, *The Communist Party of the Soviet Union* (New York: Alfred A. Knopf, Inc., 1964), pp. 538, 543.

[9] Arnold L. Horelick, *The Political Character of Soviet Anti-Semitism*, Rand Corporation Paper P-2945 (Santa Monica, California: The Rand Corporation, 1964), pp. 2, 7.

[10] "Under the Dark Vaults of the Synagogue," *Minskaya Pravda*, April 4, 1961, trans. in *Russia in Revolution*, ed. Stanley W. Page (New York: D. Van Nostrand Co., 1965), p. 287.

[11] Jan Romein, *The Asian Century: A History of Modern Nationalism in Asia*, trans. R. T. Clark (Berkeley: University of California Press, 1963), p. 147.

[12] Richard A. Pierce, *Russian Central Asia, 1867–1917. A Study in Colonial Rule* (Berkeley: University of California Press, 1960), pp. 277, 293.

[13] V. I. Lenin, *Sobranie Sochinenii* (Moscow and Leningrad: State Printing Office, 1925, XIX, 35.

[14] Hans Kohn, *Nationalism in the Soviet Union* (London: George Routledge and Sons, 1933), pp. 105–107, 136.

[15] Romein, *op. cit.*, p. 143

[16] Fainsod, *op. cit.*, pp. 495–496.

[17] Report by Stalin to the Central Committee of the Russian Communist Party, June 10, 1923, reproduced in Joseph Stalin, *Marxism and the National Question* (New York: International Publishers, 1942), pp. 164, 168.

[18] Report by Stalin to the Seventeenth Party Congress, January 26, 1934, extract in Stalin, *op. cit.*, p. 215.

[19] Olaf Caroe, "Soviet Colonialism in Central Asia," *Foreign Affairs* (October 1953), 141.

[20] Vassau-Ghiray Djabagui, "Soviet Nationality Policy and Genocide," *Caucasian Review* (Munich, 1955), I, 74, quoted in Strausz-Hupé and Hazard, *op. cit.*, p. 320.

[21] Article by William Odell Nowell, *The Pittsburgh Courier*, April 5, 1947, p. 10, cited in William A. Nolan, *Communism versus the Negro* (Chicago: Henry Regnery Co., 1951), p. 32.

[22] Roi Ottley, *No Green Pastures: The Negro in Europe Today* (London: John Murray, 1952), pp. 64–67.

[23] Nolan, *op. cit.*, pp. 160–166.

[24] *Daily Worker*, May 15, 1947, May 16, 1947, August 3, 1947, cited in Nolan, *op. cit.*, p. 177.

[25] Robert Goldwin, Ralph Lerner, and Gerald Stourzh, eds., *Readings in World Politics* (Chicago: American Foundation for Political Education, 1957), pp. 67–68.

[26] Hermann Rauschning, *The Voice of Destruction* (New York: G. P. Putnam's Sons, 1940), pp. 130, 185–186, 193.

[27] Peter Viereck, *Metapolitics. The Roots of the Nazi Mind* (New York: Capricorn Books, 1961), pp. vii–viii.

[28] "Farben" Tribunal, Flick Judgment, English Record, p. 10993, quoted in August von Knieriem, *The Nuremberg Trials* (Chicago: Henry Regnery Co., 1959), p. 484.

[29] Jawaharlal Nehru, *The Discovery of India* (Garden City, N.Y.: Doubleday and Co., 1960), p. 204.

[30] J. J. Heydecker and Johannes Leeb, *The Nuremberg Trial*, trans. and ed. R. A. Downie (Cleveland: World Publishing Co., 1958), pp. 80–81.

[31] *Ibid.*, pp. 314, 319, 325.

[32] Robert H. Jackson, *The Case Against the Nazi War Criminals* (New York: Alfred A. Knopf, 1946), p. 149.

[33] Heydecker and Leeb, *op. cit.*, pp. 330–331.

[34] Raul Hilberg, *The Destruction of the European Jews* (London: W. H. Allen, 1961), pp. 724–727; Robert E. Sherwood, *Roosevelt and Hopkins, An Intimate History* (New York: Harper & Row, 1948), p. 717.

[35] Hilberg, *op. cit.*, pp. 29, 32–33, 39.

[36] *Ibid.*, pp. 641–643.

[37] *Ibid.*, pp. 649–653.

[38] Richard S. Cromwell, "Rightist Extremism in Postwar West Germany," *Western Political Quarterly* (June 1964), 284–291.

CHAPTER IX

[1] A. Grenfell Price, *The Western Invasions of the Pacific and its Continents* (Oxford: Clarenden Press, 1963), pp. 45–46.

[2] Richard M. Brace, *Morocco, Algeria, Tunisia* (Englewood Cliffs, N. J.: Prentice-Hall, Inc., 1964), pp. 105–106.

[3] *Ibid.*, pp. 130–131.

[4] Kenneth Ingham, *A History of East Africa* (New York: Frederick A. Praeger, 1962), pp. 410–411.

[5] Edward Roux, *Time Longer Than Rope* (Madison: University of Wisconsin Press, 1964), pp. 368, 393.

[6] *Ibid.*, pp. 355, 411.

[7] *Ibid.*, pp. 406–408.

[8] *The New York Times*, July 10, 1965, p. 7; July 15, 1965, p. 4; September 9, 1965, p. 2.

[9] John Marlowe, *Arab Nationalism and British Imperialism* (New York: Frederick A. Praeger, 1961), pp. 102, 104.

[10] *The New York Times*, June 29, 1967, p. 14; June 7, 1967, p. 21; June 8, 1967, p. 21.

[11] *The New York Times*, June 23, 1967, pp. 1, 15, 36.

CHAPTER X

[1] Raul Hilberg, *The Destruction of the European Jews* (London: W. H. Allen, 1961), pp. 658–662.

[2] Robert Strauz-Hupé and Harry W. Hazard, eds., *The Idea of Colonialism* (New York: Frederick A. Praeger, 1958), p. 468.

[3] Barun De, "A Preliminary Note on the Writing of the History of Modern India," *Quarterly Review of Historical Studies*, III, 1 & 2, p. 43.

[4] Lecture by Professor Leslie Fiedler, "Indian and Negro Themes in American Literature," Colorado College, May 10, 1965.

[5] J. J. Heydecker and Johannes Leeb, *The Nuremberg Trial*, trans. and ed. R. A. Downie (Cleveland: World Publishing Co., 1958), p. 241.

[6] Rudolf W. Leonhardt, *This Germany: The Story since the Third Reich* (Greenwich, Conn.: New York Graphic Society, 1954), p. 150.

[7] New York *Herald Tribune*, March 15, 1964.

[8] Arnold J. Toynbee, *The World and the West* (New York: Oxford University Press, 1953), pp. 67–68, 70.

[9] James Baldwin, *Nobody Knows My Name. More Notes of a Native Son* (New York: Dial Press, 1961), p. 33.

[10] C. G. Jung, *The Archetypes and the Collective Unconscious* (New York: Pantheon Books, 1959), p. 22.

[11] Colin M. Turnbull, *The Lonely African* (Garden City, N.Y.: Doubleday and Co., 1962), p. 12.

[12] Jawaharlal Nehru, *Toward Freedom, The Autobiography of Jawaharlal Nehru* (New York: John Day Co., 1942), p. 264.

[13] Dominique O. Mannoni, *Prospero and Caliban: The Psychology of Colonization*, trans. Pamela Powesland (New York: Frederick A. Praeger, 1956), pp. 61–62.

¹⁴ Donald L. Wiedner, *A History of Africa South of the Sahara* (New York: Random House, Inc., 1964), pp. 182, 185; Turnbull, *op. cit.*, p. 35.
¹⁵ Anthony F. C. Wallace, "Revitalization Movements," *American Anthropologist* (April 1956), 264–281. Cf. Anthony F. C. Wallace, "Stress and Rapid Personality Changes," *International Record of Medicine and General Practice Clinics* (December 1956), 761–774.
¹⁶ Ssu-yu Teng and John K. Fairbank, *China's Response to the West. A Documentary Survey, 1839–1923* (Cambridge, Massachusetts: Harvard University Press, 1961), pp. 193, 189.
¹⁷ Edwin O. Reischauer, *Japan Past and Present* (New York: Alfred A. Knopf, 1958), p. 194.
¹⁸ Captain Rikihei Inoguchi, Commander Tadashi Nakajima, with Roger Pineau, *The Divine Wind* (New York: Bantam Books, Inc., 1958), pp. xiv–xv.
¹⁹ The word "juramentado" means "sworn," that is, the fighter was sworn to fight on until death. He was anticipating no invulnerability, but usually the Moslem fighter was promised instant bliss in heaven as his reward for dying for the cause.
²⁰ William J. Foltz, "Malagasy: Patterns and Prospects," *Current History* (March 1964), 165–166. Mannoni, *op. cit.*, also provides an interesting account of the revolt with psychological interpretations.
²¹ New York *Herald Tribune*, June 6, 1964 and January 11, 1965; Colorado Springs *Gazette Telegraph*, November 25, 1964; and *The New York Times*, February 5, 1965.
²² John Demos, "The Antislavery Movement and the Problem of Violent 'Means,'" *New England Quarterly* (December 1964), pp. 502–503, 505.
²³ Louis Fischer, *Gandhi* (New York: New American Library, 1962), p. 39.
²⁴ M. K. Gandhi, *Non-Violence in Peace and War* (Ahmedabad: Navajivan, 1942), I, 147–153, extract in *The Gandhi Reader*, ed. Homer A. Jack (Bloomington: University of Indiana Press, 1956), pp. 309–312.
²⁵ *Ibid.*, p. 316.

CHAPTER XI

¹ S. Chandra-sekhar, *Red China, An Asian View* (New York: Frederick A. Praeger, 1961), p. 216.
² George McT. Kahin, *The Asian–African Conference, Bandung, Indonesia, April, 1955* (Ithaca, N.Y.: Cornell University Press, 1956), p. 38.
³ There appears to have been no lending of funds for economic aid to China since 1954. The withdrawal of technical and military assistance personnel in 1960—there had been 10,000 or more of them—brought the Soviet commitment down to almost nothing.

[4] *Time* (April 21, 1961) describes the Sino–Soviet trade agreement of that year as putting trade on a cash basis, with no Russian grain to spare for China. Instead, the U.S.S.R. offered sugar, which was little help, since China was even then committed to take one million tons of sugar from Castro. It is worth noting that while Sino–Soviet trade, even on a cash basis, shrank greatly in the past five years, Soviet shipments of oil continued. This was truly an essential item for China. Their dependence on Russia for it has given the Soviet Government a certain influence over China even when relations were very unfriendly. Note also that many of the Soviet technicians withdrawn from China in 1960 had gone there to help develop the local oil-producing capability. New York *Herald Tribune*, August 6, 1962.

[5] Donald S. Carlisle, "The Changing Soviet Perception of the Development Process in the Afro-Asian World," *Midwest Journal of Political Science* (November 1964), pp. 391, 397, 401–402.

[6] *U.S. Department of State Bulletin*, December 16, 1963, p. 930.

[7] *Time* (March 29, 1963), p. 15.

[8] *Communist Affairs* (April–May 1963), p. 7.

[9] *National Observer* (February 11, 1963). Cf. my article, "Sino-Soviet Relations as Conditioned by Competition of Factions and Pressure Groups in the U.S.S.R.," *Studies on Asia* (1964), 29–47.

[10] *The New York Times*, August 25, 1965, p. 1 C; New York *Herald Tribune*, January 4, 1965.

[11] *U.S. Department of State Bulletin*, May 20, 1963, p. 783. It is true that segregation in the United States was a legitimate concern of the Department of State, because Afro-Asian diplomats accredited to Washington or to the United Nations in New York often complained about discriminatory treatment by U.S. citizens. Rayford W. Logan describes the problem very well in his "Discrimination: Weakness of our African Policy," *Current History* (January 1962).

[12] *Communist Affairs* (May–June 1964), 24, 29.

[13] New York *Herald Tribune*, January 15, 1964.

[14] *The New York Times*, August 16, 1965, p. 8 C. Cf. my article, "The Sino–Soviet Rivalry in Africa, 1960–65," *Rocky Mountain Social Science Journal* (April 1967), 115–24.

[15] *U.S. Department of State Bulletin*, November 11, 1963, p. 755.

[16] Barbara Ward, *The Interplay of East and West* (New York: W. W. Norton Co., 1962), pp. 94–95.

[17] Harrison Brown, "The Combustibility of Humans," *Saturday Review* (June 24, 1967), 14.

[18] Why would this thinning process be better than a simple competition for food? One reason is that the latter might too often eliminate the children and youngest adults. In the former, the mature males tend to eliminate the less qualified of their group. Also, among grazing animals or simple foodgathering creatures, the whole population is

exposed to death if the food of the region is grazed away or otherwise generally depleted.

[19] *The New York Times*, August 17, 1965, p. 17 C.

[20] Sripati Chandrasekhar, *Hungry Peoples and Empty Lands* (London: G. Allen & Unwin, 1954), pp. 48–49.

[21] Eric Fromm, *Beyond the Chains of Illusion* (New York: Trident Press, 1962), pp. 180–181.

[22] Guenter Lewy, *The Catholic Church and Nazi Germany* (New York. The McGraw-Hill Book Co., Inc., 1965), *passim*.

Bibliography

BOOKS

Adams, Brooks, *The Law of Civilization and Decay*. New York: The Macmillan Co., 1896.

Arendt, Hannah, *The Origins of Totalitarianism*. Cleveland: World Publishing Co., 1958.

Ardrey, Robert, *The Territorial Imperative*. New York: Atheneum, 1966.

Baldwin, James, *Nobody Knows My Name. More Notes of a Native Son*. New York: Dial Press, 1961.

Ball, W. Macmahon, *Nationalism and Communism in East Asia*. Carlton, Australia: Melbourne University Press, 1956.

Beveridge, Albert J., *The Russian Advance*. New York: Harper & Row, 1904.

Bigelow, John, ed., *The Complete Works of Benjamin Franklin*. New York: Letter-Press, 1887–1889, Vol. II.

Bond, Horace Mann, *Negro Education in Alabama: A Study in Cotton and Steel*. Washington, D.C.: Associated Publishers, 1939.

Brace, Richard M., *Morocco, Algeria, Tunisia*. Englewood Cliffs, N.J.: Prentice-Hall, Inc., 1964.

Burns, Sir Allen, *In Defence of Colonies*. London: George Allen & Unwin, 1957.

Chandrasekhar, Sripati, *Hungry Peoples and Empty Lands*. London: George Allen & Unwin, 1954.

———, *Red China. An Asian View*. New York: Frederick A. Praeger, 1961.

Curti, Merle E., and Thorpe, Willard, *American Issues. The Social Record*. Philadelphia: J. B. Lippincott Co., 1960.

336

Darwin, Charles, *The Descent of Man*. New York: Appleton-Century-Crofts, Inc., 1883.

Davis, Philip, ed., *Immigration and Naturalization*. Boston: Ginn and Co., 1883.

Eisenhower, Dwight D., *Crusade in Europe*. Garden City, New York: Doubleday and Co., 1948.

Elsbree, Willard H., *Japan's Role in Southeast Asian Nationalist Movements*. Cambridge, Mass.: Harvard University Press, 1953.

Fainsod, Merle, *How Russia is Ruled*. Cambridge, Mass.: Harvard University Press, 1959.

Fischer, Louis, *Gandhi*. New York: New American Library, 1962.

———, *The Life of Mahatma Gandhi*. New York: Harper & Row, 1950.

Freud, Sigmund, *Civilization and its Discontents*, trans. by James Strachey. New York: W. W. Norton Co., 1962.

Fromm, Erich, *Beyond the Chains of Illusion*. New York: Trident Press, 1962.

Furneaux, Rupert, *Massacre at Amritsar*. London: George Allen & Unwin, 1963.

Goldwin, Robert, Ralph Lerner, and Gerald Stourzh, eds., *Readings in World Politics*. Chicago: American Foundation for Political Education, 1957.

Goshal, Kumar, *People in Colonies*. New York: Sheridan House, 1948.

———, *The People of India*. New York: Sheridan House, 1944.

Gossett, Thomas F., *Race: The History of an Idea in America*. Dallas, Texas: Southern Methodist University Press, 1964.

Gruening, Ernest. *The State of Alaska*. New York: Random House, 1954.

Gunther, Frances, *Revolution in India*. New York: Island Press, 1944.

Gunther, John, *Inside Latin America*. New York: Harper & Row, 1941.

Hall, H. Duncan, *The British Commonwealth of Nations*. London: Methuen & Co., Ltd., 1920.

Hayden, Joseph R., *The Philippines*. New York: The Macmillan Co., 1942.

Hayes, Carlton J. H., *A Generation of Materialism, 1871–1900*. New York: Harper & Row, 1941.

Heydecker, Joe J., and Johannes Leeb, *The Nuremberg Trial*, trans. and ed. by R. A. Downie. Cleveland: World Publishing Co., 1958.

Hilberg, Raul, *The Destruction of the European Jews*. London: W. H. Allen, 1961.

Hobson, J. A., *Imperialism. A Study*. New York: James Pott and Co., 1902.

Hochhuth, Rolf, *The Deputy*. New York: Grove Press, 1964.

Holland, William L., *Asian Nationalism and the West*. New York: The Macmillan Co., 1953.

Hutchins, Robert M., *The Power of Reason*. Santa Barbara, California: Center for the Study of Democratic Institutions, 1963.

Ingham, Kenneth, *A History of East Africa*. New York: Frederick A. Praeger, 1962.

Inoguchi, Captain Rikihei, Commander Tadashi Nakajima, with Roger Pineau, *The Divine Wind*. New York: Bantam Books, Inc., 1958.

Irving, David, *The Destruction of Dresden*. New York: Holt, Rinehart and Winston, 1964.

Jack, Homer A., ed., *The Gandhi Reader*. Bloomington: University of Indiana Press, 1956.

Jackson, Helen Hunt, *A Century of Dishonor. The Early Crusade for Indian Reform*, Introduction by Andrew F. Rolle. New York: Harper & Row, 1965.

Jackson, Robert H., *The Case Against the Nazi War Criminals*. New York: Alfred A. Knopf, 1946.

Jung, Carl G., *The Archetypes and the Collective Unconscious*, trans. by R. F. C. Hull. Bollingen Series XX, *The Collected Works of C. G. Jung*, Vol. 9, Part I. New York: Pantheon Books, 1959.

———, *Essays on Contemporary Events*, trans. by Elizabeth Welsh, Barbara Hannah, and Mary Griner. London: Routledge and Kegan Paul, 1947.

———, *Modern Man in Search of a Soul*, trans. by W. S. Dill and Cary F. Baynes. New York: Harcourt, Brace and World, Inc., 1933.

Kahin, George McT., *The Asian-African Conference, Bandung, Indonesia, April 1955*. Ithaca, N.Y.: Cornell University Press, 1956.

———, *Nationalism and Revolution in Indonesia*. Ithaca, N.Y.: Cornell University Press, 1952.

Khrushchev, Nikita S., *The Crimes of the Stalin Era. Special Report to the Congress of the Communist Party of the Soviet Union*. New York: The New Leader, 1962.

Knieriem, August von, *The Nuremberg Trials*. Chicago: Henry Regnery Co., 1959.

Knowles, L. C. A., *The Economic Development of the British Empire*. London: George Routledge and Sons, 1924.

Kohn, Hans, *Nationalism in the Soviet Union*. London: George Routledge and Sons, 1933.

Leech, Margaret, *In the Days of McKinley*. New York: Harper & Row, 1959.

Lenin, V. I., *Sobranie Sochinenii*, XIX. Moscow and Leningrad: State Printing Office, 1925.

Leonhardt, Rudolf W., *This Germany: The Story Since the Third Reich*. Greenwich, Conn.: New York Graphic Society, 1954.

Bibliography

Lewy, Guenter, *The Catholic Church and Nazi Germany*. New York: McGraw-Hill, 1965.

Liu, Kwang-ching, *Americans and Chinese*. Cambridge, Mass.: Harvard University Press, 1963.

Logan, Rayford W., *The Negro in American Life and Thought. The Nadir 1877–1901*. New York: Dial Press, 1954.

——, *The Negro in the United States*. Princeton, N.J.: D. Van Nostrand Co., 1957.

Lorenz, Konrad, *On Aggression*, trans. by Marjorie Kerr Wilson. New York: Harcourt, Brace and World, Inc., 1966.

Lyman, Richard W., and Lewis W. Spitz, eds., *Major Crises in Western Civilization*, II. New York: Harcourt, Brace and World, Inc., 1965.

Mahan, Alfred T., *The Interest of America in Seapower, Present and Future*. Boston: Little, Brown and Co., 1897.

Malone, Carroll B., *History of the Peking Summer Palaces under the Ch'ing Dynasty*. Urbana: University of Illinois Press, 1934.

Mann, Thomas, *Essays of Three Decades*, trans. by H. T. Lowe-Porter. New York: Alfred A. Knopf, 1947.

Mannoni, Dominique O., *Prospero and Caliban: The Psychology of Colonization*, trans. by Pamela Powesland. New York: Frederick A. Praeger, 1956.

March, Francis A., *History of the World War*. Philadelphia: United Publishers, 1919.

Marlowe, John, *Arab Nationalism and British Imperialism*. New York: Frederick A. Praeger, 1961.

Maurois, André, *Lyautey*. New York: Appleton-Century-Crofts, Inc., 1931.

May, Rollo, Ernest Angel, and Henri Ellenberger, eds., *Existence: A New Dimension in Psychiatry and Psychology*. New York: Basic Books, 1958.

Miller, Perry, ed., *The American Puritans. Their Prose and Poetry*. Garden City, New York: Doubleday and Co., 1956.

——, *American Thought*. New York: Holt, Rinehart and Winston, 1961.

——, *Errand into the Wilderness*. Cambridge, Mass.: Harvard University Press, 1956.

Montagu, Ashley, *Man's Most Dangerous Myth: The Fallacy of Race*. Cleveland: World Publishing Co., 1964.

Montaigne, Michel de, *Complete Essays*, trans. by Donald M. Frame. Stanford, California: Stanford University Press, 1958.

Moon, Penderel, *Warren Hastings and British India*. London: English Universities Press, 1946.

Morgan, Edmund S., *The Puritan Dilemma. The Story of John Winthrop*. Boston: Little, Brown and Co., 1958.

Morgan, Murray, *Bridge to Russia*. New York: E. P. Dutton and Co., 1947.

Murray, Henry A., ed., *Myth and Mythmaking*. New York: George Braziller, Inc., 1960.

Nehru, Jawaharlal, *The Discovery of India*. Garden City, N.Y.: Doubleday and Co., 1960.

――――, *Glimpses of World History*, 2 vol. Allahabad, India: Kitabistan, 1935.

――――, *Toward Freedom. The Autobiography of Jawaharlal Nehru.* New York: John Day Co., 1942.

Nolan, William A., *Communism versus the Negro*. Chicago: Henry Regnery Co., 1951.

Ottley, Roi, *No Green Pastures. The Negro in Europe Today*. London: John Murray, 1952.

Page, Stanley W., ed., *Russia in Revolution*. New York: D. Van Nostrand Co., 1965.

Parry, J. H., *The Establishment of the European Hegemony: 1415–1715.* New York: Harper & Row, 1961.

Pettigrew, R. F., *Triumphant Plutocracy*. New York: Academy Press, 1921.

Pierce, Richard A., *Russian Central Asia, 1867–1917. A Study in Colonial Rule.* Berkeley: University of California Press, 1960.

Pike, Douglas, *Australia, the Quiet Continent*. Cambridge: Cambridge University Press, 1962.

Price, A. Grenfell, *The Western Invasions of the Pacific and its Continents.* Oxford: Clarendon Press, 1963.

Priestley, Herbert I., *The Coming of the White Man, 1492–1848*, Vol. I of *A History of American Life*, ed. Arthur Schlesinger and Dixon Ryan Fox. New York: The Macmillan Co., 1929.

Progoff, Ira, *Jung's Psychology and its Social Meaning*. New York: The Julian Press, 1953.

Rauschning, Hermann, *The Voice of Destruction*. New York: G. P. Putnam's Sons, 1940.

Reik, Theodor, *Myth and Guilt*. New York: George Braziller, Inc., 1957.

Reischauer, E. O., *Japan Past and Present*. New York: Alfred A. Knopf, 1958.

Richardson, James D., ed., *A Compilation of the Messages and Papers of the Presidents, 1789–1908*, n.p. 1909.

Romein, Jan, *The Asian Century. A History of Modern Nationalism in Asia*, trans. by R. T. Clark. Berkeley: University of California Press, 1963.

Roosevelt, Theodore, *The Winning of the West*, I. New York: G. P. Putnam's Sons, 1889–1896.

Roux, Edward, *Time Longer than Rope*. Madison: University of Wisconsin Press, 1964.

Schapiro, Leonard, *The Communist Party of the Soviet Union*. New York: Alfred A. Knopf, 1964.

Schwarz, Solomon M., *The Jews in the Soviet Union*. Syracuse, N.Y.: Syracuse University Press, 1951.

Scott, Ernest, *A Short History of Australia*. London: Humphrey Milford, 1930.

Seton-Watson, Hugh, *The Decline of Imperial Russia, 1855–1914*. New York: Frederick A. Praeger, 1961.

Sherwood, Robert E., *Roosevelt and Hopkins. An Intimate History*. New York: Harper & Row, 1948.

Smith, Henry Nash, *Virgin Land. The American West as Symbol and Myth*. New York: Vintage Books, 1957.

Stalin, Joseph, *Marxism and the National Question*. New York: International Publishers, 1942.

Stamp, A. H., *Other Nations' Colonies*. Tunbridge Wells, England: Courier Press, 1957.

Stillman, Edmund, ed., *Bitter Harvest*. New York: Frederick A. Praeger, 1959.

——— —, and William Pfaff, *The Politics of Hysteria. The Sources of 20th Century Conflict*. New York: Harper & Row, 1964.

Strausz-Hupé, Robert, and Harry W. Hazard, *The Idea of Colonialism*. New York: Frederick A. Praeger, 1958.

Stringfellow, William, *My People is the Enemy*. New York: Holt, Rinehart, and Winston, 1964.

Teller, Edward, *The Legacy of Hiroshima*. Garden City, New York: Doubleday and Co., 1962.

Teng, Ssu-yu, and John K. Fairbank, *China's Response to the West. A Documentary Survey, 1839–1923*. Cambridge, Mass.: Harvard University Press, 1961.

Townsend, Mary E., *European Colonial Expansion Since 1871*. Chicago: J. B. Lippincott Co., 1941.

Toynbee, Arnold J., *Civilization on Trial*. London: Oxford University Press, 1957.

Turnbull, Colin M., *The Lonely African*. Garden City, New York: Doubleday and Co., 1963.

Verrill, A. Hyatt, *The Real Americans*. New York: G. P. Putnam's Sons, 1954.

Viereck, Peter, *Metapolitics. The Roots of the Nazi Mind*. New York: Capricorn Books, 1961.

Ward, Barbara, *Five Ideas that Change the World*. New York: W. W. Norton Co., 1959.

————, *The Interplay of East and West*. New York: W. W. Norton Co., 1962.

Washburn, Wilcomb E., ed., *The Indian and the White Man*. Garden City, N.Y.: Doubleday and Co., 1964.

Webb, Walter P., *The Great Frontier*. Boston: Houghton-Mifflin Co., 1952.

Wells, H. G., *The Outline of History*. Garden City, N.Y.: Garden City Publishing Co., 1930.

Wiedner, Donald L., *A History of Africa South of the Sahara*. New York: Random House, 1964.

Willison, George F., *Saints and Strangers*. London: William Heinemann, 1946.

Winks, Robin W., *British Imperialism. Gold, God, Glory*. New York: Holt, Rinehart, and Winston, 1964.

Woodward, C. Vann, *The Strange Career of Jim Crow*. New York: Oxford University Press, 1957.

Woolf, Leonard, *Empire and Commerce in Africa. A Study in Economic Imperialism*. London: George Allen and Unwin, 1920.

Zinkin, Maurice and Taya, *Britain and India*. London: Chatto and Windus, 1964.

OTHER SOURCES

Bowles, Chester, "What American Negroes Can Learn from Gandhi," *The Saturday Evening Post* (March 1, 1958), pp. 19–21.

Brown, Harrison, "The Combustibility of Humans," *Saturday Review* (June 24, 1967), pp. 14–17, 66.

Caroe, Olaf, "Soviet Colonialism in Central Asia," *Foreign Affairs* (October 1953), pp. 135–144.

Cantor, Milton, "The Image of the Negro in Colonial Literature," *New England Quarterly* (December 1963), pp. 452–477.

Carlisle, Donald S., "The Changing Soviet Perception of the Development Process in the Afro-Asian World," *Midwest Journal of Political Science* (November 1964), pp. 385–407.

Communist Affairs, 1962–1967.

Cromwell, Richard S., "Rightist Extremism in Postwar West Germany," *Western Political Quarterly* (June 1964), pp. 284–293.

Current Affairs Bulletin, University of Sydney, Australia. "The Outback Aborigines," December 1958.

De, Barun, "A Preliminary Note on the Writing of the History of Modern India," *The Quarterly Review of Historical Studies* (Calcutta), III, 1 & 2 (1963–1964), 39–47.

Demos, John, "The Antislavery Movement and the Problem of Violent 'Means,'" New England Quarterly (December, 1964), pp. 501–527.

Duvall, Severn, "Uncle Tom's Cabin: The Sinister Side of the Patriarchy," New England Quarterly (March 1963), pp. 3–22.

Fiedler, Leslie, lecture: "Indian and Negro Themes in American Literature," Colorado College, Colorado Springs, Colorado, May 10, 1965.

Foltz, William J., "Malagsy: Patterns and Prospects," Current History (March 1964), pp. 163–168.

Gazette Telegraph, Colorado Springs, Colorado.

Government of India, East India. Report of the Committee Appointed by the Government of India to Investigate the Disturbances in the Punjab. London: His Majesty's Stationery Office, 1920.

Herald Tribune, New York.

Hong Kong Tiger Standard.

Horelick, Arnold L., The Political Character of Soviet Anti-Semitism, Rand Corporation Paper P-2945, n.d.

India News, Washington, D.C.

Izvestia, Moscow, U.S.S.R.

Langer, William L., "A Critique of Imperialism," Foreign Affairs (October 1935), pp. 102–115.

Logan, Rayford W., "Discrimination: Weakness of Our African Policy," Current History (January 1962), pp. 28–48.

Lumby, E. W. R., "Lord Elgin and the Burning of the Summer Palace," History Today (July 1960), pp. 479–487.

National Observer, Washington, D.C.

The New York Times.

Pravda, Moscow, U.S.S.R.

Samuel, Herbert, "The Congo State and the Commission of Inquiry," The Contemporary Review (July–December 1905), pp. 873–883.

Thornton, A. P., "Decolonization," International Journal (Winter 1963–1964), pp. 7–29.

Time.

Toumanoff, Cyril, "Caesaropapism in Byzantium and Russia," Theological Studies (June 1946), pp. 213–243.

Tucker, Frank H., "Sino-Soviet Relations as Conditioned by Competition of Factions and Pressure Groups in the U.S.S.R.," Studies on Asia (1964), pp. 27–50.

——, "The Sino-Soviet Rivalry in Africa, 1960–1965," Rocky Mountain Social Science Journal (April 1967), pp. 114–124.

Union of South Africa, House of Assembly, The Price of Appeasement in Africa. Speech of H. F. Verwoerd, March 10, 1960. Pretoria: South African Information Service, n.d.

U.S. Chief of Counsel for the Prosecution of Axis Criminality, *Nazi Conspiracy and Aggression*, 10 vols. Washington, D.C.: Government Printing Office, 1948–1958.

U.S. Congress, Senate, *Congressional Record*, Vol. 21, Part 1, 51st Congress, 1st Session, p. 802. Washington, D.C.: Government Printing Office, 1889.

———, Vol. 33, Part 1, 56th Congress, 1st Session, pp. 704–712. Washington, D.C.: Government Printing Office, 1900.

U.S. *Department of State Bulletin*, May 30, 1942, May 20, 1963, November 11, 1963, December 6, 1963. Washington, D.C.: Government Printing Office.

Wallace, Anthony F. C., "Revitalization Movements," *American Anthropologist* (April 1956), pp. 264–281.

———, "Stress and Rapid Personality Changes," *International Record of Medicine and General Practice Clinics* (December 1956), pp. 761–774.

Wilson, Harold, speech delivered in London, November 16, 1964, "United Kingdom View of World Affairs." *SEATO Record* (February 1965), pp. 7–11.

Zviaza, Minsk, U.S.S.R.

Index